*High-Minded and Low-Down*

*Music advisor to Northeastern University Press*

GUNTHER SCHULLER

# High-Minded and Low-Down

MUSIC

IN THE LIVES

OF AMERICANS

1800–1861

## Nicholas E. Tawa

Northeastern University Press

*Boston*

Northeastern University Press

*Library of Congress Cataloging-in-Publication Data*

Tawa, Nicholas E.
    High-minded and low-down : music in the lives of
    Americans, 1800–1861 / Nicholas E. Tawa.
      p.  cm.
    Includes bibliographical references (p.  ) and index.
    ISBN 1-55553-443-0 (cl : alk. paper)—
    ISBN 1-55553-442-2 (pa : alk. paper)
     1. Music—Social aspects—United States.
     2. Music—United States—19th century—
History and criticism. I. Title.

  ML3917.U6 T39   2000
  780'.973'09034—dc21        99-089419

Designed by Gary Gore

Composed in Photina by Wellington Graphics. Printed and
bound by Maple Press, York, Pennsylvania. The paper is
Maple Antique, an acid-free sheet.

MANUFACTURED IN THE UNITED STATES OF AMERICA
04  03  02  01  00    5  4  3  2  1

*To the memory of Alan Buechner,*

*a fine friend and dedicated scholar*

# Contents

## Contents

# Preface

This book is primarily a documentation of music in the lives of people. It is not about composers and musical compositions. To be specific, I attempt to discover the relevance of music to the lives of Americans active during the formative years of the United States. The decades of interest extend from the beginning of the nineteenth century to the Civil War. To achieve this end, the pages that follow examine not only the ways of early musical life but also the thoughts about music that characterized antebellum Americans. The focus remains on those cultural interests and values that point up the men and women of the time, educated and uneducated, wealthy and poor, sophisticated and uncultivated alike. All these people contributed to the shaping of the American democracy that has come down to us. Their loves and hates, successes and ordeals, desires and frustrations, preferences and indifferences were reflected in their music, are embedded in our national character, and overspread our national civilization. Every constituency contributed something to our national makeup.

Two types of literature on music are available to today's readers on American culture: (1) accounts describing the contributions of important composers and musicians to American culture, and (2) analyses of the music itself, from song to symphony. Neither type helps us to see into the inner character or underlying truths that informed the antebellum period and a citizenry struggling to define their government and the nature of their society. Some writing is also available on the musical inclinations of the ordinary citizenry, it is true, but too often such knowledge is narrowly channeled or conveyed by opinionated individuals. For example, the love for emotional hymns and sentimental balladry of the era is usually disvalued; its discussion turns judgmental and dismissive. The role of such music in people's lives and in the capturing of the tenor of the times has rarely been satisfactorily considered. Nevertheless, such prominent figures as Henry Thoreau, Walt Whitman, Abraham Lincoln, and Harriet Beecher Stowe sang sentimental songs in all sorts of settings. Why did they? When did they? Where did they? Their tastes and views should be taken seriously.

Under no circumstances do I wish to urge any particular cultural or social view on the reader. I would rather, if I can, see matters as contemporary men and women saw them. What did they have to say about themselves, is the question I ask myself. For me to employ a principle of the present time, based on present concepts, as a yardstick for assessment of this period, not to mention as a general gauge of human taste, would be pointless, if not unfair. There is no doubt in my mind that each society's set of shared attitudes harbors within itself its own inherent cogency. I would prefer to understand these attitudes, not pass judgment upon them.

The claim is not made that these Americans required music as a necessity for living. This is patently not so. Such a conclusion would amount to a declaration of belief and is scarcely verifiable. Even so, these men and women, like all humans throughout recorded history, made and reacted favorably to music. Music might not have been a necessity but was always present. This is without question verifiable. Whatever their living conditions, even at the most primitive, men and women wanted to sing, dance, and play musical instruments. And they did so in their homes, churches, theaters, and concert halls. Moreover, American waterways, fields, forest trails, and camps rang with musical sounds. Why? For entertainment, of course. Nevertheless, what comes through as well from the evidence is that expressing ideas and emotions through the elements of rhythm and melody was also a constant in their day-to-day existence. Music had to have added something vital to their lives, otherwise it would never have been present. What that something was is a large part of this book's subject.

A further aim is to reveal how the musical behavior and standards of Americans, their expectations from music, and their cultural objectives evolved from the daily lives they led. We can thus obtain a more insightful depiction of early American society and its makeup, and get some idea of the interaction between its different economic and social classes. Music, as we shall see, was part of the cultural tie that united citizens, making American society a viable entity, even as other factors were emerging to tear the country apart. If the society had had no shared culture, the nation would have fallen apart long before the Civil War. There was always the danger that our nation might succumb to oligarchical tyranny or mob rule, or whirl itself into dizzying chaos. In understated fashion, music acted to counter that danger.

In documents published in antebellum America survives an immense amount of unutilized information that pictures the uses of, and articulates the opinions about, music in the homes and communities of a still youthful United States. Some documents are hidden away, remaining in private hands or uncatalogued in library cellars; others remain neglected on library shelves. This study rests chiefly upon whatever of such documents were retrievable, and purposely includes many selections from them. Their insertion in this study allows a reconstruction of the era and a better understanding of the functions of music within various social contexts. What these particulars give us are not only the facts but also the flavor of early musical life, as reported directly by the contemporary Americans who experienced it. For this reason, I have incorporated numerous passages describing that life. Almost everything that I quote was published during the antebellum period or shortly thereafter. Most of the quotations that come from more recently edited and published books had already seen print in the last century.

Among the cited documents are the autobiographical narratives of former slaves. A large majority of these eyewitness accounts have to do with the last twenty years of slavery, before the Civil War ended the enslavement. They were taken down by white interviewers engaged in the WPA Federal Writers Project during the late 1930s. I have considered it preferable to give the quotations exactly as they were put down by the interviewers or modified by white editors—that is, in dialect. In so doing, I am aware that interviewers chose dialect formats that reflect their own interpretations of black speech patterns, influenced by their own backgrounds and biases. The same holds true for what is included in the narrations—those matters that are stressed and those downplayed by both the interviewer and interviewee. The careful researcher must always also consider what may have been excluded, first by the interviewee and second by the interviewer. Several published accounts were written by the African Americans themselves. Even here, the same caution must apply. Why were they written? Was it to advance a cause? Who sponsored their publication? Was there a ghostwriter in the background?

The problem for a music historian like myself is to separate out, from the millions of words confronting him, whatever information most faithfully and thoroughly calls attention to the character of American people, white and black, at a crucial time in our history. If successful, this endeavor eases the way toward restoring the link between the smaller sphere of musical activity and the countless societal pursuits of which music forms a part. I am therefore dedicated to discovering the musical thinking that the various men, women, and communities of antebellum America held in common. In order to achieve this, every manner of music making has significance, has its own appeal, and has ties to the larger society. In this scheme, playing the guitar and singing minstrel ditties around a western campfire are as noteworthy as opera attendance in New York City.

I take seriously an observation made by David Grimsted: "Because of the suggestive tentativeness of the answers cultural history gives, there is particular value in presenting not its conclusions, but some of its facts, the documents of cultural history—songs, stories, poems, sermons, diaries, paintings, cartoons, photos—to let the reader search for meanings and connections in their diverse subject matter and varied intimations. . . . The documents present both a panorama of the types of sources a cultural historian may use and a kind of introduction to the period that does not preclude answers and observations different from my own."[1] Readers, if they wish, can draw their own conclusions from the evidence I present.

At least thirty years of reading and note gathering have gone into the preparation for this book. Hundreds of documents have been studied. The search for information has consumed incalculable hours and days. For every examined document that supplied a nugget of information, there have been three or four that supplied nothing at all. Because few secondary sources proved helpful to me, I found it necessary to devote several months to blind reading in the stacks of Harvard's Widener Library, going systematically through book after book on the shelves in the American literature and American history sections. Fortunately, the notes did accumulate and point me in rewarding directions. Whatever selections appear in the following chapters, they are representative of other like observations for which there was no room.

I recognize that lacunae exist. Some subject matter has been explored more thoroughly than others. One reason for this is that not enough reliable information was discoverable in some areas of inquiry. Eventually, I had to decide to break off and start putting together what I had unearthed. It is left to future researchers to fill the gaps.

The layout of the chapters is straightforward. First, there is a look at the United States as it was in the antebellum period, at the composition of its population, and at the considerations that guided what men and women of the time thought about music. Second, the question I try to answer is why, given all the other demands on their attention and time and the lack of musical means, Americans would foster music at all. Third, because childhood environment had a great deal to do with the types of compositions that would be cultivated, my investigation turns to how boys and girls first became acquainted with music, learning about it at home, at church, at school, and in the community. Fourth, the highly circumscribed access to professional performances by well-trained musicians is also taken up. Following this comes the core segment of this study, an exposition of the myriad ways that people used music, and how it functioned in their lives. Scenes of domesticity, worship, wooing, and recreation; of work in shops, factories, and farms; of travel on roads and trails—all of this is grist for our mill. Finally comes a summation of previously stated information, with a few reasonable inferences that can be drawn from the data.

If the reader comes away enlightened about a people of an earlier time and thoughtful about the more universal aspects and ramifications of what took place, then my task has been accomplished.

# High-Minded and Low-Down

# Shaping Music for an American Society

T HE MUSICAL TRAITS OF ANTEBELLUM AMERICA, while fascinating in themselves, are important to understand because they showed themselves during a formative stage of American society. These traits appear in real and imagined events that early nineteenth-century Americans found significant enough to write about and, frequently, to publish for their contemporaries to read. They are described mainly in memoirs, autobiographies, diaries, reminiscences, travel reports, and letters, but also in articles, poetry, short stories, plays, and novels. The question I ask is, simply, What did people have to say about themselves and their relation to music? The postulate is that whoever lives in a culture acts upon, and is acted upon by, that culture. Whatever the answers that come from the Americans who lived in antebellum times, they deserve respect. Encumbering them with today's political, social, and psychoanalytic theories requires a great deal of caution.

The extant private records do need careful handling. They inadequately mirror the diverse strata of the populace. The majority of them favor those fortunate ones who were prominent, educated, and affluent. They say little about the millions who were obscure, unschooled, and had few possessions, and least about the enslaved African Americans. Moreover, they represent selective memories, what the contemporary writer or future biographer or editor considered consequential enough to relate, at the same time leaving much suppressed. Then too, the availability of these records, provided they still exist, is uncertain. Published and unpublished sources may remain un-catalogued, forgotten, or lost. Many have been removed from library collections. Today's descendants of antebellum figures may hold family papers close, not permitting their scrutiny.

In available sources, events of consequence are normally to the fore; the

4     intimacies of private life are missing. Music often is scarcely mentioned, though a significant part of bread-and-butter existence. To fill out the musical picture we sometimes must turn to fiction, where family life and the thoughts and feelings of individuals are more or less held up to the candle of truth and, at the least, indicate prevalent modes of living and thinking. Even here caution is in order, because the author may try to heighten an effect, enhance a dramatic situation, or draw out an emotion to an excessive degree.

The most difficult picture to fill out truthfully concerns black Americans. African Americans, most of them slaves during the antebellum years, were usually seen through white eyes, when seen at all. Too many descriptions were either the apologies for slavery of white Southerners or the antislavery propaganda of Northern abolitionists. We must keep in mind that most masters, whatever the beliefs of some Southern whites, regarded their slaves not as insensate objects but as persons capable of nourishing moral feelings. However, the morality that white Southerners preached was the morality of respectful and obedient conduct due a white superior. The morally praiseworthy slave obeyed faithfully and without question. This last stemmed from the attitude that black persons were also chattels, that is to say, human property. Slaves were lesser humans owing to inborn deficiencies, claimed their owners.

All this said, many plantation owners experienced ceaseless misgivings about their slaves. For one, the blacks in servitude outnumbered their overlords and had little reason to be grateful to those domineering over them. The gangs of field hands, controlled with the whip, might turn at any moment on their subjugators. As for the house servants, they did have superior positions and more polish vis-à-vis the field hands. They were regarded more warmly for belonging to their owner's household. The white family might claim to cherish their black cook, nanny, housekeeper, and butler, from whom it exacted tractability and affection as a right. Nevertheless, whatever the slave's standing, the state of affairs existing between all black servants and the master was uncertain as well as perilous. For blacks, affection toward white owners often meant accommodating to circumstances over which they had no control. Devotion of this sort was undependable and could change to extreme hostility without warning. Numerous slave revolts certainly underlined this view.

Comparatively few publications contain the reminiscences of former slaves, and many of these, too, are written to prove a point. In the case of those black Americans who were once slaves, I found that they sometimes concealed the truth about their days of servitude when interviewed by a white person. As one ex-slave, Martin Jackson, remarked: "Lots of old slaves closes the door before they tell the truth about their days of slavery. When the door is open, they tell how kind their masters was and how rosy it all was.

You can't blame them for this, because they had plenty of early discipline, making them cautious about saying anything uncomplimentary about their masters."[1] For example, one slave was probably using an excess of imagination in describing the prolonged Christmas holidays granted the African Americans on the plantation by the kindly master. It extended from Christmas Eve to the first day of February. During these weeks, all the workers did was dance, sing, and otherwise enjoy themselves, at the same time feasting on a never-ending supply of ducks, geese, squirrels, opossums, rabbits, pigeons, chickens, foot-and-a-half-high pound cakes, and whiskey. What was verifiable, from several other slave statements, was the additional claim that the plantation contained its own musicians. Another description that is not entirely believable involves corn huskings, where "about midnight the huskin' would be over and plenty of food would make its appearance—roast sheep and roast hogs and many other things—and after they had their fill they would dance till morning." That the food was comparatively plentiful and the dancing went on until morning is consistent with other accounts; that there were always plenty of roasted sheep and hogs on hand is doubtful.[2] Yet, whoever the black spokespeople, they consistently depict African Americans as adept singers and instrumentalists, devoted to music. This was true whether they were domestics in the plantation house, toilers in the plantation fields, servants of town dwellers, or urban laborers and artisans.

Many events involving music were unimportant ones experienced by the common run of humanity, whether white- or dark-skinned. Yet among them were occurrences that, taken cumulatively, indicated crucial modifications in cultural behavior when compared with that of Europeans. Writing about the antebellum musical situation in America, Richard G. Parker observed, in his biography of the nineteenth-century piano manufacturer Jonas Chickering, that such modifications could be advantageous to society: "The history of the world is full of proof that the world is more indebted to apparent insignificance for the greatest changes in its physical condition, and the history of man records a great number of beneficial changes from the operation of humble and apparently insignificant means, than from all that is called great and wise and learned."[3] Whether for the good or not, states David Grimsted, every aspect of American cultural behavior should be considered in order to obtain a meaningful view of people's lives. The first sixty years of the nineteenth century, he says, produced an extensive American information base. The historian must sift through this information for those cultural elements that genuinely and fully indicate the substance "of a given society at a particular point of time." It is vital to rediscover the link "between the chosen little historical world and the diverse complexity from which it was wrenched," to unearth the ideas that make "a unit of the diverse individual

**6**  and groups and aspects of a given society." Grimsted insists that in order to arrive at a true cultural history, "no subject matter can be blocked arbitrarily from the field of vision; everything has fascination in itself, and, if one could detect truly, offers clue to, has connection with, everything else."[4] To this I add James Russell Lowell's admonition to the publisher James Fields, who was preparing to bring out his reminiscences of Hawthorne: "Be sure and don't leave anything out because it seems trifling, for it is out of these trifles only that it is possible to reconstruct character sometimes, if not always."[5] The character of the American people is also arrived at only by not leaving anything out.

The music chronicler finds that from the beginning of U.S. history, ordinary men and women were engaged in musical activities (mostly Lowell's "trifles") and were carving out the cultural attitudes, values, and biases that would also characterize much of the musical civilization to come. Their cultural behavior illustrates the various needs for and the uses of music in the stripped-down society in which they lived and affords an understanding of the basic functions of music for any people. In a crucial way, music making offered these men and women a certain intimacy with each other, a sense of a shared humanity. It was a cement, however trifling at times, that acted to unite family, community, and nation, even as the issues of slavery, states' rights, industrialization, and westward settlement pushed Americans apart. As Americans struggled to define themselves politically, socially, and economically in the first half of the nineteenth century, they also had to define themselves culturally—that is to say, to define the intellectual and artistic features of their society. This was a matter of great urgency to them. The one thing they did know, and European travelers kept emphasizing, was that for better or worse, Americans *were* a different people—not English, French, Spanish, or German.

What indeed was similar or different in the musical practices of Americans and Europeans? This question, which I try to address, forms an essential part of a cultural concept that, Stuart Chase says, gives "the closest fit to the truth about mankind." Regrettably, the histories handed down to us, Chase continues, whether from the distant or recent past, hardly ever emphasize this "truth." Instead, they concentrate on individuals, "the great men who rise out of the group, often to torment it." The customary chronicle, "with its Caesars and Napoleons, tends to be a record of the abnormal, the geniuses." Here we find the social pyramid standing "on its apex." In contrast, "the cultural concept puts it back upon its base."[6]

And that base of plain American citizens was by no means a wretched one, despite the negative remarks of several antidemocratic European visitors. When Harriet Martineau visited the United States in the mid-1830s she had already read the many adverse criticisms of the young country. She was prepared to encounter a barbaric, uncivilized, crude sort of people. Instead, she was amazed by the intellectual ability at all levels of American society, whatever the education or lack of it. (Her attention of course was concentrated on European Americans.) She was struck by "the absence of poverty [as Europeans knew it], of gross ignorance, of all servility, of all insolence of manner." Everyone acted like an independent citizen. Landownership was much more widespread than in Europe. Newspapers were everywhere available and read. She was astonished to find that even "the factory girls" had "their libraries."[7] What follows on these pages is an attempt to put the American musical chronicle back upon its base.

### Backgrounds

Although the population of the United States grew rapidly and urban centers burgeoned during the antebellum period, national life remained predominantly rural. Most Americans lived on farms or in small villages and towns. For instance, in 1840, of the 5,420,000 "gainful workers" in the nation, 3,720,000 were employed in agriculture, and only 790,000 in manufacturing, hand trades, and construction.[8] Loosely defined geographical areas were appearing: New England with its earnest Puritan background and people of predominantly British descent; the South with its huge population of African slaves and commitment to the cultivation of cotton and tobacco, which would soon include Cajun-French Louisiana and the former Mexican territory of Texas; the middle states of Pennsylvania, New Jersey, New York, and Kentucky, where representatives of the British Isles, Germans, and Dutch coexisted; and the rude western settlements toward the Mississippi River and beyond, eventually to California. Beginning with the late 1840s, an immense inflow of Irish and Germans would add to the population mix. It is needful also to keep in mind the mix of black and white Americans in the antebellum period, as shown in table 1.[9]

Members of rural society tended to be conservative. They had strong ties to land, were inclined to stay put, saw few people in any given day, and maintained fairly close relationships with nearby residents, however few they might be. Neighbors depended on each other for most diversions, which of necessity remained of the simplest, most undemanding sort. They lived within a confined circle; they rarely roamed more than a few miles from their homes. However, some people had little or no land or were restless. These discontented ones longed for the free and sizable homesteads that the federal government offered them in the empty territories to the west, or, after 1848, for the California gold that promised them riches. Most migrators departed

TABLE I

| Free African Americans | 1820 | 1840 | 1860 |
|---|---|---|---|
| United States | 223,504 | 386,303 | 488,070 |
| North | 99,281 | 170,728 | 226,152 |
| South | 124,223 | 215,575 | 261,918 |
| *Slaves* | | | |
| United States | 1,538,125 | 2,487,455 | 3,953,760 |
| North | 19,108 | 1,129 | 64 |
| South | 1,519,017 | 2,486,326 | 3,953,696 |
| *White Americans* | | | |
| United States | 7,861,931 | 14,195,695 | 26,957,471 |
| North | 4,970,371 | 9,563,165 | 18,860,008 |
| South | 2,891,560 | 4,632,530 | 8,097,463 |

from the more crowded northeastern seaboard. When they removed themselves permanently to unsettled parts of the West or South, they carried with them the uncomplicated musical customs of their villages and towns.

At the same time, cities grew at a breathtaking rate. Manhattan went from 33,141 inhabitants in 1790 to 60,515 in 1800, then leapt to 813,669 in 1860.[10] Boston went from 25,000 in 1800 to 200,000 in 1850; Chicago, from 4,000 in 1837 to an astonishing 300,000 by the end of the Civil War.[11] Villages and towns, too, expanded. J. G. Holland speaks of the changes that took place in one New England village between 1830 and the mid-1840s: "Ten years ago, Crampton had but one church; now it has five. The railroad has introduced 'the foreign element' and there is a new structure, with a cross upon the top, as a result. The Methodists and Baptists and Episcopalians have all built churches. . . . There are new streets cut in all directions, and there is a flowing row of stores."[12]

Urban people often lived on rented properties, were less rooted to place, and shifted around more, from street to street or city to city. They had more impersonal relationships and were accustomed to crowds. They also had numerous diversions available, including musical entertainments taking place in concert halls, opera houses, variety theaters, and dance establishments. Urban growth was making costlier and more sophisticated musical ways possible that were unrealizable in the thinly settled areas. Ceaseless immigration from Europe augmented the native urban population, especially after 1830. For example, of Manhattan's population of 166,000 in 1825, only 11 percent were born outside the United States. Thirty-five years later, of

Manhattan's 813,669 residents, 45 percent had come from Europe: 200,000 Irish, 120,000 Germans, 27,000 English, 9,000 Scotch, and 8,000 French.[13] Other population centers revealed similar growth and change patterns. With the foreign-born came different views of and uses for music that would carry over into the everyday existence of the native-born, especially those living in or near cities.

It follows that every musical scene must be visualized as to what is appropriate to it. A symphony concert would have been not only beyond the resources and comprehension of rural audiences but also inappropriate, that is, incongruous in a milieu that set great store by playful frolics and hospitable husking bees. On the other hand, eastern seaboard metropolises containing wealthy and highly educated inhabitants and large German populations would more easily find a place for art music. Therefore, the question of the propriety of a music to a situation, people, and desired expression must be kept in mind.

This was a period where everything, personal and shared, was marked with unprecedented nationalistic fervor. The incursion of fresh national emblems into all aspects of American life was fundamental to the birth of a democratic tradition. Patriotic paintings and wall ornaments adorned the residences of well-to-do supporters of the nation. Everyday utensils and bric-a-brac came decorated with democratic patterns or miniature illustrations of democratic import. Any object was apt to be covered with a rampant eagle or with a fanciful scene depicting American independence. Other decorations illustrated the equality promised every citizen, the prosperity for all that arrived with democracy, or the triumph of common man. Beautiful allegorical figures symbolizing democracy or liberty, likenesses of Washington and other admirable leaders, and pictures of the events shaping America's brief history replaced the reproductions of nymphs, shepherds, and shepherdesses in bucolic settings.

This was also a period of belief in progress, hope in the future, and radical change in technological processes. At the same time economic depressions came that afflicted rural homesteaders and urban workmen indiscriminately. Time-honored conventions and behavioral patterns were subject to considerable modification or were becoming outmoded. Therefore, a number of less encouraging mental burdens produced uneasiness of mind and misgiving. These encroached on the prevalent attitudes of self-assurance and optimism. One worried about potential insurrection, the undisciplined rabble, financial disaster ever on the horizon, dissolution of the family unit, and unexpected death.

A moneyed aristocracy—merchants, financiers, manufacturers, and large landowners—was contesting politically, economically, and culturally

*10*   with a broad multitude of ordinary men and women. The less affluent classes worked the farms, operated the machines in mills and factories, labored as underlings in merchants' offices, struggled to maintain modest retail stores, and performed the hundreds of humble tasks required by society, such as carpentering, shoe making, and tailoring. This struggle would come to a head after Andrew Jackson was elected president in 1828 and took on Nicholas Biddle, the Bank of the United States, and the entrenched interest group it represented. From the earliest years of the United States through the Jacksonian era, the middling classes assumed more and more power. There was also a rise of individualism and capitalism. No aristocratic ties, no inherited rights, no hereditary customs based on class prevailed. People felt free to accept or reject, and to spend on whatever they wished. At the same time, the age's romantic spirit and the rise of the emotional factor, with links to idealism and poetic expression, counteracted the suffocating features of humdrum everyday life.

What sort of music could possibly exist among this unrelenting human endeavor, turmoil, and paradox?

## The State of Musical Culture

The term *musical culture* as used here relates to all the approved and characteristic modes of musical activity of the American people during the period under investigation. This expression of shared musical perceptions constitutes an aggregate of all American ways of hearing, imagining, feeling, and behaving musically. To a certain extent, the songs and dances of the New World were those transported across the Atlantic as a legacy from Europe. This music making tended toward the ordinary and simple, without aiming at higher and more sophisticated attainments. Impoverished musical conditions and the need to satisfy a broad spectrum of humanity determined its direction. In addition, a great deal of cultural self-sufficiency existed; that is to say, whatever music was produced often originated in or centered on the community, mainly in the form of amateur singing or playing for dances. It was the sound of music in small parlors, austere churches, plain halls, and convivial taverns. Family members, neighbors, and fellow townspeople produced and listened to it. America's unresolved class structure, where social status was hazy and no sophisticated praxis had established itself, encouraged an accessible and easily produceable art. Because so many people were moving from place to place, that art had to be not only readily portable but also flexible enough to adapt to any situation. To sing and dance did not demand great skill, much practice, or unchanging residential living. The Americans of the eastern seaboard and the farmers, settlers, and pioneers to the west had

an abundant stock of songs and dances from which to draw. In every part of
the nation, people nourished these two types of expression. For them, verses
were meant for singing, and singing frequently accompanied dance. No one
city had yet become the focal point for national culture, as with European
countries, despite Boston's and New York City's self-appointed attempts to act
in that capacity.

Returning to this state of affairs in 1833 after a residence in England,
James Fenimore Cooper saw the country as lacking any clean-cut cultural
direction. He commented: "While nothing was vulgar, little even approached
to that high standard" set by Europe.[14] He, like most European visitors, found
America's culture wanting. And to be sure, the United States had more than
its share of boors, know-nothings, and crass individuals guided by material
rather than artistic values. Nevertheless, Dr. Thomas Nichols, an American
who eventually went to live in England, confidently stated in the early 1860s:

> Music is more cultivated in America than in any country in the
> world except Germany. I am sure there are ten pianofortes in every
> American town or village to one in England. Singing is taught in
> the public schools, and the number of bands and amateurs is very
> great. As to a national music, I can say little. The negro melodies
> [minstrel songs] are nearly all we have to boast of. These have a
> charm that has made them popular everywhere.[15]

To some extent, both Cooper's and Nichols's commentaries were equally
valid. What Cooper should have realized was that no American authority
could decree that only compositions deemed artistic be allowed to engage the
general public. Worthwhile musical recreation did not have to center on
artistic works. Nonetheless, the potential for exchange between popular and
artistic music did exist, because people of differing tastes were still conversing
with one another. Many a symphony or opera aficionado also enjoyed the
popular ditties of the day, and many a commoner on occasion would leave
aside his ballads and join the symphony or opera audience.

Aware of criticism like that of Cooper and bragging like that of Nichols,
Harriet Martineau once made the qualifying observation, after traveling
through America in the mid-1830s, that

> the popular scandal against the people of the United States that they
> boast intolerably of their national institutions and character appears
> to me to be untrue; but I see how it has arisen. Foreigners, espe-
> cially the English, are partly to blame for this. They enter the United
> States with an idea that a republic is a vulgar thing, and some take

no pains to conceal their thought. To an American, nothing is more venerable than a republic. The native and the stranger set out on a misunderstanding. The English attacks, the American defends, and, perhaps, boasts.[16]

Offering further enlightenment, the French economist Michel Chevalier wrote, after visiting America from 1832 to 1835, that most English travelers in America saw only the bad and drew caricatures of the country, including America's lack of cultural attainment. Yet these travelers have usually belonged to the aristocracy and have judged the American people by aristocratic standards when it would have been fairer to compare them to, say, Yorkshire farmers or Birmingham mechanics:

> Democracy is too much a newcomer in the world to have been able as yet to organize its pleasures and its amusements. In Europe, our pleasures are essentially exclusive, they are aristocratic like Europe itself, and cannot, therefore, be at the command and for the use of the multitude. In this matter, then, as in politics, American democracy must create everything anew.[17]

"Creating everything anew" was the American challenge. Abetting the new creation was the fact that millions of Americans were almost completely self-taught and distrustful, if not scornful, of the refined gentility championed by those who aspired to be their superiors. They took umbrage at the sneers hurled in their direction from the English and Continental presses. In reaction, they delighted in their crude Americanisms, even overstating them for transatlantic visitors, and never missed any excuse to lampoon Europeans and the pretensions and posing of the would-be gentry in their own society.

## Art Music and Opera in the Young American Democracy

To reach a wide public in the antebellum period, music had to be democratic, that is, represent cultural equality and address the interests and choices of unexceptional people, not of sophisticates. The primary postulate involving this democratic music was that the shared views of a group that sponsored a specific music must finally and inevitably determine the music's historical importance. One must keep in mind that during much of the antebellum period, men and women lived who had watched or participated in the American Revolution, a widely unifying event. (It is noteworthy that the Civil War arrived in the 1860s, when this age group had died off.) They had already shared a significant experience that permitted their young nation to function as one, an experience symbolized in many ways, such as the planting of "trees of liberty" in public places. Music was a part of this network of symbols. For example, in 1840, Texas was awaiting admission to the United States and had several trees of liberty commemorating both the American and Texan wars for independence. That year, Houstonites found their tree in such poor condition that it needed cutting down. The decision to proceed was upsetting to reach. This they finally did with a solemn public ceremony and staid national songs appropriate to the occasion. The proceedings were brought to an end with a patriotic dance to the tune of "Old Rosin the Bow." The tune, popular over many years, was sung and whistled everywhere in the United States. It had the ready capability to adapt to different requirements of most native music. As illustration, a few years later an old African American on a Galveston wharf made it into a work song when he hauled cotton bales and reconstituted it into an entertainment when idle, as he accompanied his singing with the clanking of two steel bale hooks.[18] Tree ceremony and tune were basic expressions familiar to all Americans.

The post-Revolution American majority, an ordinary citizenry of modest means and attainments, was unhampered by the class-driven inclinations toward artistic cultivation that characterized some members of the urban middle and upper classes. This opened the way for people to contribute the necessary yeast for fermenting the singular sounds that became the new American popular music—a potpourri of traditional and freshly minted songs and dance tunes.

So much of what came to Americans as the higher forms of musical culture from Europe seemed unrelated to their lives. In contrast, the new music they were sponsoring was lively, danceable, and stripped to essentials, or it was slow, grave, and designed to deliver a graspable emotional homily. Margaret Fuller in the mid-1840s saw the dawning era of the American popular arts as essential for the eventual production of great artistic works:

> The spirit of the time, which is certainly seeking, though by many
> and strange ways, the greatest happiness for the greatest number, by
> discoveries which facilitate mental no less than bodily communica-
> tion . . . [and] by the simultaneous bubbling up of rills of thought in
> a thousand hitherto obscure and silent places, declares that the ge-
> nial and generous tendency shall have the lead for the present. We
> are not ourselves at all concerned lest excellent expression should
> cease because the power of speech to some extent becomes more
> general. The larger the wave and the more fish it sweeps along, the
> likelier that some fine ones should enrich the net. It has always been
> so. The great efforts of art belong to artistic regions where the boys

in the street draw sketches on the wall and torment melodies on
rude flutes. . . . The electricity which flashes with the thunderbolts
of Jove must first pervade the whole atmosphere.[19]

Fuller found the music making of antebellum America to embody tremendous variety, from the simplest folk song to the most complex Beethoven
sonata, a variety about which she thought Europeans were not sufficiently
aware. She would have agreed with Cooper when he said in a perceptive
moment: "Taste, whether in the arts, literature, or anything else, is a natural
impulse, like love. It is true both may be cultivated and heightened by circumstances, but the impulses must be voluntary, and the flow of feeling, or of
soul, as it has become a law to style it, is not to be forced, or commanded to
come and go at will."[20] Fuller was aware of prejudices that passed as wisdom,
like those of the unbendable D. R. Hundley. Hundley extolled Southern
women for their modesty, virtue, industry, and devotion to husband and
family. Among their virtues, he claimed, were unfamiliarity with such subver-
sive subjects as woman's rights, free love, and free thinking. Nor had Southern women "ever visited the Opera—never hung entranced on the warbles of
a Strakosch or a Piccolomini—never heard of *andante, allegro ma non troppo,*
or *prestissimo;* and only acquaint [themselves] with such old-fashioned songs
as 'John Anderson My Joe,' and the psalms of David by good Dr. Watts."[21]
Here and elsewhere in his writings, Hundley was a smug advocate of the
commonplace and conventional in art.

Such prejudices were, in part, reflections of the lack of cultural knowledge that inhibited cultivation of the more complex arts. The hordes deficient
in this knowledge threatened to overwhelm the cosmopolitan handful that
sincerely cherished the enrichment brought by art music and opera. In 1820
John Rowe Parker acknowledged that the absence of musical knowledge and
experience was true for most Bostonians. Charles Congdon admitted it was
true for himself when he succumbed to "the Jenny Lind lunacy which came
in 1851." He paid a "dozen dollars," which he could then ill spare, "for the
privilege of seeing the extraordinary woman, when I might just as well have
stayed at home, and listened to a dear voice singing something which I could
understand, to the honest accompaniment of the old, well-worn piano-
forte."[22] He implied that there was more affectation than virtue in the repertoire Lind brought with her from abroad.

Nevertheless, as some Americans increased their exposure to the arts,
they also found their tastes changing. When a young man, George Templeton
Strong preferred Scotch songs to oratorios and symphonies, but he deliberately sought to familiarize himself with art works through repeatedly hearing
them. Fortunately, he lived under urban conditions that made artistic compo-

sitions available to him. In 1844 he finally was able to take the fullest pleasure in Beethoven's Fifth Symphony: "I expected to enjoy that Symphony, but I did not suppose it possible that it could be the transcendent affair it is. I've heard it twice before, and how I could have passed by unnoticed so many magnificent points—appreciated the spirit of the composition so feebly and unworthily—I can't conceive."[23]

Art-music concerts and opera performances open to anyone able to afford the ticket price was commendable, but producing a continuously widening demand for such fare was difficult to achieve. Only in a few large cities were such performances available at all. Further inhibiting the strengthening of art music in our early democracy (in addition to what has already been said about availability and the need for greater experience, cultural education, and urban concentrations of population) was the high cost of attendance. Entrance prices were usually much too dear for the ordinary person to afford, frequently three to six times as high as tickets for a minstrel show or a family singing troupe's performance. Carl Arfwedson, a Swedish visitor to the United States who attended Italian opera performances in New York City during the fall of 1833, said that although New Yorkers might have "a real taste for music," the house "was seldom more than half filled." He attributed the apathy to high admission prices, the depression in the money market, and the hegemony of European performers of limited ability. "However much Fashion may endeavor to take unappreciated music under its special protection," he said, "still New York is not ripe for an Italian Opera." John Neal seconded this view twenty-five years later, when he wrote in *True Womanhood* that during the economic depression of 1858, while millions went hungry, the privileged few of New York spent money on musical entertainments "regardless of expense." While thousands wandered the city's streets "literally starving and freezing," the opera was "in full blast, all the theatres, the Academy of Music . . . and all the magnificent balls," a situation not likely to endear opera and art music to the general public.[24]

Not only was overpricing the problem, but so too was the effort to keep art enterprises alive by promoting a superstar atmosphere. The boosting of European opera singers and virtuosi, despite the mediocrity Arfwedson decried, led to the boosting of their salaries and hence the need to increase entry prices. European domination of the musical stage also aided in stifling local talent, making art music seem the importation of a European luxury. For a long while an attempt was made to keep symphony and opera performances commercially viable. To be sure, both did develop a following among all classes of people in the few places where they were presented, and men and women did pay the posted admission prices to attend. Interestingly, this audience showed little interest in separating what was artistic from what was

*16*    plebeian. Most people paid to be entertained, not elevated. Nevertheless, opera in particular proved costly to produce. Wealthy Americans had to keep artistic ventures such as opera afloat.

Unfortunately, too many moneyed men and women espoused a highfalutin culture of slight substance, one based on the glory reflected on them through association with acknowledged celebrities and not on the love of music, and based on the higher social status given them and not on the enrichment of American life. European musicians, too, formed connections with the rich and well educated, rejecting what they regarded as the vulgar multitude. They allied themselves usually to the affluent patrons who provided their bread-and-butter support. The populace, including those who genuinely enjoyed attending the musical theater, found these musicians constantly in the company of the elitists, who busily set up walls between themselves and the rest of America.

Most contemporary Americans who sat in on opera were dismayed by the sung Italian language, which remained unintelligible to them. They were annoyed at the private loges, which demonstrated snobbery and flaunted upper-crust superiority. W. Dermot Darby makes a noteworthy comment about Ferdinand Palmo and his earnest attempt to establish an opera house "for the people" in 1844:

> Palmo's splendid experiment had only served to show that . . . democratic opera was a delusion. Opera in Italian or in any other language foreign to the masses of the people was foredoomed to failure. Only the glamour of social prestige could save it. And, just as opera needed society, so did society need opera. It was out of the question, of course, that persons of social pretensions should patronize Palmo's or Niblo's or Castle Garden or any other place geographically outside the social sphere and appealing largely to the common herd. Society is a jewel which shines only in an appropriate setting.[25]

English and American ballad operas, where tuneful ditties in the English language reigned supreme, had been enjoyed for several decades, beginning in colonial times. More recently, some English companies had appeared that not only performed continental operas such as *Don Giovanni* and *The Barber of Seville* in English but even dared to modify text and music to suit their audience's tastes. The Seguin English Opera Troupe was one such company that won a respectable following. But in November 1825 Manuel Garcia had brought a continental European company to New York and with it an Italian operatic repertoire sung in the original language. The higher echelons of society soon came to see Italian grand opera as the perfect embodiment of their aspirations. After the novelty of Garcia's presentations wore off, and despite the obvious talents of his daughter, the future Maria Malibran, general attendance lessened because of unfamiliarity with the language and musical style. There followed repeated attempts to establish symphony orchestras and opera companies after the continental model on our shores. Always it was a moneyed minority that sponsored these attempts. The successes were few.

The common citizens who composed the American electorate continued to contend with a small elite for economic and political power. They suspected art music, and opera especially, of representing antidemocratic elements. Such music seemed allied to the overweening rich, to those who assumed special privileges and considered themselves above the masses. A consequence was the assumption among many that art music, whatever its merits, represented the taste of a high-handed elite.

Observers such as Michel Chevalier confirmed the existence of this alliance. He noted in January 1834 that "there is a sort of aristocracy founded on knowledge of commercial distinction. This aristocracy, somewhat prone to entertain a contempt for the vulgar multitude, causes a strong reaction against itself in the popular mind." He said further that, in Europe, "the middling and higher classes" were a minority but could determine public opinion and taste. This *haut monde* had elevated the fine arts to considerable importance. In the United States a similar minority was able to influence opinion "only in a few salons in the larger cities" and had "no greater power than is allowed to minors, women, and idiots."[26]

This American minority, "all inhabitants of the large commercial cities [and] . . . more or less connected with the conservative Stock Exchange of London and Paris," alone could afford to travel to Europe, where it fawned on aristocrats. Aping them, it learned to sponsor the musical arts, especially opera, claimed Francis and Theresa Pulszky in 1853. Opera was contrary to the spirit and genius of the United States, added Isaac Pray in 1855, and an entertainment Americans would not tolerate because it fostered the idea of a superior class.[27] Heedless of such criticism, this small group of aristocrats *manqué*, replicating what it interpreted as the trappings of Europe's privileged classes, seized on symphony and especially opera as bases for fashionable activities. Writers in newspapers and magazines mentioned the fashionable and wealthy set almost exclusively as making up the audience for artistic events, heedless of the hundreds of ordinary attendees who might love the music and who contributed to making paying propositions of the presentations. The thousands of democratic readers without direct access to symphony and opera could not help wondering about an art that, they were told, was allied to snobbery. To be sure, this indictment was not prevalent in the first years of the century. But little by little the branding of the musical arts as unrepresentative of the common man increased.

Art music and opera could not help becoming stigmatized in the eyes of the general public. Even though the importation of complex and polished European compositions to America was inevitable and potentially invigorating, they seemed in the antebellum years to be inassimilable attachments to American culture, not something to enhance it, integrate with it, and excite further musical growth. No trained American art composers were ready to add a native dimension to the sound. No native educational institutions were ready to produce these composers. No group of sincere art-music lovers was of sufficient size to absorb Europe's offerings and merge them into the native scene. Not until the end of the century did the alien character of art music and opera begin to wear off. A certain symbolism can be read into a comment of Solon Robinson about the Swedish violinist Ole Bull, in the *Albany Cultivator* for April 1845. Robinson hints at the artificiality of an "American" composition by the violinist, as follows:

> I soon concluded to "put out" and brave the terrors of a threatening
> snow storm upon a prairie 15 miles across, as upon the other side
> lay the town of Carlinsville, the seat of justice in Macoupin county. I
> am of opinion that if that fellow [Ole Bull] who is astonishing the
> "down easters," fiddling the "solitude of the prairie," had been with
> me this evening, that he would have been able to play the tune in
> much greater perfection.[28]

As for the admirers of European artists, art music, and opera, their tastes struck most Americans as teetering toward overrefinement. John Sullivan Dwight of Boston, an ardent advocate for German music and hater of America's popular-music idioms, was once spotted attending a performance of Mozart's *Don Giovanni*. His appearance gave rise to the comment that seated in the audience was "one of the most genial, dainty, and philosophic musical critics of the country. If he could once break through the shell of his library and mingle a little with the world, he would become a glorious fellow—yet after all, perhaps, not so *precious* as now. So we will even let him vegetate."[29]

John Neal enjoyed satirizing "precious" aesthetes like Dwight. Without a scrap of evidence, he accused them unfairly of disdaining utilitarian work and cultivating a "poetic temperament." They intentionally tried to break "the shackles of conventionalism" and discovered philistinism in every American act and feeling. In reality, Neal continued, they were always in debt and unhappy and had learned that "there are no Maecenases in these modern times to help those who will not help themselves." He quoted an imaginary aesthete, who lamented: "Must the Aeolian harp of genius be so rudely swept by a Charley [an ignoramus]—must that harp, as I may say, play mere banjo jigs, when it should only respond in Lydian measures to the southern breezes of palpitating imagination?"[30]

These were censures, though manifestly unjust, that would persist from generation to generation in America. In rebuttal, Dwight might easily have replied with the words of Thomas Grattan, an English visitor who crossed the Atlantic in the summer of 1839: "The public taste is at a low par, and the pursuits of the population afford scanty opportunities for its culture. As a general rule in concert or auction rooms the worst music and inferior pictures are the most popular."[31]

Grattan would have been well advised to mention the existence, however few in relation to the total population, of Dwight and other musically inclined Americans who had the opportunity to attend, and had developed a genuine love for, opera and symphony. These men and women had had to accept that America in the antebellum years was already a pluralistic nation. They recognized that the absolutist approach to culture, which "purified" European taste, would have weakened the tolerance essential for holding a democratic society together. Where and when they could, they advanced the superior merits of the symphonies, operas, and chamber music that they truly treasured. From 1852 to 1881, for example, John Sullivan Dwight published *Dwight's Journal of Music,* in which he furthered the cause of Beethoven and Mendelssohn and criticized the popularity of Stephen Foster's tunes. For him a Beethoven symphony was an ultimate of human experience, a Foster song an irritant to the ear.

John Francis was another early believer in opera. He wrote in 1858 that he had passionately loved Italian opera from his first introduction to it by Manuel Garcia in 1825. He and his circle of New York friends discovered that their greatest happiness came when attending an operatic performance:

> The opera, whatever may be the disputes touching its origin, was known to be the offering of genius. It had universal approval as an exalted mental recreation to recommend it; its novelty here secured prompt attention to its claims, and its *troupe* of artists who honored us with their *entrée* were considered the recognized professors of the highest order in the art. It captivated the eye, it charmed the ear, it awakened the profoundest emotions of the heart. It paralyzed all further eulogiums on the casual song-singing heretofore interspersed in the English comedy, and rendered the popular airs of the drama, which had possession of the feelings, the lifeless materials of childish ignorance. Something, perhaps, was to be ascribed to fashionable

emotion, for this immediate popular ascendancy. . . . From the moment that [Garcia's] first night's entertainment closed, I looked upon the songs of Phillips (which had made Coleman, the editor, music-mad), the melodies of Moore, and even the ballads of Scotland, as shorn of their popularity, and even now I think myself not much in error in holding to the same opinion.[32]

The songs that Francis rejected had all come from the British Isles and were introduced to Americans by British vocalists. He did not deign even to mention the more vulgar songs written and sung by Americans—the homely sentimental ballads and jaunty minstrel songs. With the musical exclusivity approved and practiced by a frustrated aristocracy and by Neal's "Charley," and countenanced by a few sincere music lovers such as Dwight and Francis, art music and opera threatened to become more cut off from the lives of a broad public, even more grounded on class, and increasingly separated from the populace to which the upper crust professed to minister—a condition that unfortunately would persist throughout the nineteenth century. Attempts to counteract it would be made later by such private benefactors as Henry Lee Higginson, who established the Boston Symphony Orchestra and a policy of low-priced tickets for attendance, and by President Franklin Delano Roosevelt, whose WPA acts included the organization of music education classes for the multitudes and symphony orchestras offering free concerts to all comers.

## Common Patterns of Thought and Feeling

The music historian quickly learns that every member of the general public has personal ideas, wishes, and requirements that are brought to bear on a piece of music. In the background is the effect of physiological and behavioral influences, the circumstances of living, and previous encounters with music. When a citizenry interacts with music intelligible to it, it cannot help but assess, absorb, and use the encounter as a basis for future experiences. However traditional their mindset, people find that every musical experience spins a fresh pattern for their community's employ. A cultural break and a sudden change of musical values hardly ever take place. Modifications usually occur imperceptibly.

Charles Fraser, reviewing the history of Charleston in 1854, wished to explain the gradual changes that took place in the St. Cecilia Society, which had been founded in 1762 to entertain Charlestonians. It had also been founded to encourage a taste for and a nurturing of worthwhile music. To this end, an orchestra was assembled and subscription concerts initiated. Slowly, however, the society found its financial and audience base shrinking and had to shift its focus away from art-music concerts to more popular fare, especially dancing:

> Change, which is always at work, was silently preying upon [the St. Cecilia Society's] prosperity. As the old members fell off, their places were supplied by younger ones. A rival Society had sprung up [the Philharmonic Society, incorporated in 1810]. Musical entertainment could be enjoyed elsewhere—new tastes were formed—new habits came into fashion. The love of dancing increased. At length, viz. in February 7, 1819, the board of managers reported that they had found it impracticable to procure an orchestra for the Society, and therefore ordered a ball to be given. After that, one more effort was made to obtain performers, when the committee reported to the Society that they could only procure a quintette. Finally, about the year 1822, the concerts were given up, and the Society substituted dance assemblies.[33]

Admittedly, Americans, even when offered them, were not normally addicted to symphonies. True, their tastes were sometimes coarse, and a community's cultural pattern could reveal this coarseness, but only to the extent that living conditions forced indelicacy upon them. Again and again we come upon men and women yearning for greater humanity, knowledge, and refinement, though not necessarily for symphonies. Sad to say, they could only be as humane, knowledgeable, and refined as the existing conditions that affected them allowed. That is why Alexis de Tocqueville in 1836 cautioned: "It is . . . not true to assert that men living in democratic times are naturally indifferent to science, literature, and the arts; only it must be acknowledged that they cultivate them after their own fashion and bring to the task their own peculiar qualifications and deficiencies."[34]

The perception of indelicacy often depended on the eye of the beholder. For example, the slaves of the South, found to have brutish ways by some observers, were found noble in their own way by others. African Americans attempted to defy and rise above the harsh circumstances imposed upon them. West Africans arriving in America had brought with them the disposition to work jointly, rhythmically, and frequently with responsive singing, which helped build a feeling of community in their native lands. In America, they labored in the fields in groups. In groups, too, they went singing to and from the fields and when engaged in tasks such as corn shucking. They declared their humanity through the outlets allowed them by, and often in defiance of, their owners. They affirmed it through their stories and clowning. They advanced their own interpretation of civilized behavior when they sang

22 and danced. They taught themselves to play musical instruments, many of which were of home manufacture. Whatever they turned their hand to in music they did with a flair. Thus did they cultivate music "after their own fashion and bring to the task their own peculiar qualifications and deficiencies." Listeners who heard the singing of slaves, and in fact the slaves themselves, describe the songs as representations of tender feelings, work activities, punishments, states of mind, and instances of oppression. Some are satirical or bitingly sarcastic, others rebellious. An example of the first type was provided by Cornelius Garner, a former slave:

> One day Charlie saw ole Marsa comin' home wid a keg of whiskey on his ole mule. Cuttin 'cross de plowed field, de ole mule slipped an' Marsa come tumblin' off. Marsa didn't know Charlie saw him, an' Charlie didn't say nothin'. But soon arter a visitor come an' Marsa called Charlie to de house to show off what he knew. Marsa say, "Come here, Charlie, an' sing some rhymes to Mr. Henson." "Don't know no new ones, Marsa," Charlie answered. "Come on, you black rascal, give me a rhyme for my company—one he ain't heard." So Charlie say, "All right, Marsa, I give you a new one effen you promise not to whup me." Marsa promised, an' den Charlie sung de rhyme he done made up in his haid 'bout Marsa:
>
> > Jackass rared,
> > Jackass pitch,
> > Throwed ole Marsa in de ditch.
>
> Well, Marsa got mad as a hornet, but he didn't whip Charlie, not dat time anyway. An' chile, don' you know he used to set de flo' to dat dere song? Mind you, never would sing it when Marsa was roun', but when he wasn't we'd wing al roun' de cabin singin' 'bout how ole Marsa fell off de mule's back. . . . But ev'y'body sho' bus' dey sides laughin' when Charlie sang dat las' verse:
>
> > Jackass stamped,
> > Jackass hupped,
> > Marsa hear you slave, you sho' git whupped.[35]

A goodly number of songs describe the dread of and cruel encounters with the nighttime patrols, called "patterrollers" by the slaves. Gangs of whites patrolled their area looking for slaves acting suspiciously or wandering about without passes from their masters. When caught, these slaves endured

brutal punishments. Many ditties concerned themselves with the slave's various predicaments, as in the following corn-shucking song:

> Shuck corn, shell corn,
> Carry corn de mill.
> Grind de meal, gimme de husk;
> Bake de bread, gimme de crus';
> Fry de meat, gimme de skin;
> And dat's de way to bring 'em in.[36]

What might seem repulsive in both white and black Americans' conduct
to a European visitor such as Frances Trollope might seem a joy to the
Americans themselves. Mrs. Trollope hated public inns, the "boors" inhabit-
ing them, and the raucous music emanating from their common rooms;
Anne Royall, a western Pennsylvanian of ordinary education, took delight in
the friendly common rooms of inns and the bluff comradeship of the country
people found in them. The drinking there warmed her. The joking and story-
telling she found entertaining. The flawed and unrefined music from the
self-taught musicians playing damaged violins and off-pitch melodeons gave
her pleasure.[37]

Young Walt Whitman reveled in the simple songs of a raw America. He
wrote in 1845:

> Great is the power of Music over a people! As for us of America, we
> have long enough followed obedient and child-like in the track of
> the Old World. We have received her tenors and her buffos; her oper-
> atic troupes and her vocalists, of all grades and complexions; lis-
> tened to and applauded the songs made for a different state of soci-
> ety—made, perhaps, by royal genius, but made to please royal ears
> likewise; and it is time that such listening and receiving should
> cease. The subtlest spirit of a nation is expressed through its music—
> and the music acts reciprocally on the nation's very soul. Its effects
> may not be seen in a day; or a year, and yet these effects are potent
> invisibly. They enter into religious feelings—they tinge the manners
> and morals—they are active in the choice of legislators and high
> magistrates. . . . No human power can thoroughly suppress the
> spirit which lives in natural lyrics, and sounds in the favorite melo-
> dies sung by high and low.[38]

In order to be sung "by high and low," the favorite serious and comic
songs had melodies and lyrics that captured "every-day feeling." The musical

24    language had to strike the auditor as unaffected, sincere, and listener-friendly.[39] Hence the popularity of hymns such as Lowell Mason's "Nearer My God to Thee" and "From Greenland's Icy Mountains"; parlor ballads such as Henry Russell's "Woodman! Spare That Tree" and George Root's "Rosalie, the Prairie Flower"; and minstrel songs such as Dan Emmett's "Dixie" and Stephen Foster's "Camptown Races."

When in May 1837 the curmudgeonly George Templeton Strong attended New York's St. Paul's Church on a Sunday, he was delighted with the inclusion of "Old Hundred" among the sacred music selections. Although normally he found much fault with popular taste, the sound of this ancient and still personally favored hymn was irresistible owing to its "noble, plain, simple, and majestic" melody. Everybody loved the hymn and joined in the singing. Some voices quavered and cracked, others had a nasal twang, but nothing could "murder" the tune in his estimation.[40]

Parlor ballads were also irresistible owing to their splendid simplicity. Augusta Evans wrote about a Georgia scene in which a young woman, Beulah, sang for her guardian and a guest and his wife. She first presented an air from Donizetti's *Lucia di Lammermoor,* but the guest said he preferred simple ballads. His wife suggested "something after the order of 'Lilly Dale,' Beulah; he hears nothing else in his country home." Beulah then performed "that exquisite ballad 'Why Do Summer Roses Fade.'" It was a song that her guardian loved to sing, with his "deep, rich, manly voice."[41]

Minstrel songs, first appearing in the 1830s, and the minstrel shows that incorporated them quickly won special favor with audiences. Words and tunes were immediately accepted on both sides of the Atlantic as distinctively American. Their roots were in the traditional verbal imagery, song, and dance of African and European Americans. Minstrelsy adapted itself to the facts of American life through its indigenous strain of jest and caricature, albeit with a sinister undercurrent of weird pity and built-in resentment of economic wrongs and social hypocrisy. Most Americans felt psychological empathy with the black-faced minstrels who exploited the power of laughter to further the reordering of the new culture. Like the performers, the writers of minstrel songs, even if they gave barely any thought to political debate, could not escape from this larger obligation—to represent their nationwide constituency.

As proof of the closeness of American performers, and minstrels in particular, to the general public, we have the testimony of several contemporary observers. As an example, when the Englishman William Hancock visited the United States during the 1850s, he was amazed at how the "Ethiopian 'minstrels' and 'serenaders' flourish in full vigor." Trying to account for the wide acceptance, he said: "The songs, and jokes, and eccentricities of the negro race are the growth of the soil, and the hyperbole and extravagance which mark the performances of their stage representatives are the distinguishing characteristics of native humor, as a glance at the 'funny' column of any American journal will testify, and bear the impress of the national taste and temperament."[42]

A major part of the music from abroad that Americans relished were the Irish and "Scotch" airs coming from people such as Thomas Moore ("'Tis the Last Rose of Summer"), F. Nicholls Crouch ("Kathleen Mavourneen"), and Robert Burns ("Auld Lang Syne"). These airs, of course, shared a common ancestry with America's own approved songs and like them addressed American temperaments directly, intelligibly, and affectively.[43] To American ears, they and America's own music had as their distinguishing virtues not only candor and sincerity but also freedom from obstructive ornamentation. To quote Josh Billings: "'Korrect taist' iz anuther big wurd; ive herd folks uze it whose finger nales wanted cleaning. Music, after all, is sumthing like vittels, the mor cooking and seasoning we uze, the more we have to have, till after awhile we kant enjoy ennything ov the vittels but the pepper."[44]

### To Serve a Useful Purpose

Music is not essential for survival. Theoretically, one can live without it. On the other hand, after the problem of staying alive is under control, then invariably every society reaches out for music. Even a superficial survey of mankind's history reveals that the love and need for it is constant. The uses that influence its shaping are many—among them, for work, worship, play, psychological relief, entertainment, social intercourse, and the capturing of personal and communal feeling. What differs from people to people and age to age are the resources available for making this music and the particular ways people choose to employ it.

For example, its use as handmaid to religion suggests that music helped worshipers cope with fundamental questions and events: the origins of life, birth, marriage, catastrophe, suffering, and death. These are enigmas and occurrences for which there are no rational answers and questions that demand answers in all cultures. They and other questions concerning life's mysteries were responded to in religious chant, hymn, and musical ritual. Samuel Goodrich is informative in this regard when he describes the aftermath of the destruction by lightning of the meetinghouse in his hometown of Ridgefield, Connecticut. The church was rebuilt, but a high wind blew it down again. What were the people to do?

It was now proposed by Deacon Hart that they should commence the performances [of the neighborhood raising a new church building] by a prayer and hymn, it having been suggested that perhaps the want of these pious preliminaries on former occasions had something to do with the calamitous results which attended them. When all was ready, therefore, a prayer was made, and the chorister of the place gave out two lines of the hymn thus:—

> "If God to build the house deny,
> The builders work in vain."

This being sung the chorister completed the verse thus, adapting the lines to the occasion:—

> "Unless the Lord doth shingle it,
> It will blow down agin!"[45]

During the antebellum period, therefore, music could be consciously or unconsciously esteemed not only in itself as something aesthetically pleasing and emotionally "good" but also for its utility. It served to satisfy biological wants—those natural needs that affected all human life. It satisfied social wants—those requirements for enhancing community and domestic life. It also satisfied personal wants—unpredictable demands made by the psyche. Emerson provides further testimony of music's utility when he states that "we are lovers of rhyme and return, period and musical reflection. The babe is lulled to sleep by the nurse's song. Sailors can work better for their *yo-heave-o.* Soldiers can march better and fight better for the drum and trumpet."[46] All Americans had musical needs, no matter when or where—in the roughest wilderness camps, in the tidy New England villages, in plantation slave quarters, and in various city settings.

Bearing witness to these needs is a letter that William Atson wrote to his wife in 1856. Unlike Charles Congdon, he was one of the thousands who enjoyed Jenny Lind's singing:

> [Music is] a necessary component of every sound soul. You know I
> can neither whistle nor sing, nor play a tune on any instrument;
> that I have not the ability to learn to do these things; and that I can-
> not even tell when a tune is properly "turned." Yet who more easily
> is swayed by sweet sounds? The fiddle shakes my foot. The flute
> soothes and softens; the drum and fife make all that is martial stir
> within me. Out of the vast crowds that heard Jenny Lind at the St.
> Charles and Odd Fellows' Hall, I was the only one utterly devoid of a
> musical ear. But was any one present more completely unwrapt,
> transfixed, intoxicated by the passing melody? The man who has no

poetry in his soul is just as fit "for treasons, stratagems, and spoils," as he who has no music there. They are sister senses. And he who possesses them not is as morally maimed, as he is physically who has not the senses of sight and hearing. I claim, therefore, to possess them. Who does not? Without them, how dreary, how icy, would the cold reality be? Who could live under the prospect of the monotony of three meals a day for twenty or more years, did not the fancy picture the table radiant with the visions of human countenances, and vocal with the music of human voices?[47]

Art music was not entirely immune to the test of practicability, and to what extent it served a utile rather than an abstract purpose was still unclear to contemporary music lovers. As Margaret Fuller once wrote: "Whether the arts can be at home among us; whether the desire now manifested to cultivate them be not merely one of our modes of imitating older nations; or whether it springs from a need of balancing the bustle and care of daily life by the unfolding of our calmer and higher nature, it is at present difficult to decide." She thought that the practical had to be its predominant purpose: "The first question should be, What ought we to expect under the circumstances? There is no poetical ground-work ready for the artist in our country and time."[48] Clearly the concept of an art for art's sake had to bow to the imperative of art for life's sake, particularly when the recipients of this art were living closer to the bone than would be later generations.

No such question arose to bother George Root, a songwriter whose fingers were always on the democratic pulse. He left art songs to the German composers and busied himself with writing more rudimentary songs, such as "Hazel Dell," that achieved a nationwide success but were criticized for not aiming at "a higher grade." He replied that "there were tens of thousands of people whose wants would not be supplied at all if there were in the world only such music as they (the critics) would have."[49] Alexis de Tocqueville thought similarly:

The general mediocrity of fortunes, the absence of superfluous wealth, The universal desire for comfort, and the constant efforts by which everyone attempts to procure it make the taste for the useful predominate over the love of the beautiful in the heart of man. Democratic nations, among whom all these things exist, will therefore cultivate the arts that serve to render life easy in preference to those whose object is to adorn it. They will habitually prefer the useful to the beautiful, and they will require that the beautiful should be useful.[50]

28      That the beautiful had to be useful was certainly on Lowell Mason's mind when in 1836 he petitioned the Boston School Board to allow music into the public schools. He knew that aesthetic reasons alone would not persuade the board. Mason gave intellectual reasons for its introduction (music enlivened memory, comparison, attention, and intellect); moral reasons (it effected happiness, contentment, cheerfulness, and tranquillity); physical reasons (singing strengthened the lungs and other vital organs); and entertainment reasons (it recreated without idleness).[51]

The enlivenment of memory and intellect, a practical utility that Mason mentioned, was an accepted attribute of music during the antebellum years. Certainly Charles Leland thought so when he described himself as a four-year-old, in 1828, "stringing" his "thoughts to it" because he was "moved by melody." One rhyme often sung to him to the tune of "Over the Water" went thusly:

> Charley Buff
> Had money enough,
> And locked it in his store;
> Charley die
> And shut his eye,
> And never saw money no more.

This "and other tunes" influenced his thought so much that he often wondered whether anybody ever realized how much was owed to music "acting on thought." As far as he was concerned, "I do not believe that I ever penned any poetry in my life unless it was to a *tune.*"[52]

One of music's most utilitarian functions was in the furtherance of causes. D. R. Hundley has earlier been cited as criticizing the women's rights movement. In the 1840s and 1850s this campaign had employed music to encourage supporters and to call attention and win new adherents to its cause. Another man was as irked as Hundley over the presumption of "emancipated" women, among them the bluestockings of Boston, in demanding enfranchisement and was also bothered by music's role in promoting their goals. Instead of grumbling, however, he chose satire to describe a "Women's Rights March" that included a

> band of the muses, under the direction of Madam Fugleman, fife
> and drum major. . . . Next to Miss Fanny Fairy-Finger, who "touched
> the light guitar"—the leading instrument of the band—was promi-
> nent Mrs. Thumpemhard, a very portly lady, and the most extraordi-
> nary *base*-drummer in all America. . . . Last, though not least, either

in magnitude or celebrity, was Aunt Philice, the Ethiopian Min-
streless, executing the most exquisite antics on her Banjo.

Two of the marches heard were "The Bloomer Gallopade" and "Onward, Ye
Braves." The marchers stopped to listen to a speech from their leader, after
which all voices joined in singing "The Lords of Creation."[53]

## The Shaping of Lyric and Tune

Songs whose lyrics were based on the ordinary American's own experiences were the most favored form of musical expression. The verses that most
succeeded were kept deliberately lucid in order to express the genuine feelings
of a plain citizenry. This was the consensus among musicians sensitive to the
sentiments of the general public, and obviously what sold best.[54] Aside from
the cognoscenti, whose numbers were minuscule and whose sponsorship was
a now-and-again affair, an American musician knew that music in the antebellum democracy had to wear a mantle recognizable by the "unwashed
masses." This was the means to their success.

The growing numbers of native singers and instrumentalists who gave
public concerts, scarcely any of them with more than a modicum of formal
musical training, courted the masses to remain viable as performers. This
meant tailoring their repertoire to suit the cut of their audiences. The composers, whether commanding a modest musical language, as with Stephen
Foster, or a more sophisticated one, as with George Root, had no choice but
to become plainspoken tunesmiths, their offerings reflecting the tastes of
America's millions.

For the masses, it was the singing voice's guileless expression of feeling
and the listening body's sensing of refreshing rhythm that allowed music its
hegemony. There had to be an unambiguous tune and a clearly defined beat.
When music departed too far from this requirement, it lost its meaning. In
May 1830 the *Village Herald*, a rural journal in southwest New Jersey, printed
a piece from one of its readers. He spoke up for honest songs with "pure and
simple melody" in preference to compositions boasting complex harmonies.
He said that neither instrumental concerts, nor oratorio presentations, nor
operatic moments impressed people like him as much as "a single song or
unsupported air; & Bonny Doon or Logan Water [two popular ballads of the
day] give more sensible pleasure than the most labored passage of Handel or
Pleyel."[55]

Influencing the direction that music was taking in the United States, at
one extreme were such people as the backwoodsman David Crockett: "He was
remarkably fond of music, but his idea of the classic hardly went beyond the

30 'Arkensaw Traveller,' or 'Coony in a hollow.' Lively airs or humorous Ethiopian melodies pleased him; but he could not abide what he called the 'scientific touches.' He compared the Italian school of singing to the howling of a wild-cat." The Quaker poet John Whittier was less extreme but cautious about expressing his preferences. Uncomplicated songs sung in domestic circles won him completely, though his Quaker upbringing discouraged his musical inclinations. He and some Quaker children heard a Mr. John Gough sing a pleasing comic song one day. The circumspect children asked on the next day: "John Gough, will thee tell us that same story thee told us yesterday, in the same tone of voice." A request to repeat a song "in the same tone of voice" would also come from Whittier "when some sweet young girl had sung to him a Scotch ballad." Acknowledging the popularity of uncomplicated songs, the fairly fastidious New Yorker Nathaniel Willis said that one evening "three successive boys have gone under my window whistling 'Dance, boatman, dance!'" He agreed with the populace about the draw of "negro melodies" such as this one, but he was happier when one of these melodies was reshaped to accommodate a more exacting taste. This the composer Charles Horn and the lyricist George Morris had done to "As I was gwyin down Shinbone alley," transforming it into the highly successful sentimental ballad "On the lake where drooped the willow." At the other extreme from David Crockett was the poet Henry Wadsworth Longfellow. When he could, he availed himself of symphony, oratorio, and opera performances in Boston and Cambridge. Yet he too "had a great love for simple and expressive melodies," said his brother Samuel.[56] "Simple" and "expressive" were the going criteria for much of the music heard in the United States.

To Americans such as A. B. Longstreet, this simplicity carried over to the performance. In Georgia he praised a Mary Williams for coming to the piano to sing without taking on any pretentious airs. She kept her enunciation clear and free of affectation, her expression appropriate and unexaggerated, and her manner natural.[57] When the Hutchinson Family Singers of New Hampshire left their parent's farm and sought to launch their professional careers, N. P. Rogers, editor of the *Herald of Freedom*, published in Concord, New Hampshire, attended an early performance in 1842. He came away delighted and praised the Hutchinsons in similar terms to those Longstreet had used in praising Mary Williams:

I am enamored of unaffected, natural music and am disposed to speak of the performance of these young persons in the highest terms. In singing, they are truly eloquent and overpowering. . . . They are all modest in their singing, pronounce language well, and as though they understood and felt it. There is no affectation or grimace about them, or contortion, as some singers display.[58]

After this first hearing of the Hutchinsons, Rogers continued to applaud their singing, at the same time constantly admonishing them to "ever cultivate home affections." In 1846 he was on his deathbed and sent for the Hutchinsons "to sing him to sleep." They rushed to his home in Concord but found him dead when they arrived.[59]

Sometimes the absence of pretentiousness went to the utmost. Sol Smith, an amateur trying to turn professional in 1824, found himself penniless. He tried to recoup his fortune with a concert in Princeton, New Jersey. Only one young man came. About to give up in despair, Smith heard the sympathetic young man say he would go out and "rouse up the boys." On returning, the youth stood at the door and collected an admission fee of fifty cents from the young acquaintances he had rounded up. Smith's monetary relief was welcome but temporary. Later, on a very cold night, Sol Smith tried to give a concert in a Perth Amboy tavern. Only seven men and boys came. They invited Mr. Smith to sit with them by the fire, and he finished his concert "with my heels cocked up over the fireplace!"[60] In contrast to the thousands that turned out for Jenny Lind, this meager and highly informal audience was more the usual lot of the unassuming American singer.

# Why Americans Did or Did Not Cultivate Music

THERE IS NO QUESTION THAT A LARGE MAJORITY OF Americans did cultivate music, if not secular, then religious. At the same time, some individuals had difficulty experiencing music at all and for a variety of reasons. Included among these individuals were those who were tone-deaf or close to it. The author Nathaniel Hawthorne, for one, admitted that he was insensible to music, unable to distinguish between the ubiquitous "Yankee Doodle" and "Hail Columbia." John Calhoun, vice president of the United States from 1825 to 1832, did only a shade better; he could recognize one tune, "Yankee Doodle," but try as he might he could not whistle it. Apparently some Americans were unaware of his disability or refused to believe it true. What seems incongruous is that directly after Calhoun's death, Mr. Talmadge, a medium, claimed he had communed with Calhoun's and heard his ghostly presence play "Lilly Dale" on a guitar.[1] A third figure and a prominent Unitarian minister, Theodore Parker, upset over his unresponsiveness to music, tried to remedy the defect through diligent study but failed. Julia Ward Howe reports on the effort:

> Parker's ideal of culture included a knowledge of music. His endeavors to attain this were praiseworthy but unsuccessful. I have heard the late John S. Dwight relate that when he was a student in Harvard Divinity School, Parker, who was then his fellow student, desired to be taught to sing the notes of the musical scale. Dwight volunteered to give him lessons, and began, as is usual, by striking the dominant *do* and directing Parker to imitate the sound. Parker responded, and found himself able to sing this one note; but when Dwight passed on to the second and third, Parker could only repeat the note already sung. He had no ear for music, and his friend ad-

vised him to give up the hopeless attempt to cultivate his voice. In like manner, at an earlier date, Dr. Howe and Charles Sumner joined a singing class, but both evincing the same defect were dismissed as hopeless cases. Parker attended sedulously the concerts of classical music given in Boston, and no doubt enjoyed them, after a fashion.[2]

Evidently, all three men had listening impediments whose correction was beyond their own or their contemporaries' abilities. Men and women like these should not be numbered among those who actively sought music because they enjoyed the listening experience, nor among those who disassociated themselves from secular music and, far more rarely, religious music.

### Americans Who Shunned Music

The singing of hymns was accepted almost everywhere; not so the performance of worldly song and dance. The most frequent reasons for not engaging in secular music making, especially, were the demands of work, whether in or outside the home, the decision that music was useless and to become involved with it was a waste of money, the discounting of any musical accomplishment as merely a dispensable frill, the perception that its practice indicated a fault in character and effeminacy in men, and, above the rest, the equating of music making with idleness and sinfulness.

Many men of the time were like Horace Greeley, about whom Thurlow Weed commented after meeting Greeley in 1838: "He had no habits or tastes but for work, steady, indomitable work."[3] The Greeleys of this nation were able to pay music little attention. Their occupations consumed most of their hours and exhausted their energy entirely. The same can be said of many women after they married. Children and unending household chores prevented them from continuing a pursuit that may once have occupied countless hours of their adolescence. They took no positions for or against the art; they simply had scarcely any leisure for its exercise. This problem would be gradually ameliorated as labor-saving devices for the home were introduced over the decades.

There was out-and-out hostility, as well. Grant Thorburn, a New Yorker, opposed giving any attention to music and declared attendance at operatic performances to be the "entering wedge" to every vice, and its attendees also to be frequenters of "gambling and prostitution houses." This was by no means just one individual's opinion. However, he betrayed a mercenary narrow-mindedness when he added: "Were one-tenth of the money that is spent in buying and tuning piano-fortes laid out in knitting-needles, and one-fourth part of the time that is lost in jingling the machine [the piano] employed in

34    making stockings, I verily believe the *balance of trade* would be in our favor, and you would not see so much splendid misery walking up Broadway."[4] He was not alone in believing that production of saleable goods and making money should be the sole occupations of Americans. Countless men of the first half of the nineteenth century felt it their door to fortune. In addition, it was their duty to advance a still undeveloped land by forwarding the means of transportation and communication, developing America's natural resources, and engaging in manufacture and commerce. Refinement of taste and the arts were, at best, secondary considerations.

This indifference to music was not confined to the Northern states. Mrs. Sue Bowen tells the story of a recently married South Carolina woman, Addy Gilmore, who wrote to a friend, Caroline Bloomfield, in 1847, that her husband was very kind but hated music and had made her stop singing and give up the piano: "John has not the slightest ear, and he says, besides, that a woman becomes too much public property when she has people racing after her to listen to her playing and singing. My two children show very little musical taste, and their father rejoices in it. He says that a good housekeeper had better be in her kitchen than practicing love ditties."[5]

Shedding more light on this sort of viewpoint is the "Dialogue on Music," an essay left unfinished by Charles Brockden Brown, one of America's first novelists. He had a character, designated as "L," stand for those men he knew who called music a "low" pleasure, one consisting of singing meaningless sounds to the prattling words of others. "L" declared firmly that music exhibited "neither virtue, nor talent, nor social feelings." A person wasted time acquiring a vain skill that could lead to "sensuality, caprice, and folly." If one had to indulge in music at all, one should do so when alone, at night, and only if impossible for others to hear.[6]

The sentiments of Brown's "L" are similar, though more severe, to those of the Virginia statesman John Randolph. Though he might enjoy singing to himself in private, he nevertheless wrote to his relative, Theodore Dudley, on 8 January 1807 about the vanity of excelling in such worthless pursuits as music, since they did not imply merit nor demonstrate real education. He cited one young man whom he knew who had mastered several superficial accomplishments without any "proper cultivation" of his mind. Among them, "He sang a good song and was the envy of every foolish fellow, and the darling of every silly girl, who knew him."[7] The young man weighed very lightly in Randolph's scale of virtue.

Randolph's judgment was that of the elegant set to which he belonged—music was a diversion to be indulged in for relaxation so long as it did not interfere with what was considered really important in life. In particular, he was admonishing young men to take care that it did not diminish their manliness. His assessment was prevalent among men of the upper classes in all the states. Writing from New York City on 25 November 1854, an English visitor, Amelia Murray, wrote home: "People here are not at all less exclusive than in London—only the differences of rank and wealth are evinced by more minute and elaborate attention to dress and to trifling conventionalities, than with us. I have been surprised to hear some men of business, but of wealth, assert that the cultivation of the fine arts is a proof of national effeminacy!"[8]

The valuation of music as only a frill that should be allowed scanty or no study was also prevalent among the working classes. Charles Quill said that he found it in parents of apprenticed boys as well as their employers. He was worried because impressionable boys were allowed to sing and play whatever they wished, without supervision and regard for principle: "They [parents and employers] set no proper value on music, either as a pleasure, or a moral instrument," and did not supervise what boys might whistle or sing. Here, according to moralistic Quill, was an infallible road to depravity.[9]

Although some music was though to foster the good in people, certain types of secular music were regarded as potential corrupters of one's integrity. This last was a perpetual concern among religious people. Opera particularly excited their disapproval. Its plots sanctioned illicit behavior; its music, if understood at all, had an unduly sensual appeal; and its professional singers led dissolute personal lives—so they believed. They opposed opera, if only because it transgressed against what they claimed were the decrees of God. In addition, a suspicious foreignness invested a music that seemed overly elaborate and an Italian language that nobody understood. The objections were vehemently expressed, though it was remarkable how many of those objecting had never witnessed an opera performance nor heard an aria sung. Their opinions rested on hearsay.

Julia Ward Howe says that her mother allowed her to attend the opera performances of Manuel Garcia twice when she was seven years of age, but after her mother's death she was no longer allowed to go to performances. Her father, like many devout people that she knew, disapproved of opera and the theater in the belief that they violated divine law.

Reading Thomas Hastings's commentary on musical taste, one discovers that the religiously inclined, who had some knowledge of secular vocal music, had reservations about the lyrics in more than a few operatic arias and secular songs. Those texts dealing with reckless if not profligate love, or condoning the sway of passion over reason, or dwelling on overly sentimental scenes that brought on enervation of spirit, they found especially objectionable. Even the songs set to the poetry of Burns, Moore, and Byron, however revelatory of genius and taste, were viewed as paying court to licentiousness.[10]

The religious old guard even worried about the introduction of instrumental music into the church service, since it associated instruments with the worldly and profane. At the beginning of the century, an uphill battle was fought to allow even organs into New England churches. As late as 1842–43, when Augustus Longstreet advocated musical instruments for Southern churches, he was denounced in the *Southern Christian Advocate*'s pages, where critics called such music making useless and its indulgence "on the level of whiskey, whist, and polygamy, theaters, circuses, and dances." One writer said he was appalled to visit a house where he saw the latest pieces of music in the parlor: "They were *dancing* pieces—and Miss [Fanny] Elssler at the top of all, in dancing costume—and her skirt came down, a *little below the knee!*"[11] These were examples of compositions intended for playing on musical instruments.

Dancing and dance music came in for frequent religious condemnation among the stricter Christian sects. Dancing was not an amusement for the serious and mature, but was perhaps allowable to a small innocent child: "How agreeable is it to see [childish] motions modulated by music, touched by the sentiment of sound. A dancing child is like a bright rose-tree waved by a breeze."[12] In particular, the new dances that had male and female holding each other closely were censured. A respectable and moral person was not supposed to learn them. When the overly bold "fast set" of girls took up the novel waltz, polka, and mazurka in Charleston, in the mid-1850s, they were judged to have transgressed all proper bounds. Girls who wished to preserve their reputations did not so behave.[13] The proscriptive church denominations were the Presbyterians, Methodists, and Baptists; the most lenient, Episcopalians. And the strictest years of the century were the earliest ones—as the century progressed, the strictures against dancing and secular music grew less harsh.

For a long while, the first three sects not only regarded many of the pleasures of life, such as dancing and secular music making, as potentially sinful, but also felt that indulging in these pleasures on Sunday would bring on certain damnation.[14] A greater tolerance of new ideas and behavior irreversibly set in during the Jacksonian years. The Civil War would unravel church authority even more. The following advice, offered in the early 1860s to a Hiram Meeker by a relative, would scarcely ever have been given by anyone at the beginning of the century. Richard Kimball writes that when the young Meeker arrived in New York City from Connecticut, his city cousin advised him to leave the Presbyterians and become an Episcopalian: "The fact is, Hiram, I can't stand the [Presbyterians]; they make a hypocrite of you, or a sniveler. Now, I don't profess to be a good person, but I think, after all, my neighbors know about where to find me. As to the Episcopalians, they give us good music, good prayers, and short sermons. They don't come snooping around to find out whether you sometimes go to the theatre, or if any of your family practice the damnable sin of dancing at parties."[15]

Slaves on Southern plantations were again and again cited by visitors to the South as enjoying all sorts of secular music making and dancing. Yet they too, on numerous occasions, were influenced by the more inflexible religious sects. To give one instance, in the 1840s the slaves on one plantation had loved playing instruments, singing, and dancing, especially during Christmas week and other holidays: "The sound of the fiddles and banjos, and the steady rhythm of their dancing feet, floated on the air by day and night to the Burleigh house." Soon, though, all this joyous celebration ceased: "The whole plantation joined the Baptist church. Henceforth not a musical note, nor the joyful motion of a negro's foot was ever heard again on the plantation. 'I done buss' my fiddle an' my banjo, an' done fling 'em 'way,' the most music-loving fellow on the place said to the preacher." Or, as the former slave Dora Franks said, she had not sung secular songs for so long that she remembered scarcely any of them: "You see when I got 'ligion I asked de Lord to take all de foolishness out of my head and make room for His word and you know since den it's the hardest thing in de world for me to remember dose songs we useter dance by."[16]

However much we may disagree with the judgments of the religious, we must acknowledge that most of their criticisms were sincere and arose from strongly held beliefs. It was in the adamant denial of music to others who did not hold to these beliefs that they were wrong.

### Superficial Justifications for Music

After the arrival of the Garcia opera company in America in the mid-1820s, Italian opera, far more than Central European symphony, became the focus of attention for quite a few Americans. It appealed both to those with comfortable incomes and a degree of sophistication and others of limited means and having an instinctive love for music. New York City and New Orleans offered operatic performances on a fairly regular basis. Regrettably, most Americans living in other sections of the country had to be satisfied with occasional visits to a city that offered an operatic performance or with the home presentation of arias from sheet music. However few their numbers, music lovers were found throughout the United States who were devotedly attached to the sonorous and sophisticated musical works imported from Europe. Nonetheless, they were not sufficiently numerous to make opera and art music a going concern in antebellum America. A far more influential number took up the cause of these cosmopolitan arts because it became the fashion to do so. Theirs was a weathervane allegiance. True appreciation was

*38*    not part of the bargain. Yet fashion, too, served a need arising from the circumstances in which affluent Americans found themselves. They wished to make a statement about themselves and chose music to convey their message. Much as we may criticize the shallowness that fashion implies, it was instrumental in establishing a complex art in the American land that went beyond simple song and dance.

John Rowe Parker wrote in 1820 an indictment against the rule of fashion and the lack of sincere commitment to the art for its own sake:

> Since the exhibitions of Messrs. Philipps and Incledon, we have heard their songs sung by every one who possesses a Piano forte. Among many pretenders to musical knowledge and taste, fashion possesses an irresistible sway, and the enjoyment of it does not proceed from the music itself, but from the self-gratification of being able to play what is new or in vogue, without the possibility of deriving pleasure from the beauties of what is before them.

The highly fashionable Margaret Smith professed to a love of music, but when she wrote to a friend from Washington on 12 January 1829, she revealed a commitment only skin deep. On the previous night, she said, the Asbury Dickenses had given a "small social party," which half of Congress had attended. In the course of the evening, she herself had sat "next to the Pianno [*sic*], where the Miss Fultons (from New York) were playing and singing in high style—Italian in perfection. Madam Garcia over again. But charming as the musick was, it could not interrupt our conversation." The songwriter John Hewitt fumed when remembering an invitation to a dinner in South Carolina, where John Calhoun was a guest. Instead of being allowed to join the men for an after-dinner cigar and sherry, Hewitt was forced to go with the ladies and entertain at the piano. He played and sang for an hour while the women gossiped with each other without listening to a single note. George Templeton Strong said that he attended a concert of the New York Philharmonic in 1847 where Mozart and Beethoven were heard, but much to his annoyance the ladies around him "kept up an animated conversation rising and falling in loudness with the music all the evening." In a letter sent to John Sullivan Dwight in 1845, George Curtis bewailed New York's "fashionable circles" who had elevated Italian opera into eminence not out of love but because it was their latest craze, one that had caused them to repudiate the instrumental music of Schubert and Mendelssohn as beneath notice. A recent convert to opera, Walt Whitman complained, in 1851, of how sick he was of "the superficial crowd who saunter here [Castle Garden, where Donizetti's *La favorita* was being performed] because it is a fashion; who take opera glasses with them, and make you sick with shallow words upon the sublimest and most spiritual of the arts."[17]

Social standing in polite company was made conspicuous by attendance at opera performances and by the production of arias at private social gatherings, activities that were two of the most approved vogues of the 1840s and 1850s. Among the well-to-do and educated, only a few men and women adhered to religious principles that prohibited being present at such affairs. The pastimes of the wealthy people who sponsored operas and symphonies and gave imposing dinners and parties, American critics said, manifested "an artificial state of society," that of the pampered and privileged few, and did not reflect "the deep and settled sentiments" of the millions of contemporary Americans who would have nothing to do with "the frivolities of human life."[18]

Even if "fashionable young folks" could not whistle "Yankee Doodle," they nevertheless pursued opera because it "was essential for their social success and happiness." Eliza Ripley said this of New Orleanians in the 1840s, but she was echoing what other commentators said in other areas of the country. Moreover, fashionable people had no musical opinions of their own, claimed A. B. Longstreet; they allowed European musicians and European society to determine what they would favor.[19] An amusing Josh Billings "saying" took apart musically modish people:

> Let some Prime Donner, or Mezzer Soapraner, or Barrytown Base, or
> some sich latin individul, come into this village, and histe their flag,
> and have a programmy ov singing as long as a search warrant, and
> as hard to spell out as a chinese proklamashun ritten upside down,
> and taxed seventy-five cents for a preserved seat, and moste evry-
> body will go tu hear it, bekause moste evrybody else dus, and will
> say, evry now and then (out loud) "how bewitching! how delishus!
> how egstatick! and nineteen out ov evry twenty-one ov them
> wouldn't kno it if the performance was a burlesk on their grand-
> mother.[20]

Max Maretzek arrived in New York in 1848 to manage the opera there, hoping to cater to the democratic public that formed a large part of his audience and that he found to be hardworking and desiring amusement after satisfying its basic needs. This was not possible, he complained. Instead, he found himself having to cater to an "aristocracy of money" that cherished fashion more than the arts, and that was instrumental in making opera seem an antirepublican institution, with their plush private boxes and insistence that all opera attendees wear proper dress. Nathaniel Parker Willis agreed, for he had witnessed time and time again the privileged people seated in the boxes

*40*   ogling each other's dress for three hours and snubbing the commoners in the cheaper seats, rather than attending to the stage presentation. "To the main object of an Opera," in the fashionable view, "music is, in a certain sense, secondary." The wealthy chatter while "the connoisseurs" try to hush them in vain and "the audience, above and below" try to listen while remaining "breathlessly still and attentive." Unfortunately, too, refined and respectable people of more modest means were deterred from going to opera performances because of the need to attend in full dress or feel declassed. A "Young Gent" observed that for many in the elite audience, "the *entr'acte* intervals are the only pleasant parts of the performance," when attendees could gossip and ogle most freely. He went on to explain the origins and progress of a typical member of the "New-York aristocracy," who had achieved "wealth and position." The husband may have begun as a modest retail hog butcher, then advanced to become a wholesale dealer and speculator. Having earned a great deal of money, he bought a boardinghouse, which he expanded into an aristocratic mansion. His daughters "exchanged the rolling-pin for the piano, and magnificent weekly entertainments almost made the whole family forget that all their greatness is derived from" dead hogs. The family at last arrived at its full glory with a box at the opera. To keep up this distinction, this wife might prefer, as did another wife, to conceal the husband's humble origin by leaving him home, since his manner and speech would betray the family's vulgar origins.[21]

It has already been pointed out that in these years men were duty bound to busy themselves in commerce and industry, a task that left them used up by day's end and impeded whatever close personal relationship they could offer their wives. Theirs was a utilitarian learning only. Women, genteelly brought up, had a more miscellaneous education that was much more likely to embrace the arts. Indeed, the businessman's "requisites for a wife" included "a smattering of French" and the ability "to drum the music out of a piano, to sing and dance, or all in one word, she must be *genteel*." Such a woman, of course would have been next to useless in a more humble household. When William Ryan urged women to come out to underdeveloped California at midcentury, he warned: "I must not be understood as asserting that every class of female would do well in California. Young ladies, whose accomplishments have been confined to acquiring proficiency in music, or in fancy-work, would do better to remain at home."[22]

Yet the "requisites" did exist and were honored in the settled areas of the nation. Mrs. Sigourney once gave the following advice to young ladies:

> Music, at present [ca. 1830] the most popular of all accomplishments, is a source of surpassing delight to many minds. From its

power to sooth the feelings and modify the passions, it seems desirable to understand it, if it does not involve too great expense of time. Vocal music is an accomplishment within the reach of most persons. "I have a piano within myself," said a little girl, "and I can play on that, if I have no other."

Like all writers of the time, Mrs. Sigourney advised young ladies never to flaunt what they had learned, because doing so would repel the very people one wished to impress. Witness A. B. Longstreet's cantankerous report on a Georgia-born and Philadelphia-educated Miss Crump, who declared with false modesty "that she was out of practice" when invited to go to the piano. Eventually, "she seated herself at the piano, rocked to the right, then to the left, leaned forward, then backward, and began" an exhibition of keyboard gymnastics, with the two hands seemingly battling each other. "Anyone, or rather no one, can imagine what kind of noises the piano gave forth during the conflict." Miss Crump finished and "moved as though she would have arisen, but this was protested against by a number of voices at once: 'One song, my dear Aurelia,' said Miss Small, 'you must sing that sweet little French air you used to sing in Philadelphia.'" Again she showed a false reluctance before commencing a boring and unending piano prelude. Then "my ear caught, indistinctly, some very curious sounds, which . . . seemed to be compounded of a dry cough, a grunt, a hiccough, and a whisper." Shortly thereafter, Miss Crump entered a different phase of her performance:

> She now threw away all reserve, and charged the piano with her whole force. She boxed it, she clawed it, she raked it, she scraped it. Her neck-vein swelled, her chin flew up, her face flushed, her eyes glared, her bosom heaved; she screamed, she howled, she yelled, she cackled, and was in the act of dwelling upon the note of a screech-owl, when I took the St. Vitus' dance and rushed out of the room.[23]

Eliza Foster, Stephen Foster's mother, once reminisced about a down-to-earth character named Molly Murphy, who said at a social gathering in western Pennsylvania: "All the spare money nowadays is given to that French woman to learn their daughters foreign airs, to make fortune hunters of them, and set themselves up to catch strangers. . . . Play the harp forsooth! Who in the name of commonsense will you play the harp for here? Our young men care no more about the sound of a harp than if it was a brass kettle!" A sly young woman, Mary O'Hara, replied: "We don't want young men, we only learn the accomplishments for our own amusements. At least, I speak for myself." and all the while looked "cunningly" at the other young women in the room. But Molly Murphy had the last word: "Pshaw! Your fathers expect you to marry some rich man of some great family, when you settle yourselves to their liking. But just as likely as not, you will run off with some strange fellow that they never heard of, because he plays on the guitar and sings songs, or writes rhymes or some such nonsense."[24]

The attainments of genteelly educated young women did serve to attract men, among them future husbands. Shortly after the Charleston gentleman William Simms met his future wife, Chevillette Roach, for the first time, he wrote to his friend James Lawson on 27 May 1836: "You ask about the lady. . . . She is young—just 18—a pale, pleasing girl—very gentle and amiable—with dark eyes and hair, sings sweetly and plays upon piano and guitar."[25]

Mary O'Hara was quite aware of how useful a musical accomplishment might be to catch a prospective suitor's attention and to torment a rival. A somewhat unusual instance of this use is provided by Marion Harland. Her mother had married in Virginia, although her father had originally come from Massachusetts. In the summer of 1825 her parents, newly wed, traveled north to visit her father's mother. One evening of the visit, Marion Harland's mother told her, a Miss Topliffe called, who had expected an offer of marriage from her father and was disappointed when he chose her mother instead.

> Miss Topliffe was rather handsome and very lively, and she was in
> high feather that night, directing most of her conversation to my
> husband. She played upon the piano, and sang love-songs, and alto-
> gether made herself the attraction of the occasion. I felt small and
> insignificant and dull beside her, and I could see that she amused
> your father so much that he did not see how I was pushed into the
> background.[26]

If there was leisure in a fortunately circumstanced family, it was more probable that women possessed it. Therefore, they would be the ones to initiate the cultivation of music, whether out of conviction or fashion or both. In all probability, the butcher already referred to, like Harriet Beecher Stowe's Mr. Van Arsdel, knew and cared nothing for art and did not pretend in the least to understand or enjoy it. On the other hand, he was "quietly indulgent to the tastes and whims of wife and daughters, of whose superior culture he is secretly not a little proud." As for the wife and daughters, according to *The Young Lady's Own Book*, the best most of them would achieve was a negligible proficiency in music, perhaps the execution of "a few romances on the guitar, a few waltzes on the piano-forte." Furthermore, they would exhibit "no taste, no love of knowledge, no real desire for improvement."[27]

Some parents inducted their young daughters into the rank of snobs by spurning a useful common school education for them, instead sending their girls to a private academy for genteel indoctrination in subjects considered refined and stylish. A young woman thus conditioned was irreparably harmed, according to several observers. She "goes to bed when other people are getting up, dotes upon Don Juan, and thinks he must have written Walker's Dictionary . . . covers the legs of her piano . . . adores Italian music, and never could live through an English opera, calls mamma 'our cook' and wonders whom her dirty little brother belongs to."[28] She had "nothing to recommend her as a sober, industrious, frugal housekeeper. She knows how to dance, to play on the guitar and sing, and that is all."[29]

Warnings were given not to marry such women. But marry them men did. John Neal provides a devastating sketch of this kind of young woman, whose manners her fiancé hoped to correct after marriage, although he never did manage to do so:

> He knew that her musical education terminated in an operatic
> crash, the lady having in a fit of impatience demolished the guitar
> over the head of her teacher; but, in this instance, the mitigating
> plea must be allowed that it was done because the instrument
> "wouldn't play good," a perversity to which instruments, like lessons
> "which won't learn," are lamentably prone.[30]

Usually the poor teacher was a hapless and needy woman who had turned to music teaching as one of the few means she had for making an honorable living. She was often given short shrift by the affluent families she tried to please. George Lippard mentions a poverty-stricken young woman struggling to make ends meet in New York who was forced to give up music teaching to work in a shirt store: "She had taught music, and had been a miserable dependent upon the rich; been insulted by their daughters, and been made the object of the insulting offers of their sons."[31]

In Virginia a music teacher might fare no better. Anna Dorsey writes of a pampered girl on a plantation who was being given a harp lesson by a Signor Uberti. The girl hated the drudgery of learning music systematically and announced: "'I will not practice this morning, Signor.' 'It is Signor Shirley's orders. Two hours, *caro mio*. The harp is ready!'" The girl clutched at the strings in a fit of rage, snapped them with a bang, yanked the music book from Signor Uberti's hands, then pitched it as far out on the lawn as she could.[32]

Early on, these girls must have heard the admonishment: under no circumstances should a well brought up young person bestow too much time in studying voice or piano "scientifically," only enough to entertain polite society

44    and parade an embellishment that made the performer more interesting—
so advised Donald Fraser in 1808. Musical accomplishments, warned Mrs.
Sigourney, should never impede "solid learning"; one studied what was necessary, then what was useful, and, only after these were completed, what was
ornamental. John Pintard wrote to his daughter about the "modern tinsel &
frippery usually taught in Boarding schools." He conceded that "something
might be bestowed on the pianoforte" to qualify a person "to perform & sing
an air, but no scientific performance." To achieve the latter, one had to put an
incredible amount of time into practicing. To be too skillful in musical performance was an error; no one selected a companion for marriage because of
proficiency in playing a concerto, said the author of *The Young Lady's Own
Book.*[33] Despite the advocacy of people such as Mrs. Sigourney and John
Pintard, the advice to give greater attention to more solid learning was rarely
realized.

    Notwithstanding what was just said, Americans had read and were stung
by Frances Trollope's much publicized 1832 accusation that the nation was
so dominated by provincial religious prejudices, the pursuit of money, and
boorish behavior that there was a total want of refinement everywhere,
whether in manners or the appreciation of the arts. Although public rebut-
tals to her allegations frequently found their way into American newspapers
and journals, she and other social critics from abroad helped spur the movement toward greater discernment of what it meant to appear civilized. Thus
we find Walt Whitman in the antebellum period continuing to advocate the
teaching of singing in the schools, convinced that music did influence
"manners and conduct, and Americans needed this refining influence."
Representing the hinterland, Charles Smith, of northwest Georgia, remarked
that he knew some people who cared little for music and dancing, while
others liked both because it was in their nature and they could not help
themselves. Children especially loved to dance and for them it was an innocent amusement. Church people, said Smith, were wrong to condemn music
and dance for encouraging a dissolute way of living. Americans should enjoy
what the good Lord had given them "and be all the more thankful for His
Goodness." Smith believed in the civilizing influences of music and in the
healthy enjoyment that dance provided. His affections encompassed music
from minstrel song and parlor ballad to hymn and gospel song. His conviction
was that

> Music is the only employment that is innocent and refining, and
> that cannot be indulged into excess. It stands by itself as the pecu-
> liar gift of God. It is the only art that is alike common to angels and
> to men. It has a wonderful compass and variety, and yet from the

grandest to the simplest, it is all pleasing and all innocent. Every other pleasure can be carried to dissipation, but not music.[34]

Charles Smith stands for the great majority of Americans who found music refining and enjoyed it in all its variety. His words signal the belief that music could be cultivated for interior, personal, and positive reasons.

## An Agreeable Recreation

In contrast to the pursuers of fashion and superficial accomplishments, other Americans did express a sincere love for music, whether of operas or symphonies or unassuming ditties. "R. L. B." of Boston declared, "I passionately loved music. So intensely indeed as often to sit with closed eyes, that no attendant 'stage' circumstance might distract from the harmony itself." The Maryland-born William Wirt, who became attorney general of the United States, "was passionately fond of music, and devoted a portion of his life to its cultivation throughout every period of his life." An early partiality toward music drove some into trying to make their living from it. Dan Emmett, who became a noted songwriter and minstrel show performer, says that as far back into his childhood as he could remember, he wholeheartedly loved music, constantly hummed favorite tunes, made up melodies of his own, and invented new words for what he hummed. Then there was the experience of a girl named Jenny, about whom Fanny Fern tells us. She could hum melodies before she could speak, and as soon as her little hands could reach the piano keys, she began to play "by ear." To hear anyone singing threw Jenny "into an ecstasy of pleasure."[35]

Countless other men and women might not have been so fervently involved with music but were music lovers nevertheless. Without question, one of the primary amusements of Americans, whether rural or city dwellers, consisted of making their own, or listening to others make, music. Sophie Damon tells of a Vermont girl, Elsie, who had studied music because she enjoyed it, thus fitting her for cultivated society, earning a living out of music teaching if need be, and providing her with an entertainment that afforded constant pleasure. Samuel Upham describes gold-seeking "Forty-Niners" as always starved for musical entertainment. At every moment of leisure, they provided amateur concerts for themselves or, when offered it, flocked to attend a professional performance. He says Stephen C. Massett, on the evening of 22 June 1849, charged the outrageous admission price of three dollars to hear him; regardless, "the house was crowded to overflowing." An inveterate traveler, Timothy Dwight, says that everywhere he traveled on the eastern seaboard, "the principal amusements of the inhabitants" included music. The

**46**   editors of *The Singer's Companion* claimed that their collection of secular songs was intended for the amusement of those innumerable Americans "only slightly musically educated" who yearned to produce music of their own.[36]

Again and again, visitors to a neighbor's house and travelers to distant places took perhaps a violin, guitar, songbook, hymnbook, or sheet music with them to fill in their solitary hours or to contribute to the enjoyment of a social evening, whether it was an Indiana lawyer, a village elder in Maine, or a young person in a wagon train headed across the western plains.[37]

Apparent in the narrations about music making involving two or more people is the image of music stimulating a back-and-forth response that was mutually meaningful and satisfying. This accounts for the endless singing of such songs as "Auld Lang Syne," and for listeners finding themselves united in feeling when hearing an exquisite yet simple melody sung. It accounts also for the popularity of songwriters such as George Root and Stephen Foster and hymn writers such as Lowell Mason and William Bradbury, all four of whom were able to delve into what was felt in common by America's millions.

It also accounts for the many musical evenings where people gathered together to ease loneliness and share a communal delight. We hear a young Margaret Cooper, in a Kentucky village, saying to a musical friend: "Mother sent me after you to beg that you will come there this evening. Old Jenks has come up from the river, and brought a store of fine things—there's a fiddle for Ned, and Jason Lightner has a flute, and I—I have a small lot of books, Margaret, that I think will please you." We find Robert Kemp, in a Massachusetts village, saying that "the good people of Reading depend upon social intercourse for their enjoyment," and therefore "one evening I invited a few young people (singers) to my residence, to pass an evening in repeating some of the popular songs of the day, with which we were all familiar."[38] Not a little of their enjoyment derived from music's ability to help them escape worrisome thoughts and cares.

Outside the home, music could prove quite diverting. The distraction produced by a bagpiper at a Boston boardinghouse bar kept all attention narrowly channeled and allowed a thief to rob the safe of fifteen hundred dollars. The diversion provided by a one-man band and his pack of dogs kept the schoolboys in New Bedford, Massachusetts, riveted to the spectacle and sound, rather than attending classes. It earned them a whipping later. The entertainment from a band of minstrel serenaders, strumming banjos, clacking bones, and bellowing "Oh! Susannah" and "Carry Me Back to Ole Virginny" in a California gambling saloon, enthralled the miners completely and destroyed the business at the monte tables. While moving into his new home in northern Illinois, an astute doctor noticed how mystified the onlookers

were by the crate labeled "Piano Forte." He also knew that his new neighbors 47
hungered for entertainment. Three days after arrival, he invited the neighborhood to a musical entertainment, which was provided by his wife and three
daughters playing the piano and singing. The next morning, "the whole
country for twenty miles round rung with the praises of Dr. A's 'consarns' and
their 'musical cupboard.'" This immediately led to the doctor's acquiring a
huge practice.[39] These four episodes illustrate what the shrewd Phineas T.
Barnum knew—that men and women in these antebellum years wearied of
their constant toil and wanted a diversion such as music, or at worst his
freak-show humbugs, to gratify their more cheerful and carefree moments.

The desire for entertainment could take a more distressing turn among
Southern slave owners. If a slave was physically weak and unable to do
physical labor, his owner sometimes had him train on a musical instrument,
then play, sing, and dance to suit the owner's pleasure. The owner might also
rent out his slave musician for the entertainment of others. Otherwise, whoever on a plantation had musical talent was expected to provide diversion
when it was demanded of him or her. To give an example, William Brown, a
former slave, writes that when visitors in Missouri were at Poplar Farm, the
home of a Dr. Gaines, the house servant Cato was frequently ordered to
provide amusement for the company by singing or telling jokes. Cato's own
feelings, of course, were never consulted. Once, when handed a glass of wine
and asked to give a toast, the quick-witted Cato sang out:

> De big bee flies high,
>> De little bee makes de honey,
> De black man raise de cotton
>> An' de white man gets de money.[40]

The unconscionable tyranny in the demand that slaves entertain their
masters is exposed by Solomon Northup, a musician and once a slave owned
by Mr. Epps, who had a plantation close to the Red River, in Louisiana:

> At times he [Mr. Epps] would come home in a less brutal humor.
> Then there must be merry-making. Then Master Epps must needs re-
> gale his melodious ears with the music of a fiddler. Then did he be-
> come buoyant, elastic, gaily "tripping the light fantastic toe around
> the piazza and all through the house." . . . Frequently I was called
> into the house to play before the family, mistress being passionately
> fond of music.
>> All of us would be assembled in the large room of the great
> house, whenever Epps came home in one of his dancing moods. No

matter how worn out and tired we were, there must be a general dance. When properly stationed on the floor, I would strike up a tune. "Dance, you d——d niggers, dance," Epps would shout.

Then there must be no halting or delay, no slow or languid movements; all must be brisk, and lively, and alert. "Up and down, heel and toe, and away we go," was the order of the hour. Epps' portly form mingled with those of his dusky slaves, moving rapidly through all the mazes of the dance.

Usually his whip was in his hand, ready to fall about the ears of the presumptuous thrall who dared rest a moment, or even stop to catch his breath.

Northup adds that he and the other "servants" often were forced to sing and dance until almost daylight, then, exhausted, made to go out into the fields and work while the master slept.[41]

## *The Emotional Side to Music's Cultivation*

Americans in the antebellum decades heard continual warnings that they needed to prize, and make room for, leisure and should not feel uneasy when allowed it. They needed to back away from the endless commotion in their lives and treasure their moments of tranquillity. Above all, they should appreciate "feeling" and accept the guidance of the "soul." The soul was a real entity in the minds of contemporary men and women. Nor did music lovers feel embarrassed when talking about music of or for the soul. The observant Henry Tuckerman, concerned that New Englanders might stifle feeling, cautioned:

> Constant supplies of knowledge to the intellect and the exclusive cultivation of reason may, indeed, make a pedant and logician; but the probability is, these benefits, if such they are, will be gained at the expense of the soul. Sentiment, in its broadest acceptation, is an essential to the true enjoyment and grace of life as mind.[42]

An important corollary to Tuckerman's comment is the admonition of James Russell Lowell in 1855 that until the United States had learned to love poetry and the arts

> not as an amusement, not as the mere ornament of her cities, not as a supposition of what is *comme il faut* for a great nation, but for its humanizing and ennobling energy, for its power of making men better by arousing in them a perception of their own instincts for

what is beautiful, and therefore sacred and religious, and an eternal
rebuke of the base and worldly, she will not have succeeded in that
high sense which alone makes a nation out of a people, and raises it
from a dead name to a living power.[43]

Men and women stated repeatedly that to make themselves better and to
profit by the sentiments of the soul, they turned to music. Clarifying this
predilection further, they said that they prized music because it was the native
tongue of the heart or soul; that is, it summoned up feeling rather than
intellect, delineated innermost being and character, and reached the seat of
life itself. Truly meaningful music not only addressed the human core but also
evoked a response from it. The response was immediate and encompassed
emotions that would otherwise have been left unexpressed, whether grave as
in the serious ballad or joyous as in the comic minstrel song. Some Americans
would have mentioned symphony or opera alongside or instead of ballad and
song.

Almost every man and woman felt music's influence: song comforted the
babe, encouraged the downhearted, gave the timid courage, heightened the
awareness of affection, and opened the door to merriment, because it was
"predominantly the language of the heart," wrote John Moore. So much of
what men and women agreed was music's meaning arose from the prominence they gave to the emotions and music's felt ability to lead them to an
intuitive truth that could be truer than reasoned truth. Frederic Saunders
spoke for his fellow citizens when he rhapsodized:

Justly may it be said that music has its origin in the sweetest emotions of the human breast. It is not the issue of the cold conceptions
of intellect. It is inspiration—the inspiration of the heart to utter its
joys, or bewail and yet console its woes. It is the language, not of
thought, but of affections. Maternal tenderness vibrates upon its
voices, and infantile helplessness is soothed with its sound. The lorn
lover woos by its potent spell, and pours the tale of his sorrow or his
hopes into the not unwilling ear of his listening maid.
    It is music that inflames the patriotic ardor of the foot-weary sol-
dier. . . . It is the ballads of the nation that give tone to popular sentiment and add force to its laws. . . . It is music which renders vocal
the praises of the sanctuary, and the devotions of the worshipper.
The fire-side circle, too, is witness to its softening and uniting
influences, its joys awakening power and sympathetic charm.[44]

Patriotic ardor and emotional commitment to various causes, such as
political parties, women's rights, abolition of slavery, and teetotalism, were

50    certainly enhanced by music. Such specially tailored musical works sought
the unity of a populace or group. The persuasive strength of compositions of
this sort and their cementing usefulness were enormous. At the same time, all
works took part, some more than others, in the inclination to exalt the native
soil or a principle, and they reinforced the "truth" of their subject by the
attractiveness of the music. Adherents to a point of view would certainly
cultivate songs presenting their position in order to vent their own feelings.
At the same time, they hoped that the music would win converts. An indig-
nant citizen wrote to *Dwight's Journal of Music* in August 1853, protesting
John Sullivan Dwight's dismissal of the patriotic music performed on the
Boston Common during a summer evening by calling the works trifling if not
hackneyed. Dwight, who preferred an exclusive diet of German symphonies
and chamber music, belittled the popular numbers heard in the band concert,
including "Yankee Doodle" and "Hail Columbia." The citizen rebutted with:
"My dear sir, I, for one, can never listen to my country's national melodies but
with feelings of pleasure and delight; and in saying this, I feel confident that
I speak the sentiment of every true American; but I presume your foreign
ideas prevent you from thinking so." Dwight editorialized, calling the writer
"illiterate" and his criticism "ill-tempered." Then there was Lydia Child, whose
breast welled with emotion as she watched a parade of a temperance group,
the Washington Society, marching by in 1841—banners, men and boys,
women and girls, fire and military companies:

> The music, too, was revealed to me in fullness of meaning. Much of
> it was of a military character and cheered onward to combat and to
> victory. Everything about war I loathe and detest, except its music.
> . . . It is the voice of resistance to evil, of combat with the false. . . .
> Let the trumpet sound, and the drums roll! Glory to resistance! for
> through its agency men become angels. The instinct awakened by
> martial music is noble and true; and therefore its voice will not pass
> away; but it will cease to represent war with carnal weapons, and re-
> main a type of that spiritual combat whereby the soul is purified.[45]

Patriotism and attachment to a cause were two of many sentiments
captured in music. There was no discomfiture in expressing any honest emotion by means of sound so long as it brought satisfaction to the "soul." Even
girls and boys might welcome having a musical outlet for their feelings. Eliza
Southgate wrote to her sister Octavia from Mrs. Rawson's school, near Boston, on 12 June 1800: "I am learning my 12th tune, Octavia. I almost worship
my Instrument [the piano],—it reciprocates my sorrows and joys and is my
bosom companion."[46]

The belief that every variety of man and woman could receive comfort through the outward expression of sorrow, or feel loyalty to a principle, or find relief in comical sounds and song situations, is shown in the song and hymn texts and the descriptions of contemporary listeners' reactions to secular and sacred music. Worship in church, rediscovering God at a camp meeting, socializing in the family parlor, solitary occupation in a study, frolicking at a picnic, celebrating a national holiday—in all of these instances, emotion allowed people to commune within themselves and get closer to others through music. We hear a strong and seemingly self-sufficient Charles Belmont, in Mrs. Lasselle's novel drawn from life *Annie Grayson, or Life in Washington,* say: "I brought the guitar for Ella [a young woman]. Music is to me one of life's best gifts. It makes the heart more joyous in its hours of mirth, and it soothes it when oppressed with sorrow. I have deeply felt its influence." We hear Fanny Fern's praise of hymn singing at prayer meetings, however poor and out-of-tune the voices: "Those old 'come-to-Jesus' hymns! I tell you I long for them sometimes with a homesick longing. . . . You may pick up the hymn-books containing them, and with your critical forefinger point to 'hell' and 'an angry God,' and all that. It makes no difference to me. . . . I don't mind that so long as there's a heart-tone in your voice, a love-look in your eye, when I'm heart sore—don't you see?" We hear Harriet Beecher Stowe's minister father exclaiming, "I am sick because I cannot reveal the feelings of my heart!" He would lift his old violin, pluck a note or two, and unsatisfied exclaim, "If I could only play what I hear inside of me, I'd beat Paganini." We hear Lydia Child's voice in a letter written 8 September 1842: "Music, whether I listen to it, or try to analyze it, ever fills me with thoughts which I cannot express—because I cannot sing; for nothing but music can express the emotions to which it gives birth. Language, even the richest flow of metaphor, is too poor to do it." All four individuals testify to the inseparable union of music and feeling.[47]

The valuation of music for emotional reasons and the desire for its cultivation were strong even in the backcountry. A daughter of a dairy farmer in central New York State writes of her growing up in the 1830s and provides a valuable picture of music making and the exercise of feeling in humble, rural surroundings:

So far as devotional and concerted music was concerned, we were a musical family. As our only social indulgence was the singing-school, naturally singing together was an outlet for much that would otherwise have been inexpressed in our natures. We all read written music as easily as we read books, and although sacred music was our chief practice, lighter music was not under the same

ban as light literature. We could sing Moore's melodies and serenades and love-songs, although novels and romances were forbidden. My oldest brother played both bass viol and flute and had a
lovely tenor voice. My elder sister had a silvery soprano voice, and I
was a contralto, my part being what we called "second." When Father and Mother sang with us we were fully equipped, for Father
sang a good masculine bass and Mother that high fifth part which
was then called counter. I wish I could hear "Coronation" sung now
[the beginning of the twentieth century] as we used to sing it with
our five voices, the music so stately and magnetic. I think it must
have been very good music, although as different from the singing I
hear now as a clear stream of water gushing from its source is different from the same element arranged to reflect the sky in marble-
edged spaces or springing in fountains in the midst of velvet lawns.[48]

Throughout the antebellum years, human breasts teeming with feeling
are described as breaking out into song because they cannot help doing so. At
the beginning of the century, brother and sister aboard ship off the Maine
coast let out their pent-up emotions in an earnest chanting of hymns. In the
1820s a heartbroken mother tending her dying baby in western Pennsylvania
sang over the crib. In the 1830s Carol Gilman found her father in the woods
freely shouting out the hymn tune "St. Martin's" out of an "overflow of
feeling." In the 1840s a blushing Philadelphia girl overwhelmed by the joy of
newly discovered love sang a Scotch ballad, the expression of a "heart" that
was now "deeply stirred." During the 1850s Americans sang because they
could not "help singing forth, in some way, the feeling that is within" them:
"Perhaps one of the best proofs that the instinct of song lies in our very
nature, is in the fact that many who have no music for others have enough
of it for themselves, and the sweet voice within the heart itself disguises to
them the discord of their lips."[49]

Given the emphasis on music as a vehicle for feeling, there were times
when emotions seemed to overflow in excessive amounts. As the blind Fanny
Crosby heard Ole Bull play his violin she wept and found herself completely
bewitched: "the birds sang, the brooks rippled, the rain fell, the thunder
roared, the sunbeams danced, the bells pealed, the angels sang. . . . Burning
tears of joy coursed down my cheeks." John Trowbridge says his father had
ill health owing to a life of hard labor, yet "was passionately fond of music."
He was regularly overcome with emotion and obliged to sit down when
hymns were sung in the country meetinghouse. Once, after worship, he heard
his mother say to his father "that she should think he might control his
feelings a little better; she didn't consider the singing anything so very fine.

'Maybe not,' he replied. 'But it brings up something—I can't tell what!' And 53
his voice choked with the recollection." Julia Ward Howe spoke of her girlhood and the "morbid melancholy" brought on by music, "which threatened
to affect my health." She advised young people to avoid overstimulation when
great symphonic music swept over them, or a beautiful voice charmed them,
because it disturbed one's mental equilibrium and induced "a listless melancholy or, worse still, an unreasoning and unreasonable discontent."[50]

African Americans were extremely sensitive to music. Andy Brice, a slave
in South Carolina, says:

> One day I see Marse Thomas a twistin' de ears on a fiddle and ros-
> inin' de bow. Then he pull dat bow 'cross de belly of dat fiddle.
> Sumpin' bust loose in me and sing all throu my head and tingle in
> my fingers. I make up my mind, right then and dere, to save and
> buy me a fiddle. I got one dat Christmas, bless God! I learn and been
> playin' de fiddle ever since."[51]

The emotions encouraged by musical sounds often made connection to
something that they were experiencing in the real world. The experience
might be joyous, or sorrowful, or one that combined the two emotions. For
example, the slave Cato of Poplar Farm, who was mentioned earlier, when
told he was to be allowed to marry his beloved Hannah, longed to run away
with her to Canada, but instead relieved his feelings by singing a hymn that
he made up. Again, a Virginia-born slave says his beautiful mother proved
attractive to her master, who forced himself upon her and got her pregnant.
She was therefore hated by her jealous mistress, who was also a mother. After
she gave birth, his mother was required to tend her mistress's baby and give
up her own: "She use to cry more'n she laugh. She would sit and sing,
holding misssus' baby in her lap—her own would be put out to black nigger
to nurse." Incidents like the two above were certainly on Frederick Douglass's
mind when he said:

> The remark in the olden time was not infrequently made, that slaves
> were the most contented and happy laborers in the world, and their
> dancing and singing were referred to in proof of this alleged fact;
> but sometimes it was a great mistake to suppose them happy be-
> cause they sometimes made these joyful noises. The songs of the
> slaves represented their sorrows, rather than their joys. Like tears,
> they were a relief to aching hearts. It is not inconsistent with the
> constitution of the human mind that it avails itself of one and the

same method for expressing opposite emotions. Sorrows and desolation have their songs, as well as joy and peace.[52]

A direct emotional response in song to a common tragic experience, the selling and transportation of slaves to a distant plantation and the splitting of families, is described by William Brown, who was once a slave:

> The following song I have often heard the slaves sing, when about to be carried to the far south. It is said to have been composed by a slave.
>
> > See these poor souls from Africa
> > Transported to America.
> > We are stolen, and sold to Georgia,
> > Will you go along with me?
> > Come sound the jubilee!
> > See wives and husbands sold apart,
> > Their children's screams will break my heart.[53]

Various emotional articulations of sorrow and joy are found in the verses of songs that all people cultivated. A supreme love for God or Jesus is naturally found in the hymns sung in church and at home. Americans also treasured songs colored by emotion that featured love for parents, siblings, children, or friends. Animals and inanimate objects might be fiercely loved, frequently as surrogates for a cherished person—a faithful dog, a family Bible, a mother's rocking chair. Whatever the song, to be a success it had to touch someone quite personally. A typical instance of such an effect on a person took place at a fair in Charleston, South Carolina, in March 1833. A middle-aged sailor, about to take ship on a long voyage, caught sight of a ballad, "The Sailor's Daughter," hanging above a table. He read it through, unpinned it, and laid down the purchase price. Shaking his head sadly and thinking of his own daughter, he said half aloud, "I shall not see her for nine months."[54] In all probability he, or some other shipmate for him, sang the ballad more than once during the voyage.

Most songs of devotion, as has been true throughout history, expressed romantic love between a man and a woman, usually suitor and beloved. Despondency over love denied was a predictable subject of sentimental ballads and, in the following scene, penetrated the singer's being like a piercing dagger. Mary Windle, describing travel by ship from New York to Philadelphia in March 1857, said a lovesick young man was aboard who almost drove the other passengers insane:

Among the passengers was a gentleman who seemed mad with love      **55**
and despair. He had evidently been spurred into frantic activity by recent rejection. For hours during the day he paraded the deck, whistling "Love Not" in diverse keys and with so many variations, that
more than one of our party devoutly wished him overboard. As
night came on, he swallowed a tremendous glass of Cognac and disappeared below. . . . Snatches of song . . . were distinctly audible
from his berth the live-long night. The Bay, which was in a state of
unusual calm, was probably overawed by the storm raging in the
breast of this unhappy Romeo.

The same song, "Love Not," was sung by a mournful young Virginia woman
during a walk in the woods, where "I tried to warm my own heart by
chanting—'Love not, love not, ye hapless sons of clay.'"[55]
Another "unhappy Romeo" kept residents of a boardinghouse up much
of the night as he practiced dancing a "pigeon-wing," which he hoped would
please his beloved, with "each thump resounding like the report of a can-
non." When everyone thought they would finally be allowed to sleep, "the
whole house was roused by a direful, and, until then, unusual uproar in the
chamber . . . a compound of unearthly singing and of appalling knocks on
the floor." A third Romeo made his unhappiness plain at an evening party,
where he aimed the following song at the woman he loved: "Shall I, wasting
in despair,/Die because of another's fair?"[56]
Amorousness and music were joined in an overwhelming number of less
disconsolate scenes where more optimistic wooing took place. Not uncommonly, young women were sought after with flowers, sheet music, opera
tickets, and invitations to evenings of dance.[57] But the most typical spectacle
was that of a girl and her admirers or sweetheart around the piano, with an
older chaperone either present or in an adjacent room. They performed keyboard pieces, sang solos and duets, and thus telegraphed their feelings for
each other. At a South Carolina party where music took place, a gentleman
proposed to a schoolteacher, who hesitated to give her consent. He called on
her again during the next afternoon, coaxed her to the piano, sat close, and
asked her to sing. She sang Michael Balfe's "I Dreamt That I Dwelt in Marble
Halls." At its close, a long silence ensued. The gentleman then mustered his
courage and proposed again. Finding his emotions deep and sincere, she
accepted. Presumably they marked the occasion with more singing. In Indiana, a young lawyer, Daniel Voorhees, was distant from his much loved
fiancée when, in the evening, he pulled out his fiddle and started in on the
"Cracovienne" and "Arkansas Traveler." Because his mind was on the
woman to whom he was engaged, however, he soon turned to "Annie Laurie"

**56** and kept up the song for the rest of the evening. In western Pennsylvania, William Somers and Ellen Grant were waiting to be married when William asked Ellen to sing his favorite song once more, "on which he had often hung with such delight, from the earliest stage of their love. The company all listened with attention to the sweet accents, as they fell from her lips. The words spoke of the joys of true affection—and young and old seemed to feel the force of its application to the present case."[58]

The jointing of song to love was endemic to the antebellum years, so much so that even those who had no ear for music could not help subscribing to their union. Thus we find Nathaniel Hawthorne, who could not carry a tune, writing to his future wife on 5 December 1839:

Dearest,—I wish I had the gift of making rhymes, for methinks there is poetry in my head and heart since I have been in love with you. You are a Poem. Of what sort, then? Epic? Mercy on me, no! A Sonnet? No, for that is too labored and artificial. You are a sort of sweet, simple, gay, pathetic ballad, which Nature is singing, sometimes with tears, sometimes with smiles, and sometimes with intermingled smiles and tears.[59]

Those who were elderly, and well beyond the romantic emotions of their youth, kept up their devotion to love songs. Perhaps the music recalled the fires that once burned within them. Witness the ancient Mrs. Dabney, of Virginia, saying at a home gathering of family and friends in 1832 that she wished to hear someone sing sentimental love ballads because she doted on them: "I always cry my eyes out over 'Highland Mary' and 'Auld Robin Gray' and 'Lord Ullin's Daughter.'"[60]

Yet there is an obverse side to the elderly coin. James Weir, in *Lonz Powers*, warned that the elderly are not taken in by the extravagant declarations of love that were widely accepted in song and by young people. His was the matured voice of one who had lived and coped with life in the western frontier lands:

Talking of love at first sight and hearts broken by false lovers, or passion unreciprocated, do you believe there is any such thing beyond the pages of a novelist? . . . This thing of love at first sight and broken hearts will do well enough for sighing, soft-hearted (we came very near saying "soft-headed"), serenading young gentlemen, and novel-reading, moon-gazing, melancholy young misses, but as for old stagers, it wont do, in other words, you may "tell it to the

marines," but if you wish it to be believed keep clear of the "old
soldiers."[61]

## *Therapeutic and Other Reasons for Music's Cultivation*

Something beyond the emotions already described is implied in numerous statements about the effect of music on listeners. For example, H. M. Brackenbridge recollected of his Pittsburgh years at the turn of the century:

> I was also seized with a desire to play on some instrument of music,
> and took lessons on the violin, and then on the flute. But I found
> that I had a very bad ear, and was advised to give it up. Yet, I was
> passionately fond of music; it has always had a powerful effect on
> my feelings. It soothes the mind, and tames the ferocious heart. At
> church the music has often reconciled me to a dull sermon, in
> which bad reasoning and bad language were rendered almost tortur-
> ing, by bad voice and bad delivery.[62]

Soothing the mind and taming the ferocious heart—music, when understood in this fashion, conveyed psychological, physical, and moral benefits, similar to a remedy for a pathological disease. This was a widespread claim in those years.

Restoration of health and recovery from disease were rewards it was supposed to convey. If only on these grounds, several writers recommended music's cultivation. "Song is the language of gladness and it is the utterance of devotion," wrote Frederic Saunders, and "coming lower down, it is physically beneficial." Blood circulation benefited; lungs strengthened; bodily energies awakened; life and animation diffused through the body. In short, "song is the outlet of mental and physical activity and increases both by its exercises."[63]

For the secluded individual, music making in the evening provided companionship, a way to examine one's intimate concerns, and a vehicle for mental relief. Women in particular could benefit from such a routine, said the Reverend Elijah Sabin around 1816. He was convinced of music's health-restorative usefulness:

> Musick, if rightly employed, will afford a help to devotion, elevate de-
> pressed spirits, and relieve a melancholy hour. It is scarcely possible
> to conceive what effect good musick may have on a female of deli-
> cate constitution and weak nerves; for while it affords an agreeable
> exercise, the soft enchanting sounds of the piano forte or harpsi-

58    chord are perfectly congenial with refined female tenderness, and
will brace and temper the nervous system and expel the dregs of
melancholy, and prevent a worse method of spending time.[64]

That men also benefited from the sound of music is maintained by Ann
Willson. In a letter that she sent from Port Elizabeth, New Jersey, dated
20 June 1827, she described crossing a river by moonlight when she and the
oarsmen heard "a sound of melody" arising "from the shore before us." As
one person, the oarsmen paused and listened, "for even manly hearts are
touched with harmonious strains which irresistibly throw their spell upon us,
frequently tending to quiet, soothe and still an agitated mind."[65]

The extensive custom of hymn singing was often mentioned in connection with people close to psychological collapse. It was a psychotherapeu-
tic recourse, a help when confronted with dangerously debilitating situations.
Hence the popularity of camp meetings. Ordinary men and women, white
and black, who were experiencing extreme tension could bolster their mind's
health through uninhibited torrents of sacred singing and a "coming to
Jesus." Mention is often made of people, worried over a serious illness or on
their deathbeds and frightened over what was shortly to happen, who would
turn to the singing of hymns and songs of a serious nature. This activity had
a happy effect and helped compose their nerves.[66]

Music was thought to act on the psyche so that the inner being achieved
a measure of psychological purgation. Because its message was unspecific,
music was the preferred medium to bear the freight of human sentiments
from the profound to the frivolous. Once musical sounds enmeshed the mind,
anxieties were supposed to lessen, and the individual experienced relief. Thus,
music was seen as an abreactive agent that helped discharge emotion into
consciousness, culminating in catharsis. The protagonist, the "I," in a song
became a human symbol who bore the burden of one's feelings, desires, and
transgressions, a symbol with whom the singer and listener could realize total
emotional affiliation, a sympathetic identification that provided release from
tension.

Speaking in terms of the nervous system itself, Oliver Wendell Holmes
wrote that "the nerves that make us alive" to music are found to "spread out
. . . in the most sensitive region of the marrow, just where it is widening, to
run upwards into the hemispheres," and "produces a continuous" and even
"logical sequence of emotional and intellectual change; but how different
from trains of thought." Pursuing a similar course of reasoning, Henry
Tuckerman told of the "physical effects of music," where music aided in the
treatment of mental malady, as David's harp once aided Saul's troubled
mental state. He advised that "invalids of nervous temperament" could "raise
their tone of health to an astonishing degree, by frequenting musical enter-

tainments." Indeed, many witnesses testify to melody's efficacy in producing a "tranquil state" in "cases of violent insanity."[67]

Evidently the efficacy of music and dance in the treatment of insanity was a major reason why the State Hospital for the Insane, in South Boston, featured them in the institution's doctoring. After Charles Dickens visited this institution in 1842, he wrote admiringly:

> Once a week, they have a ball, in which the Doctor and his family, with all the nurses and attendants, take an active part. Dances and marches are performed alternately, to the enlivening strains of a piano; and now and then some gentleman or lady (whose proficiency has been previously ascertained) obliges the company with a song; nor does it ever degenerate, at a tender crisis, into a screech or howl; wherein, I must confess, I should have thought the danger lay. At an early hour they all meet together for these festive purposes; at eight o'clock refreshments are served; and at nine they separate.[68]

A similar report came from Fredrika Bremer, who visited the Philadelphia Lunatic Asylum in 1850:

> They frequently meet for general amusement, as for concerts, dances, and so on. . . . I heard on all hands music in the house. Music is especially an effective means of cure. Many of the patients played on the piano remarkably well. They showed me an elderly lady, who had been brought hither in a state of perfect fatuity. They gave her a piano, and encouraged her to play some little simple pieces, such as she had played in her youth. By degrees the memory of many of these early pieces reawoke, until the whole of her childhood's music revived within her, and with it, as it seemed, the world of her childhood. She played to me, and went with visible delight from one little piece to another. . . . She will probably never become perfectly well and strong in mind, but she spends here a happy, harmless life, in the music of her early years."[69]

Music had a key function in the New World, where so much of society was still raw and unsettled. If rightly conducted, it counteracted the uncivilized conduct brought on by their crude living conditions. It helped to make important aspects of human nature whole. Contemporary spokespeople cited music's ability to convey beneficial principles, promote social decorum, and encapsulate human events within a moral framework. Song acted like an inoculation against moral disease. Properly channeled, it directed a person toward right thought and conduct and thus was restorative and praiseworthy.

60   John Rowe Parker was insistent about this effectiveness when he wrote in
1820:

> Music is not only an innocent recreation, if properly directed, but is
> capable of being eminently beneficial to the younger classes of soci-
> ety. In many instances, it may be the means of preventing that vacu-
> ity of mind, which is too frequently the parent of libertinism; of pre-
> cluding the intrusion of idle and dangerous imaginations; and more
> particularly . . . may prove an antidote to the poison insidiously ad-
> ministered by the innumerable licentious novels, which are hourly
> sapping the foundations of every moral and religious principle.[70]

Moral as well as mental therapy was on Harriet Beecher Stowe's mind
when she said, "The influence of music over the disturbed nerves and bewil-
dered moral sense of those who have gone astray from virtue is something
very remarkable." She speaks of hymns as like singing angels, walking the
earth and scattering the devils before them. Hymns "watched over our cham-
ber-door, they sit upon our pillow, they sing to us when we awake" to cancel
out evil and lead to God.[71]

Moral therapy was also the object of one clergyman's employment of
music. Mrs. Sigourney depicts him as follows:

> An excellent clergyman, possessing much knowledge of human na-
> ture, instructed his large family of daughters in the theory and prac-
> tice of music. They were all observed to be exceedingly amiable and
> happy. A friend inquired if there was any secret in his mode of edu-
> cation. He replied, "When any thing disturbs their temper, I say to
> them *sing*, and if I hear them speaking against any person, I call
> them to sing to me, and so they have sung away all causes of discon-
> tent and every disposition to scandal.[72]

Charles Quill advocated music for ordinary laborers ("mechanics"), not
only because it soothed troubled minds but also because it made them receptive to every worthwhile moral impression. It knitted their families together
and boosted the pleasures of the home over those of the barroom and gaming
table. Moral therapy through music was also recommended for inmates of
prisons. The Hutchinson Family Singers derived satisfaction from their stops
at Sing Sing Prison, where they presented such compositions as "My Mother's
Bible" and saw the prisoners in tears and presumably put on the road to
moral health. Harriet Martineau spoke approvingly of the prison authorities
at the Charlestown Prison, in Massachusetts, who allowed black and white

convicts to practice the singing of works such as "The Heavens Are Telling." It could only lead to their betterment, in her estimation.[73]

For a huge number of African Americans living under duress, music was an essential for their well-being. The persistence of the songs that were sung in the antebellum years and the meanings attached to them are amenable to several interpretations. Just for them to exist gave evidence that the slave's inventive imagination would endure the harshness of servitude. A means was at hand for the slave to project his circumstances onto music, to construct extravagant and revivifying images of himself, and to form some rationale about his fate. This aspect of therapy was of paramount importance to those subjected to tyranny. Music was a part of their everyday living not normally regulated by the master. It comprehended vital influences on the mind for restraining rage. It directed overt and suppressed hostility into paths that kept the spirit unharmed and the being healthy. Thus could song entertain even as it allowed one to more usefully confront the cruelties that came with daily living. Even the slave owner recognized that music mitigated the hardship of servitude and calmed the slave's feelings of frustration and anger.[74] Jim Quattlebaum said this of his South Carolina master: "Marster lak to see his slaves happy and singin' 'bout de place. If he ever heard any of them quarrelin' wid each other, he would holler at them and say: 'Sing! Us ain't got no time to fuss on dis place!'"[75]

Solomon Northup, born in New York State as a free person, kidnapped to the South, and enslaved from 1841 to 1853, wrote of his captivity:

> Alas! had it not been for my beloved violin, I scarcely can conceive how I could have endured the long years of bondage. It introduced me to great houses—relieved me of many day's labor in the field—supplied me with conveniences for my cabin—with pipe and tobacco, and extra pairs of shoes, and oftentimes led me away from the presence of a harsh master, to witness scenes of jollity and mirth. It was my companion—the friend of my bosom—triumphing loudly when I was joyful, and uttering its soft, melodious consolations when I was sad. Often, at midnight, when sleep had fled affrighted from the cabin, and my soul was disturbed and troubled with the contemplation of my fate, it would sing me a song of peace. On holy Sabbath days, when an hour or two of leisure was allowed, it would accompany me to some quiet place on the bayou bank and lifting up its voice, discourse kindly and pleasantly indeed.[76]

Almost unbearable anguish agitated the slaves on a South Carolina plantation when a number of them were sold to a slave trader, who was taking them to a railroad station for transportation to Louisiana. Families were being split apart, perhaps permanently, and Louisiana was seen "as a place of slaughter." The news flew to all of the nearby plantations:

> While passing along, many of the negroes left their masters' fields and joined us as we marched to the cars; some were yelling and wringing their hands, while others were singing little hymns that they were accustomed to for the consolation of those that were going away, such as,
>
> > When we all meet in heaven,
> > There is no parting there. . . .
>
> We arrived at the depot and had to wait for the cars to bring the others from the Sumterville Jail, but they soon came in sight, and when the noise of the cars died away we heard wailing and shrieks from those in the cars. While some were weeping, others were fiddling, picking banjos, and dancing as they used to do in their cabins on the plantations. Those who were so merry had very bad masters, and even though they stood a chance of being sold to one as bad or even worse, yet they were glad to be rid of the one they knew.[77]

Hymns for consolation and fiddling and banjoing out of relief were complementary manifestations of the therapy offered by music under the circumstances.

### Songs for Remembrance

Ah, what a hallowing glory invests our past, beckoning us back to the haunts of the olden time! The paths our childish feet trod seem all angel-guarded and thornless; the songs we sang then sweep the harp of memory, making magical melody; the words carelessly spoken, now breathe a solemn mysterious import; and faces that early went down to the tomb, smile on us still with unchanged tenderness. Aye, the past, the long past is all fairy-land.[78]

Americans cultivated two kinds of songs for remembrance. One kind comprised songs learned in earlier years that, when sung, recalled those years. The older singer and listener found them full of "beauty which time has only mellowed, and which come down to us hallowed with associations which cluster around them like vines."[79] However old fashioned, even obsolete, such

songs might be, they often proved more delightful to older people's ears than    **63**
contemporary songs (and these included hymns), said John Pintard. For him
to hear music of his juvenile years, like "Luther's Old Hundred," "Down the
Bourne Davie Love," "'Twas When the Seas Were Roaring," and "Auld Robin
Grey," brought back the long-gone scenes with friends and family he saw no
more. On the trail to California, Lucius Fairchild heard a girl sing "my old
favorite song 'Good bye,' which seems like home and sister Sarah." Eliza
Ripley watched a party of little girls dancing and marching to music she had
not heard for forty years and said that she immediately felt joyous, was taken
back to her girlhood, and had the impulse to get up and move about with the
children.[80]

One did not have to be ancient to value the past and the music that
recalled it. Sallie Ford in 1857 described a newly wed young woman, Grace
Truman, who had moved to some austere western settlement. One day, suddenly, she heard someone sing a hymn that began "The pity of the Lord" and
recalled having sung it at her parent's home. The past became intensely
present in her mind: "We see it, we read it, we *feel* it. . . . in a moment we
escape from the realities of the living present, and wander amid the by-gones
of the resurrected past. Our mother, our childhood's home, all of joy, all of
sorrow that our heart has known, is before us with the vividness of actual
existence."[81]

A song from the past is movingly referred to by Mary Claflin in *Personal
Recollections of John G. Whittier.* She portrays a post–Civil War reunion of
antislavery associates:

> When the excitement of the hour was at its height all tongues were
> silenced by the voice of a woman singing "John Brown's body," all
> eyes were turned toward the piano where the singer was seated play-
> ing her own accompaniment. She was one of the "unfortunate
> races," and as her thrilling tones, tremulous with emotion, floated
> through the rooms, every voice caught up the song,—those who
> had a voice to sing, and those who sang with their souls, swelled the
> grand chorus, and at the conclusion there was not a dry eye in the
> room. . . . Mr. Whittier listened with bowed head, his eyes suffused
> with tears, and his flushed cheeks showing the deepest emotion.[82]

There were contemporary songs whose subjects referred to and reinforced memories of objects, people, and circumstances of the past. In them
were affectionately recalled and idealized images of yesteryear, of someone or
something cherished. The inclusion of these musical images into one's own
mind enabled a person to repossess much of the ambience of an earlier

**64**    existence. This, in turn, the individual objectified and applied as archetypes
for his own conduct in subsequent years. It introduced a degree of stability in
spite of constantly changing circumstances.

The antebellum American would never forsake the period of his childhood and adolescence, in whatever form he had experienced it, in order solely
to focus on the present and future. For him to do so would have seemed
ridiculous, even sacrilegious. Forever included amid his highly regarded treas-
ures were those memories he had cared to save, ponder, absorb, and visualize
anew.

Stephen Foster was a master of songs valued for their evocation of
bittersweet longing for the past. Americans by the thousands claimed as their
own such songs as "The Voice of By Gone Days" (1850), "Old Folks at Home"
(1851), "I Cannot Sing To-Night" (1852), "Old Dog Tray" (1853), "My Old
Kentucky Home" (1853), and "Jeanie with the Light Brown Hair" (1854). At
times, remembrance inspired the creation of a new lyric, as it did in the fall
of 1844, when Abraham Lincoln's visit to his old home and the graves of his
mother and sister awakened childhood memories. He then wrote "My Childhood Home I See Again." The memories, he said:

> Seem hallowed, pure, and bright,
> Like scenes in some enchanted isle,
>    All bathed in liquid light.[83]

James Weir maintained, in his novel on Kentucky, *Lonz Powers,* that
hardened criminals in the wild lands of western Kentucky felt the softening
effect of nostalgic musical compositions. Contemporary readers were entirely
willing to accept the picture that he drew as true to life, of young women
about to receive bodily harm from some very rough characters. Unexpectedly,
one girl sang a "home" song. So "deeply moved and affected" was an outlaw
that he broke into tears, exclaiming to the others:

> I did hear a song! and sung, too, by one of these trembling girls . . .
> a song that brought tears even to these eyes, long strangers to mois-
> ture; a song that reminded me of years ago, and of my young man-
> hood, when . . . I knew nothing of life but honesty and happiness; a
> song that determined me to protect them from injury and insult.[84]

## Musical Transcendence

The landscape of America brought up feelings of transcendence, in a
manner similar to the evocations of fine music. As Garnett Andrews wrote of
the American highlands:

On account of their vastness and magnitude, one cannot look on a
lofty range of mountains without feeling some awe and elevation of
soul that is akin to the sensation inspired by contemplating the vastness of eternity. Fine music—I know not why—inspires the same
lofty sensations. Hence, I believe, when looking on the ocean, grand
mountain scenery, the vastness of an extensive prairie, or listening
to fine music, one is as near heaven, in this world, as on any other
occasion.[85]

The ultimate gratification that music could give, even to those without
musical ability and knowledge, was its engaging but mysterious summoning
forth of an ideal world. There was an enchantment linked to its refusal to
state anything explicitly while it alluded to the universal, wrote Henry Tuckerman.[86] No better antidote to the materialism that endangered the spirit
existed. Music was "vague because the thoughts and feelings it aims to express partake of the infinite . . . it is the heart's prayer, which cannot imbody
itself so fully as in the language of tones and harmonies; it seems like the
soul's effort to speak its mother tongue in a strange land, a yearning for a
complete fulfillment of its destiny."[87]

For most Americans, such transcendence came through singing and
listening to hymns. For the cosmopolitan and educated few, it came also
through symphony, chamber works, or the music of opera. Nevertheless, all
who valued the transcendental experience availed themselves of music that
struck them as noble, impressive, and sublime. As Harriet Beecher Stowe said
of her own preferences:

I do not see the propriety of confining one's self to technical sacred
music. Any grave, solemn, thoughtful, or pathetic music has a
proper relation to our higher spiritual nature, whether it be printed
in a church service-book or in secular sheets. On me, for example,
Beethoven's Sonatas have a far more deeply religious influence than
much that has religious names and words. Music is to be judged by
its effects.[88]

Rapture or ecstatic joy, that is to say, the carrying of a person to another
sphere of existence, was an essential attribute of the transcendental musical
experience. Bronson Alcott spoke of beauty and "the overflowing of life's tides
in rapture, in music and song." James Otis, who had Handel's and Haydn's
music in mind, referred to music's higher character when "its effect is to
produce *rapture*" and when "it elevates the spirit toward the eternal source
whence all its harmony flows." Miss Mendell, a woman frequently on the road
in her capacity as book peddler, took rapturous delight in the sound of song

**66**  and hymn, saying, "How lovingly, how like a mother it draws us from our gloomy thoughts, never chiding, but with persuasive tender tones reminding us of the bright Beyond, and bidding us on."[89]

The word *soul* was given two different meanings in its antebellum use. The first usage we have already encountered when we examined how music addressed the human individual's moral and emotional nature as distinguished from his intellect. The second usage, with which we are now concerned, involved music's connection to one's immortal, spiritual nature—"its revelation as to the life of the human soul," as Margaret Fuller put it. To her, music was "the greatest of arts—expressing what was most interior,—what was too fine to be put into any material grosser than air; conveying from soul to soul the most secret motions of feeling and thought." For Lydia Child, "music was to my soul what the atmosphere is to my body; it was the breath of my inward life."[90]

Americans held to the belief that music had the capability of liberating the individual from earthly bonds and of leading him to universal harmony, order, and unity. It freed a person from the limitation of words "by speaking a language to the soul more eloquent and richer in meaning than words could express."[91] Through music, one grew intimate with a spiritual self and reached out to God.

Here, as elsewhere in this chapter, the words of antebellum Americans may seem flowery, their feeling close to the bathetic. Yet they relished the richness of words and deliberately left themselves open to feeling. They were struggling to encompass their musical experiences within the limiting framework of verbal description. They chose to speak expansively in an attempt to get their meaning across. Theirs was not the world of the later centuries, where verbiage is supposed to be leaner, sentiment moderated—at least to *littérateurs* and academics. To speak of the emotional heart and the infinite soul during the antebellum period did not give rise to confusion and shame nor make for uneasy self-consciousness. The former was only the symbolic seat of feeling to them, true, but the latter did indeed exist for them, however enigmatic its dwelling place. We can hear George Upton struggling to make comprehensible what he sincerely felt at hearing Beethoven's Seventh Symphony, when he exclaims:

> Music is full of religion! The first tidings that ever came from Heaven to man came in music on the plains of Bethlehem. It reaches far down into the soul. It fills it with longings for the Unknown. It reveals the infinite more clearly than the spoken word. Its tendency is upward. It gives birth to aspirations. It makes a true man, truer. It makes a bad man, better.[92]

He had a right to his beliefs.                                                     **67**

On a humbler level, we find Uncle Ben Horry, a former slave in South Carolina, saying:

I like good song. One I like best?

> Try us, Oh Lord,
> And search the ground
> Of every sinful heart!
> What eer of sin
> In us is found
> Oh, bid it all depart!

Reason I choose that for a favorite hymn, I was to Brookgreen doing some work for Dr. Wardie Flagg and I had to climb as high as that live oak tree, and I feel high as that tree! I lay there till I doze off in sleep. And I tell you what happen to me curious. While I was sleep I seen two milk white chickens. You know what them two white fowl do? They gone and sit on my mother dresser right before the glass and sing that song. Them COULD sing! And it seem like a woman open a vial and pour something on me. My spiritual mother (in dem day every member o the church have what they call a spiritual mother) say, "That not natural fowl. That sent you for a token." Since that time I serve the choir five or six years and no song seem strange to me since that day.[93]

George Upton and Uncle Ben Horry, each in his own way, had undergone a transcendental experience through music.

# CHAPTER 3

# Becoming Acquainted with Music

G OVERNMENT, WHETHER LOCAL, STATE, OR FEDERAL, scarcely ever intervened in the production, distribution, and vending of music. This was left to the private sector, as was thought proper for a market economy and, by extension, a market culture. Not until 1838, at the instigation of Lowell Mason and the Boston Academy of Music, did public music education begin in the Boston schools, gradually to spread to other, though not all, areas of the country. This was the first and only significant venture of governmental bodies into music's domain during the antebellum years. Otherwise, government would benefit music only indirectly, through its general services, such as improved distribution of music publications owing to new road construction and improved mail delivery.

The dissemination of musical information had to wait, first of all, for improvements in transport and travel conditions. Fulton and his successful demonstration of the steamboat in 1807 meant that serious upstream river travel became a reality. In 1811 the National Road was begun, eventually to reach from the eastern seaboard to far beyond western Pennsylvania. Along it traveled wagonloads of goods and coaches full of travelers. The Erie Canal was completed in 1825, further opening the lands to the west. Shortly thereafter, railroad construction commenced. The movement of people westward grew into a mighty flow. By the time of the Civil War, roads, railroads, and artificially improved waterways were crisscrossing the entire United States east of the Mississippi. Two consequences were a more efficient postal system and a swifter exchange of news, information, and goods. By the mid-1840s, a uniform postage rate structure had been put into place. Prepaid postage stamps, moderate in price, were offered the public, as an alternative to the customary high-cost pay-on-delivery rates. Ten years later, postage stamps became compulsory to use. Music publishers and purveyors of music goods

could more economically and efficiently reach immense, heretofore underuti-
lized audiences with sheet music, music books, notices of new publications
and wares, and offers to facilitate purchase of any music item.

Catharine Sedgwick reported on a third consequence: "The progress of
civilization, and the facilities of communication have levelled all distinctions.
There is no village so secluded now [1852] as to be surprised by the fashions
of the town, and scarcely a country-bred lady to be detected by her rusticity."
Direct imports from France and England were finding their way to shops that
were once country stores.[1] Music in its variety was also finding its way to
shops, as were music performers to village halls and music teachers to the
academies.

Little by little, residents in every part of the nation had access to music
publications and instruments and grew familiar with music teachers and
professional performers. After Eli Whitney proved the efficacy of interchange-
able parts in 1800, the mass production of low-priced music instruments
increased. Writing about a Vermont town at the beginning of the 1820s,
Sophie Damon said, "This was . . . before the piano and cabinet-organ found
their way into nearly every house where music-lovers dwelt. A few spirits, and
one or two pianos and harps, were all that the thriving town . . . could boast,
although thirty or forty years later there was a perfect frenzy for the Melodeon and Seraphine. . . . On all festive days as well as religious occasions, the
bass-viol and violin were the chief dependence, the fife and drum being of
course indispensable on Training-day." By September 1842 Lydia Child was
able to comment: "Music, like every thing else, is now passing from the few to
the many. . . . Music is taught in our common schools, and the cheap accordion brings its delights to the humblest class of citizens."[2]

It was not only the manufacture of low-cost instruments that facilitated
knowledge of music, but also the advent of low-cost sheet music and scores.
The discovery of wood pulp as an inexhaustible source for paper manufacture
and the automation of the printing press made the purchase of music affordable for most wage earners. In 1844 N. P. Willis published an article, "The
Mirror Steam Press," in which he stated:

> The improvements in printing-presses within the last ten or fifteen
> years are probably far less remarkable than some other progresses of
> mechanic invention, yet they are wonderful enough. . . . The differ-
> ence between the old Ramage press, and the steam-miracle in our
> present office, is peculiarly impressive to ourself. . . . We remember
> *balling* [inking the type by hand via a leather ball] an edition of
> "Watt's Psalms and Hymns," which took weeks to print. . . . Inven-
> tion soon after superseded the ink-boy's elbows . . . by a bit of ma-

chinery that neither required to be fed, nor committed verses to memory while inking the type! This getting rid of the *boy* was the peculiarity of the *Smith* press, and then followed the *Napa* press, which dispensed with the *man*, and needed only the tending of two girls or boys; and now (thanks to Mr. Hoe), we have a steam-press, which *puts up three iron fingers for a sheet of white paper, pulls it down into its bosom, gives it a squeeze that makes an impression and then lays it into the palm of an iron hand which deposits it evenly on a heap—at the rate of two thousand an hour.*[3]

Music stores, many maintained by music publishers for the sake of selling their own sheet music productions, were making their appearance in the cities. Newspapers and other periodicals began offering songs as supplements to their subscribers. Failing that, they printed song texts in their pages, identifying the tunes to which they should be sung. Sheet music became sufficiently modest in price that newspaper offices and general stores catering to the ordinary public began making them available for purchase. By 1845 the *Western General Advertiser* of Cincinnati was announcing that it offered sheet music (the songs "We'll Go to the Sea No More," "Thou Sweet Gliding Kedron," and "The Departed"), received from Peters and Company, for resale to its customers. Far away from the East Coast, the *Los Angeles Star* was reporting in 1858: "Our taste for music is neither innate or cultivated and unfortunately we have never been able to rightly appreciate the heavenly sounds, but we saw some this week at the book and variety of Mr. Ducommun that did excite our admiration," and, "We acknowledge with thanks the receipt of music from the publishers in New York."[4]

Advancing technology had facilitated the affordability and distribution of music for the large democratic public and thereby increased the chance that more and more Americans might want further acquaintance with music and would become curious about learning how to sing and play an instrument.

### Musical Instruments in the Home

Men and women became acquainted with music by learning how to play an instrument, which in turn led to learning music for that instrument. At the close of the eighteenth century, musical instruments were still scarce and the ability to play them negligible. Therefore, an enterprising Dr. Flagg in 1797 offered to go to Europe and return with hand organs that he would have programmed to play mechanically any desired hymns. A scarcity of instruments was not a problem in the Moravian community of Bethlehem, Pennsylvania, where music played an indispensable role in worship, leisure, and education. On 9 August 1803 Eliza Southgate wrote from Bethlehem to her mother in Scarborough, Maine, about the great fondness for music she found in the town. There was "scarcely a house in the place without a Piano-forte." The postmaster's parlor sported "an elegant grand piano." Visiting the Young Men's house, she came upon youths performing together on an organ, two bass viols, four violins, two flutes, two French horns, two clarinets, a bassoon, "and an Instrument I never heard before." When she visited the town's school, much to her astonishment, she found a piano in every schoolroom and little girls being taught music.[5]

Nonetheless, although the rest of the United States remained almost barren of pianos, the importation of pianos and other musical instruments was increasing, and their local manufacture had commenced. By 1806 a British traveler was reporting that storekeepers in western Pennsylvania were trying to keep on hand all articles possible that local residents might want, including German flutes. Nothing was said about instruction. However, the availability of musical instruments and available instruction on them increased year after year, so that by 1822 Timothy Dwight could remark: "People of wealth, and many in moderate circumstances, have their children taught music; particularly on the piano-forte; and many of the young men play on the German flute, violin, clarionet, etc. Serenading is not unfrequent." At the beginning of the 1850s Joel Ross spoke of his amazement at the proliferation of pianos: "There are forty or fifty manufactures of these beautiful instruments, which at the present day adorn nearly every mansion." Pianos were priced at $225 to $1000.[6] On the eve of the Civil War, musical instruments were in a majority of homes—pianos, melodeons, violins, flutes, guitars, banjos, accordions, and harps, mainly. Most Americans could sing, and a surprising number could play a little, that is to say, perform popular song melodies, traditional ballad airs, dance tunes, and hymns.

Americans desired musical instruments, going through considerable trouble to acquire them for their homes. To give one example, in the late 1820s and into the 1830s, pianos were appearing in Pittsburgh. A few had been carried from the eastern seacoast through the mountains to Pittsburgh by mule train and canal boat. Because the demand still remained unsatisfied, one or two enterprising local residents had commenced manufacturing them in Pittsburgh itself. To give another, in 1848–49 California gold miners avidly sought after sheet music and whatever musical instruments were available— accordions, violins, guitars, flutes, horns—in order to entertain themselves when not panning for gold. They played these instruments in the evening, however tired they might feel. By January 1850 Andrew Kohler had opened a combined grocery and music store in San Francisco, and nine months later, Joseph Atwill had arrived from New York and set up a publishing house and

72    retail music establishment with the expectation of a profitable public response to their offerings.[7] Raw as life was on the Pacific Coast, it still required music.

For a long while, the piano was a newfangled notion for most Americans. Only on the northeastern coast was it soon a common object. Pianos were either seen or known to be in households, such as that in which the young Harriet Beecher Stowe lived during the 1820s, in Connecticut. Her father was a Congregational minister and music lover:

> Father was very fond of music, and very susceptible to its influence; and one of the great eras of the family in my childish recollection, is the triumphant bringing home from New Haven of a fine-tuned upright piano, which a fortunate accident had brought within the range of a poor country minister's means. The ark of the covenant was not brought into the tabernacle with more gladness than this magical instrument into our abode. . . . Father soon learned to accompany the piano with his violin in various psalm tunes and Scotch airs, and brothers Edward and William to perform their part on the flute. So we had often domestic concerts, which, if they did not attain to the height of artistic perfection, filled the house with gladness.[8]

Henry Longfellow was living close to Harvard University when he wrote to his father on 25 October 1838: "The Commodore [Alexander Scammell Wadsworth] purchased a beautiful piano-forte: rose-wood, with a most soft, and melodious tone. I think Aunt Luisa [*sic*] will be delighted with it. If she is not, she must indeed be hard to please. Perhaps she has friends, who set themselves up for critics; and may think it necessary to find fault."[9] Aunt Louisa was a pianist, had old music, and set about getting new music for the instrument.

Across the Charles River, in Boston, Julia Ward Howe wrote to her sister Louisa on 4 August 1846 of her excitement over the arrival of her new piano:

> Yesterday was made famous by the purchase of a very beautiful piano of Chickering's [Boston] manufacture. The value of it was $450, but the kind Chick sold it to us at wholesale price. It arrived at Green Place to-day, and has already gladdened the children's hearts by some gay tunes, the rags of my antiquated musical repertory. You will be glad, I am sure, to know that I have one at last, for I have been many months without an instrument, so that I have almost forgotten how to touch one.[10]

Before less sophisticated people, who were legion, could get acquainted
with the piano's music, they had to get acquainted with the instrument itself.
Emily Barnes talks of the piano's first arrival in her village of Walpole, New
Hampshire, around 1806–10:

> The Colonel [John Bellows] purchased the first piano that was ever
> brought into Walpole. It was said that he imported it directly from
> France. . . . He lived about a mile from the village, and I happened to
> be there at the time the piano-forte arrived. That word [piano-forte]
> had not been interpreted to many of the inhabitants of that period;
> and, when the huge box in which it was brought and labelled in
> large capitals, was being unloaded, quite a number of people gath-
> ered about it, critically examining the letters and greatly puzzled as
> to what they might spell. One individual very knowingly informed
> them that it was the name of an extinct animal, whose bones had
> been dug up somewhere, and wired together, and were being carried
> about for exhibition. . . . I think it would be very amusing, particu-
> larly to those who have been accustomed to the grand piano of the
> present time [1880s] if they could see one of those instruments of
> that early period. This one that was purchased for Cousin Maria was
> a very large instrument, having a good deal of ornamental work
> about it . . . but its capacity was very limited as compared with what
> instruments of to-day furnish to our ear.[11]

People living in the country areas of Indiana in the 1840s knew hardly
anything about the piano. Lew Wallace was around twenty years old and in
Crawfordsville, Indiana, when he heard that a Major Elston had recently
imported a piano:

> What was a piano? Those of whom I asked, hardly better informed
> than myself, told me it was a big music machine. The description ex-
> cited my curiosity the more. And again I invited myself into the Ma-
> jor's home, and saw the sight without discovery; whereupon I was
> beset with a greater wonder. How was the playing done? I laid in
> wait for the solution. One evening the double parlor was a wonder
> of brilliance. A party was in progress. I worked my way, Indian-like,
> to a window through which the whole interior was in view. In a lit-
> tle while, sure enough, a young lady went to the machine, opened
> it, and began a song with an accompaniment. I remember the song:
> "One little, two little, three little Indians,/Four little, five little, six lit-
> tle Indians," and so on for quantity.[12]

The purchase of a new piano was an indulgence possible only to rather affluent people who could afford to pay out around $225 or more. For music-hungry families of more limited means, there appeared around 1810 the melodeon, a simple reed organ, also known as the seraphine, whose lightness made it readily portable and whose price, as low as $45, easily affordable.[13] By the 1840s it had become extremely popular and could be found in the modest homes and small churches of villages and towns throughout the country. Itinerant ministers and evangelists found a melodeon convenient to take along during their circuits. The melodeon even went west with the explorers and settlers and showed up in hamlets from the Mississippi to the Pacific. The melodeon was considered a superior instrument for the accompaniment of singing.

A person with scarcely any money could still find some sort of musical instrument available at minimal cost. Asa Greene tells of a South Carolina farmer who found his land had poor productivity and so turned to manufacturing wooden Jew's harps, selling them "for three halfpence a piece." They sold well, so he increased the price to "one penny three farthings." His brother objected to the higher price, although he admitted that Jew's harps answered "every purpose" for his "negroes, whose leisure hours must be amused with Jewsharps of some kind or other, to prevent them from being worse employed."[14]

Americans were a dauntless lot. When a desired instrument was unavailable, an ingenious handworker might make one for himself, as did the doctor father of William Cullen Bryant, who once made a bass viol to play upon. At least he knew what the instrument looked and sounded like. There were others who lived in isolation, far from the informed sections of the country. They, too, wanted music in their lives. Without a blueprint for making an instrument, and with unclear ideas of what instrument to make, they went ahead anyway and put something together that would produce acceptable sounds. They then set about learning how to play it by trial and error. Harriet Martineau provides an example of this sort of instrument. She tells of being in a wild part of New Hampshire's White Mountains in the 1830s when her party came upon the home of Ethan Crawford:

> We were little prepared for such entertainment as we found. After a
> supper of fine lake trout, a son of our host played to us on a name-
> less instrument made by the joiners who put the house together,
> and highly creditable to their ingenuity. It was something like the
> harmonica in form, and the bagpipes in tone; but, well-played as it
> was by the boy, it was highly agreeable. Then Mr. Crawford danced
> an American jig, to the fiddling of a relation of his. The dancing

was somewhat solemn; but its good faith made up for any want of mirth.[15]

From what has just been said, it is obvious that there was, as Charles Quill said, "a *taste* for music in our people." He noted that "in half our shops there is some musical instrument; and even though nothing but horrid discord is extracted from the ill-tuned fiddle or cracked flute, the very attempt shows the existence of a natural desire for the pleasures of melody." The fact that ordinary laborers were forming bands, and that some of the best bands were "composed of young working-men," proved to him that "music was not a luxury for laborers." Nevertheless, most of them had to learn how to play their instruments without instruction from a music teacher.[16]

African Americans, most of them in servitude and penniless, were constantly crafting plucked, bowed, and percussive instruments for themselves out of the materials at hand—gourds, reeds, sticks, tree trunks, bones, barrels, different sized containers and tins, and discarded farm and home utensils. When lucky, they possessed fiddles, clarinets, fifes, flutes, guitars, and banjos of professional manufacture. Only a handful of free African Americans could boast ownership of a piano. One of these fortunate ones, William Johnson, a Natchez barber, wrote in his diary on 22 December 1835: "I paid Mr. Maury $15 for repairing my Piano Forte and gave him orders to sell it for the Best price He Could get for it But that he must not sell I for Less than $70." On 7 April 1836 Johnson wrote: "To night I sent up and had my old Piano Brought Home from Mr. Maurys." And on 31 March 1843: "Mrs. Alexander sent up to Know what I would take for the Piano. I sent her word that I would take twenty five Dollars for it."[17]

Most musically inclined slaves, when they desired a regular instrument, did everything they could to obtain a fiddle, guitar, or banjo, however battered. Jerry Boykins, while a slave in Texas, longed for a fiddle:

> One time I wanted a fiddle a white man named Coconut Harper kep'
> tryin' to sell me for $7.50. I didn' never have any money, 'cept a lit-
> tle the missie give me, so I kep' teasin' her to buy de fiddle for me.
> She was allus on my side, so she tol' me to take some co'n from de
> crib and trade it for de fiddle. In de night I slips out and hitch up de
> mules and fetched de co'n to old Harper's house and traded for dat
> fiddle. Den I hides out and play it, so'm marster wouldn' fin' out, but
> he did and he whip all daylight outta me.[18]

Reports abound of slaves fashioning their own instruments. An ill Kentucky slave owner, who died later in the day, ordered in slaves to dance for him, and a fiddler, with a homemade instrument created from an old gourd, to play under the threat of a whipping. In New Orleans, a Congo dance was executed with music, such as it was, from an "excavated piece of wood . . . one end of which is a piece of parchment which covers the hollow part on which they beat." On a Mississippi plantation, "Some of de colored folks was pretty sociable. . . . De niggers on de plantation dance a heap—seemed ter me like hit was mos' ever' night. You takes a coon skin an' make a drum out of hit, stretch hit over a keg—a sawed-off one—dat make a fine drum. An' banjos an' fiddlers! Didn' have no mandolines an' gui-tars then."[19]

One of the most interesting of the homemade instruments, and a common one, was the panpipe. Gerry Brown says that on his Georgia plantation, "before a frolic would begin the men would go to the swamps and get long quills which would furnish music by blowing through them. The music reminded one of the music of a flute." C. B. Burton, on a South Carolina plantation, says, "We danced and had gigs. Some played de fiddle and some made whistles from canes, having different lengths for different notes, and blowed 'em like mouth organs." And Lila Coleman of Mississippi comments, "Mama an' me worked in de fiel'. We danced outdoors on de groun'. They clapped hands fer us ter dance by an' played home-made banjos an' harps. No'm, not harps you picks but harps made out of leetle pieces of reeds-like; you blow in 'em. They made purdy music."[20]

African Americans who became proficient instrumentalists usually had to gain their skill through self-instruction. White slaveholders, to furnish themselves with ready entertainment, often ordered that one or more of their slaves learn to play on his own. John Davis describes a Virginia slave, "Dick the Negro," whom he met in 1802, as saying:

> My young master was a mighty one for music, and he made me
> learn to play the Banger. I could soon tune it sweetly, and of a moon-
> light night he would set me to play, and the wenches to dance. My
> young master himself could shake a desperate foot at the fiddle;
> there was nobody that could face him at a *Congo Minuet;* but *Pat
> Hickory* could tire him at a *Virginia Jig.*[21]

At first, few instruction books for instruments were available. With the turn of the century, much music began to be imported from London and a few American music publishers had established themselves. This enabled the Franklin Music Warehouse of Boston to advertise in 1820 that it had for sale "an extensive collection of the most fashionable music, consisting of instructions [i.e., method books for self-instruction] for Piano-Forte, Violin, Clarionet,

Oboe, Flute, Fife, Flageolet, Guitar, Lyre, Bassoon, Clarion, Horn, Trumpet, Bugle, Trombone, Violoncello, Serpent and Drum." For several years the self-taught instrumental player was the norm. Consequently, we learn of Augustus Longstreet, a Georgian, who loved music and taught himself to play the flute and piano. He had a gift for hearing a piece of music, then being able to "play it off 'by ear.'" There was also a New Jersey coach painter who had taught himself French and music. The clarinet was the favorite of the several instruments he had learned to play. "He seemed to use it as the outlet for those musings which found no vent among his ordinary associations; for most of his performances were voluntaries and fitful *capriccios*."[22]

Many other instances of self-taught instrumental players could be cited, among them Jonas Chickering, the piano manufacturer, who taught himself the fife and clarinet; James Gates Percival, the poet, who learned on his own to play the accordion, flute, and guitar; a young woman of Ellisburgh, New York, who had learned so well to play the melodeon and to sing that "to send her to a music teacher is unnecessary"; and a young laborer, mentioned by Charles Quill, who was completely self-taught on the violin but without talent, so that the tunes he played sounded excruciatingly painful to the ear.[23]

In due course, as the Jacksonian democratic era lengthened, do-it-yourself instruction books, priced and written for people of limited income and musical knowledge, came into print, as did easy arrangements of music for instruments. The Philadelphia composer and publisher Septimus Winner alone turned out around fifteen hundred simple arrangements and issued a succession of short, cheaply priced, and highly popular elementary instruction methods for various instruments.[24]

### Discovering Music in the Domestic Circle

The household was a significant and indispensable school for the young. Because of the severely limited means for diversion outside the home, it was also the principal place for recreation. When the family gathered for the evening, parents and children sang, played musical instruments, engaged in games (many of them with music involved), and read aloud. These were widespread family amusements. Prayer services and hymn singing, too, were common components of religious households, of which there were more than a few.

It follows that children invariably learned a great deal of music within the home—from grandparents, parents, siblings, relatives, friends, neighbors, and, if born into well-off households, servants. Most people sang hymns if nothing else, but more often a rich mixture of songs old and new, sacred and secular, serious and comic. The youngster first heard this music coming from the lips of trusted and loved individuals, and these sounds became some of his or her earliest memories. Only on occasion did musical learning take place whose source was unidentifiable. One such instance occurred in Lucy Larcom's infancy. Even before she could talk intelligibly, she toddled about the house humming constantly: "My father and mother/Shall come unto the land," sometimes varied with "My brothers and sisters/Shall come unto the land." Nobody knew from whom she had taken words and tune.[25]

Traditional hymns and song were constantly handed down from grandmother, especially the maternal grandmother, to grandchild. Thus, Samuel Goodrich, talking about his growing up in Ridgefield, Connecticut, mentions the "plaintive songs" and ancient "ballads" he delightedly learned from his maternal grandmother, because they "were suited to my taste." Frederic Cozzens attributes his knowledge of ancient legends and songs also to his maternal grandmother. Abraham Lincoln, while still a tiny boy, learned old ballads like "Fair Ellender" and "Wicked Polly" that were once sung by his maternal grandmother, and then by his mother, Nancy Hanks Lincoln.[26]

Joanna Isom described her Mississippi childhood as a slave as follows:

When I wuz little my granny taught me some ole'd slave songs dat she sed had been used to sing babies to sleep ever since she wuz a chile. I used to sing dis one:

Little black sheep, where's yo' lam',
Way down yonder in de meado'.
The bees an' de butterflies
A-peckin' out hiz eyes.
The poor little black sheep
Cry Ma-a-a-my.

And an elderly Hector Smith said that he still remembered songs that he learned from his grandparents, including "Nobody Business but Mine," which began:

Rabbit in de hollow,
I ain' got no dog.
How can I catch 'em?
I do know! I do know!
O Me! O Mine!
Sorry dat if I leave my home,
I gwine to my shack

Wid de chicken on my back,
Nobody business but mine.[27]

It was to be expected that devout parents, however poor, would see to it
that their sons or daughters had their own book of hymns out of which to
sing, as was the case for the unidentified writer of *An Autobiography*. It was
also to be expected that parents in humble circumstances who had attended
singing school, or otherwise learned how to read music, would pass on their
knowledge to their children, as the unassuming cooper Arthur Kip and his
wife did for their son.[28]

Those fathers devoted to music, of whom there were many, invariably
passed on their love of songs and instrumental pieces, and the printed music
they owned, to their offspring. The father of Alice and Phoebe Cary was an
Ohio farmer; their stepmother, a "hard, uncultured, utilitarian woman." It
was from their deeply religious father that the children learned to read, sing
hymns, and share in the Bible readings. Elizabeth Pringle, growing up in
isolation on a South Carolina plantation, was fortunate in her "father's love
of art, and of music, and of all beauty. . . . It made all the difference in the
world to us, his children, growing up in the country, so far from picture-
galleries and concerts and every kind of music."[29]

One of the most interesting accounts of a father's musical influence on
his children comes from Susan Smedes, who grew up on a Mississippi plantation in the 1850s. Her father adored music; her mother did not:

> She had no ear for music, and understood that her children could
> hardly be expected to be very proficient in that. But Thomas desired
> and expected his daughters to perform like professionals. He was ex-
> cessively fond of music, although he never learned to play on any in-
> struments except the flute, on which he played very poorly, and he
> gave that up as soon as he heard better music from his children's
> fingers. He filled the house with musical instruments,—two pianos,
> and a harp, and a flute or so, and, later on, a melodeon for sacred
> music.[30]

Many fathers of children who later contributed to American music sang
or played an instrument and encouraged their sons and daughters to do
likewise. The farmer father of the Hutchinson Family Singers "for many years
whiled away the hours of toil singing many old ballads and hymns, in which
his boys, mowing and raking at his side, joined him heartily." Stephen Foster's
father encouraged and participated in the family's evening concerts. He liked

**80**    especially to sing merry old tunes, a few displaying vulgar humor. One that
never failed to delight the children was "The Three Rogues:"

> In the good old Colony days,
> When we were under the King,
> Three roguish chaps
> Fell into mishaps
> Because they could not sing.

Is it any wonder that the ten-year-old Stephen wrote to his father, who was
away from home, saying, "I wish you to send me a commic [sic] songster for
you promised to."[31]

For most men and women, it was especially their mother's singing voice
that recurred in their earliest memories. "How many of us can recall 'Blue-
eyed Mary'? the little ballad with which my mother always quieted me to rest.
. . . And in my childhood days, too, mammy rocked me to sleep with 'Ole
Grimes is daid, dat good ole man.'" Or, "One of my earliest recollections is of
being put early into his [father's] great bed, by which my beautiful mother sat
and sung to me in her sweetest voice to a Hebrew air—'Hush, my dear—lie
still and slumber!/Holy angels guard thy bed.'" Or, "Abby [Hutchinson] was a
born musician. As soon as she could talk she began to sing. The first songs
she learned were the hymns taught her by her mother while singing at her
spinning wheel. At the early age of four years she displayed such musical
talent that people would come from afar to hear her childish songs."[32]

The daughters of Julia Ward Howe said that their mother had given them
their earliest music lessons on the piano, which was located in the dining
room:

> We see ourselves gathered in the great dining-room, where the
> grand piano was, and the Gobelin carpet with the strange beasts
> and fishes, bought at the sale of the ex-King Joseph Bonaparte's fur-
> niture at Bordentown, and the Snyders' Boar Hunt, which one of us
> could never pass without a shiver; see ourselves dancing to our
> mother's playing,—wonderful dances, invented by Flossy, who was
> always *première danseuse*, and whose "Lady Macbeth" dagger dance
> was a thing to remember.
>
> Then perhaps the door would open, and in would come "Papa"
> as a bear, in his fur overcoat, growling horribly and chase the danc-
> ers into corners, they shrieking terrified delight.
>
> Again, we see ourselves clustered round the piano while our
> mother sang to us; songs of all nations, from the Polish drinking-

songs that Uncle Sam had learned in his student days in Germany, down to the Negro melodies which were very near our hearts.

Best of all, however, we loved her own songs: cradle songs and nursery nonsense made for our very selves. . . . Again, she would sing passionate songs of love or battle, or hymns of lofty faith and aspiration. One and all, we listened eagerly; one and all, we too began to see visions and dream dreams.

Of their lessons they said:

Probably we were troublesome children and made more noise than we should. Her accurate ear for music was often a source of distress to her, as one of us can witness, an indolent child who neglected her practicing. As the child drummed over her scales, the door of the upstairs study would open, and a clear voice come ringing down, "*B flat,* dear, *not* B natural!"

It seemed to the child a miracle; she, with the book before her, could not get it right: Mamma, studying Kant upstairs behind closed doors, knew what the note should be.[33]

If it was not from a mother's lips, then it was from her music collection that a daughter or son might learn a piece of music. A Boston girl, Kate Wentworth, was asked by her admirer, a Harvard student about to graduate, to sing again a song he had heard from her lips the year before. He played two or three notes on the piano as a reminder. She recognized the notes as "a hymn to the Virgin," which she had found "last summer among some of mamma's old music, written out on a sheet of paper, and have no way of even guessing how old it is, or who wrote it."[34]

In very rare instances, a mother's singing would have an adverse effect on a child. Richard Stoddard, for example, grew up in an poverty-stricken household with a widowed mother whose music making depressed him:

I can see myself, a boy of five or six years [ca. 1830–31], sitting on a little stool at my mother's frock. She was of melancholy temperament, as may be inferred from the hymn which she frequently sang to me at nightfall,—

The day is past and gone,
    The evening shades appear:
Oh! May we all remember well,
    The night of death draws near."

There were other even-songs no less cheerful. Indeed, I learned so to hate the hymns of Dr. Watts that I vented my feelings by often scratching the black cover of the hymn-book with a sharp pin.[35]

Slave children also learned songs from their mothers, as did James Claiborne of Mississippi, who remembered "my mammy singing 'Swing Low Sweet Chary-ot' and she rock me to sleep, she would sing: 'I Don't Care Whar Dey Bury My Body—But O! My Lil' Soul is Gwine ter Rise and Shine.'" Likewise, Katie Sutton, a child on an unidentified plantation, lived with her mother in an old cabin. "My mammy was good to me but she had to spend so much of her time at humoring the white babies and taking care of them that she hardly ever got to even sing her own babies to sleep." Yet she did recall one lullaby her mother had sung to her that began: "A snow white stork flew down from the sky,/Rock a bye, my baby bye."[36]

Uncles, aunts, and cousins also added music to a youngster's repertoire. Charles Leland, when seven or eight, visited relatives in Dedham, Massachusetts, and from the lips of his cousins Caroline and Emily Stimson learned "'The Sunset Tree,' 'Alknoomuk,' 'I see them on the winding way,' and Moore's Melodies." When Leland was thirteen, a young friend taught him to smoke Havana cigars and sing "On Springfield Mountain"; both smoking habit and song, the friend said, he had picked up from an uncle.[37]

Family circles did include persons close to parents and children. A young lady who worked in the cotton mills of Lowell credits her "Uncle Peter" (an honorific) with teaching her several songs that she knew:

There was his vocabulary of songs . . . and these, too, were all of the olden time. . . . He taught me to sing two or three dozen, or such a trifle, when I was quite a child. . . . Rainy days Uncle Peter used to shell corn in the long kitchen. Then was a favorite time for me to learn songs and listen to his stories with open-eared delight. . . . I liked to hear such songs as "The Ship Carpenter," "Major's Only Son," "The Nightingale," and others of similar import. But the song of all songs to my mind was the "American Taxation." In the performance of this, Uncle Peter seemed to be the very incarnation of music. . . . When he came to that part of the song where the "subtle arch combiners addressed the British court" . . . his eyes would kindle up with a patriotic and exultant pride.

When his widowed mother was thirty-two years of age, recalls Richard Stoddard, a sailor who loved to sing and dance often visited their home as a suitor for her hand. The boy Richard listened with fascination to his songs and stories about "witches, mermaids, and other impossible folk."[38]

Mrs. Lydia Huntley Sigourney says that, as a daughter of a gardener, she was fortunate to have been befriended by a Madam Lathrop, who needed someone to read aloud to her. Madam Lathrop's house became a second home. The elderly lady "had been taught [music] scientifically when a child. Many were the pieces in which I was instructed to accompany her, sacred, patriotic, or pathetic." She cites "Pompey's Ghost to His Wife Cornelia," "While Shepherds Watched Their Flocks by Night," "The Poor, Distracted Lady," and "Solitude."[39]

On Southern plantations, some very religious slave owners took it on themselves to teach their slaves to sing hymns, as did the South Carolina mistress of Anderson Bates: "My mistress name Nancy. Her was of de quality. Her voice was soft and quiet to de slaves. Her teach us to sing: 'Dere is a happy land, far, far 'way,/Where bright angels stand, far, far 'way.'"[40]

Almost like a second home were the nurseries for children, to which boys and girls were sent at an extremely early age. Motherly women tended the children during the daytime hours, feeding, cleaning, and singing to them. Lucy Larcom recalls that she started in "Aunt Hannah's" nursery, really her sitting room, at the age of two. Lucy would sit and watch Aunt Hannah spinning on her flax wheel and singing hymns, which were indelibly imprinted onto her young memory. One that remained most vivid in her adult years began with the words:

Whether goest thou, pilgrim stranger,
    Wandering through this lowly vale?
Knowest thou not 'tis full of Danger?
    And will not thy courage fail?[41]

Another source for new musical experiences were the receptions, dinners, balls, and other similar social functions that took place in the home, which children could not help but witness. These formal gatherings invariably called for music of one sort or another. On these occasions, children were likely to hear some music not normally performed in the more intimate family gatherings—dance pieces, operatic arias, piano sonatas, and songs not tailored to children's ears. A goodly number of such experiences are recorded in the literature of the period. For example, Julia Ward Howe says that the earliest social function she could remember was a ball that took place when she was four years of age. Late in the evening she was taken out of bed, dressed up, and brought downstairs into the drawing room, where the orchestra, com-

**84**   plete with a double bass, was playing and guests dancing. The novel music
and rhythmical motions made an unforgettable impression upon her.[42]

### Discovering Secular Music outside the Home

When the child grew into adolescence and beyond, attendance at social
functions in other homes and public halls became a possibility. Frequently, the
sheet music of the most recent songs encountered in neighbor's homes was
borrowed to make handwritten reproductions. Examples of such copying
abound in the private music collections that have come down to us from the
period. In recently settled towns, such as Pittsburgh in the 1820s, "copies of
new songs by J. Hook, R. C. Spofforth, Th. H. Bayley, and Thomas Moore were
loaned from one pioneer family to another, and handled with the reverence
accorded volumes of Holy Writ." The music encountered might easily be new
to one's experience, and at times appear more sophisticated than familiar
pieces, if not beyond understanding. As Charles Congdon admitted, when he
first attended "receptions" he heard conversations he did not understand, sad
songs unfamiliar to him, and ambitious piano compositions he found to be
"musical puzzles." Philip Hone says that he first became truly acquainted
with minstrel songs in October 1837, at an Astor House dinner where many
theater performers were present: "Rice's negro songs and melodies were exceedingly fine. I never heard them before under similar advantages, and was
perfectly astonished at Jim Crow's powers in that department." Levi Beardsley
grew up in a sparsely settled part of New York State, where no musicians
resided. Eventually the fiddler Brayton Allen was hired to come in and play for
local balls, where he dispensed hitherto unknown but eloquent dance music
and songs.[43]

Country fiddlers often mixed the traditional with the current music when
they performed for village fêtes. Indeed, there might be a preponderance of
the former. At the same time, the communities that sponsored these fiddlers
during the antebellum years, especially the earlier ones, esteemed the unwrit-
ten tunes that were handed down from one generation to the next. In a
Kentucky village, Ned, a fiddler, and John Blodget, a boatman, once presented
listeners with old Scotch pieces meant "to drive away bad humors." In a
Virginia village, Hafen Blok, a fiddler, played old dance tunes and sang ballads such as "The Manhattan Tragedy," "The Royal Factor's Garland," "The
Golden Bull," "The Prodigal Daughter," "The Yarmouth Tragedy," "Jemmy
and Nancy," and "The Gospel Tragedy." Sometimes he sang the traditional
tunes to his own words.[44]

Elderly country fiddlers were not alone in remembering the age-old ballads and dance tunes and transmitting them to young Americans. Fanny

Longfellow wrote of visiting her mother's family in Pittsfield, Massachusetts, in the summer of 1835 and hearing the village eccentric, the ancient "Crazy Sue," singing, among other things, "an old ballad of a youth crazed for love." In the same year, Charles Leland reported that "there lived in Boston some friends of my mother's named Gay. In the family was an old lady over eighty who was a wonderfully lively spirited person. She still sang, as I thought very beautifully, to the lute, old songs such as 'The merry days of good Queen Bess,' and remembered the old Colonial time as if it were yesterday."[45]

Not infrequently, the music inherited from the past and learned in childhood and youth became so much a part of an individual that he or she might inadvertently claim it as his or her own. Certainly contemporary songwriters such as Oliver Shaw, Dan Emmett, Stephen Foster, and George Root, consciously or unconsciously, had their song styles influenced by inherited melody. At times, direct quotation took place.[46] Even nonmusicians absorbed tunes from the past until they seemed their own. An informative illustration is provided in a letter sent by William Webster to Julius Ward on 19 June 1865, describing James Gates Percival in 1840, when he was forty-five years of age:

Percival was no musician, but . . . almost every evening . . . he came to my house at a very early hour (frequently before tea), and going to the piano, he would sit at arm's length, and with a single finger pick out the notes of some simple strain of his composition the previous day, and request me to record it for future use. A tedious process for him and me, as he might strike a dozen keys before the proper note would be produced, and sometimes a whole evening might be thus spent on a single theme; and after all, on playing or singing the air myself, I would find it to be only a reminiscence of his earlier days. This discovery occasionally mortified the Doctor, and sometimes he would persist in claiming it an original; but one evening, while we were going through this wearisome labor, my wife, from an adjoining room, struck up the very air he had been all day composing, and sung it through without the failure of a note. Percival stopped amazed, almost doubting the evidence of his own senses; but on calling upon Mrs. Webster, who told him that it was a song she had rarely heard since infancy, he acknowledged that many of the simple strains he thought his own might be only the impressions left in his memory in very childhood.[47]

The public streets of a community were fertile areas for the cultivation of music. Street music was almost as prevalent as street noises. Listening to the

**86**   sounds was unavoidable for all pedestrians. A verbal portrait of New York City in the spring of 1836 shows that

> its streets are cluttered with private equipages, trucks and charcoal-carts, lemonade barrels, fruit-wagons. Mingled with the noise of rush, tack, and jib in a roadway without traffic conventions are the chant of the "Hot corn" girl, the "Hot bread, who buys?" and the baker's bell, the chimney-sweep's song, the down-South voice of a "free nigger" selling hominy. . . . When the confusion in the streets is cleared, it is to make way for parades: the volunteer fire companies, with their musical bands and with their engines glorified by flags, streamers, and flowers; the militia; the Washington Market Chowder Guard, the Moustache Fusiliers, Tomkin's Butcher's Association Guard, or another of the target companies; the Cold Water Army of the Temperance Societies; fraternal orders and labor unions.[48]

All of this a child would listen to and observe with open-eyed delight.

Charles Leland retained vivid impressions of the "street-cries and sounds" from his Philadelphia boyhood, among them "a coloured man" and his "strange musical strain which could be heard a mile":

> *Tra-la-la-la-la-la-loo,*
> Le-mon-ice-cream!
> An'-wanilla-too!

In addition, there was the picturesque old hominy man:

> De Hominy man is on his way,
> Frum de Navy-Yard!
> Wid his harmony!

"Also, 'Hot-corn!' 'Pepper-pot!' 'Be-au-ti-ful clams!' with the 'Sweep-oh' cry, and charcoal and muffin bells."[49]

Wandering the streets were the ubiquitous barrel organists, playing a mixture of Italian and French arias, sentimental songs, and minstrel ditties. A barcarole from Auber's *Masaniello*, the pathetic "Woodman, Spare that Tree," the lively "Dixie" indicate the variety of sounds that came from the street musicians, which young listeners could then take up. A comic commentary about these organists was once made by Charles F. Browne, better known as "Artemus Ward":

The moosic which Ime most use to is the inspirin stranes of the
hand orgin. I hire a artistic Italyun to grind fur me, payin him his
vittles & close, & I suppose it was them stranes which fust put a
moosical taste into me. Like all furriners, he had seen better dase,
havin formerly been a Kount. But he aint of much akount now, except to turn the orgin and drink Beer.[50]

If it was not the reedy sounds of a barrel organist that "put a moosical
taste into" a youngster, it was the music coming from bands, whether playing
at bandstands on village greens or marching about the neighborhood. Nor
was it only in military parades that bands tramped the streets. They also
found employment as auxiliaries to fraternal and trade associations who took
to the outdoors to display their solidarity. Again and again, we find private
societies maintaining their own bands or hiring one when desiring to make
an important statement. Charles Haswell as a boy was a witness to the last
mentioned, when he found New York butchers around 1817 advertising the
possession of "exceptionally fine" meat by parading up and down the streets,
preceded by a spirited band. They would stop before the doors of customers,
serenade them, then wait expectantly for orders. During the warm summers
the playing of band music could not be shut out of homes, since windows
usually remained open to cool the interior. John Trowbridge states that one
could not help getting to know the compositions, whether one wished to or
not. Writing about a summer in New York around 1847–48, he remarks:

The band concert . . . should also be enumerated among the advantages of my Perrault lodging. Opposite my room, but a block or two
farther down Broadway, was the Café des Mille Colonnes, a brilliant
house of entertainment, with a balcony on which an orchestra used
to play on summer evenings, the popular airs of the period, to
which I listened many a lonely hour, sitting by the window of my
unlighted chamber, "thinking—thinking—thinking!" The throngs of
pedestrians mingled below . . . each to his or her "separate business
and desire;" while, over all, those strains of sonorous brass built
their bridges of music, from the high café balcony to my still higher
window ledge, spanning joy and woe, sin and sorrow, past and future, all the mysteries of the dark river of life. Night after night were
played the same pieces, which became so interwoven with the
thoughts of my solitary hours, with all my hopes and doubts, long-
ings and aspirations, that for years afterward I could not hear one
of those mellow, martial, or pensive strains without being immediately transported back to my garret and my crust.[51]

Marion Harland, in her quasi-autobiographical novel *Judith*, about a girl growing up in Virginia during the 1830s, states that Judith's strict Presbyterian upbringing had denied her the experience of hearing secular music and attending dances. On a trip to Richmond around 1832, however, she found herself one of a party attending a performance by a visiting circus. It revealed to her a musical world she did not know had existed: "The night was still and bland, and as we set forth upon our expedition the music of the circus band floated up the hill. I had never heard a brass band until that minute, and the lively strains infused themselves like electricity through my veins. I walked on tip-toe, fell unconsciously into dancing-steps I had never learned."[52]

Travel certainly provided the means for further musical experience. Undoubtedly, someone like Judith would share her latest musical knowledge with friends on her return home. Furthermore, family members when away from home often helped a stay-at-home person to new discoveries. Eliza Southgate wrote from New York to her sister Octavia, in Scarborough, Maine, on 23 July 1803, saying, "The two songs I sent you are all I could find that struck me; for the 'Death of Allen,' I never heard it, and bought it because it was a composition of Floyd's; 'The Wounded Hussar' I admired and knew you could not get it set for the Piano,—I don't know but 'tis different from Miss Sanford's." Also, we find William Wirt, in Baltimore, writing to his daughter Laura, on 18 April 1822, asking, "Shall I bring you a Spanish guitar, of Gilles' choosing? Can you be certain that you will stick to it? And some music for the Spanish guitar? What say you?" And again, on 15 July 1822, writing to Laura from Washington, "I send you a song, called 'They're a' Noddin,' with which, it is said, all Edinburgh is echoing; also, one of the glees sung at the Anacreontic club in Baltimore,—and some other songs,—*inter alia*, the rival airs of Baltimore to the serenade in the Pirate."[53]

Henry Wadsworth Longfellow provided similar offices when he wrote from Cambridge on 11 June 1837 to his sister Mary, who was ill in bed in Portland, "I thought, my dear, I had sent your music. But a day or two ago, I found it—in my closet. I reflected, however, that having been so long on the way, a few weeks more would be no great matter; particularly, as you cannot play much under your Dr's hands." And he wrote from Cambridge on 11 March 1839 to Samuel Ward in New York City, saying that he would send the "Anglo-Saxon Book and Music for yr. Sister Julia, as soon as I can find an opportunity."[54]

Professional musicians, in their concert and dramatic stage appearances, helped their audiences discover new music. Clara Temple Leonard, when a girl of twelve years of age, wrote from Greenfield, Massachusetts, on 25 February 1841 to her mother in Boston:

There was a concert given here Tuesday evening by Misses White,
Bailey, Pond and Wellington, and as Aunt Betsy offered to pay for
me, I went. They sang a very pretty little song there, called "Nothing
Else to do." I wish you would get it if you can, in Boston. Mrs.
Bailey has one of the sweetest voices that I ever heard and Mr.
White [*sic*] sang "Rory O'Moore" very well indeed. I do not know
when I have enjoyed anything so much; the hall was crowded. Two
of their songs, viz, "A Little Farm Well Tilled," and "A Schoolmaster
a Scholar" (which last was certainly very good) were encored, and I
liked them very much.[55]

When the minstrel craze was at its height in the late 1840s, Americans
clamored to purchase the novel songs that they had recently heard or heard
about, and publishers' presses were kept busy turning them out. Charles
Haswell remembers that

the reach of its [minstrelsy's] influence was very wide. New "negro
songs" were sent out almost daily from the publisher's presses and
were sung all over the land. . . . Households that had amused themselves with singing English opera (which had been greatly in fashion) and English glees and part-songs, turned to the new melodies.
Besides the original compositions, a crowd of parodies appeared:
"The Mellow Horn" became "The Yellow Corn;" Balfe's air, "I
Dreamt that I Dwelt in Marble Halls," was Africanized into "I
Dreamt that I Dwelt in Hotel Walls," etc. etc.

Is it any wonder, when "Daddy" Rice's song and dance for "Long Tail Blue"
swept the country, that youngsters throughout the land would mimic his
outfit and dance and sing his ditty? Only some of them had witnessed the
minstrel's performance; for others it was only hearsay. Not surprisingly, the
young Stephen Foster caught the fever and "strutted the boards in the old
carriage-house attired in Pa's best blue [broadcloth coat], with the tails
sweeping up the chaff on the floor behind him. It is not likely the Jim Crow
type of song won Stephen great approval from his mother; she certainly
would have preferred 'Come rest in This Bosom!' But Eliza Foster was very
indulgent."[56]

African Americans on plantations, of course, also learned music from
those living beside them. For example, Jim Archer of Mississippi mentioned
learning songs by listening to other slaves. In the same state, Albert Cox said
that no slave on his plantation could read or write, and whatever secular and
sacred songs he learned he either had heard others sing or made up himself.[57]

American communities were usually devout ones; prayer and hymn singing were a part of the daily experience, whether at home, at a neighbor's, or at a meetinghouse. A large portion of every American's musical repertoire consisted of sacred music, much of it acquired when young. This fact occasioned an observation by the English traveler Edward Kendall at the time of a visit to Stafford Springs, Connecticut, in 1807: "The Evenings, at the Springs, were generally spent, by the young women, in singing hymns, of which a favourite one was called the *Garden Hymn*. . . . They sing hymns because they are more familiar with the words and tunes of these, than with those of songs; and because they are accustomed to sing them in parts."[58]

If not learned at one's own home or a neighbor's, then a Sunday school, held at the church or other suitable place, was where a child obtained his first religious songs. A host of devotional songbooks aimed at youngsters attending Sunday schools came out in these years. The Reverend A. D. Merrill in the preface to his *Sunday School Melodist* states that if children heard the new religious music sung to them, they would be persuaded to join in the singing and learn the songs. This singing would also be a healthy exercise for the vocal organs and preparation for congregational singing in church. An informative description of a Sunday school in session and the teaching of sacred songs to the young comes from Maria Cummins's novel, *Mabel Vaughan*. A young woman named Rose is seen conducting a religious class in the back room of a private dwelling in New York City: "Rose was seated in her little arm-chair in the centre of the room, and around her were grouped some half dozen children, none of whom could have been more than seven or eight years of age." Rose was giving out the final verse of a hymn, and "as Rose spoke the last word, the children commenced singing. It was sweet and touching to hear their childish voices uniting in the simple melody which Rose had taught them." The last verse of the hymn was:

> Bright in that happy land
> > Beams every eye;
> Fed by the Father's hand,
> > Love cannot die.

Maria Cummins was a popular sentimental novelist of the 1850s, noted for her "lachrymations." Nevertheless, a description like the above does limn an important source for the transmission of music to the young.[59]

A passage from Augusta Evans's novel *Beulah* delineates the close association of child to religious song. At the beginning of the book, Beulah, a little girl, has finished singing a song. A man asks her who has taught her to sing. She replies: "I have never had a teacher, sir; but I listen to the choir on Sabbath, and sing our Sunday-school hymns at church." He then asks about the song she has just sung and learns that the words are those of Longfellow's "Psalm of Life." Beulah comments: "I found them in this book yesterday, and liked them so much that I tried to sing them by one of our hymn tunes."[60]

Finally, there was the experience of Harriet Beecher Stowe when a child in Litchfield, Connecticut. She heard at the meetinghouse, and never after could forget, "the execution of those good old billowy compositions called fuguing tunes, where the four parts that compose the choir take up the song, and go racing around one after another, each singing a different set of words, till at length, by some inexplicable magic, they all come together again, and sail smoothly out into a rolling sea of harmony!"[61]

Mrs. Stowe was introduced to many hymns during her childhood, at home, Sunday school, and the meetinghouse. These she continued to sing into her adult years, though perhaps not the fuguing tunes, which required several singers to execute properly. The sturdy and rough-hewn fuguing tunes were created by American and especially New England tunesmiths, in the second half of the eighteenth century mostly. This music had been to the native taste at the beginning of the nineteenth century but was gradually supplanted by the more up-to-date and "correct" hymns advocated by such European-oriented "reformers" as Lowell Mason and William Bradbury. Nevertheless, once installed in people's lives, fuguing tunes were not easily given up. Many, like Mrs. Stowe, persisted in loving and recollecting them. Mrs. Sigourney, to give a second example, kept on remembering the fuguing tunes learned in singing school at the beginning of the century, by herself and other local young men and women, who then had constituted the choir for their church in Norwich, Connecticut. She remembered also how the choir had disturbed the old-timers when it first introduced these works into the church service:

> The taste of the congregation was decidedly for that plain, slow mu-
> sic in which the devotion of their fathers had clothed itself. . . .
> Though [the singing master] taught this extremely well, he had an
> innate love for those brisk fugues, where one part leads off, and the
> rest follow with a sort of belligerent spirit.

One Sunday the choir started off with a lively, stirring fuguing tune: "Raise your triumphant songs/To an immortal tune." It startled the congregation, but the choir continued until the last two lines: "No bolts to drive their guilty souls/To fiercer flames below." She and the rest of the choir tried to give full expression to the piece:

> Off led the treble, having the air, and expanding *con spirito* upon the adjective "fiercer," especially its first syllable, about fourteen quavers, not counting semis and demis. After us came the tenor, in a more dignified manner, bestowing their principal emphasis on "flames." "No bolts, no bolts," shrieked a sharp counter of boys, whose voices were in the transition state. But when a heavy bass, like claps of thunder, kept repeating the closing word "below," and finally all parts took up the burden, till, in full diapason, "guilty souls" and "fiercer flames below" reverberated from wall to arch, it was altogether too much for Puritanic patience. Such skirmishing had never before been enacted in that meeting-house. The people were utterly aghast. The most stoical manifested muscular emotion. Our mothers hid their faces with their fans. Up jumped the tithing-man, whose office it was to hunt out and shake refractory boys. The ancient deacons slowly moved in their seats at the foot of the pulpit, as if to say, "Is not there something for us to do in the way of church government?"
>
> As I came down from the gallery, a sharp, gaunt Welsh woman seized me by the arm, saying: "What was the matter with you all, up here? You begun wery well, only too much like a *scrame*. Then you went gallivanting off like a parcel of wild colts, and did not sing the tune that you begun—not at all."
>
> How the shrill-voiced old lady, who could not sing, should know what the new tune was, or ought to be, I was not given to understand.[62]

Mrs. Sigourney's description demonstrates how the taste of a singing master and his and his fellow tunesmiths' new music were handed over to their students, so that they became a part of youthful taste and experience, and in turn how the students, when singing as a choir, transmitted this new music to the grownups in the congregation, who had to listen, willing or not.

One performing ensemble, Father Kemp's Old Folks Concert Troupe, kept on singing fuguing tunes for nineteenth-century audiences throughout the country. Moreover, these compositions formed an integral part of rural American shape-note hymnody, a singing tradition that has continued to the present day.

*The Influence of Education* 93

Parents, even in the more remote regions of the country, were determined to have music, for their daughters in particular. James Boardman visited upstate New York and said of the area around Rochester:

> Amidst all this grinding of corn, shipping of flour, unpacking and re-
> tailing of manufactures, felling of trees, and building of houses, we
> found the refinements of life were not neglected. Music was taught
> to all the young misses, as young females in the sphere of society
> above the laboring classes are styled; and, in a ball-room over the
> apartment in which we dined at the hotel, Monsieur was giving les-
> sons to a number of pupils in the art of "tripping the light fantastic
> toe." The sensations produced by hearing sounds associated with the
> most polished life, in view of the labours of the pioneer of the forest,
> would not be easy to describe.

On 18 August 1857 Henry Thoreau wrote from Concord to Daniel Ricketon in New Bedford, Massachusetts, "Please remember me to your family, and say that I have at length learned to sing Tom Bowlin [*sic*] according to notes."[63] To learn to read music "according to the notes" had been the ambition of more than a few Americans since the first viable singing schools were established in the 1720s, and it was what the "young missses" from around Rochester were learning to do.

Singing schools were the most affordable and oftentimes the only method available at the time for acquiring musical knowledge. Moreover, they introduced young people, such as Mrs. Sigourney when a girl, to a variety of new musical works, mostly sacred but some secular, one or two of which were composed by the singing masters themselves. Instruction meant vocal instruction books, and these the singing masters supplied. The books invariably contained the music for hymns, anthems, and through-composed "set pieces," which the students were expected to study. In order to keep students interested, a few secular pieces, glees and sentimental songs, were also included in the pedagogy. This was especially true in the years after 1830. For example, Francis Underwood describes the singing master who came to Enfield, Massachusetts, to conduct a singing school in the 1830s as an enthusiastic instructor, possessing a "perfunctory" voice but playing a "smooth" violin for his students. While psalmody was the main fare of the instructional sessions, he added to the musical list such English glees as "Here in Cool Grot" and "Hail, Smiling Morn."[64]

A church or a community association would engage someone purportedly knowledgeable in music to teach the essentials of singing and the meaning of written notes to beginners, usually over a period of four to twelve weeks. At the end of this time, a public performance demonstrated what the students had learned. Once in a while, a singing master would initiate his own hiring by making a proposal to potentially interested parties or even by advertising his availability. If individual fees were levied, they were usually quite modest and often were offset with the ticket sales for the final concert held at the end of the schooling.

We find Levi M'Clean—deputy sheriff, jailer, pound keeper, butcher, and constable of Cincinnati—playing the fiddle and teaching singing school. One wonders if he was the singing master who trained the children of the First District Common School in the songs sung "at the Close of the Exhibition in the School, Friday, June 27th, 1845." The parting song was "We meet a band of children young," to be sung to the tune of the minstrel song "Lucy Neal." Then there was Jonathan Fisher, a parson in Bluehill, Maine, who loved to sing but had no ear for music. He embarrassed himself again and again when he tried to sing the hymns of the Sunday service. In part to help himself, he obtained permission to have a singing master hold a singing school at the local Bluehill Academy during February and March 1805 for three or four evenings each week. A Samuel Wood received seventeen dollars from the town for his services, and the parson was a regular attendant at the sessions. Free African Americans also had their singing schools. For example, James Smith, who escaped from slavery in 1838, then lived in Norwich, Connecticut, says that he was one of the people to organize a local Methodist Church for blacks and open a singing school there.[65]

Singing schools remained prominent in American music education until their slow decline, beginning with the early proliferation of music instruction in public schools, in the 1840s. In the 1850s, however, they were still going strong in country villages and towns. One reporter, in *Dwight's Journal of Music,* June 1852, mentioned that singing masters were active and spreading out in western New York State, with results neither "particularly good" or "particularly bad." This, he said, was typical of the singing instruction that took place "in almost any of our country villages every winter." He also mentioned hearing some glees and sentimental songs in the performance at graduation. One year later, *Dwight's Journal,* which was not favorably inclined toward any of the American popular music movements, was quoting the *New York Musical World* about the $27 million musical trade, of which about $12 million went to the purchase of pianos, most of the remainder into the publication of "namby-pamby" songs and psalm books. Much of the teaching, the report went, was still done by poorly qualified music "professors" who spread their "drag-nets over town and village." A month later, the Dwight

periodical reported with special glee on the chicanery practiced by an igno-
rant singing master who proposed holding a singing school in Cincinnati and
advertised: "All those who wish to be taught music in CLASSES as it was
taught in ancient [!] times by Handel, Mozart, Beethoven, and Mendelssohn;
and as it is taught in modern times by Mason, Webb, Hastings, Bradbury, and
Ziner [Zeuner?], will meet this evening."[66]

Admittedly, few if any singing masters had thorough training in a music
conservatory or from a well-grounded musician. And one or two, like the
Cincinnati individual just cited, dispensed a great deal of hokum. Yet on
balance, their qualifications were usually adequate to their purpose—to teach
amateurs the fundamentals of note reading and singing. Moreover, without
them and their singing schools, ordinary Americans would have had no
opportunity to engage in music study; nor could they have learned any music
beyond what was transmitted orally to them. The fact that the singing schools
were so popular was evidence that people wanted them very much in their
lives and, what is more, that they believed that attendance was within their
financial means.

An excellent illustration of how a singing school was started occurs in
Seba Smith's *'Way Down East*. When Christopher Crotchet, a New England
singing master, appears at a Yankee village and offers to set up a singing
school, the local inhabitants meet at the village tavern "to see about hiring
him." A Squire Brown claims, "A singing-school won't do us no good, and I've
ways enough to spend my money without paying it for singing." But like most
youngsters, his son and daughter protest, his daughter saying, "Now, Pa, you
*will* go over and see about having a singing-school, won't you? I want to go
dreadfully."

The Squire still refuses. "It'll cost a good deal of money, and I can't afford
it. And besides, there's no use at all in it. You can sing enough now, any of
you; you are singing half your time." But Mrs. Brown agrees with her children, "Other folks' children have a chance to go to singing-schools, and to see
young company, and to be something in the world." She is adamant and
makes her husband go to the meeting.

At the meeting, the village residents accept Mr. Crotchet's terms: "Twenty
evenings for twenty dollars and 'found,' or for thirty and board himself." They
then take up a subscription and agree to board him with shifting families.
New singing books are purchased, and the long chamber in the tavern is
selected as the meeting place. A range of long narrow tables with benches
were put into place, and a singing book and a candle are supplied to every
two students. A large number of young people gather to receive instruction,
voices are tested and instruction begun, and on the tenth day, spectators are
permitted to observe the classes.[67]

That the tavern was resorted to as a meeting place, if other venues were unavailable, was true for other villages in the country. Daniel Drake remembered his boyhood in a letter he sent to his daughter Harriet on 14 January 1848. He wrote that at the beginning of the nineteenth century, Mays Link, Kentucky, where he grew up, was "scarcely a village," yet a center for the people who lived within a radius of six to eight miles. There were some "pretty rough characters around," with attendant drunkenness and brawls. At the same time, singing schools were held "in a room of Deacon Morris' tavern." He said, "I was never a scholar, which I regret, for it has always been a grief with me that I did not learn music in early life. I occasionally attended. As in all country singing-schools, sacred music only was taught but, in general, there was not much display of sanctity."[68]

The more usual meeting place was at the local church. This was where Candace Wheeler (née Thurber), daughter of a dairy farmer whose farm was close to Delhi, New York, went for music instruction before she married at the age of sixteen in 1843:

> Every Saturday night we went to "singing-school" and were trained
> in sight reading and choral music by "a professor," who lived in Al-
> bany and circled around the state setting the pitch and beating time
> for hundreds of young people whose pleasant voices created a musi-
> cal atmosphere in every small detached settlement. The singing-
> school was held in the basement of the Presbyterian church, and we
> four elder children walked our mile there and back, singing as we
> went and came, after we had left the village street and had crossed
> the little foot-bridge to our own side of the river. If any one was
> awakened from early toil-earned sleep by our fluting and singing,
> they probably explained the disturbances by saying, "Oh, it's only
> them Thurbers going home from singing-school."[69]

Mrs. Sigourney writes that the singing school she attended in Norwich, Connecticut, was held in the courthouse, with the new girls seated at a table in the front, and the older, more experienced singers in the gallery, "a few steps above." Also present were "young gentlemen of our circle . . . either as spectators or members of the choir." The local schoolhouse was frequently pressed into service for singing classes as well. Mrs. Ellen Rollins makes this point in her description of a New England village toward the beginning of the century:

> The winter diversions of the young people were just as simple as
> those of their elders. What could be quainter than the singing-

school, held in a country school-house, with its rows of tallow candles planted along the desks, and its loud-voiced master pitching his tunes? The young men sat on one side and the maidens on the other. Its wild music was heard from far away. The tunes were of long repute, and what was wanting in melody and harmony was made up by the zeal with which they were roared out. To many of the singers the walk home was the best of all, when, in undertone, they lengthened out the melodies which had been taught them.[70]

In more isolated parts of the country, in which it was not practical for persons desiring instruction to travel back and forth to a village or town, a singing class might be held in a home. Marion Harland, who grew up in rural Virginia, recalls that around 1843–44 she attended a home class:

> Once a week we had a singing-class, which met around our dining-table. My father led this, giving the key with his tuning-fork, and now and then accompanying with his flute a hymn in which his tenor was not needed.
>
> Have I ever spoken of the singular fact that he had "no ear for music," yet sang tunefully and with absolute accuracy, with the notes before him? He could not carry the simplest air without the music-book. . . . He was passionately fond of music, and sang well in spite of it, playing the flute correctly and with taste—always by note. . . .
>
> These songful evenings were the one dissipation of the week. A singing-master, the leader of a Richmond choir, had had a school at the Court House the winter before, and *The Boston Academy* was in every home in the village.

The class was held on Tuesday evenings. Not only were her family present but also neighbors, male and female, young and old, around ten to twelve visitors in all.

> We lined both sides of the long table, lighted by tall sperm-oil lamps, and bent seriously happy faces over *The Boston Academy*, singing with the spirit, and, to the best of our ability, with the understanding,— "Lanesboro" and "Cambridge" and "Hebron" and "Boylston" and "Zion," and learning, with puckered brows and steadfast eyes glued to the notes, such new tunes as "Yarmouth," "Anvern," and "Zerah." . . .
>
> In the interval of singing we chatted, laughed, and were happy.

. . . We sang until ten o'clock; then apples, nuts, and cakes were brought in, and sometimes sweet cider. An hour later we had the house to ourselves, and knelt for evening prayers about the fire before going to bed.[71]

Singing school was the especial province of the young, who attended as much for diversion and meeting people of the opposite sex as for learning. William Cullen Bryant states that the boys of western Massachusetts flocked to singing schools during winter evenings, "naturally attracted to [the] school as a recreation." A young woman working in the Lowell mills said that the singing schools in her village were held at the schoolhouse. Although she had "some deficiency in my lungs, or throat, or something else," she had "continued to attend the school, for we had few amusements, and the girls never had to pay anything." Amzi Chapman Stephens, of Morris County, New Jersey, testifies in his diary to the pursuit of singing schools for recreational reasons:

Jan 8th 1851 Went to Mt Olive to Singing-school, from thence I went to Gideon Salmons to a party.

Thurs Jan 16th 1851 I help thrash wheat, at night I went to Drakestown to Singing with four horses.

Jan 18th I help clean wheat: We cleaned 56 bushels at night I went to Mt Olive to Singing-school, from thence went to esq. Wiltses School house to Singing-school, from there I went to Gideon Salmons to see Harriet and staid there all night.

Feb 22 at night I went to A W[illegible] and took Malinda Wolfe [unclear] to Esq. Wiltses School house to Singing-school from thence I went and took M W home and staid with her a while. . . .

Sat Mar 22 . . . at night I went to Mt Olive to Singing-school from thence to Esq. Wilts [*sic*] School house to Singing-school from thence I went to M Wolfes [*sic*] and staid all night.[72]

Now and again a singing master reaped more than a monetary profit from his classes. A South Carolina and Georgia singing master, Colonel Stamper, in the dress of a bejeweled dandy, was used to strutting about as he beat the time for his classes, and bending over to sing the notes into the ears of his most attractive feminine scholars. He sang so effectively in the ear of the prettiest belle of a Georgia neighborhood that she consented to elope with him.[73]

For singing masters and the singing books they prepared for their classes, the transition from singing school to public school was a natural one. Where once they traveled to organize transitory classes, they turned to establish music teaching on a permanent basis, first in Boston's public schools, then in those of the New England towns, and finally in public schools in the rest of the United States. From Lowell Mason's first attempt to introduce music into the Boston public schools in 1838, he and most other Americans held to the belief that all children could learn and would enjoy instruction in music.

Singing books once aimed at young people voluntarily attending singing school were done over to accommodate the requirements of public school children. They were made as uncomplicated as possible, shaped for teaching purposes, and with content meant to hold children's attention, not excluding popular music. We find one singing master, Horace Bird, soliciting Longfellow's assistance in placing *The Singer's First Book, Consisting of Simple Rules and Easy Music for Common Schools* in Boston's public school classrooms. Longfellow wrote to Samuel Gridley Howe, a school board member, on 10 October 1845:

> I trouble you with this note in behalf of Mr. Bird, who will call upon you about his "Singer's First Book," which he wishes to get introduced into the Boston Primary Schools. He is an excellent man, and having been long a teacher of music, is as likely as any one to know what is wanted in that way. I am not conversant with books of instruction in music, and therefore cannot make any comparison between his and those of others;—but all comparisons apart, this of his seems to me very simple and good; and I hope he may succeed in making you see it in that light.

Interestingly, *The Singer's First and Second Book* states in its preface that it is intended for class use in the "common schools" and contains "simple rules and easy music." Book 2 includes "many of the most useful and popular melodies."[74]

Aiding in the spread of public school music education were such ardent advocates as Walt Whitman, who held "a low opinion of the average teacher's competence" but especially approved "the teaching of singing," warmly praising the Brooklyn public school singing teachers. He wanted music to be "given as much prominence as reading and arithmetic." John Moore, in his groundbreaking *Complete Encyclopedia of Music* (1854), included the following passage:

> There are said to be, at this time, not far from eighty thousand common schools in this country, in which is to be found the power which, in coming years, will mould the character of the democracy. If vocal music were generally adopted as a branch of instruction in

these schools, it might be reasonably expected, that in at least two generations we should be changed into a musical people. The great point to be considered, in reference to the introduction of vocal music into popular elementary instruction is, that thereby you set in motion a mighty power, which silently, but surely in the end, will humanize, refine, and elevate a whole community.[75]

As the years went by, the number of music teachers increased. Some of the American-born instructors were close to being musically illiterate, it is true; but others, usually Europeans, were adequately trained. The state of New Jersey, for example, in 1800 had about one teacher for every 16,240 inhabitants. By 1860 there was one teacher for every 2,560 people, and in the northeastern urban areas the ratio was one to 850 people.[76]

Those parents who could afford to pay for private lessons solicited them for their children. The girlhood of Julia Ward Howe was rich in musical instruction:

> My musical education . . . was the best that the time could afford. I had my first lessons from a very irritable French artist, of whom I stood in such fear that I could remember nothing that he taught me. A second teacher, Mr. Boocock, had more patience, and soon brought me forward in my studies. He had been a pupil of Cramer, and his taste had been formed by hearing the best music in London. . . . I learned from him to appreciate the works of . . . Beethoven, Handel, and Mozart. When I grew old enough for the training of my voice, Mr. Boocock recommended to my father Signor Cardini, an aged Italian . . . well acquainted with Garcia's admirable method [of voice training]. Under his care, my voice improved in character and in compass, and the daily exercises in holding long notes gave strength to my lungs.[77]

Southern plantation owners frequently resorted to private teachers, musical and otherwise, for their daughters, rather than send them away to boarding schools, where they might be "exposed to a false and shallow system of hot-bed culture for a few sessions," according to D. R. Hundley. On a South Carolina plantation, a Charles Duncan was hired to teach piano and voice to a girl of thirteen years of age and to supervise her daily two hours of practice. He also acquainted her with fresh songs and helped her distinguish "what was false in sentiments" in her other songs. In Charleston, South Carolina, Elizabeth Pringle said that the fresh songs that her teacher, Mr. Torriani, taught her were in the best taste, citing "a very high, lovely little song from

the opera of 'Martha.' 'Dormi pur ma, il mio reposo tu m'ai tolto, ingrato cor.
Buona notte, buon dormir.'" In the New Orleans of around 1841, wrote Eliza
Ripley, girls learned to become

> housewives and mothers, instead of writers and platform speakers,
> doctors and lawyers—suffragettes. Everybody was musical; every
> girl had music lessons and every mother superintended the study
> and practice of the one branch deemed absolutely indispensable to
> the education of a *demoiselle*. The city was dotted all over with mu-
> sic teachers, but Mme. Boyer was, par excellence, the most popular.
> She did not wander from house to house [as other teachers did], but
> the *demoiselles*, music roll in hand, repaired to her domicile.[78]

Whether itinerant or enthroned in a studio, private music teachers dotted
the landscape of the United States east of the Mississippi by the 1860s. Their
pupils were mostly girls. Boys, most of whom were destined to become bread-
winners, found that their education and later their work allowed no time for
musical study. In Sara Wentz's novel set in Boston, *Smiles and Frowns*, a young
man named Walter loves music and wishes to study it. He asks, "How can I
be a musician?" To this a friend replies, "You can begin by doing little at first.
What time do you go to the store in the morning?" "About eight o'clock," says
Walter. After the friend thinks a moment, he says, "Then if you rise at
half-past four, you will have three hours to devote to music every morning,
besides many evenings. I think I can get permission for you to play on that
fine old organ in the church; you can obtain the organist as teacher."[79] Walter
had to have loved music indeed if he was willing to subject himself to this
regimen.

Young women found it easier to take up musical study, provided of course
there was the wherewithal. Indeed, they were expected to include music as a
part of their education. If a private teacher did not come to their home or
they to a music studio, then attendance at a private academy or seminary
afforded the desired study, most often in voice and piano. Even before the
beginning of the century, several academies for girls had opened their doors
in the northeast, and there was a scattering of them elsewhere. Susan Lesley
states that her mother recollects beginning music lessons while attending a
Dorchester, Massachusetts, school at the turn of the century. Emily Barnes
remembers her sister going to an academy for girls around 1805, "the first of
that order that ever had been taught in Walpole," Massachusetts. Here she
was able to receive lessons in voice.[80]

Finding a qualified teacher of good character was sometimes a challenge
in these early days. In 1806 Leroy Anderson, in Williamsburg, Virginia, asked

*102*  William Wirt's help in finding a music teacher for his academy. Wirt wrote back from Richmond on 25 September:

> I know Vogel, he gave several lessons to Mrs. Wirt in Richmond and in Norfolk. I have also frequently heard him play alone, and I can safely pronounce him the finest male performer on the piano that I have ever heard. But like his predecessor B——— he is a son of Anacreon;—not that his potations are either so frequent or so deep as poor B———'s; but the ladies, his scholars in Norfolk, sometimes complained of neglect, which was attributed to frolics over-night. In Williamsburg he will have fewer temptations, and I dare say will do better.
>
> There is a little fellow here, by the name of ———, of whose skill in music the ladies and other connoisseurs of Richmond speak very highly. But he is only about seventeen, and they tell me (for I have not seen him) a perfect Adonis. . . . I should apprehend that such a fellow . . . might put to flight the
>
> "Quips and cranks and playful wiles
> Nods and becks and wreathed smiles"
>
> of your academy, and introduce the sigh and tear of midnight in their place.[81]

Girls of fifteen to eighteen years of age went to these academies. In addition to musical study, they acquired a smattering of knowledge in academic subjects and household management, as well as instruction in virtue, in how to conduct themselves in society, and in ways of being agreeable to others. The study of voice and an instrument was most likely to take place in the last year of schooling, as part of the final "finishing." Those young ladies who returned from distant boarding schools to their villages and towns came back with a refinement in manners, dress, and speech and a knowledge of well-bred music that were immediately communicated to their communities. Around the 1830s the residents of Enfield, Massachusetts, learned that one such young lady had returned, bringing with her the first piano to appear there. On one summer night, the people of the village from oldsters to "admiring boys," gathered outside an open parlor window to learn about the sound of this newfangled instrument and the up-to-date music she had studied while away. What proved especially fascinating to them were the scalar and arpeggiated runs her nimble fingers executed on the keyboard and the full, resonant chords, whose "magical" richness they were experiencing for the first time.[82]

From information we have about the Boston Blind Asylum and the New York Institute for the Blind, great pains were taken to teach music to those who were sightless. Fanny Crosby says the music teaching at the latter institution was both thorough and scientific. After the 7 A.M. lecture on mental and moral philosophy, students devoted the rest of the morning and afternoon to recitations and singing classes, until half-past four. She names George Root, an eminent musician, educator, and songwriter of the time, as her music teacher. She claims that he played the melodies of his newest songs to her, which she immediately learned, among them the eventually very popular "Hazel Dell," "Rosalie the Prairie Flower," and "There's Music in the Air." In addition, the school received visits from such famous singers as Jenny Lind, who performed for them.[83]

George Root lived outside the school. Not uncommonly, the female teachers of boarding academies were expected to reside at the school, not always a happy experience for them. Marion Harland, in *The Hidden Path*, describes a teacher at a Virginia academy named the Clayton Female Institute who had not a moment to herself. She shared her room and the piano in it with four girls, one of whom would execute an "unmeaning jingle" on the instrument every morning at daybreak. She managed to give one lesson before the prayer bell sounded at six. After the roll call and breakfast, she gave lessons to "three more musical pretenders," then left to conduct her French class.[84]

### The European Impact

Chances were, these "musical pretenders" at some point would try to attend a recital of opera arias or an Italian opera performance, especially if living in or close to New York City, or perhaps a symphony concert. In New Orleans it would have been French opera. The music from abroad amazed them on first acquaintance, then delighted some of them so that they wished to learn what they could of it. Thus, we find George Templeton Strong, a New Yorker, writing into his diary on 26 December 1849, "Ellie [his wife] and two Miss Maurans, her guests, are downstairs reading music, transposing, arranging, and reproducing in every form *Otello* and the *Prophète*." Regrettably, altogether too many who sang the arias knew little about the foreign language of the texts. John Cooke, in *Ellie, or The Human Comedy*, has a character, Miss Aurelia, comment, "I don't believe young ladies, generally, know a bit about Italian—they sing what is written upon their music, and that's all. I can say for myself, at least, Mr. Heartsease, that I am perfectly innocent of any knowledge of the language, and am a mere parrot—I repeat it."[85]

There were men, also, who took pleasure in the music from Europe. When in 1825 James Gordon Bennett first heard the Garcia Opera Troupe sing *The Barber of Seville*, he said, "Till that moment I never knew what music was—I never cared for singing—never valued vocal powers till then. The divine girl—for then she was a mere girl [later, the famous vocalist Maria Malibran]—carried every heart and every soul with her." Reminiscing back to 1825, John Francis remarked: "Were my individual feelings to be consulted, I would fain dwell at some length on the introduction of the Garcia Italian Opera *troupe* in this city as an historical occurrence in intellectual progress of permanent interest. It was destined to create new feelings, to awaken new sentiments in the circle of refined and social life, and its mission I believe is accomplished." Then there were the numerous gentlemen of New Orleans who attended performances at the old French Opera House—*Norma, Lucia di Lammermoor, Robert le diable, La Dame blanche, Les Huguenots, Le Prophète*—and found the music to be "so thrillingly catchy that half the young men hummed or whistled snatches of it on their way home."[86]

When Europeans came to the United States, their music came with them and their influence was cast over the Americans who interacted with them. This is what happened to Margaret Fuller. As a young girl she was befriended by an English lady who was an accomplished harpist. The lady played music to which Margaret Fuller listened in almost unbearable happiness and which revealed to her a promised land she did not know existed. In like manner was Mrs. Sigourney revealed a promise land. When an adolescent, she too was befriended by an English lady who came to live near her: "She instructed in what were termed the higher branches, including music, painting, and embroidery. She executed on the piano with great skill, and, as I had been a singer from infancy, I found much pleasure in the practice of uniting an instrument with the voice."[87]

The influx of the French into Charleston was strong in the early part of the nineteenth century, owing to the revolution in France and in Santo Domingo. The result was the introduction of French theatrical entertainments, including a French theater, into the town. The American inhabitants could not help but learn all sorts of French songs. The French influence received major reinforcement when at least thirteen French teachers set themselves up in the city to teach dancing, music, and drawing.[88]

In New England a large contingent of educated and musically inclined Germans arrived in the second third of the century, especially after the unsuccessful prodemocratic agitations of the 1840s, and with them came a taste for Central European instrumental music and lieder. A major change in taste and a reorientation of education and culture toward things German occurred. Longfellow, like others in the greater Boston area, was first fascinated

by a band of Tyrolean singers who concertized in Boston in 1840. "Their
harmony was perfect, and their national songs well sung and delightful," he
said in a letter to his father on 15 November 1840. Other Germans began to
introduce him and his circle to the joys of Beethoven, Mozart, and Mendelssohn and question the then prevalent leanings toward Italian opera.
Fourteen years later, he wrote to Charles Sumner:

> [Bernard] Rölker was here last evening. I said to him, "Who is the
> Raphael of music?"
>
> He answered without hesitation: "Mozart."
>
> "But Bellini," said I faintly, "whom does he represent? Is it Corre-
> gio?"
>
> "No; not so much as that; only Carlo Dolce!"
>
> What will become of us? I have already recanted. But you, here-
> tic, will be obliged to stand and do penance in the Music Hall, with a
> paper cap on your head. . . .
>
> Bellini, indeed! I shall begin to think you do not know who the
> Cimabue of music is—nor any of the musical pre-Raphaellites.[89]

During the Brook Farm experiment in communal living (1841–47), John
Sullivan Dwight, an ardent musical Germanophile and the later editor of
*Dwight's Journal of Music*, tried to insure the proper musical education of
everybody resident at the farm, on the outskirts of Boston, through a singing
class and the presentation of only the music of which he approved, that is to
say, the piano sonatas of Beethoven and Mozart, selections from the masses
of Haydn, and other music of that class.[90]

After the first quarter of the century, in particular, the more educated
and sophisticated Americans grew increasingly curious about European culture, and those among them who had the financial means crossed the Atlantic to visit museums, libraries, noted sights, and ancient ruins. They took in
opera performances, symphony and chamber concerts, ballet presentations,
and music recitals. They returned with the European lieder and arias that
they had heard on their lips, symphonies still sounding in their ears, and
ballet and opera scenes emblazoned on their minds.[91] Memories of European
trips would continue to fuel attempt after attempt to replicate Europe's cultural institutions in the New World.

### Interracial Exchange

Before the Civil War, white Americans wrote scarcely a word about the
music of the American Indians, and what comment there was described it as

**106** barbarous. A handful of songs, purportedly those of the earliest Americans, did come out in sheet music, but their musical characteristics were Anglo-American. Evidently, what authentic Indian music was heard scarcely made a lasting impression on European Americans, at least not enough to inspire them to discuss it intensively or to encourage a real effort to note it down. The cultural gap was too large, the cultural tolerance level too low; the lives led and territories occupied by Indians were normally cut off from those of European Americans. Most non-Indians found the music strikingly odd and harsh in sound, difficult to remember, and not worthy of memorializing. Even more enlightened people such as the Longfellows, who took an interest in the political rights of the Indians and felt sympathy for their culture, did little to propagate the music. We find Fanny Longfellow in 1832 listening to a Chero-kee youth who was in Boston to plead Indian rights. He was invited to dine at the Longfellow home and while there, she says, "sung us several real Indian songs, etc. We were all very much pleased with him." She mentions no continuation of interest in the music heard. In 1850 Henry Wadsworth Long-fellow wrote to a Cologne acquaintance, Ferdinand Freiligrath, saying, "Let me have the great pleasure of introducing to you my friend *Kah-ge-ga-gah-bowh*, an American Indian Chief of the Ojibway nation, whose English name is George Copway. . . . I shall make him promise to sing to you some of the mournful musical songs of his nation." What were these songs? To what extent did they influence his poetry? Finally, in 1856 Longfellow wrote into his journal that he had received a visit from a Mr. Tanner "and his Indian wife,—a gentle little woman, with a very soft musical voice. She sang me a Chippeway song. It was in the minor key, very plaintive and like the wind in the pines."[92] Sad and musical they might have been, yet there was little follow-up to reports like these of American Indian music.

The songs and dances of African Americans are another story. Whether as slaves or free people, they lived among white Americans, though more or less separately. They could not help frequently hearing the music white Americans made and vice versa. When they arrived in America, they brought over their African musical and dance idioms. With them came singular vocal sounds and an inventive approach to melodic ornamentation. They were inclined to promote rhythm and make syncopation prominent in their perfor-mances. This was a musical heritage not easily or willingly put aside, one that would be brought to bear on whatever musical sounds were encountered in their New World environment, reshaping them and making them fresh again.

As already mentioned for white children, black children, too, made first acquaintance with music through parents, siblings, friends, and an occa-sional traveler. They also caught songs or dance tunes from nonblacks. Some later became instrumentalists performing for balls and in concert halls. Then

again, they attended Christian religious services and learned and sang white
hymns, as often as not modifying them to suit their own needs. Their own
American tradition of black spirituals was one result. In short, a mixture of
black and white approaches to music would inevitably ensue.

During the years of Southern enslavement of African Americans, witnesses continuously reported the love of music and dance among black
Americans. At the same time, white Americans listened to the music making
and carried its memory away to influence their own musical thinking in
conscious and unconscious ways. James Weir testifies to the vivid impression
the music made on white observers:

> The negro is naturally a musical biped, and we have scarcely ever
> seen one who could not sing well, catch a tune at the first hearing,
> and [improvise] equal to any Italian poetaster, if you will only make
> his scene a "corn shucking" and give him enough of "old rye" to
> sharpen his wits. Some of the finest music I have ever heard, or at
> least so I thought when a boy (and so I still think when memory is
> busy with other days), has been the wild melody of a band of ne-
> groes around a corn-pile, or when gathered about their quarters dur-
> ing harvest-time, or when swelling up from the silent woods at the
> still hour of midnight.[93]

Whether toiling in the fields, husking corn in the barns, or trudging
home from their labors, states D. R. Hundley, black Americans sang their
novel songs, "which their fathers must have brought with them from Africa,
but the words and meaning of which are no longer remembered." To Hundley's ears the music sounded "wild and indescribable . . . with an often recur-
ring chorus" in which all joined "with a depth and clearness of lungs truly
wonderful." Hundley was also entranced by their improvisation. During one
steamboat ride on a river, for example, "the negro boatmen collected in a
squad on the bow of the boat, and one dusky fellow, twirling his wool hat
above his head, took the lead in singing, improvising as he sang, all except the
chorus, in which the whole crew joined with enthusiasm." Their religious
songs and love ballads were more conventional, although "their tamest and
most civilized efforts are surprisingly good." At camp meetings, "the whites
are constrained to surrender to the darkeys in 'The Old Ship of Zion' or 'I
want to go to Glory.'" While singing the religious songs, African Americans
usually kept time with their feet, or by clapping their hands or wagging their
head, and they often wept freely "in the fervency and rapture of their devotions."[94] Most white Americans shared in the Hundley assessment.

Several writers testify, as well, to the African American's fondness for bird

*108*  and animal imagery and sounds in their singing. Metta Victor writes of a "negro with the fiddle" who

> sang a favorite song of the plantation-lands in Louisiana and Georgia, the chorus of which is a curiously correct imitation of the peculiar cry of the turkey-cock when he calls to his distant mate—a soft, guttural, resounding utterance—and in the chorus the whole party joined—

> Chug-a-logee, chug-a-logee, chug-a-logee chug![95]

A great deal of carryover into the musical styles of all Americans ensued. The mimicking of African Americans in minstrel shows and the incorporation of elements of their dancing and music into the musical practices connected with minstrelsy was an exploratory phase that would lead to coon songs, ragtime, blues, jazz, swing, rhythm and blues, and then to various manifestations of rock music.

All the same, the exchange was never one-sided. Robert Toll, in *Blacking Up*, points out the song link between minstrels and African Americans and the giving and taking of music that ensued. He says that the American frontier saw white and black Americans working and singing side by side, each learning what the other had to offer. Black Americans took up the reels, jigs, and other lively rhythms of white dance, blending them with those of their own African heritage. Minstrels absorbed black dance and their syncopated rhythms. White hymn tunes were reshaped into black spirituals. Sentimental ballads and minstrel songs, with melodies owing much to the traditional music of the British Isles, sounded from black throats. "Daddy" Rice was entertaining people throughout the country with his "Jump, Jim Crow" imitation of a ragged black man he had once observed, and another, "Fresh Corn Meal," of a black New Orleans street vendor. Buckley's New Orleans Serenaders came upon and reproduced the song and apparel of a Savannah watermelon vendor, which made a hit with their audiences. The minstrel men made it a habit to study the black boatmen, stevedores, dancers, and singers, in order to incorporate what seemed attractive into their routines.[96] Dan Emmett and Stephen Foster were two of the celebrated white songwriters whose musical compositions with dialect texts became favored throughout the United States.

All Southern children picked up a wide mix of songs from both black and white sources. J. G. Clinkscales describes how white children on one plantation were fond of holding mock funerals for small animals and birds. After one member gave a funeral oration over the burial spot, they sang a song, whether it was fitting or not. Their repertoire ranged from "Abide with Me" to "Old Folks at Home." He explains: "From my sister we had caught Dixie and the Suwanee River; and from the grown-up negroes, 'Am I a Soldier of the Cross?'"[97]

When the English traveler Amelia Murray wrote in a letter from Charleston on 29 January 1855, "Last night I heard parties of darkies singing, as they passed the windows, those negro melodies the airs of which have become familiar in England," she was referring to the minstrel songs that black Americans had learned, mostly by ear. Other European travelers also insisted on attributing the origin of minstrel songs entirely to black Americans, either consciously or in ignorance, overlooking the contributions of white Americans. One of them, Fredrika Bremer, heard a young plantation slave sing in 1850 "with his banjo several of the negro songs universally known and sung in the South by the negro people, whose product they are, and in the Northern States by persons of all classes, because they are extremely popular." They grew out of the musical improvisations of African Americans, she claimed, and then cited six widely known minstrel songs: "Rosa Lee," "Oh! Susannah," "Dearest May," "Carry Me Back to Ole Virginny," "Uncle Ned," and "Mary Blane."[98]

A Bostonian who had gone to teach in Georgia knew differently. In a "Letter from a Teacher at the South" printed in *Dwight's Journal of Music* for 26 February 1853, the teacher claimed a residency of two years in Georgia and said that the "Negro melodies" published in the North were sung there first by white Americans and then picked up, words and tunes, by black Americans in the South:

> I have spent an evening of as hearty, if not as high enjoyment, seated in state on the wide piazza listening to a negro singing his melodies accompanied by his banjo, now grave now gay, as I ever did in Tremont Temple or the Melodeon, and as I expect to in the new Music Hall. When I heard Jenny Lind sing "Home, sweet Home," it caused such an emotion as I never before experienced; it might be *exquisite homesickness.* "Old Folks at Home," as I hear it shouted from house to house, from the fields and in the vallies, has an effect scarcely inferior. I find myself often humming the chorus and even dream at night.

> "Oh, comrades, how my heart grows weary,
> Far from the dear friends at home."

This has little to do with musical education in the main, but much in effect. A thing that speaks so to the heart is hard to be reasoned down.[99]

Mollie Watson, a former slave resident in Oklahoma, explains how she learned many of her songs:

I never knew much about music, but I sho' did like to hear Miss Betty play de piano. I never knew what she'd play unless she sung it. I recollect how she played an' sung, "Shoo Fly, Don't You Bother Me," "Granny Will Yo' Dog Bite?" "Dixie," and "Darling Black Mustache." She uster sing good songs too, sech as "Rock of Ages," "De Lord's A Rock," "Swing Low Sweet Chariot," an' lots o' others.[100]

Mollie Watson was eighty-three years old when she told the above to an interviewer. She may have mixed up what she remembered. One wonders—did she really first learn about "Swing Low" when it was sung by her white mistress? From whom did her mistress learn it?

Caroline Gilman, in her memories of plantation life on the Ashley River in South Carolina, confirmed the white–to–black American transfer. Every plantation, she said, usually had a fiddler on hand. One fiddler whom she knew, named Diggory, had a quick eye and ear and promptly learned the tunes and figures of the newly introduced cotillions in Charleston. She added:

It is amusing to observe how soon a pretty air is appropriated, in Charleston, by the negroes, by their quick musical organs. You hear the mason's apprentice whistle it as he handles his trowel, the chimney-sweep sings it between his technical cry, the nurse warbles it forth to her charge, and, almost before you know it yourself, you hear it trilling from the lips of your dressing-maid.[101]

About one matter Americans and Europeans were all agreed—black musicianship was on balance extraordinary and the musical quality of black voices commanded special attention. Not at all unusual was the sort of praise that Francis Sheridan, an English visitor, showered on a "Signor Cornmeali," of New Orleans, whose name derived from the cornmeal he sold from his wagon and whose rendition of "Old Rosin the Bow," "My Long Tail Blue," and "Nigger Jem Brown" in front of the New Orleans Exchange was perfection itself: "He sings in a manner as perfectly novel as it is inimitable—beginning in a deep bass & at every other 3 or 4 words of his song jumping into a falsetto of power & shrillness."[102] Not at all surprising, therefore, were the many black

musicians, both free men and rented-out slaves, who found places in bands, **III**
orchestras, and dance ensembles, especially in the Southern states.

There are also reports about the legal and illegal nightspots that black
Americans attended in places such as New Orleans and New York, but with
next to no information on the music played.[103] We also know that some were
present at symphony concerts and opera performances in these and other
cities and were heard in the streets humming or whistling the melodies on
their way home from the concert hall and opera house. Again, information is
scant on the extent to which they took this music to heart.

# Listening to Professional Musicians

URING THE ENTIRE ANTEBELLUM PERIOD, AMERICA'S national culture was as authentically represented in the settlements of the western frontier as in the cities sprinkled mostly along the eastern seaboard. These smaller communities, in their social lives, presented "a weird mingling of civilization and barbarism," according to Jane Swisshelm. She writes of St. Cloud, Minnesota, during the late 1850s, citing one example:

> Upon one occasion, a concert was given, in which the audiences were in full dress, and all evening in the principal streets of St. Cloud a lot of Chippewas played foot-ball with the heads of some Sioux, with whom they had been at war that day. In those days, brains and culture were found in shanties. The leaders of progress did not shrink from association with the rude forces of savages and mother nature.[1]

On the one hand, the small community of St. Cloud, with its modest resources, had a powerful inducement to succumb completely to barbarism. On the other hand, the residents did yearn to hear the more finished music that a concert might provide and to clutch onto vestiges of civilized life by attending in formal attire. It would be a mistake to assume that rough living precluded the desire for polished musical performances. Musical appetites remained lusty, and the pleasures of sound encompassed every variety of composition from the wildest music of a jig to the refined offerings of a sonata. Eager supporters of professional concerts, popular or otherwise, were to be found in every part of the United States.

From what contemporary music lovers have said about why they attended musical performances at concert halls and theaters, it is clear that many of them, though certainly not all, believed they were not doing so to avoid reality. No minds were being allowed to slip away into an illusory world or become absorbed merely in acts of entertainment. They thought that the music they paid money to hear should at least stimulate or, in certain instances, ennoble life as they found it and help them go beyond its fundamental sadness. This was certainly representative of the thinking in St. Cloud as well as in New York or Philadelphia.

The sound of music made existence for all listeners seem worthwhile. However much cognoscenti advised them to study the intellectual basis of music, in order to appreciate its structures and its purely aesthetic beauties, their ears instead persisted in extracting what was physically exciting and emotionally stirring out of the listening experience. American music lovers, on the whole, would have reacted as did Louis Moreau Gottschalk, composer-pianist from New Orleans, on seeing an earnest concertgoer and amateur pianist with his eyes glued to the score of a Beethoven piano sonata that Gottschalk was performing, "to see if I made a mistake." The man would abide only intellectual stimulation, not emotional. Such intellectuals missed the whole point of music, according to Gottschalk:

> Of all the absurdities practiced by the Anglo-Saxon race in matters of art, this is what makes me suffer the most. Their manner of playing music is wholly speculative; it is a play of the wits. They like to see such and such a chord resolved. They delight in the *episodes* of a second repetition. "They comprehend music in their own way," you will tell me; but I doubt if it is a right one. Music is a thing eminently sensuous. Certain combinations move us, not because they are ingenious, but because they move our nervous system in a certain way. I have a horror of musical Puritans.[2]

Since popular music entertainers were particularly attentive to this need for stimulation and presented the public with exhilarating works that were readily assimilable, they continued to be sought after, despite the adverse criticisms of persons who claimed a superior understanding of the arts. Their offerings came in the form of traditional song and dance that had arrived from the British Isles and recently composed music originally intended to entertain the English public. The last included the winsome pieces in English ballad operas. There was also a liberal sprinkling of reworked arias from Italian, French, and German operas and modified art songs. The original texts were abandoned for new and more suitable ones in English, and music was altered to suit the tastes of the ballad lovers. Increasingly, and especially after the 1820s, popular music would include serious and comic ballads and minstrel songs written by Americans.

The popular songs of the time were so assimilable that certain Americans devoted to art music were upset to discover that they themselves remembered the popular tunes and texts more readily than the sounds of their treasured symphonies, chamber works, and operatic scenes. There was, for example, John Sullivan Dwight's complaint, in his *Journal of Music* for 19 November 1853, that Stephen Foster's "Old Folks at Home" had one of those tunes that are "only skin deep." He claimed "that they are hummed and whistled without musical emotion . . . [but also] that they persecute and haunt the morbidly sensitive nerves of deeply musical persons, so that they too hum and whistle them involuntarily, hating them even while they hum them." Popular music became etched on Dwight's and everybody else's memory because of its lack of complication, its constant reproduction on lip after lip, and its "catchiness." Everywhere anybody went, there was popular music. Besides, unlike Dwight, some of the most cultivated people in the antebellum period were appreciative of its evocative attributes. Even for them, "Auld Lang Syne" and "When Shall We Meet Again?" were the more usual accouterments of a New Year's Eve, a college reunion, or a good-bye parting with a traveler than, say, an operatic farewell aria or Beethoven's "Farewell" Sonata, opus 81a.

John Sullivan Dwight and correspondents to *Dwight's Journal of Music* had denounced American listening habits and accused music teachers of perpetuating the taste for "inferior" music. In a statement sent to the *Journal,* one well-bred music teacher conceded the public's dedication to the popular singers but defended the teaching profession, saying the accusations were unfair and adding:

> There is music for the mass as well as the few. That this is *a fact,* I must deeply regret; but that it is the fault of teachers exclusively, I cannot believe. Whilst "Negro Vocalists," "Ethiopian Serenaders," and low priced third and fourth rate concerts are patronized by cultivated people it would take a legion of teachers to raise the musical taste of all their pupils to a higher standard.[3]

Members of the music public prized the art of professional popular musicians for its ability to raise listeners to the maximal level of emotional stimulation. When caught up in a gripping musical presentation, they insulated themselves, for the time being, from the competition of other sensations. Wholesome relief from care was provided. Minds revived, and listeners would more easily accommodate themselves to the external world. At least this was the claim. Finally, these musical performances were collective events where listeners were separate from the musicians. It was neither themselves nor people they knew singing or playing. No person-to-person involvement with family, friends, and neighbors took place as they took in a show. As music was being performed by the skilled vocalists and instrumentalists, members of the audience were required to remain silent and not participate in the presentation. Thus, each listener was able to immerse himself into his own private world of experience, without regard to the usual social amenities.

### Listening to Popular Singers

What Dwight failed to understand was that when listening to the singers of serious and comic works suited to the general masses, audiences did not believe themselves corrupted. They thought, instead, that they were provided with a surcease to the ill-mannered, grasping, aggressive, materialistic, and often cruel world they knew intimately. The popular vocalists presented serious songs of the time that upheld similar values to those of the religions with which the public was affiliated. The melodies shared many characteristics with those of their hymns. The lyrics conjured pictures where goodness and home life were extolled, as in Stephen Foster's "Happy Hours at Home:"

I sit me down by my own fireside
    When the winter nights come on,
And I calmly dream as the dim hours glide,
    Of many pleasant scenes now gone;
Of our healthful plays in my schoolboy days,
    That can never come again;
Of our summer joys and our Christmas toys,
    And rambles o'er the streamlet and plain.

I sit me down by my own fireside
    Where the children sport in glee,
While the clear young voice of our household pride
    Makes melody that's dear to me,
And by every set that can charm the heart,
    They allure my eares [*sic*] away,
To prepare my soul as the swift hours roll,
    For the duties of the bright coming day.[4]

Their comic songs laughed at and provided a corrective to the social peccadilloes engendered by a society based on money. The tune to "Sambo's Address" calls for a backwoodsman's and boatman's uninhibited hopping and

**116**  stomping. The satirical lyrics, however grotesque they may be and demeaning to African Americans, are double-edged reminders of the plight of the poor, especially those who were black slaves, and of the empty-headed life of luxury led by some of the rich:

(Verse 1)  Broder let us leave,
            Buckra land for Hettee
        Dar you be receve,
            Gran as Lafayette;
        Mak a nity show,
            Wen we lan fom steemship,
        I be like Munro,
            You like Louis Fillip.

(Verse 2)  O dat equal sod,
            Hoo no want to go-e,
        Dar we feel no rod,
            Dar we hab no fo-e;
        Dar we lib so fine,
            Wid our coch an hors-e,
        An ebry time we dine,
            Hab one, two, tree, fore, cors-e.

(Verse 3)  No more carry hod,
            No more ice ter o-pe,
        No more dig de sod,
            No more krub de sho-pe;
        But hab wiskers gran,
            An prominade de Street-e,
        Wid butys ob de lan,
            Were we in full dres meet-e.

(Chorus)   Chinger ring ching
            Ho ah ding
        Chinger ring chaw
            Ho ah ding kum darkee.[5]

As can be gathered, the performances of popular musicians allowed for tenderness and nostalgia on the one hand and laughter and burlesque on the other. They allowed for emotion to steal in and soften the hard edge of daily living. They eased the lot of the millions who had neither pleasant and lucrative employment, nor servants, nor comfortable surroundings to smooth the path through life.

The performers who were most regarded with approval had ordinary origins, comparable to the backgrounds of their public. Hardly any were highly educated or formally trained in music. None assumed the airs of an upper class to which he or she aspired. The men and women belonging to such troupes as the Hutchinson Family Singers, the Baker Family, Emmett's Virginia Minstrels, and Buckley's New Orleans Serenaders had come largely from farming, laboring, or small-craft households. They made certain that their audiences knew of the circumstances of their birth and the democratic beliefs to which they adhered. To many popular musicians and songwriters, the democratic beliefs encompassed only white Americans; to others, such as Benjamin Hanby and the Hutchinsons, the beliefs embraced all Americans, black and white alike. The Hutchinsons told of themselves in a song, "The Old Granite State:"

We have come from the mountains, of the "Old Granite State."
We're a band of brothers, and we live among the hills,
With a band of music, we are passing round the World.

We have left our aged parents in the "Old Granite State."
We obtained their blessing, and we bless them in return,
Good old fashioned singers they can make the air resound.

. . . . . . . . . . . . . . . . . . . . . .

We are all real Yankees, from the "Old Granite State."
And by prudent guessing, and by prudent guessing,
And by prudent guessing, we shall whittle through the world.

Liberty is our motto in the "Old Granite State."
Equal liberty is our motto, we despise oppression,
We despise oppression, and we cannot be enslaved.

. . . . . . . . . . . . . . . . . . . . . .

Now three cheers altogether, shout Columbia's people ever,
Yankee hearts none can sever, in the "Old Sister States."
Like our Sires before us, we will swell the chorus,
Till the Heavens o'er us, shall rebound the loud hussa.[6]

The Hutchinsons did come from a farm in southern New Hampshire (the "Old Granite State"), although their birthplace was located several miles away from the nearest mountain range. They shared their democratic credentials

**118**  with Abraham Lincoln, who came one evening in 1851 to hear them in Springfield, Illinois. He was late for the concert but elbowed his way through the crowd to get at a front-row seat, since he needed to stretch out his long legs as he listened. He enjoyed thoroughly their interpretation of Henry Russell's "The Ship on Fire" and later talked with them about his concerns over the slavery situation.[7] One cannot imagine him relaxing so informally at performances given by the opera singers in New York's Astor Place Opera House, nor of his later going backstage to hold a discussion on slavery with them.

In addition, we find the cultured poet and scholar Henry Wadsworth Longfellow present at their concerts. In October 1846 he wrote to Thomas Gold Appleton about attending concerts by the Hutchinsons and by "Leopold de Meyer, the Lion-pianist from Vienna, who when he plays seems to be dipping his hands into liquid music, and shaking the notes off the ends of his fingers like drops of water." Then he grumbled, "We made a little musical party for him but he did not come, sending instead a note." On 17 July 1849 Longfellow wrote to Charles Sumner from Portland, Maine: "Last night the Hutchinsons were here. I heard them sing 'The Old Clock [on the Stairs]' to music of their own—very striking!"[8] Did the teacher who wrote to *Dwight's Journal* consider this a low-priced third-rate concert, despite its being patronized by the cultivated Longfellow, a man whose taste it was necessary to improve?

Note, too, that the Hutchinsons sang for both the president of the United States and the inmates of Sing Sing Prison, appeared at colorful high-society soirées and at drab assemblies held in orphan asylums, came before exclusive gatherings and mixed assemblies of white and black Americans, before well-to-do and poor. They charged a modest entry fee, and anyone who had no money was still allowed to attend. And many of their appearances, including those at prisons and asylums, not to mention private homes, were gratis.[9]

Here was exercised the tenets of social equality and respect for the individual within a commonwealth, whatever his circumstances. Here was musical democracy in action. The public loved the performers' demonstrations of fellow feeling. Such generosity in time and admission prices and complaisance in performing at private homes were rare among the Europeans who purveyed high culture and high-priced works for high fees to high society.

Walt Whitman, when a young man of twenty-six years and before he discovered his enthusiasm for Italian opera, voiced important reasons why listeners like him appreciated the popular singers. He had gone to hear the Cheney Family singers at "Niblo's saloon" in September 1845 and was taken by their performance. These singers—like the Hutchinsons, from New Hampshire—consisted of four brothers and a sister who specialized in the presentation of ballads, hymns, and part-songs. Of them he said:

At last we have found, and heard, and seen something original and beautiful in the way of American musical execution. Never having been present at any of the Hutchinsons' concerts (the Cheneys, we are told, are after the same token,) the elegant simplicity of this style took us completely by surprise, and our gratification was inexpressible. This, said we in our heart, is the true method which must become popular in the United States—which must supplant the stale, second-hand, foreign method with its flourishes, its ridiculous sentimentality, its anti-republican spirit, and its sycophantic influence tainting the young taste of the republic.

The Cheney young men are such brown-faced, stout-shouldered fellows as you will see in almost any American church, in a country village, of a Sunday. The girl is strangely simple, even awkward in her ways. Or it may possibly be that she disdains the usual clap-trap of smiles, hand-kissing, and dancing-school bands. To our taste, there is something refreshing about all this. We are absolutely sick to nausea of the patent-leather, curled-hair, "japoncadom" style. The Cheneys are as much ahead of it as real teeth are ahead of artificial ones. . . . We beg these young Yankees to keep their manners plain always. The sight of them, as they are, puts one in mind of health and fresh air in the country, at sunrise—the dewy, earthy fragrance that comes up then in the moisture, and touches the nostrils more gratefully than all the perfumes of the most ingenious chemist.[10]

Significant words identify the taste of this antebellum listener with strong democratic leanings: "simplicity," "republican spirit," "plain," "health and fresh air."

No village was too small or too unpromising for these musical representatives of the ordinary citizenship to visit. Their auditors, the musicians hoped, would be law-abiding Americans willing to purchase tickets in order to defray expenses and provide a modest profit. Their auditors, unfortunately, might sometimes be rough characters and "dangerous members of the community." The professional performers tried to maintain their good names but knew that all sorts of "strolling vagabonds and impudent mountebanks" also visited the villages and compromised the whole profession with their lack of musical ability, fakery, drunkenness, and dishonesty.[11] Luckily, most Americans were starved for entertainment, cognizant of and highly amused by the charlatans, and avid listeners at bona fide concerts. More than a few listeners might be so profoundly moved by the musical encounter that a week without the opportunity to hear music was a week with little meaning, despite the inability of some to read from a music page or to play an instrument.

It is therefore no surprise to find people crowding to hear the popular performers no matter what the obstacles to doing so. Philip Hone in 1837 spoke of a nation in financial distress. Nevertheless, he was amazed to see how large the attendance was at New York's popular concerts and the vogue of "Jim Crow . . . and his balderdash song," while at the same time the Italian opera had an "unstable foot" placed at Hamblin's Theatre. Six years later, Nathaniel Parker Willis was commenting that popular music performers like the Hutchinsons were "the passion of the hour in New-York," even though "Wallace had a [opera] house that would hardly pay expenses."[12] In the same year that Willis was saying these concerts took place, the inhabitants of Richmond, Virginia, were insistent on hearing minstrel performers night after night. The *Richmond Whig,* 2 November 1843, reported about one troupe:

> The Ethiopian Serenaders have created quite a sensation amongst
> our Concert Room Visitors, and they have politically determined to
> extend it throughout all classes by taking the Theatre for three
> nights, and reducing their prices to such rates as to afford all per-
> sons the power of witnessing an Entertainment. . . . Their liberality
> in reducing their prices of admission to twenty-five cents in Boxes
> and half that sum for the Pit is certain to ensure them delighted
> and crowded audiences.[13]

When the 1820s arrived the American citizenry wanted indigenous figures, emblems, and establishments devoted to affirming the nation's special cultural character and celebrating the ordinary inhabitants of the land and not the privileged upper class. They did not want, as much as the people of high social standing did, a cultural makeover of the nation in accordance with European ideas of appropriateness. Their music should follow its own pathways, without taking too much heed of European guidelines. From their own ranks came the symbolic figures of Davy Crockett, Mike Fink, Brother Jonathan, and Mose the B'howery B'hoy. Their own ranks originated the blackface minstrel caricatures, whose singular song and dance took the country by storm. Often little difference existed between the minstrel charac-terization and that of a majority of the audience, a boisterous, demonstrative crowd given to pounding, whistling, and roaring out its delight and to raging in its displeasure.[14]

The displeasure was moderated only if ladies were present. Herman Mann, of Dedham, Massachusetts, noted in his diary for 8 July 1843:

> Concert this evening by the "Ethiopian Serenaders." They played
> and sung in character and harmony, and acquitted themselves very
> well. The Concert was in the Hall of the Norfolk Hotel, this and last

evenings, and would have been much better attended had it not
been for a company who performed a few evenings since, pretending
to be the original "Ethiopian Serenaders," but who could not sing at
all, and would doubtless have been treated as they deserved had
there been no ladies present.[15]

Throughout the countryside people awaited the minstrel men, praying
they would show up and display their musical wares. The announcements of
minstrel performances were greeted with eagerness throughout the land.
People made an effort to attend the entertainments. Educated and uneducated, sophisticated and unsophisticated, adult and child, Americans of every
type made up the audiences. They responded to the physical stimulation of
minstrel song-and-dance rhythms and to the agreeable allure of the melodies.
The significance of the sympathetic bodily response of the attendees should
not be minimized. To listen meant to release kinetic energy—a wiggling of the
head, waving of the hands, and tapping of the feet. This was a part of music's
meaning inexpressible in words. In particular, children and adolescents found
it impossible to listen without rousing some part of their bodies into activity.
When Lew Wallace was a boy in the late 1830s, and living in Brookville,
Indiana, he witnessed a single entertainer come to his town to perform in the
courthouse. The first part of the program centered on the showman's walking
on a slack wire raised only three inches above the floor. The act was mildly
entertaining. However, it was what followed that completely captured his
boyish fancy and caused him to skip about joyously:

The second part of the programme aroused the entertained, myself
included, to a white heat of enthusiasm. It was made up entirely of
plantation songs and jigs, executed in costume—burned cork, shovel
shoes, and all. Two of the songs I yet remember—"Jump, Jim Crow"
and "The Blue-tailed Fly." The chorus rang through my head for
years; and as I walked home through the night I was unconscious
of any special increase of wisdom; at the same time, I felt that the
world was full of fun and life worth living, if only for fun.[16]

African Americans also went to the minstrel performances, enjoyed the
entertainment, and got amusement from burlesques of themselves. A free
black resident of Natchez, William Johnson, records that he attended a concert of "Daddy" Rice with his ludicrously exaggerated "Jim Crow" depiction
in 1836 and a performance of the "Ethiopian Singers" in 1845. While a slave
in Kentucky, William Emmons says, "We wuz let go to shows when dey come

to Carlisle. I member goin' to see Dan Rice's Circus dat use to come to Carlisle ever yeah."[17]

Nonminstrel musicians catering to the general taste also met with an impressive welcome wherever they appeared. For example, when hundreds of miners, accustomed to toiling to exhaustion at their claims, heard that Miss Goodenow of the Alleghanians was in town, they came as they were, "sweaty and dirty, to applaud . . . and occasionally to shower her with coins. She sang *Ben Bolt* and *Kathleen Mavourneen* over and over again, until she wished the two songs had never been written." The miners, like auditors in other rough-and-tumble places, held tenaciously on to their favorite songs and demanded their constant repetition. Nor were they backward in deciding on a new favorite. The evening that a St. Louis audience heard "Dixie's Land" played for the first time, "the whole house listened with breathless silence, and without giving the usual applause, suddenly burst into one simultaneous yell of delight and astonishment, and they made the band play it over eleven times before they would be satisfied."[18]

From the viewpoint of the grubby audiences, music offered an important respite from their usual concerns. If Miriam Goodenow was tired of singing the two songs, her listeners were not. J. D. Borthwick wrote of hearing the Alleghanians about 1852, in the mining town of Downieville, California. He says that the lady of the group "won the hearts of all the miners by singing very sweetly a number of old familiar ballads, which touched the feelings of the expatriated gold-hunters." Many of their songs had a "decidedly national character." Borthwick continues:

> I was present at their concert one night, when, at the close of the
> performance, a rough old miner stood up on his seat in the middle
> of the room, and after a few preliminary coughs, delivered himself
> of a very elaborate speech, in which, on behalf of the miners of
> Downieville, he begged to express to the lady their great admiration
> of her vocal talents, and in token thereof begged her acceptance of
> a purse containing 500 dollars' worth of gold specimens.

She received similar "gold" compliments in most of the mining towns the Alleghanians visited.[19]

Noah Ludlow tried to give a fuller explanation for the strong support, in sparsely inhabited and newly settled areas, for touch-and-go drama, the everyday musical theater, and concerts adapted to the ordinary taste. He observed that the first inhabitants of the lands west of the Alleghenies were fond of amusements, and when an opportunity occurred for gratifying that fondness, they made "a general turn-out." Early migrants to a new area, he said, were generally "bold and active spirits, with an unbounded desire of novelty and excitement." They had, too, "a considerable amount of romance in their natures," and to concerts that addressed this part of their makeup they subscribed enthusiastically.[20]

However friendly the anticipated audience, the popular entertainers left as little as possible to chance. They struck no high-and-mighty poses. The performing groups could not afford just to wait for the public to come to them. Therefore, before appearing in a place, they advertised their coming in newspapers, flyers, and posted bills. On arrival, a company paraded down the main street, calling attention to their costumes, antics, and music. As Robert Kemp said of his "Old Folks" troupe, they did not depend only on advance notices, but entered a town in the costumes of yesteryear and filed along the principal thoroughfares to let the locals look them over. And look them over the people did, frequently engaging in scrutinies that were discomfortingly thorough. Yet all was in good fun, Kemp said. "The children always followed in the greatest glee, the dogs barked, business was suspended, and old men hobbled along beside us, with the light of other days shining in their eyes. Young and middle-age people smiled or laughed, and the whole neighborhood, wherever we appeared, was in an uproar,—just as we intended it should be."[21]

In the performance hall, they shaped their repertoire according to local wants, preferences, beliefs, and expectations. If some composition was locally popular, they were sure to include it. If local allusions could be made, they altered the lyrics and made them. If patriotic feeling was high, the entertainers quickly moved to exploit it in song. They did all they could to insure that everyone left for home delighted with the event. For example, Ludlow was in St. Louis in December 1820 and sensed that the residents wanted a means for expressing their pride in being Americans. He acted accordingly:

> The house was crowded to an inconvenient fullness, and all were
> anxious to discover what the peculiar performance was in which
> they were to have an exhibit of "Washington and his Family." As
> soon as all was ready for the tableau, the band in the orchestra be-
> gan the national air of "Hail Columbia." The curtain rose, strong
> white lights from behind the scenes threw a bright halo around the
> figures, and for a few moments there was the silence of astonish-
> ment,—then came a thunder of applause that sensibly shook the
> building. I do not believe I ever beheld such rapture displayed by an
> audience in my whole life. The picture was presented three times
> that night to gratify the audience, who seemed unwilling even then
> to leave the theatre.[22]

On occasion, the entertainers went almost too far in their arousal of an audience. John Hutchinson writes that in 1854 he and his siblings performed "Ship on Fire" with as graphic a rendition as possible:

> At . . . [a] point in the song, the scream of "Fire!" was heard. Judson's voice sounded it ventriloquially. Instantly I would turn my head in the direction from which it was supposed to proceed. Asa would follow with a rumble on his viol, in exact imitation of the roll and rattle of a fire-engine hurrying through the streets. The effect on the audience was always electrical. Often there would be a stampede. They would rise in groups from their seats until the whole audience was ready to start for the door. Meanwhile I would continue the song, and sometimes it would arrest their attention and they would quiet down, but usually it was with some difficulty they would be persuaded to remain long enough to find it was an illusion.[23]

The limited number of Americans likely to enjoy opera and symphony could have slight acquaintance with either if they lived distant from a handful of the largest cities. The musical fare for most American towns and villages rarely included art music. Lacking visits from professional musicians prepared to perform it, the residents of these localities had no way to experience its sound other than purchasing compositions blindly through the mails, from some distant publisher, and trying them out for themselves. Normally, they would turn to the one genre they knew about, popular music, and its enterprising performers. As one traveler pointed out in 1852, whether in Rochester, Buffalo, Pittsburgh, or Detroit, no art music performances were to be heard while he was there, and at other times were not often available. The offerings were unremittingly popular; what is more, "a few popular songs, waltzes, quicksteps, &c., seem to be generally the stock in trade both of music sellers and music teachers here."[24]

### Listening to Oratorios

Choral groups were few during the eighteenth century, and one or two had attempted to present selections from Handel's *Messiah* to American audiences. In the nineteenth century, owing to the singing school movement, more and more church choirs were formed whose members had had some vocal training. In the 1830s the musical-convention idea took hold, an offshoot of the singing school. Music teachers, church choir members, and other interested parties would come together for several days, usually sometime in the summer months, to advance their technical knowledge and study mainly religious choral selections. Directly as a result of these activities, choral societies made up of amateur singers multiplied in the more populous parts of the country. With the influx of German immigrants beginning in the 1840s, the impetus toward forming choral societies increased mightily. The ambition to go beyond hymns and attempt selections from larger sacred works or these sacred works in their entirety—oratorios, masses, and other challenging musical services—could be realized through these societies.

One of the earliest choral societies was Boston's Handel and Haydn Society. On Christmas Eve 1815 one hundred singers, solo vocalists, twelve instrumentalists, and an organist presented selections from Haydn's *Creation* and other sacred works to an audience of about one thousand people in what is now King's Chapel. The *Columbian Centinel* praised the "most judicious selection of pieces from the fathers of sacred song" and observed that "some of the parts electrified the whole auditory." Some solos seemed particularly "sublime and animating."[25]

Before long, New York City had its Sacred Music Society; Philadelphia, the Musical Fund Society; Pittsburgh, the Philharmonic Society; Cincinnati, the Cecilia Society; St. Louis, the Sacred Music Society; Chicago, the Choral Union; and Milwaukee, the Musical Society. The membership consisted mainly of musical amateurs who loved to sing. Not wanting to keep their talents private and knowing the public's interest in sacred music, the larger church choirs and the choral societies in all of these cities started to appear in concerts open to the general public, offering large sacred works for chorus and solo vocalists—most often, Handel's *Messiah* and Haydn's *Creation*. When available, professional singers usually took over the solo parts.

The admission charge to a concert was customarily around one dollar, and at least some of the proceeds went to defray the expense of instrumentalists, professional vocalists, hall rental, and cost of music. In several instances, the choral members also faced assessments. The Milwaukee Musical Society in 1857 solicited new members, stating the monthly charge would be forty cents, plus a two-dollar initiation fee. These were "but a moderate tax to pay towards the support of an organization which ministers so largely to the enjoyment of our citizens and which reflects such credit upon our city."[26]

Americans, including those whose religious convictions would never have allowed them to attend a secular concert, turned out in gratifying numbers to listen to the choral societies. In a sense, attendance might be regarded as a form of worship. (One needs to add that many came also because family members, relatives, and friends were members of the chorus.) The auditors felt to some extent that they were hearing the voice of God, who was revealing himself through musical sound. It should be remembered that

126    these were people unwilling to consent to just living life as they found it, but also wishing to find a clarification and vindication of their existence and reinforcement for their religious beliefs. In part, listening to sacred concerts aided in meeting this need. Besides, there was the magnificence of the music to satisfy them. Frequently the playing and singing were not without blemish. Criticism of the technical side of performances was left to the connoisseurs, however. The usual music lover came to be moved, expected to be moved, and wished to reach for what was then termed "the sublime." He or she willingly forgave flaws in singing and playing if this goal was achieved.

Audiences shrank when financial crises shook the nation, when too much repetition of one or two works occurred, or the presentation was so poor that nothing of the sublime could be achieved. In addition, they might be introduced to a new work whose music was unfamiliar, confusing, and too distant from the much simpler diatonic hymns to which they were accustomed. Thus the adverse notice of the performance of the unknown Haydn *Creation* by Philadelphia's Musical Fund Society in 1822:

> It was attended by a numerous and respectable company of ladies and gentlemen, who appeared to be more pleased than it was expected they would be. Some, indeed, were heard to say that, "if they were not fearful of their taste being called into question, they would not be pleased at all," and it may be supposed that others would have made similar declarations, if they had been equally candid.[27]

Mirthful and even hilarious moments did also occur, despite the solemn nature of text and music. An amused Longfellow tells of witnessing Boston's Handel and Haydn Society do Sigismund Neukomm's *David* in 1837, "where the part of David is sung by a very fat man, and the part of Goliath by a very small one; and when the pebble hits Goliath on the head it is represented by a great blow on a bass-drum, and for fear there should be any mistake, *explained* in the bill!"[28] In a later year, *David* was done again by the Society, with Marcus Colburn, of gigantic stature, as David, and George Root, a youngster, singing Goliath. Root writes:

> It was absurd enough when we went forward together to begin [their duet], for this giant was David, and I, a stripling in comparison to him, was Goliath; but when I had to sing, in the most ponderous tones I could assume, "I can not war with boys," the audience [at the Odeon] broke out into irresistible laughter, in which Colburn, who had the most contagious laugh in the world, joined and that "broke me all up," as they say now-a-days.[29]

The audience, too, put aside its usual stance of piety and also "broke all up."

A few people seated in the audience could not be reached at all by the music, though they might attend with a degree of faithfulness. Ralph Waldo Emerson was one of these. He attended a Handel and Haydn Society performance of the *Messiah* in 1843 and said he liked the chorus best when the choristers sang at length and made his ear "insensible to the music" or "made it as if there was none."[30] On the other hand, another resident of the Boston area reminisced about his boyhood in the early 1840s and about listening to the Handel and Haydn Society:

> Those were halcyon days (or nights, rather) to me. My older sisters sang there and took me along as company, not infrequently discarding me on the return in favor of some gallants who desired to see them home. . . . I recall the dramatic *timbre* of Richardson's voice. . . . I recall how sweetly Caradori-Allen sang, and what an impression our earliest imported soprano created. . . . How Charles Zeuner *did* bring out the music from the Appleton organ, too!
>
> Oh, those boyhood days! How full, earnest and gleeful our joys were, and how poignant our griefs! Nothing in mature life reached a similar stage.[31]

On balance, the sacred concerts did please numbers of listeners and had a much wider following than did Italian grand opera and symphony. John Moore, in his *Encyclopaedia of Music* (1854), referred to oratorio as telling a scriptural story "treated by music of the sublimest character." He said that oratorio listening had achieved great popularity, thanks to the music being rendered familiar "through the means of large societies in the cities." He summarizes what Americans felt about listening to oratorios:

> Like all other tastes, the love of music may be nourished from the smallest germ into large and vigorous life; the habit of attending to its beauties, and the desire of appreciating them, lead to a conviction of its truth; whilst its effect upon the mind is to elevate and refine, perhaps beyond all other sensuous enjoyment. If you doubt, go listen to the "Creation," or any other sublime oratorio, and mark the potency of many impassioned scenes upon a people who, as yet, are but in the first chapter of what may become to them a noble volume. Listen to the heavenly sounds, and acknowledge that it is in moments like these that the heart expands in its sympathies, stretches out the hand to the weak, whispers encouragement to the depressed, and applauds the strong; that men grow gentler and bet-

ter, determine upon goodness, and build up hopeful resolves. . . . It is looking at art with such feelings that we desire to see it encouraged in the midst of a population whose labors, in spite of their noble tendencies, are apt, without recreation, to lower the tone of the mind; and because we are anxious that every attempt should be in a right direction—emanate from the best feelings; not a mockery of art, but a true worship.[32]

After attending an oratorio performance by the Sacred Music Society of New York in November 1835, Philip Hone commented in his diary on "the avidity with which people crowd to hear these oratorios," while at the same time "the Italian opera does not succeed, and the proprietors are about selling their opera-house." He praised the "respectable persons in the middle walks of life, who select with careful deliberation the kind of amusement which suits them best, [and who] are fond of music and patronize it in preference to any other public or theatrical entertainment."[33]

### Listening to Opera and Other Imported Vocal Music

"The Italian opera does not succeed"; this observation was made year after year in New York during the antebellum period. One can advance several reasons to explain the failure. The artistic music heard in concert hall and opera house, invariably the product of European composers and performed by European musicians, was a gloss on American culture rather than a part of it. At first, the absence of urban centers, the scarcity of capable vocalists and instrumentalists, and the lack of disposable income severely limited the formation of musical institutions. Before long, especially after 1840, several large urban centers had taken shape and could provide huge populations from which to draw. Competent musicians began to remove themselves in large numbers from Europe to America. Wealth had accumulated to a level heretofore unknown. In short, though art music institutions might fail to establish themselves on a permanent basis, they would constantly find music aficionados ready to reseed the cultural ground. Opera, in particular, was an expensive proposition, calling for complex stage machinery, scenery, costumes, corps de ballet, chorus, vocal soloists, and orchestra. Performances could not always pay for themselves. Someone had to come forward and make up for the deficits. Not until after the Civil War had the number of opera lovers and affluent patrons in New York grown sufficiently to establish and maintain the new Metropolitan Opera on a permanent basis.

For a long while the strangeness of the music, the empty-headed fashionables who turned out for performances, and the incomprehensibility of the language caused many people, in the areas where it was available, to shun opera. Some concerned citizens condemned it wholesale, finding it morally corrupting and supported by the false-hearted. One accuser, Augustus Longstreet of Georgia, enjoyed the more popular forms of music but was closeminded when it came to opera and symphony. Whenever he listened to either, he said, the sound was foreign and un-American, a hodgepodge of unintelligible tones that could not really interest the men and women who praised such music. These listeners were frauds who counterfeited delight in something that they despised deep down. Longstreet was clearly denying the legitimacy of the claims of art-music lovers because of his own inadequacy in hearing what they heard.[34]

On the other hand, Americans made no hard and fast distinctions between different sorts of music, and attendees at operatic performances included men and women from ordinary walks of life who could afford the entry fee. Yet at first, even the potential opera lovers hesitated about giving this new art form a wholehearted embrace. It took a while for them to become acclimated to the novel music. This was certainly so when Italian opera was first brought to the American shore by Manuel Garcia and his company of singers in November 1825. Over the next several months, around eighty performances were given at the Park and Bowery theaters, with one singer being Garcia's daughter Maria, later the famous Maria Malibran. William Cullen Bryant went to hear *Don Giovanni* in July 1826 and thought Garcia a good actor but his lower notes a bit worn and husky. Maria had "a liquid voice and skinny arms," Angrisani's bass voice was fine, but the other singers were poor. Bryant's last comment: "There was another, however, young Garcia, who enacted the servant of Don Juan, who was passable.—So much for the Italian Opera!"[35]

Charles Francis Adams heard the Garcia company in the same month and was pleased with Rossini's *Barber of Seville*, less pleased with Rossini's *Tancredi*, and least pleased with Zingarelli's *Guilietta e Romeo*. He says the last was not a very remarkable opera and too noisy. "Watkins was with me who knew nothing whatever about music and merely went for fashion's sake. He troubled me considerably at first, but as this sort of performance is not one which is often presented to us Americans, I could not afford to lose it."[36]

Garcia's opera company, especially the young Maria, met at first with exceptional success. Her glowingly unspoiled voice, astonishing verve, and superior deportment aroused a frenzy of admiration in New Yorkers. Moreover, when encores were demanded of her, she complied with familiar ballads in English. Regrettably, once the initial curiosity and faddish frenzy had worn off, opera remained a novel and unassimilated art form for Americans. On the sidelines, straitlaced critics set in motion attack after attack against the alleged decadence of foreign musical theater. Maria notwithstanding, fewer and fewer listeners attended performances. The Garcia troupe quickly was entangled in financial troubles and was forced to leave the United States.

Three visitors to America's shores took the first steps toward correcting the prevalent negative attitude toward art music: Ole Bull, who appeared in the United States from 1843 through 1845; Jenny Lind, in 1850 to 1852; and Louis Jullien in 1853 and 1854. Ole Bull was a magnificent violinist, but what is more, a dedicated democrat and an upright, manly hero when facing down bullies. He could not help but appeal to Americans, and by extension, his art did also. Jenny Lind was not only an extraordinary singer but was seen to personify purity and virtue, an image she and her publicist, P. T. Barnum, carefully cultivated. Her angelic manner infused rightness into the arias she sang. Louis Jullien, a knowledgeable orchestral conductor, brought with him from Europe several exceptional instrumentalists as the nucleus of an outstanding orchestra capable of playing the more difficult symphonic literature of Europe with finesse. At the same time he was a consummate showman. Compositions of the highest caliber were mixed with pieces meant solely to amuse. He was skilled at staging musical spectacles that dazzled the public. When he led his players, Jullien showed the sentiments the music was supposed to convey through his conducting mannerisms. He was endlessly entertaining and made it a pleasure to listen to art music. All three musicians triumphed also because they were emotional, not intellectual, performers. They mixed profound pieces with entertaining trifles. Their artistry encouraged wonder and enchantment. In short, they spurred the imagination of their listeners.

To these three should be added Louis Moreau Gottschalk (1839–69), born in New Orleans, musically educated in Paris, and one of the finest pianists in Europe and America. He was also a composer about whom most Americans could feel proud. In Europe he gained the reputation of a virtuoso gifted in presenting music in a theatric manner. He returned from Europe in 1853 and swept through the United States playing many of his own piano works to full houses. He captivated the women in the audience wherever he appeared and presented a living argument for the possibility of excellence in a native musical performer and composer. True, several of his compositions were salon pieces, meant mainly to entertain or astonish. On the other hand, he pioneered the use of song and dance from the United States and the West Indies in music of lasting interest: "Le Banjo," "Bamboula," "La Savane," "Union," "La gallina," and the Symphony No. 1 ("La nuit des tropiques") to name six.

The realization grew in men and women of new musical possibilities that promised a greater richness than they had ever before experienced. Art music evoked expression not possible from the simpler fare of popular song and dance and made listening potentially into a highly rewarding encounter. To be sure, not everyone was won over; nor did all who were won over become permanent devotees. Yet enough Americans remained enthralled to allow art music to become far more viable than it ever had been. At first, quite a few Americans remained skeptical about the three aforementioned Europeans. The *Richmond Whig*, for example, warned local citizens of the imminent debut of Jenny Lind in Richmond, late in 1859:

> "The Nightingale," "The Queen of Song," the "Divine Jenny," will soon be among us, and her advent promises to be celebrated by the usual quality of Humbug, extravagance, and insane folly. As the world goes, so will Richmond go, and Dame Rumor has already announced that we have some consummate asses here, who are ambitious of playing second fiddle to the asses of New York and Boston, who gave the extravagant sums for the premium seats.[37]

The newspaper was objecting to the ballyhoo about Lind put out by Barnum, the reported price tag of five dollars per regular seat, and the outrageous bidding at auction for the best seats that had taken place in the Northern cities. Nevertheless, wherever she appeared, people attended her concerts in droves.

Perhaps for a majority of the men and women who were present at the Lind concerts, theirs was indeed a transient infatuation and little more. Charles Congdon spoke for thousands of Americans when he wrote of the Jenny Lind madness that began in 1851. He said that tens of thousands of dollars were spent just to see, and boast of hearing, her. He wondered why he, too, had been caught up in the insanity: "Where are the dozen dollars which I myself took from a flaccid purse, and cheerfully laid down for the privilege of seeing the extraordinary woman, when I might just as well have stayed at home, and listened to a dear voice singing something which I could understand, to the honest accompaniment of the old, well-worn pianoforte?"[38]

In contrast to Congdon, an eighteen-year-old apprentice to a clock maker walked sixty miles to Wheeling, West Virginia, to hear Lind sing. The journey took three days and the youth keep himself in funds along the way and earned his entrance fee by repairing clocks. His father, a poor clergyman, was angry at his son's absence because no permission to leave had been requested. When the son returned and told his father where he had been, however, the anger turned to satisfaction over a boy who had proved he "was made of good stuff" by going to hear Lind.[39]

Interestingly, those who enjoyed her singing praised mostly the non-operatic compositions. Bronson Alcott admired her singing in October 1850

132   but said, "The 'I know that my Redeemer liveth' and 'The Herdsman's Song' were the most impressive pieces." He added that Daniel Webster had come to hear her and was "only courteously attentive" when she sang operatic arias for the first two-thirds of her program, but ecstatic when she finally sang a simple mountain song.[40] A further report on Lind comes from the *Philadelphia Record*, concerning a concert at Washington's National Hall with Daniel Webster and John Howard Payne, who wrote the lyric for "Home, Sweet Home," in the audience. She had begun by rendering "Casta diva," "The Flute Song," "The Bird Song," and "Greeting to America."

> But the great feature of the occasion seemed to be an act of inspiration. The singer suddenly turned her face to the part of the auditorium where Payne was sitting and sang "Home, Sweet Home," with such pathos and power that a whirlwind of excitement and enthusiasm swept through the vast audience. Webster himself almost lost his self-control, and one might readily imagine that Payne thrilled with rapture at this unexpected and magnificent rendition of his own immortal lyric.[41]

Like Lind, other singers of opera wisely mixed well-known and beloved pieces with the arias they presented. For example, when Madame Feron advertised that she would do selections from operas such as *The Marriage of Figaro*, she knew that this by itself would encourage a small turnout. Consequently, she also promised to include such popular songs as "I Pray Thee Now List to Me," "The Soldier Tired of War's Alarm," and "The Milk Maid."[42]

Charles Browne, using the pseudonym of Artemus Ward, wrote of hearing Adelina Patti sing "suthin or ruther in a furrin tung. I don't know what the sentiments was," but "when she sung Cumin threw the Rye, and spoke of that Swayne she deerly luvd," he was enraptured. He then expressed the sentiments of a great majority of Americans who had listened to operatic arias: "But Miss Patty orter sing in the Inglish tung. As she ken do as well as she kin in Italyun, why under the Son don't she do it? What Cents is thare in singing wurds nobody don't understan when wurds we do understan is jest as handy?" Furthermore, while in Cleveland, he attended a "musical sorry at the Melodeon," given by "Maria [i.e., Marietta] Piccolomini," where she wisely included two extremely popular ballads of the 1840s: "When, in tellin how she drempt she lived in Marble Halls, she sed it tickled her more than all the rest to dream she loved her feller still the same, I made an effort to swaller myself; but when, in the next song, she looked strate at me & called me her Dear, I wildly told the man next to me he mite have my close, as I shood never want 'em again no more in this world."[43]

Relishing music other than the songs and dances with whose character    *133*
one was well acquainted from infancy was not easily done, in fact taxing, for
most people, including the most educated and sophisticated. Nevertheless, the
number of Americans taken with the operatic repertoire grew with acquaintance. After Lind had been in America for several months, Longfellow went to
a concert of hers and found he had a real taste for an operatic aria. He wrote
to Charles Sumner from Cambridge on 7 December 1851:

> Last night (Saturday) in town to be present at Jenny Lind's Farewell
> Concert. She sang divinely! The finest piece of all was "Deh! Vieni,
> non tardar!" The most delicious singing I ever heard or conceived. It
> is from Mozart's Nozze di Figaro! And I beseech you if ever you see
> it advertised, and she to sing it, do not fail to go, though the Union
> be in danger. Love, tenderness, longing, never found a more com-
> plete and triumphant expression than in that music and Jenny
> Lind's face while singing it![44]

During his early adulthood, Walt Whitman had been a sharp critic of
Italian opera. Yet he did continue to listen to it. By the middle 1850s he found
himself a convert and proclaimed "the supremacy of Italian music," finding
its melodies original, its harmonies rich, and its grand and tumultuous effects, as in the finales of the acts, "one of the greatest treats we obtain from
a visit to the opera."[45]

Americans could be found in the 1850s who had come to be dominated
by powerful feelings when attending performances of this newfound musical
import. A few were not altogether comfortable with the way the music took
over their emotions. John Neal, in his novel *True Womanhood*, describes a New
York drawing room scene in the 1857–58 winter in which an Uncle George
tells young Julia to go to the opera because it will maker her happier:

> "Happier, Uncle George! Happier at an opera, where I never go, but
> for your sake, and you never go but for mine, I believe."
>
> "Ah, but you are so passionately fond of the opera, Julie," added
> Arthur [Julia's cousin].
>
> "*Passionately!* Cousin Arthur? No, no, not so bad as that, I hope.
> That I am fond of opera music, and of the great masters, Meyerbeer,
> and Mozart, and Von Weber, I acknowledge; but I have serious objec-
> tions to the opera, and really am not altogether satisfied with my-
> self, when I give way to my *passion* for music, as you call it, Cousin
> Arthur."[46]

The most ordinary of people, neither well educated nor well to do, could certainly be found who also took pleasure in opera. New Orleans seems to have had more than the average of such music lovers, white and black, in the opera audience. Eliza Ripley tells of two seamstresses in New Orleans who discoursed knowledgeably about the merits of the prima donnas appearing in the local opera house. One of them said that she never failed to attend performances on Sunday. Ripley also mentions Mme. Casimir, the wife of an assistant at a barbershop near the French Market, who loved opera, and "dusky Henriette Blondéau," a hairdresser who "had to tell how fine was 'Robert,' but she prefers De Vries in 'Norma.'" Ripley says that "such were the gallery gods" who attended opera on Sunday nights, "and no mean critics were they."[47]

Further north on the Mississippi lived the free African American William Johnson, who attended a presentation of Italian opera in Natchez in June 1836 and, nine years later, listened to Ole Bull on the violin. Hundreds of miles distant from New Orleans lived Pete Williams, the black owner of a "low-down dance-house" in New York City. Well to do because of his profits, although he gambled much of it away, he was also an avid theater- and operagoer who abominated Macready, supported Forrest, and said that he was willing to die for Charlotte Cushman.[48]

Nevertheless, the mounting of an opera continued to be an unusual event during the antebellum years. Most Americans who came to discover what opera was all about went away less than happy. In particular, they found the conversations in musical recitative bizarre. Henry Wikoff summed up American reaction to Italian recitative when he remarked on the reception of Saverio Mercadante's opera buffa *Elisa e Claudio* in Philadelphia in 1832:

> The music was expressive and full of melody, and the situations afforded scope for effective acting. . . . The only thing that struck me as a disagreeable novelty was the recitative, which was neither singing or talking. It was amusing to note the effect on the audience. At the end of the first act people glanced at each other, afraid to divulge their impressions. Some looked grave, others perplexed, and not a few struggled to conceal symptoms of weariness. "Is this Italian opera?" said one. "Why, I have heard these airs before." "What is it all about, I wonder?" ventured to inquire another; for the *libretto* was not published in English, as nowadays [around 1880]. A few of the more audacious set fashion at defiance, boldly declaring, "It was a bore," and would gladly have sold their subscriptions at half-price. The majority, more forbearing, remarked mildly, "It might be pleasant after you get used to it," and displayed a patient resolve

to "worry it" out. After the first performance the pit and gallery vanished, frankly admitting the fun was beyond their comprehension.
. . . The subscribers were finally abandoned to their operatic immolation and, without meaning to libel them, I often suspected that a hornpipe occasionally danced between the acts would have been found quite refreshing.[49]

The faith of the advocates for opera was in those attendees who thought opera might be pleasant after one got used to it. Unfortunately the costliness of mounting opera and the need to charge high ticket prices to cover expenses prevented all but a minority of this potential audience from getting used to it.

## Listening to Instrumental Art Music

The United States was still a young country in the years under examination, its inhabitants engaged in carving their way through what was once wilderness. Even in 1862 Louis Moreau Gottschalk was forced to admit the "immense lacunae" in America's civilization. "Our appreciation of the *beaux-arts* is not always enlightened," he said, "and we treat them like parasites occupying a usurped place." Americans worshiped money too much and tended to try to drag down what was fine in the arts to their own unrefined level. "These little faults happily are not national traits," he concluded; "they appertain to all young societies."[50]

The United States had produced no celebrated musical art works, admitted Thomas Hastings in 1822. Of necessity, it turned to Europe to supply them. Yet the great symphonic and chamber music compositions of Europe had frequently revealed themselves to be beyond the discernment of the most well-disposed listeners. This lack of understanding was found even in the majority of their original European audiences, including those in nations where such music was broadly nurtured and executed by fine professional instrumentalists. "One would suppose," said Hastings, "that the most refined and complicated of these productions would be ill suited to the untutored taste of Americans." And they were. Americans, he said, wanted the best in music, but what they selected as the best and brought to the American shore they had to take on trust, since their own judgment was insufficiently developed.[51]

Throughout the first half of the nineteenth century, native musicians were usually fairly inept executants of art music, incapable sometimes of playing the least intricate works in acceptable fashion. Yet, prodded by the more fastidious listeners, they repeatedly programmed works that called for great playing ability if they were to make any impression at all. As a result,

*136*  great symphonic compositions were left to the mercy of poorly taught or self-taught musicians who promptly made travesties of them. Nonetheless, audiences were expected to find merit in music produced thusly, lest they invite the accusation of barbarity and simplemindedness, if not from America's musical connoisseurs then from European visitors. This was the conclusion of Hastings.[52]

What may have been true in the early 1820s gradually ceased to be as true in the years that followed. The few musicians, mainly from London, and the scarcer American instrumentalists who had enlivened the concert scene at the turn of the century slowly enlarged their ranks. Increasing numbers of trained players emigrated from the European continent. They had noted the lack of properly trained musicians in the United States and hoped to find employment as music teachers and membership in instrumental ensembles. The count grew steeply from the 1840s onward, especially with the crop failures of 1846–47 and the unsuccessful revolution of 1848 in Central Europe.

To the German and Austrian migrants to America must go a great deal of the praise for the formation of musical societies, immediately on their arrival, that featured the finest music of their countrymen, prominent among them Bach, Mozart, Beethoven, and Mendelssohn. When touring in the west in 1862, Gottschalk said of Milwaukee that it was "one of those Western towns of the United States which, born but yesterday, are built as if by magic." It was "peopled principally by Germans (in a population of sixty thousand souls they number forty-five thousand)." Already it possessed "a Philharmonic Society, a theater, a concert hall, and a magnificent hotel. Do not forget that we are one thousand miles from New York and very close to the Indian territories."[53]

The Germans notwithstanding, throughout the first seventy years of the nineteenth century, ensembles, some better than others but generally lacking proficient instrumentalists and constant support from an informed public, led an unstable existence. For example, in Charleston a St. Cecilia Society had been organized in 1784 to give concerts. Yet after 1822 dancing assemblies were replacing many concerts. The Union Harmonic Society was started up in 1822 to give concerts that might prove attractive to the public, mostly in the form of oratorio selections. It struggled to stay alive. The Charleston Harmonic Society in 1843 announced it would give a vocal and instrumental concert, its third of a series. In 1853 the Charleston Philharmonic Society proclaimed it had come into existence to raise taste. It, too, struggled to survive. Impermanency was the rule.[54] In Philadelphia the Musical Fund Society commenced life in 1820 and experimented with a variety of concert formats to remain financially viable—symphony concerts, opera singers' appearances, and performances by popular ballad singers. In New York the Philharmonic Symphony Society was formed in 1820, a cooperative enterprise operated by the players themselves. The quality of its performances varied widely from concert to concert, and these occurred sparingly during a season. Underrehearsing and defective performances were the norm; the Philharmonic's instrumentalists showed up to play only if no other, better-paying job was available. Listeners were likely to come away disenchanted with the musical experience. Boston's Academy of Music and the Musical Fund Society offered symphonic concerts of a sort. Music lovers enjoyed what was offered as best they could. Excellence in execution was rarely the hallmark of any of its participating instrumentalists.

It was therefore a revelation when Henri Vieuxtemps and Ole Bull demonstrated what fine violinists could do, after they arrived for visits in 1843. John Sullivan Dwight spoke for many lovers of art music when he said that Ole Bull "does inspire. . . . The most glorious sensation I ever had was to sit in one of his audiences, and to feel that all were elevated to the same pitch with myself, that the spirit in every breast had risen to the same level. My impulse was to speak to any one and to every one as to an intimate friend."[55]

Louis Jullien demonstrated what a fine orchestra could do when he crossed the Atlantic in 1853 with some forty excellent instrumentalists and added around sixty more players after his arrival. He presented symphonies and overtures, as well as dance music, quadrilles, and operatic selections. He provided the audience with fine amusement. The *New York Courier and Enquirer* called him a humbug, but a humbug who gave good value. Showmanship was to the fore when he waved a jeweled baton around or sat on a velvet throne before a music stand in the shape of a fantastic gilt figure, but musicianship was at a high level, said the *Courier and Enquirer:* "The discipline of his orchestra is marvelous. He obtains from fifty strings a pianissimo which is scarcely audible and he makes one hundred instruments stop in the midst of a fortissimo which seems to lift the foor, as if a hundred men dropped dead at the movement of his hand."[56]

In 1853 Gottschalk began to appear in public at the keyboard, but he flitted in and out of the United States, now here, now in Cuba, Haiti, Puerto Rico, Jamaica, Venezuela, Panama, or Brazil. A far more lasting impression was made by a group of musicians from Berlin who emigrated in a body as a well-trained though small orchestra to settle permanently in the United States. They would make a tremendous difference in the buttressing of art music in America. Calling themselves the Germania Orchestra, they first appeared in New York City in October 1848. Despite the orchestra's competence, it failed to win a following, owing principally to a lack of knowledge about and interest in its repertoire. Listeners again failed to appear when the

*138*    Germania tried concertizing in Philadelphia. The players were at the point of breaking up when appearances in Washington, then in Baltimore, changed their fortunes for the better. Finally they investigated Boston, where their success was so great that they decided to remain. Longfellow heard them in April 1849: "A charming concert by the 'Germania,' some fifteen young Germans, who gave us overtures and parts of symphonies, etc. We had the finale of the C minor of Beethoven, and Mendelssohn's Overture to Midsummer Night's Dream. After the concert a *petit-souper*."[57] In February 1853 James Higginson wrote from Boston to his brother Henry Higginson, the future founder of the Boston Symphony Orchestra and then in Europe, "The Germania brought out a new symphony of Beethoven last Saturday evening, the first time it has ever been performed in this country. Dwight, I believe, says it was very fine, beautiful, etc., but no doubt most of the audience thought it terribly dull."[58] The Germania was educating New Englanders and, in their tours, other Americans to fine music, winning accolades from such influential cultural leaders as the editor of *Dwight's Journal of Music*, and seeding the ground for the growth of permanent symphony orchestras. Tired of touring, they disbanded in 1854. Nevertheless, individual musicians from the orchestra provided the leavening for the formation of instrumental ensembles throughout the nation after the Civil War.

It took years of indoctrination before dependable audiences arose to sustain permanent orchestras, let alone chamber groups and instrumental recitalists. When Ole Bull appeared in Richmond at the end of 1843, a writer for the *Richmond Whig* admitted, "We cannot boast of a highly cultivated musical taste, and it is probable, therefore, that much of Ole Bull's performance was lost upon us."[59] For a long while almost all Americans, including the writer just quoted, were fixated on melody of the customary ballad or minstrel type. Any music that did not have a suggestion of this style was criticized as uninteresting because untuneful. Virginia Clay-Clopton once forced a Congressman Dowdell to go to a Gottschalk concert in Washington, at a time when the pianist was at the height of his popularity and young women everywhere were incorporating his sentimental "Last Hope" into their repertory. Asked the next day about his reaction to the concert, Congressman Dowdell said he thought that Gottschalk played prettily and with dexterity, but was not impressed by his music. Why? Because he did not play a single tune.[60]

Thomas Ryan tells an amusing story of how the chamber music concert of his Mendelssohn Quintette Club was reviewed in Washington in 1859:

> In next morning's paper we found . . . a glowing article; but,—
> *miràbile dictu!*—we were all singers instead of players!—a kind of
> Hutchinson-family arrangement; that being the sort of music then

most enjoyed by the public. The notice in question contained ecstatic
praise of the soprano, and also of the sympathetic alto, declaring
that so good a voice had never before been heard in Washington.
The tenor "had the true timbre of a tenor voice,"—there was no sus-
picion of a light baritone.

Writing the above at the end of the century, Ryan continued by conceding,
"Classic music is still *caviare* to many people, and thirty-six years ago it was a
thing of dull and dubious character to the uninitiated."[61]

Although the American musical public was uninitiated, it did sense an
urge for music, however one defined that urge. When George Templeton
Strong attended a concert at Castle Garden in July 1846, the evening was a
warm one and crowds of commoners made up the audience:

> Tonight I've spent comfortably at Castle Garden. . . . Heard the over-
> tures to *Masaniello* and *The Bronze Horse,* just the kind of music
> one wants to hear in hot weather. . . . The visitors to the place are
> mainly milliner's girls and their adorers, who look spoony and senti-
> mental, and sigh out the aroma of shocking bad cigars by the hour
> together.[62]

Naïve these "visitors" might have been, and revealing a lack of musical
sophistication. A mix of reasons, some having little to do with music, caused
them to come to listen. Nevertheless, they did choose the concert at Castle
Garden over a host of alternative entertainments available to them in New
York City.

Innocent though some music lovers might be, they did desire to enter the
art area. The traveler Harriet Martineau relates her astonishment when in
1835 she visited Cincinnati, still new and raw, and attended the first serious
concert ever given there. A quiet and well-mannered audience sat patiently
through the offerings. Those who came to listen had yearned to hear music
beyond the ordinary. Whatever the deficiencies of the performers, all was
forgiven them:

> One of the best performers was an elderly man, clothed from head
> to foot in gray homespun. He was absorbed in his enjoyment; so in-
> tent on his violin that one might watch the changes of his pleased
> countenance the whole performance through without fear of discon-
> certing him. There was a young girl, in a plain white frock, with a
> splendid voice, a good ear, and a love of warbling which carried her
> through very well indeed, though her own taste had obviously been
> her only teacher. If I remember right, there were about five-and-

twenty instrumental performers, and six or seven vocalists, besides a long row for the closing chorus. It was a most promising beginning. The thought came across to me how far we were from the musical regions of the Old World, and how lately this place had been a cane-brake, echoing with the bellow and growl of wild beast; and here was the spirit of Mozart swaying and inspiring a silent crowd as if they were assembled in the chapel at Salzburg.[63]

Unformed taste sometimes kept company with an eagerness to continue hearing art music. In 1846 the Viennese pianist Leopold de Meyer gave a concert in Buffalo to a crowded concert room of uninitiates and swiftly generated "an outbreak of popular enthusiasm." So excited were some listeners that they were preparing to follow him to Niagara Falls, where his next concert was scheduled.[64]

Until the 1840s, Americans had been little exposed to virtuosic performance. When suddenly the violinist Ole Bull had appeared among them, he was aware of the prevailing musical innocence and willingly took advantage of it. His American listeners rapidly made fools of themselves; "they thought nonsense, talked nonsense, and printed nonsense about this Norwegian." To give an example, enthusiasm and naïveté described what Mrs. Lydia Child brought to the musical experience. In so many other ways, she showed herself to be a good-hearted and quick-witted woman; in music, she showed herself to know next to nothing. Although honestly devoted to music, she wanted to feel what she was supposed to feel. When Ole Bull played a composition named "The Mother's Prayer," she grew prayerful forthwith, found "aspiration in every trill, trust in God in each vibration of the G string, all the experiences of human life in shake or *pizzicato*, and the sweet innocence of childhood laughing now on the E and now on the A."[65]

Nonsense about art music was perpetuated in the program notes offered to audiences. Those responsible for these less-than-edifying analyses recognized that without a sung text to go with it, a composition would yield up its meaning with difficulty to uninitiated concertgoers. Frequently, the printed explanations were far-fetched, lofty balderdash to quiet the audience's unease. George Curtis told John Sullivan Dwight in a letter dated 20 October 1843 that he had just attended a concert given by the New York Philharmonic that was attended by gentlemen in full dress and their ladies. None of them knew beforehand what the program would include, since no previous announcement had been made. They just went. Among other things, they listened to the Beethoven Seventh Symphony, which the notes depicted as "a musical presentment of the mythological story of Orpheus and Euridice. That did very well as a figure to represent it, but it was taken by the audience as a theme; and they all fixed their eyes upon the explanation, thereby to judge the symphony."[66]

George Derby, employing the pseudonym John Phoenix, wrote satirical burlesques for the *San Diego Pioneer* in the 1850s on the sorts of fodder fed to contemporary concert audiences. Once, under "Programme Notes," he explained a Beethoven symphony:

> The basses begin with a mystified, questioning phrase which is answered in higher harmony. Soon the horns enter with a defiant call.
> . . . We seem to hear a kind of sardonic blasphemy—unholy jesting with unspeakable things. Is it really jest? The trio is in the spirit of rough boisterous humor (one thinks of a dancing elephant).[67]

At another time, under "Musical Review Extraordinary," he explained the meaning of a program symphony called *The Plains: Ode Symphonie par Jabez Tarbox*. He begins by saying it should have a "soul-subduing, all-absorbing, high-faluting effect upon the audience, every member of which it causes to experience the most singular and exquisite sensations." He goes on from there:

> The symphonie opens upon the wide and boundless plains in longitude 115° W., latitude 35°21′03″ N., and about sixty miles from the west bank of the Pitt River. These data are beautifully and clearly expressed by a long (topographically) drawn note from an E flat clarionet. The sandy nature of the soil, sparsely dotted with bunches of cactus and artemisia, the extended view . . . are represented by the bass drum.[68]

The piece ends with a sound of rejoicing to the "God of Day," sung by the "Sauer-Kraut-Verein," which crescendos into the minstrel piece "Hey Jim along, Jim along Josey."

Uncertain of themselves, men and women cautiously entered areas of musical experience that had once been completely off-limits and sought to improve themselves culturally. They were taking their first steps toward the formation of audiences that would eventually support the superb symphony orchestras still to come. For the most part, Americans shared a similar point of view concerning musical culture, but a point of view that was gradually bifurcating. By the 1850s a dichotomy would become obvious between the art of the popular ballad and minstrel singers and that of the artistically sophisticated operatic and instrumental musicians.

# Amateur Music Making at Home

USIC THROUGH ITS OUTPOURING FROM HUMAN throats and through human fingers—more accurately, the sound of music in its nonprofessional social setting—was a vital component of the American cultural patterns that emerged in the early nineteenth century. Like amateur sketching, painting, and poetizing, music making had to make itself suitable for use in domestic and communal circles.

When we read contemporary European accounts of American music making, caution must prevail. Many reporters proved unsympathetic with American cultural patterns and disagreed with the values that Americans affixed to their music. European travelers came almost always from the upper classes and usually had an art-centered view of what music merited praise. More often than not, they offered sweeping conclusions based on the few scenes they had observed. They usually socialized with only a particular class of society and only during a limited period of time—perhaps six months to two years. Like Frances Trollope, they may have had reason to feel anger over their treatment on American shores. She arrived in the United States at the end of 1827, failed in a business venture, and after three years returned to England to write:

> I never saw a population so totally divested of gaiety; there is no trace of this feeling from one end of the Union to the other. They have no fêtes, no merry-makings, no music in the streets, no "Punch", no puppet-shows. If they see a comedy or a farce, they may laugh at it; but they can do very well without it; and the consciousness of the number of cents that must be paid to enter a

theatre, I am very sure, turns more steps from its doors than any religious feeling.[1]

While she sharpened her knives against all things American, she chose to
overlook the moneygrubbing of English businessmen, the oppressive exploitation of the British working classes, and the irrelevance of gaiety and fêtes
when British life proved to be a hardscrabble.

Occasionally, another European visitor came forward to contradict her, as
did Francis Baily. He claimed that New Yorkers, when he had visited that city
just before the nineteenth century, had loved music, dancing, and the theater.
What is more, excellence in music had been "considerably promoted by the
frequent musical societies and concerts which are held in the city, many of
the inhabitants being very good performers."[2] On balance, Americans did try
to take whatever pleasures were possible for them. Though few aimed for or
achieved the cultural heights of Europe's upper classes and intelligentsia,
they derived joy from paintings, plays, musical performances, and social
dancing. New World conditions put major obstacles in the way of musical
cultivation. There was a virgin land to develop. Moreover, democratic attitudes forestalled exploitation of the many to support the cultural preferences
of an elite.

Gaiety, merrymaking, music in the street—these did exist when the environment allowed them to exist. Through the years of the eighteenth century
and into the next century, the environment proved more and more hospitable
to good cheer, festive moods, and music. Whatever dourness the rigidly religious had promoted, it gradually abated even as softer feelings were allowed
to enter. At the time of Mrs. Trollope's sojourn in the United States (1827–30)
and in the years immediately following, most contemporary American perceptions of New World existence were the opposite of hers. Deficiencies existed, to be sure, but cumulative wealth and leisure were providing correc-
tives. Samuel Osgood, for example, remarked that the significant stages of life
were all commemorated with music in the United States. Infants listened
delightedly to the melodies of lullabies and nursery rhymes; the dead received
dignified burial to the singing of hymns; workmen sang cheerfully as they
labored; and newlyweds happily celebrated their marriage with festive song.[3]
The *Philadelphia Mirror of Taste and Dramatic Censor* was reporting as early as
1810 that the practice of music was already extensive in the United States,
though its science was little understood. People of every class played pianos,
violins, flutes, and clarinets, though not always skillfully: "Europeans, as they
walk our streets, are often surprised with the flute rudely warbling 'Hail!
Columbia!' from an oyster cellar, or the piano forte thumped to a female voice
screaming 'O Lady Fair!' from behind a heap of cheese."[4]

144      Speaking for the plain folk of North Carolina during the 1820s, Hardin Taliaferro observed that music and merriment prevailed far and near. Young people came together endlessly to sing, play instruments, and enjoy themselves. Events like corn shucking, log rolling, and quilting called for song and dance after the day's tasks concluded. Christmas was a notable festival, with an entire week's round of visits from house to house for singing, feasting, dancing, and "sparkin'." Virginians said similar things about themselves, stating that "somebody was always getting up a frolic of some sort," or a musicale, or a picnic.[5] Mrs. Anna Pratt's description of the celebration of Lizzie Alcott's birthday at her Fruitlands home on 24 June 1834 is touching in its display of the Alcott family's and their friends' mutual affections: "I rose before 5 o'clock and went with Louisa and Willy Lane to the Grove, where we fixed a little pinetree in the ground and hung all our presents on it. . . . After breakfast we all . . . marched to the wood. Mr. Lane carried his violin and played, and we all sung first."[6]

To the north, in Plymouth, Vermont, Sally and Pamela Brown wrote into their diaries about the occasions giving rise to music—the fun they and their neighbors had in visiting to and fro, the celebrations that went with the farm year, the spelling bees and singing schools, and the dances and picnics. Even pioneer villages, such as New Salem, Illinois, where the boy Abraham Lincoln was growing up, had its music at dances, house raisings, quiltings, and camp meetings that were as much joyous occasions as solemn religious assemblies.[7]

It would certainly seem from the above descriptions that Americans were inclined to make music and enjoy themselves, in contradiction to the Trollope statement. Exceptions existed, to be sure. African American slaves were less disposed to feel joyous. In the words of Sarah Ford, a slave in Texas, "Us don't have much singing' on our place, 'cepting at church on Sunday. Law me, de folks what works de fields feels more like cryin' at night."[8] Yet, for whatever the reasons, slaves too had their entertainments and observances, when allowed the opportunity, and did sing and dance when given the chance.

In addition, Americans made music to console rather than just to enjoy themselves. Mrs. Lydia Sigourney writes that when her mentor, Mrs. Lathrop, was eighty-eight years of age, sick, and awaiting her end, the elderly lady had the young Lydia come to the bed and sing simple songs for comfort "in low, soothing tones." Mrs. Bowen writes of a similar episode, this time of a dying father asking for old-fashioned ballads and his daughter singing them for him "in a low, soft" voice.[9]

And then there was Stephen Foster's dying sister Charlotte. Another sister, Ann Eliza, wrote:

The night of the morning when she died (Oct. 20 [1829]), I sat up and was frequently in her room. She was more tranquil, yet did not sleep, but seemed as attentive as at any time during her illness to the movements of her friends, occasionally speaking to them, and about an hour before day, when all were silent, she sang a song preserving with much melody & great accuracy, every note, but her voice was so thickened that she did not articulate sufficiently plain for the words to be heard, or for the song to be recognized.[10]

### The Nonprofessional Approach to Musical Performance

In one respect, Mrs. Trollope was right. Before the Civil War, the national culture made no allowances for competent professional practitioners of music who were American, whether as composers, singers, or instrumentalists. They were neither nurtured nor condoned. People were supposed to engage in musical study and activities for recreation rather than for monetary payment or professional purposes. This had a consequential effect on the sorts of musical behavior in which Americans engaged. For one young Virginian, music "was a passion from his cradle." He begged to be allowed serious violin study, but his parents refused, "uneasy lest he should be unfitted for life." The youth had to wait until after college graduation and a trip to Europe to give himself up to violin study. "It was a very uncommon thing in those days for the sons of American parents to be taught music."[11] In another part of the United States, North Reading, Massachusetts, George Root heard again and again as he grew up that music as a career "wasn't reputable. . . . Indeed, any line of music, as a business, in those days was looked down upon, especially by the more religious and respectable portion of the community."[12]

To this, J. Marion Sims adds his boyhood experience of 1822, when he was nine years of age in Lancaster, South Carolina. He was suddenly "carried away" by music, acquired a Jew's harp, and constantly practiced on it to the detriment of his spelling lessons. His schoolmaster, furious at Sims's wasting time on music, mortified him by saying bitingly, "Marion, you appear to-day in a new character; I presume you intend to become a musician." He was even more mortified when he spelled "Jew's harp" as "juice-harp," to the amusement of the rest of the class. He wished to ward off the laughter and ridicule. Then and there, he decided it would be his "first and last experience with learning music, even with a jew's-harp. I never played it afterward."[13]

Women, much more than men, exercised caution over a musical career. A good reputation might easily be lost. For this reason, potential musicians of high excellence avoided a musical calling. One of these was a Miss Anna

*146* Stone, whose father worked in Boston as a piano builder alongside the young Jonas Chickering. Despite an extraordinary voice and talent, Anna declined "a finished musical education" because she thought it would have exposed her "to temptations, dangers, difficulties, and trials inseparable from the profession of an artist of the first class." During her travels in New England, Lady Emmeline Wortley heard several amateur musicians whose playing and singing capacities were exceedingly fine, but who kept out of the public eye either out of modesty or a desire to preserve their good name. Eliza Ripley tells of a Tennessee woman "who had a powerful voice, and she sang 'Old Rosin the Beau' and 'Life on the Ocean Wave' with all the abandon of a professional." No thought was given to public concertizing.[14]

Though they retained their amateur status and exercised caution about public appearances, some men and women did take their musical studies seriously and did achieve tremendous competency as players and singers. This is made clear in Jessie Frémont's description of the role music played in her young life in Washington, as one of Senator Thomas Benton's four daughters.

> Music was a serious study among us. We had the happiness of one
> noble contralto, and in another sister such gift of expression on the
> piano that it afterward made her a favorite guest of Rossini when
> she lived in Paris. At his Tuesday evenings he always had her play
> the *Sonate Pathétique* and the "Moonlight Sonata," and declared she
> was the only woman he had ever heard who could play Beethoven's
> music.[15]

Nevertheless, it remained the opinion of a majority of Americans that music was easy enough to perform satisfactorily with only a fair degree of skill, and this ease would facilitate its spread from village to village. The immense number of instrumentalists and singers whose abilities were acceptable to their compatriots and the high degree of pleasure taken in their musical efforts were witnesses to this idea. The employment of a music teacher was tolerable so long as no student devoted himself or herself excessively to musical study. Even then, those people to whom religion meant a great deal protested, believing that indulgence in any study of secular music was a vain activity and indicated an alliance with the devil.

For these reasons, among others, minimal musical proficiency and maximum incompetence were everywhere to be met. One could not blame Abraham Lincoln for his inability to get his mouth around the tune of a favorite minstrel song, bellowing off-key instead. He had no musical training. Nor the father that Joseph Neal knew, who upset his more musical son "because that respectable individual, with a perseverance peculiar to the incompetent, was always subjecting poor 'Hail Columbia' to the Procrustean bed of his musical capabilities, and, while whistling to show his own light-heartedness, did anything but communicate corresponding pleasure to his auditors." James Percival tried to teach himself the accordion, but whatever tunes he played were recognizable only by him; everyone one else was fortunate if they could "catch one note in three." But the young lady of Norfolk, Virginia, whom Miss Mendell took on as a student was a different matter. She was a natural incompetent. Lessons could not help her: "I can see now a pupil I once had in music. Poor girl! She could not tell when she made a discord—she had no idea of music . . . but she must learn because all ladies play the piano. . . . But she did not learn music."[16]

Those people who were particular about their music constantly complained about the sounds they were subjected to. The cantankerous George Templeton Strong suffered torments while studying at home, when

> I was aroused by a fearful yelling, which I took at first for the cry of
> murder and then for the last dying speech and confession of some
> hopeless cat in the agonies of strangulation. But on going to the
> window I found that the unearthly noises in question proceeded
> from a "feminine," or, as Tom Cringle calls it, a "young female lady,"
> at a house a considerable of a way off, yelling forth "The Mellow
> Horn" at the top of her voice, with a running accompaniment of
> what had been (probably) a piano, but now sounded more like a
> band of narrow bones and cleavers. . . . Some boarding school miss,
> probably. She's at it still, and some one of her beaux has just joined
> in the second verse at full stretch of his lungs, like a chimney
> sweeper or Stentor himself. Horrible! What a noise![17]

Unfortunately for Strong, a majority of his contemporaries would not have minded this singing. What they would have minded more was what they perceived as excessive melodic ornamentation and extravagant harmonies, and vocalists mimicking the facial casts and gestures of Italian operatic singers. "To put on airs" while performing was unforgivable. Expressing the music's meaning visually was acceptable if sincere and unexaggerated. To exhibit one's self immodestly was unforgivable. Typifying this thinking is the comical commentary in Frances Whitcher's *The Widow Bedott Papers:*

> Well, Sam Pendergrasses wife axed Miss Coon to play on the pian-
> ner. They've got a pianner for Ann Elizy—piece o' extravagance in
> my opinion—don't see how Sam Pendergrass can afford such
> things—besides, I don't b'leve Ann Elizy'll ever make much of a mu-

sicianer, for she can't play but a few tunes yet, and she's been a takin' lessons amost three months. I spent the day there one day, and she thumpt away on the consarned thing half the time. 'Twas enough to split a body's skull open. Well, Miss Coon she sot down to the pianner—and o' all things! I wish you could a ben there! If't wa'nt *killin'*, then no matter. She throw'd back her head, and she rolled up her eyes, and she thrum'd it off with the tips o' her fingers. But good gracious! Her singin'! you'd a gin up, I know, if you'd a heerd it! The way she squawked it out was a caution to old gates on a windy day! See, what was it she sung? O, I remember—a dretful nonsensical thing, that kept a sayin' every little while "*Jimmeni fondly thine own.*" I was perfectly disgusted.[18]

The purchase of the piano seen as an extravagance, the expectation of a finished performance after three months of lessons, the irksome mannerisms of Miss Coon, and the nonballad style of singing—these were matters for serious criticism in other commentaries. On the other hand, here and there, an educated and introspective American did question what struck him as his own cultural bias. In the mid-1850s Oliver Wendell Holmes wrote:

I have often seen piano-forte players and singers make strange motions over their instruments or song-books that I wanted to laugh at them. "Where did our friends pick up all these fine ecstatic airs?" I would say to myself. Then I would remember My Lady in "Marriage à la Mode," and amuse myself with thinking how affectation was the same thing in Hogarth's time and in our own. But one day I bought me a Canary-bird and hung him up in a cage at my window. By-and-by he found himself at home, and began to pipe his little tunes; and there he was, sure enough, swimming and waving about, with all the droopings and liftings and languishing side-turnings of the head that I had laughed at. And now I should like to ask, WHO taught him all this?—and me, through him, that the foolish head was not the one swinging itself from side to side and bowing and nodding over the music, but that other which was passing judgment on a creature made of finer clay than the frame which carried that same head upon its shoulders?[19]

Most people were accepting of a certain nasal quality in their singing. Not so Europeans and the few Americans exposed to the accomplished singing of trained vocalists from overseas. Fredrika Bremer offered an amusing explanation for this New World trait, after she had listened to American Indians near Fort Snelling, Minnesota, in November 1850:

> I observed in the conversations of these Indians many of those
> sounds and intonations which struck me as peculiar among the
> American people; in particular, there were those nasal tones, and
> the piping, singing, or lamenting sound which often annoyed me in
> the ladies. Probably those sounds may have been acquired by the
> earliest colonists during their intercourse with the Indians, and thus
> have been continued.

It should be added that Fredrika Bremer did report hearing now and again an American musician play and sing "remarkably well, with extraordinary power, like a real musician."[20]

Americans also accepted the idea that no piece of music was sacrosanct and should be modified to accommodate personal or local requirements. For this reason, we find the finical George Curtis taking great liberties with music he selected to perform for the knowledgeable audience gathered at Brook Farm of a Sunday evening. Georgiana Kirby says that at first she failed to recognize the operatic aria, it was so modified. A sad and touching theme and music slowly executed replaced the original rapid-fire words and fast tempo; the accompaniment consisted of simple chords and arpeggios.[21]

When George Root admitted that he freely modified and simplified and transposed music to suit his performance capacities and desired expression, he was acting as did all other Americans. When a writer in Boston's *Columbian Centinel* described what seemed to him to be excessive modulation, chromatics, ornamentation, and detailed expressive directions in music scores as nonsense, he was suggesting that this "flummery" would be improved through modification. When the editor of *The Singer's Companion* allowed that the performer's decision to change any music "should be wholly arbitrary" and that "he should give time, emphasis, pause, &c., in a manner most easy and natural, and best calculated to produce effect, no matter whether the music is written in that particular way or not," this editor was acknowledging a practice prevalent throughout the country.[22]

New lyrics to favorite tunes were constantly being written in order to represent experiences not captured in the published sheet music. Therefore, the Mormons in Salt Lake City recast the words of "Sweet Betsy from Pike" to begin:

> Oh, once I lived in Cottonwood and owned a little farm,
> But I was called to Dixie, which gave me much alarm.

**150**   And those of "The Camptown Races" to begin:

> Old Sam has sent, I understand, Du dah!
> A Missouri ass [Governor Cummings] to rule our land,
> Du dah! Du dah day![23]

Further west, in San Francisco, "The Camptown Races" had acquired a different text:

> A bully ship and a bully crew
> Doo-da! Doo-da!

"Oh! Susannah" began:

> I came from Salem City
> With my washbowl on my knee.

"Pop Goes the Weasel!" was altered to:

> You go aboard a leaky boat,
> And sail for San Francisco.[24]

Americans unversed in music found it easier to modify the texts rather than the melodies or harmonies of songs. Especially popular among young woman was the composition of original verses to favorite tunes. Most of these verses are of the loving sort, showing tender affection for another person. The protagonist in these effusions is often a forlorn lover in despair over unreciprocated affection or a dead beloved. For squeamish singers who were fond of a minstrel tune but not its dialectal lyrics, rewriting the text was mandatory. The privately bound volumes of sheet music belonging to young women in the years under examination abound with such verses.[25]

Men, too, composed verses meant to be sung to extant tunes. Their themes differ from that of the women in the variety of topics covered. Although a large number are protestations of undying love, more than a few are nonsensical or topical with a tendency toward the comically satirical. Julia Ward Howe writes of her Aunt Eliza's husband, Dr. John W. Francis, and how the children loved him. He not only made up pet names for each of them but also invented "odd snatches of song which were to delight and exasperate later generations":

To a woodsman's hut one evening there came
    A physician and a dancing-master:
The wind did blow, io, io,
    And the rain poured faster and faster.[26]

Commenting on his boyhood years in the town of Mount Vernon, Ohio, Dan Emmett said that the fashion then prevailed for him and the other young people of the locality to discover how deftly they could fashion original verses and sing them to popular tunes. In Richmond, Virginia, a favorite pastime among gentlemen was the writing of new words to ballad tunes and then singing them at social occasions. Some were even published as broadsides and in newspapers. Altogether typical, also, was the meeting of businessmen for dinner and drinks at the end of the day and, after dining, singing new verses to old songs, as did a companionable group in Augusta, Georgia. When finished with talk about the burgeoning cotton market, these Georgians listened to one of their number huskily sing, "And Whitney's little cotton gin did it all, did it all, did it all," as he drummed the table with his fingers.[27]

A smitten lover was expected to demonstrate his affections in stanzas that extolled the charms of his beloved. Less expected was the continuing remembrance of these stanzas after years of marriage. And this is what Thomas Dabney, a Mississippi planter, did when gazing at his wife, Sophia. Their daughter Susan recalls:

He delighted in teasing her, too, because she looked so young and pretty when her blushes were brought up by his raillery. One unceasing occasion of blushing on her part was when he would playfully threaten to sing to their assembled sons and daughters now growing to be great boys and girls, the song that had won her heart. He called this a "Die-away," and the first line was, "Sweet Sophy, the girl that I love." It seemed to be the paraphrase of some song that he had adapted to suit his needs when he saw that a rival lover was in higher favor than himself—this was the account that he gave of it, and he said that it turned the scale in his favor.[28]

At times a professional songwriter or singer would take over an amateur effort at versification, add music, and publish the song over his own name. Ossian Dodge, who as a publicity stunt once bought an auctioned ticket for a Jenny Lind concert in Boston for $625, was notorious for doing this. John Trowbridge asserts that Dodge pirated the words and music of other men, claiming them as his own. He did pay some authors, including Trowbridge himself, for the privilege, but he "paid peanuts." A more astute amateur versifier, Frank Butler, lived in San Francisco. The Custom House had burned down in 1851, and Collector King had transferred the treasury to another building, employing ragtag assistants armed with ancient muskets and pistols and rusting cutlasses and swords. Onlookers found the display ridiculous, as did Butler. He made a song about the incident and sang it wherever he went. Soon, he was issuing lithograph copies of the composition, entitled "The King Campaign, or Removal of the Deposits," selling them at one dollar each. King offered Butler a sinecure position if he would cease singing and selling the song. At the same time, the collector took umbrage at Custom House employees who sang the satire and "cut their heads off as though they had been so many cabbages." Unfortunately for King, the satire was unstoppable, the damage done permanent, and his career ruined.[29]

The incidence of amateurs composing music is low, despite the early example of Francis Hopkinson, lawyer and signer of the Declaration of Independence. Also exceptional was the publication of some of Hopkinson's songs under his own name. Normally, in those rare instances when such publication took place, the author was designated as "a Gentleman" or "a Lady." It was perhaps likely that Fanny Crosby, receiving more than average musical training at the New York Institute for the Blind, would attempt the music for a song or chorus to commemorate special occasions at her school. It was far more surprising in those years to discover men composing music for pleasure rather than for professional reasons, as did Robert Montgomery Bird (1806–54). From boyhood to the year he died, he had a strong interest in music. Playing the flute, copying music, and composing the lyrics and music for songs occupied much of his leisure. An opera, *The Imp of the Rhine*, was contemplated. In the 1830s he wrote several patriotic songs or hymns, and had in mind to put out a volume of original American hymns.[30] Nevertheless, amateur composers like Hopkinson, Crosby, and Bird were scarcely to be found in America.

### Eulogies to the Home

Americans everywhere saw their homes as providing life's purest happiness. Husband and wife felt this happiness dissimilarly, however. Husbands went from the responsibilities, concerns, and gratifications of working in the outside world to the private pleasures afforded by wives and children. They encountered different scenes and diverse acquaintances every day. They could expect a refreshing shift in their routines when they returned to the home circle. For women, confinement was the rule. Their horizons were narrower than those of men. Wives seldom experienced anything outside their own homes and those of their friends and relatives. Their home was almost their entire life, the customary sphere for most of their activities. The fortunate ones, usually women in affluent circumstances, might attend an occasional concert, theater presentation, or ball, but the time spent on these activities paled when compared with time spent in domestic surroundings. Very few women threw off the restraints imposed on them by their society to lead independent lives.

All men and women were agreed that the home circle, with its grandparents, parents, children, and visitors, enveloped America's true core. Americans of the antebellum period inhabited their home circles more profoundly than later generations. This they did despite the modest size of most residences. Aggregations of home circles became villages and towns. Society high and low gathered mainly in these private abodes, rather than public places. Here would come neighbors to chat, possibly to play games, make music, or dance. Here births were celebrated and deaths were mourned. Here special days such as Sundays, birthdays, anniversaries, and holidays like Thanksgiving and Christmas were observed.

In contemporary minds, a perceptible sacredness enveloped the home, at least in theory. It was a refuge from worldly peril and distress, a sanctuary where moral life was strengthened, a safety zone warding off the hedonistic traffic of the primrose path. Entering it, one was supposed to reclaim the sensibility at his human core and to banish the domain of commerce and labor and dealings that were burdensome, coarse, and selfish. The following representation of what the crowds bound for home wished to find after a day's work is overly gushing but nevertheless typical of what most men and women regarded with reverence:

> Light of welcoming hearth-fires, shadows of children's play upon the walls; light of affections in which there are no decay and no deceit; shadows of sacred retirement where God alone is; light of joys which this world's storms cannot utterly quench; shadows of sorrows around sick-beds, and in vacant places, that still make home the dearer as the arena of earth's purest discipline and of its most triumphant faith![31]

In the domestic circle, said Mrs. Sigourney, music and dance were entirely appropriate to promote health and "the cheerful flow of spirits" among children, "while the parents and even grand-parents, mingling with the blooming circle, gave dignity to the innocent hilarity in which they participated."[32]

Sarah Holmes, mother of Oliver Wendell Holmes, allowed her minister husband his hymns and her children the secular music that she and they

**154**  loved. She herself probably talked her husband around to purchasing for $150 the London-manufactured Clementi piano, which was immediately brought into the south parlor. The son remembered the occasion years later in a poem entitled "The Opening of the Piano:"

> In the little southern parlor of the house you may have seen
> > With the gambrel-roof and the gable looking westward to the
> > > green,
> At the side toward the sunset, with the window on its right,
> > Stood the London-made piano I am dreaming of to-night!
>
> Ah me! How I remember the evening when it came!
> > What a cry of eager voices, what a group of cheeks in flames,
> When the wondrous box was opened that had come from over-seas,
> > With its smell of mastic-varnish and its flash of ivory keys!
>
> Then the children all grew fretful in the restlessness of joy,
> > For the boy would push his sister, and his sister crowd the boy,
> Till the father asked for quiet in his grave paternal way,
> > But the mother hushed the tumult with the words, "Now, Mary,
> > > play."
>
> For the dear soul knew that music was a very sovereign balm,
> > She has sprinkled it over Sorrow and seen its brow grow calm,
> In the days of slender harpsichords with tapping tinkling quills,
> > Or caroling to her spinet with its thin metallic thrills.
>
> So Mary, the household minstrel, who always loved to please,
> > Sat down to the new "Clementi" and struck the glittering keys.
> Hushed were the children's voices, and every eye grew dim,
> > As, floating from lips and finer, arose the "Vesper Hymn."[33]

In a second poem, "For the Moore Centennial Celebration, May 28, 1879," Holmes recalls the family parlor as a "song-haunted room" where the "warm love-songs of fresh adolescence" were heard. Four songs by Thomas Moore are cited.[34]

Likewise, Samuel Longfellow writes of his and Henry Wadsworth Longfellow's childhood parlor where a piano resided to be played upon by their sister. As with Holmes, the vision is nostalgic and envisioned as the best of times:

In the home parlor the sister's piano had replaced the spinet of his mother's youth. The Battle of Prague, Governor Brooks's March,

Washington's March, and other music of the period were familiar;
to such songs as Henry's Cottage Maid, Brignal's Bank, Bonnie
Doon, The Last Rose of Summer, Oft in the Stilly Night, Henry lent
his voice and the training of the singing-school; while the lessons of
the dancing-school were repeated in the parlor, to the tunes of
Money Musk, the Haymakers, or Fisher's Hornpipe.[35]

More humbly situated families could not afford pianos but made do with
less expensive instruments. A factory girl employed in a Lowell mill once
described life in her village and the home of the Crosbys there, with its
"simplicity and beauty." The eighteen-year-old daughter, Abby Crosby, sang
sweetly, and in the sitting room were found her sheets of music and much
used flageolet and accordion.[36]

Despite the aura of reverence, homes had to endure the wild and mischievous antics of the young. Children's play served as an antidote to the sacrosanct rites alleged to take place there. William and Thomas Lincoln, the sons
of Abraham Lincoln, were known for their liveliness and unruly antics. They
organized the songs, dances, and acts for at least one minstrel show that
presumably their father witnessed.[37] M. E. Dodge tells a story of a mischievous
little boy, Tom, who came upon his sister Lulu with her doll and cat in the
parlor. Tom promptly danced about the cat, bowing and scraping at the end
of every line, intoning:

A cat came fiddling out of a barn,
    With a pair of bagpipes under her arm;
She could sing nothing but fiddle-cum-fee,
    The mouse has married the bumble-bee,
Pipe—cat—bee—mouse—
    Who'll go quickest out of the house?

Thereupon he kicked the cat.[38]

## Secular Music within the Home Circle

The locale for music making in the home is named variously as the
parlor, drawing room, sitting room, living room, and, rarely, music room. In
only the mansions of the wealthy were music rooms found. "Drawing room"
was a more or less pompous way of referring to a house's formal reception
room for guests and usually is mentioned in connection with mansions. One
could be synonymous with the other, as in the letter that Edgar Allan Poe sent

to Mrs. Marie Louise Shew in May 1847. He starts by mentioning her "music room," whose furnishings are a credit to her taste, and then continues:

> During my first call at your house after my Virginia's death, I no-
> ticed with so much pleasure the large painting over the Piano,
> which is a masterpiece. . . . The scrolls, instead of set figures—of the
> drawing room carpet—the soft effect of the window shades also the
> crimson and gold, etc. and I was charmed to see the Harp and Piano
> uncovered. . . . The Guitar with the blue ribbon, music stand and an-
> tique jars. I wondered that a little country maiden like you had de-
> veloped so classic a taste and atmosphere.[39]

The parlor was the most stiffly furnished room of the house, a place for entertaining guests and for important social gatherings. The sitting room or living room was a household's focal point, where the family met daily and carried on companionable activities. The term most frequently used in connection with the room for musical diversion was the "parlor." Contemporary Americans subjected the designation to loose usage, however. Generally, and especially in humbler homes, the parlor was also the sitting room, meant for the regular gathering of company and family and not at all reserved only for special occasions. Almost invariably, if there was one, the piano was located here, as much for display before guests as for playing.

Each musical member of the family had a designated role in the evening's entertainments, according to his or her talents. It did not matter whether the family was in affluent or humble circumstances, music entered the hours of leisure. In Edgefield, Connecticut, lived Deacon Hartwell, his wife, and children Wilder (married), John, Angeline, and Jonas. Jonas and Wilder, who constantly dropped in at their parents' house, appeared together to regale the home circle with melody. Regrettably, the others lacked aptitude for music. "Angeline was a bright, gay, intelligent young lady, who seemed to know everything, and could do everything but sing. The deacon was no singer." In contrast, "Jonas was a musician, and very fond of the flute. Wilder, the elder . . . was also fond of music. . . . Wilder and Jonas belonged to the [church] choir. Jonas played the flute, while Wilder sang bass."[40]

In Philadelphia, Charles Quill writes of a workman's family:

> I reached the steps of John Hall, the cabinet-maker [and] . . . found
> his front room illuminated, and occupied by a little religious meet-
> ing. But I proceeded, and stepped into the house of Dukes, my next
> acquaintance, and was near spending the whole hour there; for he
> and his wife and children were engaged in a little music concert,

which was most enviable. Mary Dukes sung over her knitting, and
Robert sung over his bass-viol; while the two boys, one with a flute
and the other with a violin, added a good accompaniment.[41]

The daily routine of one or more members of a household, and especially
adolescent girls of good family, often ran to music. In some homes the sound
of the voice or a musical instrument was heard at odd hours of the day. The
fifteen-year-old Margaret Fuller even at that age took life seriously and wrote
in a letter, dated 11 July 1825:

> I rise a little before five, walk an hour, and then practice on the pi-
> ano, till seven, when we breakfast. Next I read French,—Sismondi's
> Literature of the South of Europe—till eight, then two or three lec-
> tures in Brown's Philosophy. About half-past nine I go to Mr.
> Perkins's school and study Greek till twelve, when, the school being
> dismissed, I recite, go home, and practice again till dinner, at two.
> Sometimes, if the conversation is very agreeable, I lounge for half
> an hour over the dessert, though rarely so lavish of time. Then,
> when I can, I read two hours in Italian, but I am often interrupted.
> At six, I walk, or take a dive. Before going to bed, I play or sing, for
> half an hour or so, to make all sleepy, and, about eleven, retire to
> write a little while in my journal.[42]

The daily routine seen from the viewpoint of a father with daughters, one
of them fourteen-year-old Louisa May, is cryptically detailed by Bronson
Alcott:

> Rise at 5—Light fires—Bathe (Shower bath)—Call children, assist in
> their bathing and dressing—Shave and dress—Breakfast at 6. Read-
> ing of a hymn with Conversation. Music—Prepare wood—7, Read,
> Study, write till 10. Instruct the children—12, Dinner. Labour till 3
> in Garden—Readings with mother and children. 5, Bathe and help
> children's bathing. 6, Supper. Music and Conversation. 7 till 9, Read-
> ing and writing. 9, Bed.[43]

The morning custom on antebellum South Carolina plantations, stated
an 1851 issue of the *Charleston Courier*, was to arise at daybreak, hold early
prayers, and have breakfast. The women then adjourned to the drawing
room, where, "like daughters and wives of country gentlemen," they practiced on the guitar, copied music, wrote verses in albums, and played games.
The morning practice at her girlhood plantation home, writes Susan Smedes,

was for her mother to awaken her father, who arose from bed gay as a bird, greeting his wife with lively tunes but not otherwise speaking to her. When she protested his avoidance of conversation, he sang the more gaily and would not go in to breakfast until he "had danced the Fisher's Hornpipe for the baby, singing along with the steps and drawing an imaginary bow across imaginary strings."[44]

Most citations of everyday activity that included music connect it generally with the evening hours. These were the usual moments for relaxation, when the mother's household chores were done, the father was not at his office or shop, and the children alternately played and begged for a parent's attention. Susan Lesley's mother had little time for practicing her music following marriage. As was true for a host of mothers, a major effort was required daily to keep her house in order and regulate the activities of the children. Mechanical aids to lighten housekeeping were limited in number, and servants assisted only in the few households that could afford them. Nevertheless, regularly, after tea or at twilight, Susan Lesley's mother gave the children a prebedtime treat by playing pieces such as the "Copenhagen Waltz" and "The Battle of Prague" on the piano in the parlor and by singing. On Sunday evenings she confined herself to singing hymns. Lew Wallace said his wife, accompanied by her guitar, loved "to soothe vexed children with lullabies, and set old people to living their lives over again with ballads," in the evening.[45]

When the children entered into adolescence, it was their turn to provide music. An overseas visitor, Carl Arfwedson, expressed his delight over the summer evening walks he took in Boston's Public Garden. The houses surrounding the park had their windows open because of the heat, and he and other passersby delighted in listening to the customary music making that took place. Out from the open windows flowed the sound of "very fine music and many excellent voices" as the young people sang or played on an instrument for their parents.[46]

Perhaps on the other side of one of the windows that Arfwedson speaks of was the parlor of people like the Moreys, a Boston family. Here, after the tea things had been removed, the two little boys of the house played games. Then daughter Louisa sang "and played her father's favorite songs, and, accompanied by Mr. Lassar's flute, performed the plaintive airs her mother loved best." Nor was such singing confined to Boston. Eliza Ripley named similar situations in New Orleans, where her mother sat in an arm chair "waving a turkey tail fan warm summer evenings" and was "soothed by sweet warblings" of her girls at the piano, and where her tired father, who sat nearby, called for his favorite "Oh! Would I Were a Boy Again" or "Rock Me to Sleep, Mother" or Mrs. Hemans's "Bring Flowers, Fresh Flowers." These were "the sweet old flowers that all girls were singing sixty years ago" (ca. 1850).[47]

The heat of a summer evening drove families out to the porch in search of a breath of air. Here, too, music was apt to be heard. On one such evening, on a Virginia plantation, the Erskines adjourned to their large porch, where the following exchange took place:

"Come, Mary, can you not sing me that sweet favorite of yours, or is it too cruel to ask you, when the air is so oppressive?"

"The air is never too oppressive to gratify you," replied the daughter, and reached for her guitar. . . . She fingered her light instrument, and he listened to its plaintive but ecstatic strains, as she sang, in the richest melody, the following simple lines of Shelley:

Good night? Ah! No; the hour is ill,
Which severs those it should unite.[48]

In Walpole, New Hampshire, Judge Vose's three daughters, his son, and their friends went to a nearby hillside in hope of finding a cooling breeze. Emily Barnes depicts them as a congenial circle of young men and women:

Among them were some very fine singers. I can distinctly remember, it was often proposed on warm bright summer evenings, to go up on the other hill, and sit under those magnificent old trees in the front yard, where were always seats for the family and friends, and there we would exercise our vocal powers, knowing how very fond the judge was of music.

One evening, especially, I recall when the court was in session, at that time in Keene. The judge usually returned home every night, and frequently brought some of his professional friends with him. I remember at this particular time, the pleasure he expressed in the unexpected entertainment given to himself and his several guests. Nearly all the old songs they called for were happily quite familiar to us; "Scots Wha Hae" and "Jephtha's Daughter," finding great favor; but we adjourned to the house to sing our parting song, and a glass of wine was presented, according to custom, with which we took a cup of kindness yet, for auld lang syne.[49]

Writer after writer from the pre–Civil War years mentions the evening music making in the parlor with singing of best-liked songs and sounding of piano, guitar, or flute.[50] This was particular true of the winter months when outdoor activities were limited and the desire for coziness prevailed. For the most part, the music was of the traditional and popular variety. On only rare occasion did a writer of cultivated taste mention a more artistic music, as did George Templeton Strong. His wife, Ellen, had had a miscarriage and a long convalescence. To his relief, he heard her open the piano after six months of silence, and sing "*Batti, batti,* the *Pietà,* Schubert, *Di piacer,* and a long catalogue of the old songs of a year ago."[51] The twenty-year-old George Curtis, still subject to the ardors of youth, wrote from Concord, Massachusetts, to John Sullivan Dwight:

> For the last three evenings I have been in the village, hearing Belinda Randall play and sing. With the smallest voice she sings so delicately, and understands her power so well, that I have been charmed. . . . Last night I saw her at Mr. Hoar's, only herself and Miss E. Hoar, G. P. Bradford, Mr. and Mrs. Emerson, and myself and Mr. Hoar. She played Beethoven, sang the "Adelaide Serenade," "Fischer Mädchen," "Amid this Green Wood." I walked home under the low, heavy, gray clouds; but the echo lingered about me like starlight.[52]

The occasions were many when mothers or fathers are mentioned singing lullabies or other simple songs to their children, when not playing dances for them. In addition, nursemaids crooned to their charges and girls to their dolls. The letters of Julia Ward Howe often allude to her children during the 1840s. In 1845 "I have not been ten minutes this whole day, without holding one or other of the children. I have to sit with Fo-jo on one knee and Dudie on the other, trotting them alternately, and singing, 'Jim along Josie,' till I can't Jim along any further possibly." In 1846 she complains of busy young motherhood, "Must I sew and trot babies and sing songs, and tell Mother Goose stories, and still be expected to know how to write." And in 1847, "My children are coming on famously. Julia, or as she calls herself, Romana, is really a fine creature, full of sensibility and of talent. . . . She remembers every tune she hears, and can sing a great many songs. . . . I play for them on the piano, Lizzie beats the tambourine, and the two babies take hold of hands and dance."[53] A similar description of other mothers could easily be supplied.

As for fathers, there was the Mr. Holmes that Sallie Ford wrote about, who found his little son, Eddie, sleepy and then "with great tenderness and a slight degree of awkwardness . . . lays him on his lap, and sings him 'Rock-a-by baby on the tree-top,' until he falls asleep." There is also the picture of a western father hugging his baby to his chest in a rough cabin and improvising a simple song: "Sleep, Willie, dear! Sleep, Willie, dear!/A father holds thee closely now"; and of Stephen Foster's father, who played the violin so the children could dance.[54]

Anna Dorsey describes a Mother Jennet, nanny to a ten-month-old baby, singing:

Charlie loves a cup of tea;
He loves sugar-candy O!
Charlie loves a pretty girl
And Charlie loves the brandy O!
    Over the river and over the river
    And over the river to Charlie O![55]

And M. E. Dodge speaks of a little girl that tells her doll to go to sleep and sings to her a song she may have learned from her mother: "By! By! Never fear—/Mamma's watching. Baby dear."[56]

It was common during these years to entertain not only children but guests with music. Daughters were constantly pressed into service and brought into the parlor to sing and play for their mother's friends. This, for example, was an important duty of Charlotte Foster before her death at a young age: "Charlotte . . . did not whine, nor look affected, nor did she undertake to excuse herself by saying she had a cold, or other such reprehensible device, but walked modestly to the piano, and seating herself, sang" works such as Oliver Shaw's "There's Nothing True but Heaven."[57] A father's guests were similarly entertained. Susan Lesley remembers an 1836 visit to her Northampton, Massachusetts, home by Daniel Webster, when her sister was called upon to play the piano and sing ballads for him. Mary Eastman and Caroline Hentz talk about similar events.[58]

Henry Thoreau, returning to Concord, after visiting Daniel Ricketson and his family in New Bedford, wrote a thank-you note on 12 October 1855: "I feel very much in debt to you and your family for the pleasant days I spent at Brooklawn. . . . Methinks I still hear the strains of the piano, the violin, and the flageolet blended together. Excuse *me* for the noise which I believe drove you to take refuge in the shanty."[59] Note that Thoreau, a guest, contributed to the music making, though he describes it as "noise." He appeared again at the Ricketson home in April 1857, where he sang songs such as Moore's "Row, Brothers, Row" and Dibden's "Tom Bowling" and danced to the accompaniment of Mrs. Ricketson on the piano. When she played the lively "The Campbells Are Comin'," he pranced about like an uninhibited Indian dancer, much to her amusement.[60]

Clearly, Thoreau had a share in the musical entertainment, an ordinary

*162*  practice for guests. A much better singer than Thoreau, Dominick Lynch, often visited Julia Ward Howe's father and, while visiting, sang popular ballads in a most affective manner. She remembers creeping under the piano to hide her tears when Lynch sang "Lord Ullin's Daughter."[61]

To an extent not practiced after the Civil War, family and friends persisted in gathering informally in their homes for congenial employment of mind and body not possible elsewhere. The callers not only conversed but teamed with family members in their games, partnered dancers, sang or played instruments, and enjoyed light refreshments. This was especially true outside the comparatively few cities, in the thousands of towns and villages with no theaters, concert halls, or ballrooms. Sporadic performances by traveling entertainers was the best these places could hope for. Therefore, everybody who could play or sing had to be ready to favor the company with a display of his or her abilities. Nor did the typical evening that ordinary people spent with music feature secular compositions exclusively. To cite an instance, one evening in the 1830s, Deacon Rawson visited Mr. and Mrs. Grant of Enfield, Massachusetts, whose two daughters had just returned from boarding school, bringing with them a small square piano. All gathered in the parlor for some music making. Deacon Rawson took up the bass, Mr. Grant tenor, and the two girls soprano and alto. They first sang "Hamburg," whose first line is "Kingdoms and thrones to God belong," and whose "noble Tune is based upon an ancient choral." This was followed with Pleyel's hymn, "To thy pastures fair and large." Then the uplifting "Coronation" was sung. Only after its conclusion did they proceed to the secular portion of the evening's entertainment. One girl performed a piano romance; the other, a song then in vogue, "Oh! had I wings like a dove!" Other songs came next, and also "marches, *andante* movements, and variations on familiar themes."[62]

Elders in every section of the United States entertained the domestic company by singing the traditional ballads that they still remembered, to the joy of all who were present. For example, in the New Hampshire village where Horace Greeley had grown up, Jack Larkin writes, his mother, her neighbors, and her friends from more outlying areas still sang "old ditties" like "Barbara Allen," without the accompaniment of any musical instrument.[63] Greeley himself recalls his childhood home in Amherst, New Hampshire, around 1820, and the evening visits of neighbors and confirms Larkin's statement:

> When neighbors and neighbors' wives drew together at the house of
> one of their number for an evening visit, there were often inter-
> spersed with "Cruel Barbara Allen," and other love-lorn ditties then
> in vogue, such reminiscences of the preceding age as "American
> Taxation," a screed of some fifty prosaic verses. . . . The ballads of

the late war with Great Britain [War of 1812] were not so popular
in our immediate neighborhood, though my mother had good store
of these also, and sang them with spirit and effect, along with
"Boyne Water," "The Taking of Quebec" by Wolfe, and even "Wearing of the Green."[64]

Middle-aged company might sing some of the more au courant songs,
but they also relished the Scotch and Irish ballads that had been in vogue
during their youth and that continued to have a wide following. Mrs. Fitzpatrick, wife of an Alabama senator, for one, liked to present "'Roy's Wife of
Aldivalloch' and other quaint Scotch ditties" to her circle; providing variety,
Mr. Dowdell, an Alabama congressman, "sang with lusty enjoyment the
simpler ballads of the day." At the drop of a hat, anybody was likely to
produce "Auld Lang Syne," which, claimed John Pintard, was "a favorite air
and peculiarly appropriate" to most occasions.[65]

The more up-to-date children pranced about in imitation of minstrel men
and mouthed their dialect ditties. Young men and women sent forth popular
songs depicting the various stage of love, or they danced. If a piano was in
the parlor, young people clustered around it for amusement, if not for courtship. Decorum was the rule in the relationship between the sexes. People
expected that a healthy youth would have a hankering for a complaisant girl
and visa versa. At the same time, they thought that the best way to restrain
the more urgent amorous feelings was through the comings-together in a
parlor, where music might act as a safety valve, while married adults monitored conditions nearby.

Pamela Brown's diary records several gatherings of young people around
the piano in Plymouth Notch, Vermont. She also reports a liberal use, for
1836, of a Sunday's free time, with no mention of attendance at church:
"Elmina [a friend] and I laid a bed very late. We had hardly got the [house]
work done before James Merrill, Joel Slack and Thomas Fletcher came in.
They staid and talked and sang an hour or two. Then we all walked down to
the 'Five Corners' where we met Solomon Carlisle, H. Willis, the two Briggs
and Charlotte Duncan. Staid there and sang a few tunes and then walked to
Mr. Pinney's." Back in Boston from travel in Europe in 1853, the nineteen-year-old Henry Lee Higginson made frequent calls at the home of his friend
James Savage to enjoy good company and "informal singing and playing." In
the same year in Richmond, Virginia, the twenty-three-year-old Marion Harland was especially delighted of a winter evening, when her friend Ned
Rhodes dropped by with new music, so that both "fell to work with piano and
flute soon after my father's exit."[66]

There were two aspects to African American music making at home (and

**164**  elsewhere). On the one hand, it kept faith with its African origins. That is why the music that Letitia Burwell heard in slave cabins on Virginia plantations, sung and performed on banjo and fiddle in the evening, gave off a "wild, melancholy cadence" to her. A more specific wildness is mentioned by Edmund Kirke. One Sunday night, during a visit to a North Carolina plantation around 1850, he was talking to an elderly black woman in her shack when suddenly she stood erect and began shivering. Her son, Joe, told Kirke that "de power am on har." Shortly, while

> swaying her body back and forth with a slow, steady motion, she commenced humming a low chant. Gradually it grew louder, till it broke into a strange, wild song, filling the room, and coming back in short, broken echoes, from the adjoining apartments. Struck with astonishment, I was about to speak, when Joe, laying his hand on my arm, said:
>
> "Hush, sar! It am de song ob de kidnap slave!"
>
> It was sung in the African tongue, but I thought I heard as it rose and fell in a wild, irregular cadence, the thrilling story of the stolen black; his smothered cries and fevered moans in the slaver's hold; the shriek of the wind, and the sullen sound of the surging waves breaking against the accursed ship; and, then—as the old negress rose and poured forth quick, broken volumes of song—the loud mirth of the drunken crew, mingled with what seemed dying groans, and the heavy splash of falling bodies striking the sea.[67]

What Kirke says he heard are the mental images he formed during the course of the singing and did not necessarily correspond to the song's subject matter. Yet the chanting did go back to the singer's African roots and represented an idiom unfamiliar to the white listener, who was as likely as not to misinterpret what he heard owing to ignorance. The episode also illustrates how the connection with a cultural past, though weakened, may endure, and through a thread that gets constantly thinner the musical past may link with the present and the present with the future. Moreover, because so many black Americans lived in comparative isolation from white society, they were able to continue to preserve their African traits.

On the other hand, whatever the inheritance from a more distant past, the immediate past has an undeniable influence. The music performed in the slave cabin might well have been caught from encounters with white music making, albeit altered subtly in response to the slave's own background. Thus, Metta Victor pictures the cabin home of a slave:

The supper was cleared away, the fire flashed up cheerfully, and the
whole company [family and friends] joined in singing song after
song, accompanied by a banjo played by Scipio. . . . Hyperion sang
some songs which his ready ear had caught from the parlour—fashionable airs which had not yet descended to the kitchen; hymns,
also, of the vigorous and exciting character liked by the race, were
given with great fervour.[68]

Free blacks, usually urban residents and middle class, who had some
formal education and disposable income, often displayed musical habits that
coincided with those of whites. Although they experienced all sorts of restric-
tive treatment from whites, they nevertheless had at least some formal education and derived a great deal of contentment from their home lives. Joseph
Willson, in *Sketches of the Higher Classes of Colored Society in Philadelphia*
(1841), states that most such households possessed pianos and most young
ladies had received piano and singing instruction:

Music is made a prominent part of the amusements on all occasions
of social meeting together of friends. . . .
    It is rarely that the Visitor in the different families where there
are 2 or 3 ladies will not find one or more of them competent to perform on the pianoforte, guitar, or some other appropriate musical instrument; and these, with singing and conversation . . . constitute
the amusements of their evenings at home. The love of music is
universal; it is cultivated to some extent—vocal or instrumental—
by all.[69]

Like formal education, however, the expression of unalloyed contentment
in music was for slaves exceedingly rare. Happiness for a slave, if it existed,
had its specific nature determined by relation to the misery that surrounded
it. A female slave in Kentucky, who had been maltreated and had almost died,
was sold to a kind master. In her new situation, she met and grew to love
another slave, Henry. He came to her "during the long, cheerful autumnal
evenings, when a fire sparkled in the grate," and after work he would "bring
his banjo and play for me; whilst his rich, gushing voice warbled some old
familiar song. Its touching plaintiveness often brought the tears to my eyes.
. . . [On one evening] seated near me, with my hand in his, was the one being
on earth whom I best loved. He was singing in a low, musical tone, the
touching Ethiopian melody of 'Old Folks at Home.'"[70]
    Some songs may have had a black or white provenance, like those Emily
Burke says were sung by an "untutored slave" in Georgia as she rocked "the

*166*  cradle of its infant master." Two of her pieces were "Old Dan Tucker" and "Lucy Long." Their origins are obscure; white and black Americans sang them; cultural interchange was unremitting. Who taught whom? The question is amenable to several different answers.

There were countless made-up songs with African American subjects and tunes of mixed parentage. In the examples of them that I have seen, the texts are in a black variety of English; the subjects involve slave life; the tunes have many white and some black features; the rhythms are syncopated and more African but have a straightforward meter indebted to white music. Ann Drake, once a slave in Mississippi, relates:

> On Sundays, de slaves jes sot 'round de cabin doors an' talk an' wrap hair, an' sumtimes dey wud sing. Sum times slaves from udder plantashuns wud cum an' jine de crowd, but dey all toted passes ter keep de patterroller from ketchin' 'em. Yes, dey sung—

> > Run, nigger, run, de pat'roller' ketch yo'
> > Run, nigger, run, it's almos' day. . . .

> When de African [preacher] wud cum dat is when we all went ter church an' den dey wud sing—

> > Old time 'ligion, old time 'ligion,
> > It's good 'nouf fur me.[71]

Ann Drake's interviewer did not take down or identify the tune. The "patterroler" denominates the white patrols established throughout the South who policed rural areas, searching for slaves who seemed unruly or were away from their plantation without passes permitting them to leave. The patrols were empowered to deliver instant punishment, usually in the form of severe whippings. A large number of black songs concern themselves with the slave's fear of these patrols and efforts to avoid meeting with them.

The young people did not have pianos, to be sure, but they did come together either indoors or before their cabins to play games, make music, and carry out their own kind of courtship. Katie Holloway, a Kentucky slave on the Holloway plantation (slaves frequently took on the surname of their master), says that she and her friends loved to socialize when given the opportunity. They enjoyed a dance game called "Rock Candy." Girls stood in two lines facing each other with their hands on each other's shoulders; young men stood at the foot of the two lines. To the rhythm of the song and keeping time, all sang, as the men "rock candied" up to the girls:

A poor man he sold me,
And a rich man he bought me
And sent me down to New Orleans,
To learn how to rock candy.
Rock candy, two and two.
Rock candy, two and two.
Rock candy, two and two.
For it's no harm to rock candy.

Katie Holloway says that "Rock Candy" became popular with white Americans as well. Churchgoing people hated this dance game and the singing that went with it but could not stop the practice.[72]

Preadolescents played their own games and sang their own music. One game that appears several times in the slave narratives is described by Mary Johnson of South Carolina. "Us slave children played base and jumped from one base to another before we could be caught; and we sing:

Can I git to Molly's bright?
Three course and ten.
Can I git there by candle-light?
Yes, if your legs are long and light.[73]

## Religious Music within the Home Circle

To form an opinion about the music heard in the home, we must keep in mind that however much many Americans enjoyed their secular songs, an even greater number of them were singing hymns, either alongside these songs or exclusively. The United States was still largely rural; most Americans persisted in seeing themselves as country people even if they made their homes in villages and towns. They took their religion seriously and not only sang in church on Sunday but also at prayer meetings during other days. These sacred compositions in praise of God were frequently melancholic, consistent with life as they found it and the death they anticipated.

Sunday after church attendance was a home day where noise and activity were kept at a minimum, tranquillity permeated the family's thoughts, and domestic and religious harmony were at one with the Creator. This was the condition of the Longfellow home on Sunday evenings in Portland, Maine, when familiar hymns "of the old 'Bridgewater Collection,'—St. Martin's, and Dundee, and Brattle Street" sounded in the parlor. Several hundred miles to the south, the Sabbath evening on a South Carolina plantation was conducted similarly, despite the reservations of an adolescent boy. He interrupted

**168**   the hymns and requested a popular song from a songbook, which he claimed was "a very *sacred* air." However, he was rebuked and told that "it's a day to be devoted to God."[74]

Daily prayer sessions with music were common in antebellum homes. Ever present to spur their devotions was an evangelical awareness of sin, culpability, and the need for deliverance. The goal was to reform one's being by way of prayer and psalmody. An additional benefit was the solid unity that praying and singing together encouraged between parents and children, and between siblings. Home assemblies for prayer on rising in the morning and before retiring in the evening were frequently the norm. Mrs. Sigourney states, "Young voices around the domestic altar, breathing sacred music, at the hour of morning and evening devotion, are a sweet and touching accompaniment" to prayer. In the log cabins of a western settlement, near Louisville, Kentucky, morning prayer was a time when "every member was expected to be present, from the oldest to 'little Neddie,' who, though not able yet to read, could hold his hymn-book in his hand and look on while the others sang."[75]

Emily Barnes's cousin Sally and parents were visiting the Hartwells of New Ipswich, New Hampshire, and learned that "morning devotions" were held there every day for everyone in the house, including guests.

> There was the same observance before retiring at night; the addition
> of a hymn would often be proposed, in which all who could sing
> would join. When, for the first time, Sally's clear, sweet voice rang
> out, they were all surprised and delighted; it seemed like an inspira-
> tion. She did not sing with a trained and cultured voice, but she
> sang as the birds do, for the gift of song was native as her breath;
> and she took great delight in the exercise of this power.[76]

Everyone who sang might include the sick, however debilitated they were. It was the conviction of many Americans who were ill that it was essential to establish contact with Divinity and the best way to do so was through participation in hymn singing. Thus, Elizabeth Oakes Smith speaks of Sunday evening prayers and "the evening songs" in the home of a family named Cleveland, with an extremely ill and anxious grandfather listening from his bedroom.

> After having sung various hymns adapted to the capacities of the
> children, Mr. Cleveland commenced the grand and appropriate notes
> of Old Hundred, to the words,
>
>     "Be thou, O God, exalted high,"—

and the trembling voice of age joined with touching pathos in the
melody.[77]

The Americans who insisted on praying and singing, it should be stressed, included not just women, girls, and invalids but also hale men and boys. Indeed, William Cullen Bryant, writing of his young life in Cummington, Massachusetts, states that the men then (ca. 1810) took worship far more seriously than they would sixty-five years later. Their daily religious cravings could be satisfied only after three services, in the morning, afternoon, and evening. At these services, "some lay brother" gave out a prayer, another read a sermon, and all were invited to join in the hymns.[78]

Apparently, by 1845 religious preoccupation had become less intense. Typically, a young woman employed in the Lowell mills says of her village home that her family assembled in the kitchen during the first part of the evening "for evening devotions," when "Old Hundred" and another hymn were sung. Thereupon the scene metamorphosed. The second part of the evening saw "apples, beer, walnuts, and hard cider" served, and a request for secular songs. She remembered one evening singing two: "Fanny Gray" and "Rory O'Moore," after which a male friend sang "The Ship Carpenter" and "Dick the Joiner Lad."[79]

In no way were activities like the one just described to be taken as overly worldly, says Harriet Beecher Stowe. The recreational music heard before or after devotional hours, whether mentioned or not, often did have sacred songs interspersed among the secular pieces. She mentions tea-time gatherings, with a woman seated at the piano and playing tunes from a Sunday school songbook or hymnal, while the entire company sang "with might and main." Having such events in mind, she warns: "Let those who will, talk of the decay of Christian faith in our day [ca. 1873]; so long as songs about Jesus and his love are bursting forth on every hand . . . so long as the little Sunday-school songbooks sell by thousands and by millions, and spring forth every year in increasing numbers, so long will it appear that faith is ever fresh-springing and vital."[80] Like Mrs. Stowe, Emily Barnes says that in Walpole, New Hampshire, hymns and secular songs appeared interchangeably during recreational time. She recollected her Uncle Ben, a farmer whose passionate love of music drove him constantly to seek out her mother with his songbook under his arm. Her mother would joyfully join him in singing the old sacred music he loved. Barnes's cousin Caleb had a wife who was also devoted to music and continually refreshed her mind with singing. She "would often invite friends who could sing to come and practice sacred music with her, when Uncle Josiah would usually join them with his bass-viol."[81] Finally, Alice Carey speaks of a husband and wife, in an Ohio village, clearing away the tea

170 things. The wife was smiling as she removed the empty tea-pot from the table and sang, "When I can read my title clear/To mansions in the skies." Her husband then removed the sugar bowl, joining in with: "I'll bid farewell to every fear,/And wipe my weeping eyes."[82]

Indeed, seen from a proper perspective, even the widespread practice of holding Sunday evening prayer and hymn sessions could be described as both devotional and recreational—a renewal of devotion and a source of spiritual pleasure. They were seldom dour and solemn occasions. John Trowbridge's boyhood home of the 1830s, near Rochester, New York, never failed to witness a Sunday evening gathering of the family in the sitting room for prayers and religious song. These meetings took place owing not only to duty but because all present, and his father especially, delighted in the music and was happiest "when neighbors would sometimes come in and unite with him and my sisters (one of whom had an unusually good voice) in singing the old-fashioned hymns."[83]

Novelists of the time, their fingers on the public pulse, pictured again and again the Sunday evening session of refreshing hymn singing that participants found so pleasant. Susan Warner, in *The Wide, Wide World*, points out the delight given the Montgomerys, in New York, when they sang sacred songs at this hour ("the sweet airs" that offered "wisdom and consolation"). Maria McIntosh takes us first to a Southern plantation to describe "the Sabbath evening with sacred music" that Mr. Donaldson took especial delight in when he and his family sang

his favorite evening hymn:

> Father! By Thy love and power
> Comes again the evening hour . . .

Then she has a Georgia plantation owner visit New York City and happily contribute to the Sunday evening music making, where "Captain Moray always asked for sacred music" and "August played, and added her rich contralto to the pure soprano of Mrs. Moray, the deep bass of Hugh, and the full, soft tenor of Charlie." Finally, Caroline Hentz has a Mr. Hastings and his daughter Eulalia receive a Southern visitor, Mr. Moreland, in their home a few miles out of Boston. Mr. Hastings, a lover of hymns, advises his guest:

> It is our custom, Mr. Moreland, to have some sacred music every
> Sunday evening. We have no instruments but those which God has
> given us, and which we try to tune to His glory. My daughter, here,

has a tolerable voice, my son sings a pretty good bass, and I myself
can get through a tune without much difficulty.

When Mr. Moreland took up the singing book and sang with the family, he
was reminded of his own home, his childhood and mother, who had taught
him sacred songs like the ones before him.[84]

Writers of the period make more than a few references to the enjoyment
of not only recent but also old hymns and other venerable sacred compositions in the home. When these compositions go back to the end of the
eighteenth century, chances were that some of them were the fuguing (or,
more accurately, "fuging") tunes composed by New England singing masters.
These normally encompassed contrapuntal singing and the entry of music
and text at different time intervals in the second half of the work. Though
usually learned at the old singing schools and sung in church by the choirs
trained at those schools—a practice that continued at least into the first three
decades of the nineteenth century—they were also attempted by vocal ensembles and even solo singers at home. Reflecting on his boyhood years in
Ridgefield, Connecticut, Samuel Goodrich speaks of a Molly Gregory, daughter of the town carpenter and a choir member, who sang fuguing tunes when
by herself:

> In her solitary operations aloft, I have often heard her send forth,
> from the attic windows, the droning hum of her wheel, with the
> fitful snatches of a hymn, in which the bass began, the tenor fol-
> lowed, then the treble, and, finally the counter—winding up with ir-
> resistible pathos. Molly, singing to herself, and all unconscious of
> eavesdroppers, carried on all the parts thus:—
>
> *Bass.* "Long for a cooling—
> *Tenor.* "Long for a cooling—
> *Treble.* "Long for a cooling—
> *Counter.* "Long for a cooling stream at hand,
>      And they must drink or die."[85]

It was more usual to attempt fuguing tunes when a vocal quartet was
available. Interestingly, they would be sung not at a prayer session but as
recreational music performed in the parlor. Marion Harland describes just
such an occurrence in Richmond, Virginia, around 1832. After Sunday supper, the family and guests "adjourned to the parlor, and had sacred music for
an hour," which caused a recollection of old times, when a quartet of friends
used to sit on the porch steps, also to sing "fuging tunes." On Sundays in this

172 Richmond home, the piano was not used to accompany religious music, since it was connected with things worldly. They sang their hymns unaccompanied, until at last they came to the fuguing tunes they had practiced together— "Denmark" and "Lenox." The head of the house gave the "key and chord" to the others; next he began singing from his chair, which he tilted "back and forth, raising heels and toes alternately, enjoying his own performance with all his might." The others followed. Harland then comments:

> How they—our forebears—loved those pealing fugues, with their bil-
> lowy rush and chase, [which] continued with increasing energy un-
> til to the uninitiated it seemed inevitable that the tune must be
> beaten to death by the quickly succeeding surges—and the "diapa-
> son closing full" upon the long open note where counter and tenor
> met together, base and treble kissed each other![86]

Thanksgiving was an eminently suitable occasion for enjoying the old hymns, as old and young alike looked back to the first settlers and gave thanks for the bounty they had received. Harriet Beecher Stowe gives a detailed account of a Thanksgiving celebration from around the mid-1820s. She states that when the dinner concluded and everyone still sat at the table, all sang the hymn "Let children hear the mighty deeds/Which God performed of old." She continues:

> This we all united in singing to the venerable tune of St. Martin's,
> an air, which, the reader will perceive, by its multiplicity of quavers
> and inflections gave the greatest possible scope to the cracked and
> trembling voices of the ancients, who united in it with even more
> zeal than the younger part of the community. Uncle Fliakim . . . out-
> did himself on the occasion in singing *counter*, in that high, weird
> voice that he must have learned from the wintry winds that usually
> piped around the corners of the old house. But any one who looked
> at him, as he sat with his eyes closed, beating time with head and
> hand, and, in short, with every limb of his body, must have per-
> ceived the exquisite satisfaction which he derived from this mode of
> expressing himself.

Later in the evening, she says, everyone engaged in dancing, which made her wonder how the story about it being considered sinful to dance arose. She could not believe it to be true.[87]

There was an opposite face to the one above, the occasion when hymns to alleviate grief, suffering, or the confrontation with imminent death were more appropriate than celebratory ones. Certainly, the singing of proper sacred music at the bedside of those who were dying was without question a widespread practice during the years under consideration. Most often, an adult did the singing. For example, Fanny Fern (Mrs. Sara Payson) mentions a little boy, ill and facing death, whose mother sat close by and sang to him accompanied by her guitar. On rarer occasions, a youngster sang. Lucy Larcom says that when she was a child her father died and her mother felt devastated. Lucy wanted to talk her out of her depression but thought she "was too small a child to do that." Therefore "I did the next best thing I could think of—I sang hymns as if singing to myself, which I meant for her." In her "chirping voice" she sang, as best she could, hymns that did comfort her mother.[88]

Also found are portraits of the dying themselves singing, such as Marion Harland's of her dying friend Mary Ragland:

> Music—a passion of her life—was a solace in the fearful restlessness of the dying hours. She would have us sing to her—first one, then the other, for an hour at a time—lying peacefully attent, with that unearthly radiance upon her face that never left it until the coffin-lid shut it from our sight, and joining in, when a favorite hymn was sung, with the rich contralto which was her "part" in our family concerts.
>
> "She is singing herself away," said my husband, at twilight on the ninth of May—my mother's birthday. At nine o'clock that evening the swan-song was hushed.[89]

Henry Wadsworth Longfellow's wife, Fanny, wrote in her journal on 7 February 1833, "Mother continues very ill; the doctor has been afraid she would not survive the night. . . . She sang a hymn last night in her sleep, in a clear, sweet voice, although she had great difficulty in speaking." Add to this the account that Sophie Damon gives of a young Vermont girl, named Aseneth, who was on her deathbed: "A song was often on her lips. Her voice, one of peculiar quality, possessed wonderful clearness and strength, in contrast with the frail tenement from which it came. Even until the day when Death's shadow rested upon her, and all felt his unseen presence near, she was able to join Lucy in singing a favorite hymn."[90]

Lastly, Richard Fuller, brother of Margaret Fuller, states that just before his mother's death, "when she could hardly articulate," he sang with her the hymn "There, at my Saviour's side." Next, his brother Arthur sang with her "We are passing away." Richard continues: "Mother had the truest delight in sacred music. When she taught our infant lips to pray, she also encouraged us to join her sweet voice in singing. She accompanied the tune with a gentle motion of one hand." He concludes: "She was not exclusive, but loved all beautiful hymns, and bade me sing by her bedside in her last sickness."[91]

Sacred music functioned in the homes of black people from birth to death in similar ways to those of white people, but with some crucial differences. The great majority of African Americans were still slaves bound to the Southern soil. They toiled long hours in the fields with barely enough time left over during the week for sleep and were completely bent to their owner's will. Obviously, their leisure hours at home were severely limited. Only a more fortunate few were house servants, who usually labored less intensively and were allowed extra privileges. A large but undetermined number of blacks made hardly any or no declaration of religious belief. In many instances, their masters forbade them any religious observances. Not surprisingly, their moments of relaxation, including the Sunday hours, were given simply to resting and to completing domestic tasks, or to idle pleasures such as dancing, drinking, and other worldly activities.

On the other hand, an equally large number, if not a majority, took another direction. To preserve their humanity, these slaves discovered schemes for abating the most harmful effects of their bondage. Religious worship was one such resource. When their masters allowed it, and secretly if they did not, blacks created their own fellowships centered on religiosity, by merging beliefs and customs embedded in their African ancestry with the Christian ones of the America they inhabited. Their sacred songs would not just console them and offer surcease from their hours of drudgery, nor would they just furnish an alternative to the present in the assurance of a happier afterlife. They would also give voice to their hunger for freedom and to their revulsion at the conditions under which they lived.

We are told of one Virginia slave, Esther, who, "like her mother, was a great Methodist" and who "had committed to memory a vast number of hymns," among them, "There Is a Land of Sweet Delight." These hymns she and her sister "often sang in the kitchen, or at her mother's cabin." Because cabins were tiny and blacks felt overly cramped in them, however, a great deal of living took place just outside their doors—their open-air "parlor". Thus, we find Jennie Hill, born in Missouri in 1837, testifying that slave parents loved their children and were happy, when conditions allowed, to have the entire family sit at the cabin door and sing "slave songs" such as "Swing Low Sweet Chariot" and "Nobody Knows What Trouble I've Seen."[92]

Hymn-singing sessions were commonplace events, during which the home circle often expanded to take in adjacent families, sitting before their own doors. All shared in the music making. The hymns might receive unison renditions. Not infrequently, voices sounded in harmony. That some of this

vocalizing was exquisitely done is affirmed by many white witnesses, including Fredrika Bremer. While visiting a plantation near Columbia, South Carolina, in May 1850, she heard blacks singing hymns "in quartette" that
sounded "glorious." She had wanted to hear them in "their own *naïve* songs,
but was told that they 'dwelt with the Lord,' and sang only hymns."[93]

The delight in hymn singing at home was also characteristic of free
blacks. The singing, however, took place mostly within the confines of the
sitting room itself rather than the outdoors.

# CHAPTER 6

# Parties, Frolics, and Other Celebrations

ORMAL SOCIAL GATHERINGS OF INVITED GUESTS AT A
private home for refreshments, conversation, and entertainment, as contrasted with casual visits of one or two callers on
a family, were a prominent feature of communal living for every group of
people, whether urban or rural. There could be as few as ten or as many as
fifty or more persons in attendance. Always prominent at these events were a
select number of instrumentalists or singers who afforded diversion to the
partygoers.

Clara Leonard, like other Americans, maintained that music was an
essential feature of parties and made them joyous occasions. Descriptions of
urban parties almost always included music making. Moreover, life in villages
and small towns, many of them fairly isolated, would have been boring, even
dreary, if convivial gatherings with somebody singing or playing an instrument had been lacking. Those who could, and oftentimes those who couldn't,
were expected to perform. Fortunately, plenty of people were able and willing
to sing and play, too. Family and guests never ceased importuning the amateur musicians for songs and instrumental pieces. In Leonard's village of
Greenfield, Massachusetts, in 1828, as elsewhere, certain performers stood
out at these parties. First, there was a Miss Davis of Boston. Whenever she
visited her Greenfield cousins and attended a party, songs were requested of
her, which she sang in a pleasingly dramatic style. Then, there was a Mrs.
Chapman, a highly regarded musician with such an excellent ear and skilled
touch on the piano that "she was always in great demand, both as an
accompanist for singers and to play for dancing. She was also ready to dance
gaily when not in requisition at the piano." Mrs. Chapman's sister, Mary
Temple, was another vocalist noted for her fine voice and agreeable contributions to the entertainment.[1]

Men also sang at these gatherings. John Pintard of New York City wrote to his daughter in January 1822 and mentioned a Mr. Searle, "a gentleman, pure homely, but of many attainments, speaking 7 languages, very musical, and a humorist, who kept the company alive with his songs, Duets, etc." His ability to liven up a party caused him to be much sought after. His piano performances "excited astonishment & unbounded applause. My friend Francis, who is a musical enthusiast, said that he would relinquish his profession to perform as well."[2]

The crotchety Frances Trollope had an opposite view of American parties, finding them dismal attempts at jollity and their participants doltish and musically untalented. She looked about the American social landscape, in the years 1827 to 1830, and decreed that all American social gatherings were impossible for anyone of any sensitivity to attend:

> The large evening parties are supremely dull; the men sometimes
> play cards by themselves, but if a lady plays, it must be for money;
> no écarté, no chess; very little music, and that little lamentably bad.
> Among the blacks I heard some good voices, singing in tune; but I
> scarcely ever heard a white American, male or female, go through
> an air without being out of tune before the end of it; nor did I ever
> meet any trace of science in the singing I heard in society.[3]

Who was right, Clara Leonard or Frances Trollope? The testimonies of most Americans and of European visitors more attuned to democracy bolster Leonard's argument and give little support to the view of Mrs. Trollope.

### The Customary Evening Parties at Home

David Macrae, Mrs. Trollope's countryman, did not share her aversion to a society that was characterized by an unabashed adherence to principles of equality in rights and privileges. After his arrival in the United States, he attended several evening "socials," which twenty to forty guests attended, scarcely any of them wearing formal dress. "There are charades, readings, talk, songs, music, just as the spirit moves," he said. Every class of person appeared at these parties, from senator to shopkeeper. "Some of my happiest evenings in America were spent at these delightful gatherings," where were met "every variety of character."[4]

Sides of a person's personality that might otherwise have remained hidden were on show at parties. For example, here and there were ministers, ordinarily viewed as serious and God-dominated, who might reveal themselves at parties to have a fine social talent for entertaining conversation and friendly music making. Mrs. Stowe mentions a Rev. St. John, grave in the pulpit, but with "a gift in conversation" and a tenor voice of "feeling and refinement" at parties. During these evenings, he cast aside his usual gravity and sang as one of a harmonious vocal quartet that sounded "quite magnificent for non-professionals," and gave delight to rooms full of people.[5]

Predictably, current musical favorites were aired repeatedly for the company. In 1821 William Cullen Bryant told his sister Sarah that around 1818–19 "Highland Mary," "Forever Fortune," and "When Bidden to the Wake or Fair" were "worn out by being sung over and over at the parties in our village [Great Barrington]." Now a new song, beginning "Come here thou blue-eyed stranger," was becoming "all the rage, [and] was admired and encored, and the young ladies were all dissolved in ecstasy" over it. Someone had picked up additional stanzas for the tune and "the raptures of the young ladies were redoubled. . . . Parties were made up for the purpose of singing *Blue-Eyed Mary.* Young ladies were on a visit here from neighboring towns—*They* must hear *Blue-Eyed Mary,* too." He and a few others thought the song to be utter nonsense.[6]

Almost twenty years later, Francis Sheridan was at an evening party in Velasco, Texas, one of twenty-four guests, with both sexes equally represented. He enjoyed hearing the overture to Rossini's *Tancredi* on the piano and the singing of the first two or three songs. But then a winsome Miss Warner and an attendant young man did "that difficult duet 'The last links are broken.' I wish to God they really were, for I have been told the same thing at every piano I ever listened to."[7] Some vocalists pressed into service or volunteering their services for these social occasions invariably knew what songs were going around the concert circuit and had prepared themselves to produce them for company.

Undoubtedly Mrs. Trollope was right when she said that parties were occasions looked forward to, when young men and women could come together around the piano, although she did also comment sarcastically about the negligible attempts at music making that ensued and the persistent way "the half-grown pretty things" compared "how many quarters' music they had." On the other hand, this last comment applied mainly to the privileged young people who could afford to pay for these quarters of music. Going a step further than Mrs. Trollope, Mrs. Sigourney was conscious of the danger surrounding superficial music study and the overvaluation of "what we call *accomplishments*" when performing for others of an evening. If one sang or sat at a piano on social occasions, she said, the purpose should not be for vain display but "to sooth and enliven other spirits as well as your own, with those strains of melody, whose perception is a source of bliss, both to earth and heaven."[8] Most accounts of social evenings describe amateur musicians who fitted Mrs. Sigourney's bill or at least counterfeited the behavior she advanced.

Presumably, Mrs. Sigourney would have approved of the young Lucy of Vermont about whom Sophie Damon writes. She was an amateur singer whose repertoire included a large number of Scotch songs. During the 1820s:

> Lucy . . . was in great demand at all parties, large or small, in or out of the neighborhood; she was always so obliging and ready to suggest social pastimes. Her voice was sweet and strong, either in ballads, or for games into which singing entered; and she rarely refused to help, for she honestly acknowledged that it gave her great pleasure to be of service to her friends.

Musical instruments were scarce in Vermont homes at that time, many containing none.

> It therefore required more courage to entertain a room full of people by singing songs, than it does nowadays [1887], when the voice is usually accompanied by some sort of musical instrument. [Lucy's] memory for songs was remarkable; the grave and gay, the lively and severe, were stored away therein, for the future pleasure of her friends.[9]

Harriet Beecher Stowe saw that an utterly wasted life resulted from dwelling on accomplishments as if they were the end-all and be-all, engaging in an uninterrupted round of parties and other amusements and nothing else. Unfortunately, empty lives were plentiful among women who had had a modish education and were given no responsibilities. Her example is a Miss Eva Van Arsdel, who had "come out" in New York society and realized that nothing of true value had entered her life of festivities, balls, operas, and concerts in New York during the winter, and parties and balls in Saratoga during the summer.

> Now I live in a constant whirl—a whirl that never ceases. I am carried on from day to day . . . with nothing to show for it except a succession of what girls call "good times." I don't read anything but stories; I don't study; I don't write; I don't sew; I don't draw, or play, or sing, to any real purpose. I just "go into society" as they call it. I am an idler, and the only thing I am good for is that I help to adorn a house for the entertainment of idlers; that is about all.[10]

This sort of danger, however, threatened mostly urban young women from well-to-do families for whom frivolity and idleness were concomitants of social living. For the majority of young people, a party with music and dance was a respite from work and offered mental and physical refreshment. If one lived alone, it was an invaluable diversion to compensate for lack of domestic companionship. It was also an important means for getting out of the house and doing something different. For Sally Brown, a twenty-two-year-old schoolteacher in Cavendish, Vermont, social gatherings were gladsome affairs. She was delighted on a Tuesday in September 1832 when "Asa sent us an invitation to a party at his house." She found about thirty people and a violinist at Asa's house. Music and dancing commenced "at candle lighting time and continued until three in the morning, when the party broke up." Like Sally Brown, the hardworking men and women of a western village welcomed parties with music and dancing, and for identical reasons. Henry Riley writes that about 9 P.M. a fiddle that had seen rough handling was "tinkered up" until something resembling music came out of it. This was the signal for old and young to participate in the merriment. The fiddler played such lively airs as "Over the Hills" and "Fisher's Hornpipe," then started on a string of country dances.[11]

The fiddler, if the party was in a plantation home, was apt to be a slave, and other slaves might be made to sing or dance or both for the white company's entertainment. A description of such a party was once given by Gabe Emanuel, a Mississippi house slave who belonged to a Judge Stamp.

> De Judge was a great han' for 'tainment. He always had a house full
> o' people, an' he sho' give 'em de bes' o' food an' licker. . . . Ever'
> now an' den he'd throw a big party an' 'vite mos' ever'body in Mis-
> sissippi to come. Dey was of' Niggers in der Quarters what could
> sing to beat de ban', an' de Judge would git 'em to sing for his
> party.[12]

Compare this with the rough-and-ready, do-it-yourself parties of the western lands. Keokuk, Iowa, had grown from a crude, almost lawless village to a good-sized town by the end of the 1840s. Little by little, party giving increased, often gotten up on short notice. Men predominated in the community, and the place boasted a band of only two instrumentalists. Nevertheless, they managed to have "a good time" singing and dancing, and would usually wind up the night "with Monie Musk or the Virginia Reel." Louisville, Kentucky, had also grown similarly and had commenced small invitational parties in the early years of the nineteenth century. Not all of them were decorous as yet, since the town was still growing out of its rude beginnings. On the one hand, the more civil residents did enjoy congenial diversions with secular music on weekdays; on Sundays they conducted their assemblages "with greater propriety, and hymns and spiritual songs often made a part of the entertainment." On the other hand, and especially "among the laboring classes," these assemblages might incline toward greater dissoluteness, irreligion, and riotous behavior.[13]

Westerners thoroughly enjoyed the music making at their parties. Stephen Foster's sister Charlotte wrote to her mother from Cincinnati on 29 May 1828, saying how much she was pleased with the music at a party given by a Mrs. Kilgore. "Music, conversation and promenading were the amusements. Miss Curry and myself play'd and sang several songs and a duett together; she is a young lady from Virginia on a visit here, who has one of the sweetest voices I ever heard." There is an account, from Henry M. Russell, of Abraham Lincoln and fellow lawyers attending court in Bloomington, Indiana, in the late 1840s and early 1850s. Lincoln loved the parties given in the evening by the ladies, to which he was invited. At one of them, he teased Edward Baker for overly praising his son and for trying to "kill" everyone with his songs. Then

> Mr. Lincoln asked if there was any one present who could give us a song. Mrs. [David] Davis, ever ready to accommodate, sprang to her feet and with the remark that she would give us a ditty, in her sweet voice, to the keen enjoyment of her listeners, especially Mr. Lincoln, sang these verses:

> > So Miss Mirth is going to marry—
> > What a number of hearts she will break.[14]

The more fastidious English invitees to these western parties were less enthusiastic about the music they heard. A tone of condescension is evident in Amelia M. Murray's letter to England of 24 May 1855 from Indianapolis:

> Mrs. Wright gave an evening party of invited acquaintances; a great many agreeable people from this and the adjoining State. One lady sang some of Moore's Melodies very sweetly; but, as yet, music is not much cultivated in America: either the ladies do not devote sufficient attention to it, or there are not good masters. This is almost the first time I have heard an American sing with taste and expression. This party did not conclude before midnight.[15]

## The More Imposing Parties

Dinner parties were quite the go, usually for men who were better-off and better educated or for those meeting on business. William Wirt, then attorney general of the United States, wrote from Washington to his daughter Laura in May 1820 about an ambitious banquet given by a Mr. Law for almost a hundred men, including the capital's "gentry" and certain farmers from Prince George's County, at which President James Monroe was present. He describes the occasion as "festive," "playful," and "informal," and the dinner as extraordinary.

> Then such excellent songs after dinner! Graff has a Dutch parody on Jessie of Dumblane, which is admirable. The President laughed 'till he cried, and I believe he would have danced, if a fiddle had struck up. The good old man sat at table beating time with his fork to the songs sung by Graff and others, with all the kindness and amiability of his nature.[16]

Men's fraternal associations were widespread during the nineteenth century, and dinner meetings seasoned with songs their usual manner of coming together. Philip Hone, once mayor of New York, wrote in his diary for 25 December 1838 of the dinner meeting of his "Club" "yesterday at Mr. Crumby's Bond Street. Of the members, Messrs. Grinnell and Duer were absent; a good dinner, good singing, and plenty of wine." He had written an "Ode," which the composer C. E. Horn had set to music, and this was sung for the first time by Major Tucker. The diary entry for 7 January 1839 was about another club dinner, with Daniel Webster as guest: "We sat until eleven o'clock, and broke up after a grand chorus of 'Auld Lang Syne.'" Then, on 20 January 1840, Hone notes still another club dinner party, "with all its pleasant rules and social observances." The "Ode" was again "sung by Major Tucker, with a full chorus; and other songs and pleasant converse and good fellowship made us forget the bad times which have caused a suspension of our meetings."[17]

Hone was an inveterate party giver. Fanny Kemble reported on a formal dinner party she attended at his house on 15 September 1832. Among the guests was Dominick Lynch, who had facilitated the bringing of the Garcia Opera Company to New York City (1825). She called him "the Magnus Apollo of New York" and "a musical genius" who sang "as well as any gentleman need sing," enunciated Italian correctly, and accompanied himself "without false chords." All these virtues caused him to be someone to whom the women listened and over whom they languished. "He sang the 'Phantom Bark.' The last time I heard it was from the lips of Moore."[18]

Because everyone was expected to contribute to the singing, the unmusical could find ceremonial parties to be a trial. H. M. Brackenbridge had no ear for music, nor a passable voice. When he was a lawyer in Baltimore, he frequently attended the city's large dinner parties; there, sing he must. His bitter comment was: "Nothing annoyed me so much as to be called upon for a song or a story; and when compelled, in order to escape *ill-bred importunity*, to render myself in this way ridiculous in my own estimation and perhaps that of others, it always affected my spirits."[19]

Some gatherings, sometimes called "routs," were very elegant affairs, where people came luxuriously dressed and things were done in a tastefully superior fashion. They took place not only in times of prosperity but also during economic decline. As with Philip Hone's club members, "songs and pleasant converse and good fellowship" helped the wealthy "forget the bad times," however afflicted their less fortunate compatriots. In the winter of 1857–58 banks failed, jobs were scarce, and many lacked food and adequate shelter. Unrest, crime, and beefed-up police patrols were everywhere in evidence on the streets of New York. Yet here and there on Fifth Avenue a house blazed with light in the evening, and laughter and music rang out. In the freezing outdoors, huddled together for warmth were "scores of little ragged children . . . watching the windows." They looked with open-mouthed amazement at the feasting, gaiety, and dancing.[20]

Theodore Fay, in *Norman Leslie*, gives a detailed account of a "rout" at an elegant New York mansion. Guests arrived around ten o'clock—old and young, people of great wealth and fine education. The "highest *ton*" was present in force. There was singing. An orchestra "ever and anon breathed a low air that banished care and gravity, inspired wit and pleasure, and animated rather than interrupted conversation." Later the instrumentalists intoned a "waltz—that airy child of fashion and caprice." Eventually, a young woman sat at the piano and sang several operatic arias, displaying a bravura that astonished all with its brilliance. Next, she produced a "plaintive ballad" with such agreeable tones and sincerity that the company sat up and quietly listened.[21] The last would indicate that despite the sophistication and relatively advanced cultivation of the crowd, nobody present had yet spurned their less pretentious cultural roots.

A contrary scene is described in a sketch of party life in Virginia, with visitors from New York City and England. A young woman, Mary Hopewell, who was mostly self-taught musically, was made to sit at the piano by her father, who insisted she sing to her own accompaniment. She played an uncomplicated accompaniment and sang a simple air with a "soft and plaintive" voice. This did not satisfy one New Yorker, who immediately played "a celebrated concerto," executed "in a masterly manner." After this, a "local friend," to redeem local honor, performed a difficult prelude before singing an elaborate duet with her sister.[22] The sympathies of the anonymous observer of this event clearly lay with Mary Hopewell.

184     Americans whose tastes continued to welcome the popular and at the same time value the artistic increased during the first half of the nineteenth century, although they remained a distinct minority. One was Julia Ward. Once, when seen walking along Broadway with her future husband, it brought forth the comment, "They say she dreams in Italian and quotes French verses. She sang very prettily at a party last evening, and accompanied herself on the piano." For her and others who shared her preferences, parties included the artistic but did not spurn the simpler ballads. Henry Wadsworth Longfellow, who also enjoyed ballads, saw her at "a musical party at Mr. Ticknor's" in March 1846 and heard her sing "the 'Stabat Mater' of Pergolesi; and beautifully she sang it. Afterwards, some of Beethoven's sublime music, on two grand piano-fortes, by four young ladies." Three months later, Longfellow talked of "a small musical party at our house. We had music of Chopin, Schubert, De Meyer, Liszt, and some German songs. A delightful evening." Cultivated coteries in other cities were also sensitive to art in all its aspects. Anne Botta's New York salon was famous for its weekly gatherings of scientists, writers, artists, musicians, and intellectuals. People such as Edgar Allan Poe, Horace Greeley, Bayard Taylor, and Ole Bull were among her guests. Discussions, readings, and music filled out the evening hours.[23]

Some men and women who enjoyed singing decided on exclusively musical parties, at which the attendees could indulge in music making for their own enjoyment. The desire to meet in order to sing or play instruments was already evidenced in the eighteenth century and grew with some rapidity from the 1820s on. As usual, several English visitors proved themselves ill informed and rather sharp tongued about American musical parties. Their judgments were based usually on their own limited experience or on the partisan opinions of the American minority among whom they circulated—the hoity-toity Americans, everyone an aristocrat-manqué. One visitor, Thomas Grattan, who arrived in the summer of 1839 for a short stay, concluded that "musical parties are rare. There are very few tolerable *amateur* performers; but a great fancy for music itself good, bad, or indifferent, and not much taste to discriminate between them."[24]

The evidence of the period shows that opinions like those of Grattan require considerable modification. In February 1824 Charles Francis Adams, then sixteen years old, wrote of a musical party he had attended that included a senator and two sisters from the West Indies. He treats it as a usual occurrence, where he heard some excellent and some poor singing ("The West Indian ladies . . . sung a great while without much effect; they have singular voices in tone similar to frogs."). And indeed, for quite a few Americans, musical parties were common events, in which the participants generally came away feeling the compositions heard were of excellent quality and

the performers commendable. Julia Ward Howe was proud of her "little musical parties on Saturday evenings," which regularly took place in her "little
parlour." She told her sister Annie in an 1846 letter:

> I have found some musical friends to sing with me—Lizzie Cary, Mrs.
> Felton, Mr. Pelosos and William Story. . . . Agassiz, the learned and
> charming Frenchman, is also one of my *habitués* on Saturday eve-
> nings, and Count Pourtalés, a Swiss nobleman of good family, who
> has accompanied Agassiz to this country! I illuminate my room with
> a chandelier and some candles, draw out the piano into the room,
> and order some ice from Mrs. Meyer's—so that the reception gives
> me very little trouble. My friends come at half-past eight and stay un-
> til eleven. I do not usually have more than twenty people, but once I
> have had nearly sixty, and those of the best people in Boston.[25]

George Templeton Strong was also proud of the musical parties that he,
his wife, and their friends, all representative of the more sophisticated stratum
of New York society, began to put together in February 1854. At the first
meeting, his wife, Ellie, and five other people sang selections from Haydn's and
Mozart's masses and a chorus from Haydn's *Seasons* to organ accompaniment. Later in the same year, some less cultivated music lovers advertised in
the *New York Daily Times* for people interested in forming "a small musical
party to meet weekly at their house, uptown, and sing glees, etc., under the
charge of a professional leader." Any expenses incurred would be shared.[26]

There were casually organized meetings of amateur "Jews-Harp Clubs,"
of barely competent "Philharmonic Societies," and of plebeian "Singing Societies," some to produce oratorios and masses, others to indulge in more
humble fare. Herman Mann's diary entry of 22 March 1839 refers to a
musical group's meeting in a Dedham, Massachusetts, tavern owned by Francis Alden to perform compositions by William Billings, the eighteenth-century
Boston singing master and composer:

> *Old Billings once more!* A very full meeting of lovers of "sweet sound"
> was held at Alden's Hall this evening. A full and efficient orchestra
> was present and the different societies in the town were well repre-
> sented. Mr. Calvin Ellis presided this evening by request. About 80
> partook of the supper after the sing. A toast offered by Abijah
> Smith, an old veteran singer, was well received: "*Billings Music—half
> century singers*—may the rising generation hold fast to old times—
> eat, drink and sing with moderation, temperance and perfection—
> and each one be at liberty to license himself."[27]

The last category of grand party to be mentioned is the ball, whose purpose was elegant social dancing to instrumental music of a cosmopolitan nature. From the earliest days of the nation, a majority of Americans had demonstrated a devotion to dancing. It is therefore not surprising to learn that the days before Lent were a merry period in Charleston, with three or four balls a week. The Saint Cecilia Society alone gave three balls at ten-day intervals, which were attended by the fashionable and refined set; the Jockey Club sponsored a huge ball at the end of race week. Other organizations followed suit.[28]

When the first wave of luxury swept New York City, members of the affluent class fell into the habit of hiring a small band, such as a clarinetist, bass player, and violinist, and often coming from the rank of black Americans, for their entertainments. This action they deemed "the only preparation necessary for the most distinguished ball." At the turn of the century, the ladies and gentlemen of Georgia were already making merry at balls, dancing "the minuet, which was introduced only to teach us the graces, and the congo, which was only to chase away the solemnities of the minuet." Waltzes were unknown at that time. Likewise, New Orleanians were constantly getting up public balls, even coupling them with concerts and musical theater. The streets were apt to be muddy in New Orleans. It was not unusual to see women walking barefoot to a ball, then, on arrival, washing their dirty feet, putting on their fancy shoes, and changing into their dancing costumes at the door. As often as not, if an opera were mounted, it was made to end early enough that the audience could go dancing afterward.[29]

Although Americans had heard of the waltz by the 1820s, they only cautiously accepted it, leery of a couples dance that allowed partners to hold each other closely. City dwellers gradually introduced it into their balls during the 1830s and 1840s. Those living in less urban areas lagged a decade or so behind the city. As late as 1850 Grace Greenwood was describing a young gentleman, Jack Richards, as just getting around to learning the steps and enjoying its "delicious delirium." Sophie, to whom Jack was engaged, had also taken up the waltz, despite opposition from moralists. She wrote to Jack about dancing with her cousin Mortimer: "Now, some people think it shocking for me to waltz with Mortimer, but I smile at their old-fashioned notions, and away we whirl!"[30]

The upper social stratum of small towns and villages also had to have balls, though not necessarily waltzes. In 1807 Edward Kendall was staying in Litchfield, Connecticut. On one evening he was taken "to a little village ball" held in the courthouse. Those attending were "the younger members of the most respectable inhabitants of the place." Similarly, Christopher Baldwin of Worcester, Massachusetts, wrote into his diary on 27 February 1829 that a

ball had been held at a public house belonging to a Mr. Thomas, with sixteen  *187*
ladies and nineteen gentlemen present, each of whom had paid the three-
dollar admission. "Nero Powers on the Fiddle and old Peter Rich on the
Tamborin are the Musick." Powers said that he had "a fine time. Ladies in gay
dresses and musick always pleases me." Ten years later, Walter Austin was
describing the social assemblies held in the Alden tavern of Dedham, Massachusetts, where the music was supplied by Kendall's Cotillion Band: "E-flat
Bugle, Harp, Violin, Clarionette, Ophicleide." And a year later, Francis Sheridan was reporting on "a very good ball" held in the small community of
Galveston, Texas, which opened with the singing of the national anthem of
the Republic of Texas, whose tune came from Thomas Moore's "Will You
Come to the Bower." Then followed "God Save the Queen," in honor of the
several British guests present, succeeded by "Hail Columbia," after which the
actual dancing began.[31]

For balls held on Southern plantations, slaves almost invariably supplied
the music. On the Texas plantation to which she had once belonged, said the
former slave Betty Bormer, her white master was quite broadminded. Some
slaves were permitted to study how to read and write, and her aunt was
allowed to learn the piano:

Dere am lots of music on dat place; fiddle, banjo and de piano.
Singin', we had lots of dat, songs like Ole Black Joe and 'legious
songs and sich. Often de marster have we'uns come in his house
and clears de dinin' room for de dance. Dat am big time, on special
occasion. Dey not calls it "dance" dem days, dey calls it de "ball."[32]

That the term *ball* could accommodate a variety of music-and-dance
situations was made obvious when Charles Dickens wrote about a visit in
1842 to the State Hospital for the Insane, located in South Boston, where a
"ball" took place once a week. These balls were successful. The inmates looked
forward to them and even practiced their dancing beforehand.[33]

## Frolics: Revels for Commoners

Jonathan Slick (pseudonym of Ann S. Stephens) vividly portrayed the
difference between the unbuttoned revels of the ordinary folk and the more
decorous entertainments just discussed, when describing a "posh party" held
in New York City. Slick, who had come to town from the country, had dressed
himself as a "fashionable" in order not to be taken as a rube at the high-toned
evening event. On arrival, a young woman immediately approached him:

"Do you dance quadrills, Mr. Slick?" sez the black eyed gal, as if she wanted me tu ask her to dance.

"Wal, I don't know," sez I, "I never tried them kind of things; but I ruther guess I can, if you'll show me how."

With that, I took the tip end of her white glove between the fingers of my yeller one. . . . I didn't know what they were a-going tu dance, but I warn't much affeard, anyhow—for there warn't a chap in all Weatherfield could beat me in double shuffle, or could cut so neat a pigeon-wing without music, as I could.

Wal, the music begun, and one of the fellers . . . begun tu slide about with his eyes half shet and his hands a hanging down, and looking as doleful as if he'd jest come away from a funeral. . . . The gals all stuck out their little feet, and poked about just in the same way. Think, sez I, when it comes my turn, I'll give you a little specimen of ginuine dancing. . . . I took two steps for'ward and then cut a peeler of a pigeon-wing, and ended off with a little touch of the double shuffle, but my trousers were so plaging tight that I couldn't make my legs rale limber all I could do, besides, the music warn't much more like a dancing tune than Greenbank or Old Hundred. At last I went up tu the gal that was playing, and sez I—

"Look a here—jest give us something lively—Yankee Doodle, or Money Muss, or the Irish Washerwoman, or Paddy Carey."[34]

Slick represented the commonplace Americans who danced, sang, and played musical instruments with slight or no formal instruction and no pretensions to cultivation. They attended parties, denominated as frolics, without bothering with fashionable dress, and made no to-do over formal manners. The parties that took place closer to the eastern seaboard and especially in the northern states tended to be more controlled affairs and favored good fellowship. Those taking place toward the west and south, while inclining toward friendly relationships, were more unpredictable, more raucous, and contained more rowdy characters always ready for a capital fight.

In the first half of the nineteenth century, the usual run of young American men and women commanded a privilege of intimate companionship unusual in the social life of prim "polite" society. Most of them lived in rural areas. They strolled, boated, picnicked, rhythmically skipped about a dance floor, vocalized ditties with and without accompaniment, and took pleasurable excursions freely together. They could enjoy their leisure time, whether day or night, with little restraint, and without the occurrence or even the sense of indecorum. A few of the stricter Christian sects advised their adherents to avoid indulgence in dancing, but the advice was frequently disregarded. Even though religion and church attendance were strong with **189** common Americans, most thought nothing of riding horseback, driving a surrey, or walking five miles or so to attend a country frolic. They worked hard and played hard and would not willingly forgo opportunities for getting away from the monotony of their everyday lives.

In contrast to the New York party that Slick attended, an 1838 frolic held in a split-log house in a frontier county of Georgia, said A. B. Longstreet, was a straightforward and "honest" event and had nothing "fashionable" about it. All furniture had been removed from the room; rough planks on trestles held "plain fare" for those who were hungry; the attendees, many of them farmers and their wives, came neatly and plainly dressed, in clothing of their own manufacture. Their music and dances were their own—traditional songs, reels and other country dances—and not those of French or Italian manufacture. A black fiddler energetically plied his trade before the assemblage.[35]

Frolics were scenes of gaiety, lively gatherings that called for singing and games along with the dancing. Davy Crockett, when he settled in western Tennessee with his second wife, found that his neighbors held frolics that generated a great deal of excitement. The tunes flew out at lightning speed: "Forked Deer," named after a local stream; "Knob Dance," after the great knobs seen in the area; "Natchez-under-the-Hill," after the rude village on the Mississippi; and "Rocky Mountains," after the peaks that few had seen. There were "dance-tunes that sounded like the baying of hounds in full cry. And lively Irish reel tunes were played, like 'Miss McCloud.'" A writer in the *Spirit of the Times*, in an article entitled "Dick Harkin's Tennessee Frolic," recounted one episode where a fiddler, Jo Spriggins, sponsored his own frolic, not an uncommon action for fiddlers. He charged "a 'jip' for a reel and two 'bits' for what corn-juice you suck." The frolic was set for Saturday night at his house and was announced beforehand by Jo, who rode about the neighborhood singing:

> Oh, I met a frog, with a fiddle on his back,
> A axin his way to the fro-l-i-c-k,
> Wha-a-he! Wha-he! Wha-he! Wha-ke he-ke-he!

Everyone came to it carrying food for a potluck meal, which was laid out on a plank table in the yard. The same pieces as those Crockett had heard were played ["Rocky Mountains" is called "Rocky Mounting"], and people worked up an appetite as they danced, courted, and drank whiskey and beer. The festivity continued until 3 A.M., when two young men started to fight over a girl; the fight expanded into a free-for-all, and the party broke up.[36]

Rarely was the latest music heard in the more isolated rural communities.

In one remote district, a Connecticut man was a guest at a frolic where, for a portion of the evening, every person took his or her turn at singing. When it came to the Yankee's turn, "he gave them the pathetic ballad of Ben Bolt, sung feelingly and well," and "all hearts were instantly captivated. Immediately they passed him the bottle of old rye, pressing him to wet his whistle and try again, and so kept him singing and telling of the great world of which they knew so little, until near upon the peep of day."[37]

Most rural communities treasured, indeed insisted on, their romps, and each neighborhood somehow managed to shelter at least one musician, good, bad, or indifferent, whose services were vital for these functions. Usually the musician was a fiddler. George Harris, drawing on his knowledge of the American South, described a North Carolina fiddler named Bart Davis, who possessed a three-string instrument, gave parties at his own house, and made himself available for frolics anywhere within a five-mile radius of his home. At one frolic, a hard-shell preacher appeared, who did not object to loading his insides with whiskey but did object to the music and dancing. He confiscated the fiddle and commenced preaching a sermon on sinning. Everyone in attendance soon grew angry at his fulmination. After a while, one young woman had taken all that she could. She pounced on him, knocked him down, pulled his hair, and kicked him. When she began to stick pins into him that she snatched from her collar, the preacher thought it best to flee the place.[38]

The services of a musician were required even in the raw gold-mining communities of the California forty-niners. W. E. Woodward reported on one such musician, Fanning Plunkett, who "had never engaged in useful toil" but "was by no means an idler." He could be found at evening festivities, at picnics, and at other frolicsome affairs, "playing the banjo or guitar, singing songs and teaching new games to those present."[39]

Frolics were also a significant part of life in slave communities. Amid the indignities and miseries inflicted upon them, African Americans occasionally had some cheer let into their lives. To keep their slaves from becoming too restive, many masters allowed their blacks to relax with music and dance on Saturday nights. When the master and his family were away, those left behind immediately took a wonderful holiday from labor and care. If blessed with a benevolent master, they might be granted passes to attend a party at a neighboring plantation. If denied passes, they attended anyway, sneaking out at night and avoiding the surveillance of the patrols. Once the frolic began, the plantation locals, and those visitors with and without passes, set about enjoying themselves as best they could with pooled refreshments and musicians. "I wants yo' all ter know, us had had gran' times at de frolics," said Manda Boggan, who added that her master was a preacher. "On Saturday nites us would dance all nite long. I can hear dem fiddles an' guitars yet, wid dat loud 'swing yo' pardners.' Hit wuz all gran'."[40]

However unfortunate their circumstances, those held in servitude had plenty of musicians in their midst for their own frolics, musicians who were often also summoned for white entertainment. One of these, the Louisiana fiddler Solomon Northup, gave it as his opinion that "the African race" was "a music-loving one," and that many of his "fellow-bondsmen" were extraordinary singers, ingenious fiddlers, gifted guitarists, and dexterous banjo players. He performed gladly for his friends, and his master frequently rented him out to play at white affairs, from which he would return with a pocket full of tips.[41]

Another musician, Daddy Tony, was a carriage driver on a South Carolina plantation. "He wore his tall hat and fine clothes [livery]," said his son Richard, "and he was a musician—played the violin" for white assemblies, "at the Academy on the 'Old Ninety-Six Road,'" and for the parties of his black comrades. A frequenter of jollities on or near her Mississippi plantation, the ex-slave Manda Edmonson explained: "Us wont taught no learning' but wuz let to go to frolics an' picnics now an' then. Us would dance an' meet boys from other plantations an' court an' have our fun. We went to church at de white folks meeting house, an' sing an' shout in de fields. Some of dem ole songs wuz mighty purty." A fuller description of slave frolics was given by William Adams, who lived in Texas:

On Sat'day and Sunday nites dey'd dance and sing all nite long. Dey didn' dance like today, dey danced de roun' dance and jig and do de pigeon wing, and some of dem would jump up and see how many time he could kick his feets 'fore dey hit de groun'. Dey had an ole fiddle and some of 'em would take two bones in each hand and rattle 'em. Dey sang songs like "Diana had a Wooden Leg," and "A Hand full of Sugar," and "Cotton-Eyed Joe." I dis'member how they went.[42]

Because slaves did not command the resources to load their tables with food at frolics, they regularly resorted to thievery in order to acquire a hog or a few chickens. Thus supplied, they could "cook, eat, and, with dancing and music, enjoy a big time generally." To have a hog actually given to a slave was a cause for astonishment and high anticipation in the entire black community. The customary consequence for such a gift was a request for a frolic. Andrew Gill states that at one time such a gift giving took place on his Mississippi plantation:

I 'member one time Missus Rosa give one of de niggers a nice fat hog fer doin' somethin' special fer her. Dat nigger was sho' proud of dat hog. Yas Suh! Come Saturday Mornin' an' he asked Missus Rosa could he have a celebration on dat hog. Missus Rosa say she guess so. Lord 'a mercy were dem niggers full of 'citement all day. Dey sang out in de fiel's all day long an' I heah dem way up at de Big House.

> We's gonna kill a pig,
> We's gonna kill a pig,
> Glory be Hallealuh!
> We's gonna kill a pig.

Dat night de Quarters was jes' bustin' wid merriment, an' wid de Gill niggers helpin', dat pig sho' didn' las' long.[43]

## Excursions and Picnics

Americans everywhere, when they could get away from work, resorted to brief pleasure trips during warm weather. A fortunate few who had the leisure and financial means would leave for a favorite resort, such as Saratoga Springs, and remain there from two weeks to an entire summer season. Whether people were away for a few hours or a few weeks, music came away with them. Every resort employed some sort of ensemble for the entertainment of its guests. As a case in point, in the summer's heat of 1830, wrote James Boardman, fashionable people from urban areas, as in other years, were fleeing in droves to their favorite watering places, hillside resorts, and country houses. Those who could not get away spent the evenings at public gardens, walks along the shore of the ocean or a river, and visits to pleasure grounds, where music was a "never-failing attraction." Rural dwellers, too, appreciated getting away from their labors and workaday stresses, if that were possible. N. Parker Willis, on 21 August 1848, was on a visit to the hamlet of Trenton Falls, on the Mohawk, between Utica and Niagara, when he noted:

> It is a very popular place of resort from every village within thirty
> miles, and, from ten in the morning till four in the afternoon, there
> is gay work with the country girls and their beaux—swinging under
> the trees, strolling about in the woods near the house, bowling,
> singing and dancing. . . . We have had songs, duets and choruses
> sung here by village girls, within the last few days, in a style that
> drew all in the house to listen very admiringly.[44]

A vacationing group made a side trip to visit Kentucky's Mammoth Cave **193** in 1849. Within the underground chambers they listened with delight to the echoes when a gentleman regaled them "with 'The Arkansas Hunters,' 'Uncle Ned,' 'O! Susanna,' and other far-famed works of the great masters, finishing with 'Yankee-doodle.'" In the same state, young people were on a picnic and, as was the custom, taking turns singing. A young woman was asked to sing a favorite song, but she insisted on singing verses written by her escort, which she had put to a popular tune of the day: "O, would I were a girl again!/When life was love, and sunny hours."[45]

In 1836, after picnickers beside Lake George had finished eating and drinking, singing was in order. A robust "Uncle Johnny began to growl in a horrible bass" the air of "The Old English Gentleman": "I'll sing you an old ballad,/That was made by an old pate!," to which a mockingbird answered. After the conclusion of this man-bird duet, a lady sang "Let every flower yield up its fay," and again the mockingbird joined in. The unexpected dueting gave added entertainment to the listeners.[46]

Quite a few occurrences connect music to recreations taking place on ponds, lakes, rivers, and oceans. By rowboat and steamboat, Americans took to the water as often as they could during the summer. Rowing across the Hudson for a picnic, a woman sang "Home, Sweet Home" while a man accompanied her on the flute. Walt Whitman and fifteen friends embarked on the waters of Long Island's South Bay, to fish and picnic, and passed away the time pleasantly singing, among other things, "the popular melodies of 'Auld Lang Syne' and 'Home, Sweet Home.'" In Lynn, Massachusetts, a group of sixteen people went for a fishing excursion and picnic on a fishing smack and had "songs, speeches, and toasts, with mirth unmeasured and laughs unmeasurable." Mrs. Sigourney talked of a summer's short boat ride after tea in Norwich, Connecticut, where the oars kept time "to the favorite melody of 'Row, vassals, row!' or the Canadian Boat-Song." Saco, Maine, was proud of its evening singing parties aboard boats of varying capacities. The *Maine Democrat* reported: "Saco is getting to be as celebrated as Venice in olden times. We have singing in gondolas on the water, from the 'village choir,' and music in the balconies on moonlight nights from the 'Social Band.'"[47]

Steam and sailing ships were called into service by larger groups bent on warm-weather diversion. Residents of Savannah liked to take trips, sometimes in parties of one hundred, to an ocean island, where they picnicked, played music, sang, and danced before returning late in the evening. Lydia Child said that a favorite way for New Yorkers "to relieve the oppressiveness of summer in the city" was to take steamboat excursions on the Hudson, and the most pleasant of all were those taken with glee clubs and bands aboard. One that she went on, in July 1844, left the pier at 5 P.M., went upriver for eighteen miles, then turned back to stop for a picnic on Staten Island, with music supplied by a band. On the return, "the choir of singers gave us 'Auld lang syne' in full chorus; and strangers as we were to each other, every one found a response in the memory of his heart." Then came "choruses, glees, and songs, with occasional interludes of the band." At midnight, when they were close to docking, all sang "Home, Sweet Home." A harder-to-please excursionist, George Templeton Strong, also of New York, said the band on board his ship consisted of two violinists (the captain and a sailor), a professional clarinetist, and two guitarists (one of them a mulatto), who played jigs with energy and ferocity and "squeaked, twanged, and tooted" forth "Hail Columbia."[48]

Further to the west, Dr. Thomas Nichols took an extended excursion over the Great Lakes on the new ship *Erie:*

A very nice party it was. We had a band of music, and danced every pleasant afternoon and moonlit evening. Every day was a festival. We chatted, played, sang, ate excellent dinners, drank the captain's wines, enjoyed beautiful scenery, visited the flourishing cities springing up around the lakes . . . [and had] a good time generally.[49]

Even further west, Californians also enjoyed shipboard excursions, such as the one that took place on 2 June 1850. Captain Sutter and one hundred invited guests went from Sacramento to his Hock Farm residence on the steamer *Governor Dana*, with the band playing continuously on the upper deck. As they approached the farm, "Hail Columbia" sounded. After arrival, the band continued its efforts much to the astonishment of the Indians, who crowded the banks and listened "thunderstruck," because they had never "heard anything of the kind."[50]

The winter season, with its snow, made possible a special type of excursion that was extremely popular in the antebellum years—sleighing jaunts. Buffalo robes, bearskins, or other soft furs kept the passengers warm and comfortable. The journeyers were most often young men and women bent on pleasure, although men and women of all ages were in attendance on many trips. John Cooke tells of a sleighing expedition by residents of Richmond, Virginia, some of them older adults, others children. Songs were sung during the ride, among them, "Where Are the Friends of My Youth" and "The Children's Prayer to Maia."[51]

The destination for these outings was normally a rural house, most often a tavern with a large room, which was kept in a state of readiness to receive excursionists. The tavern's proprietor had a supper ready for his guests. If musicians had not come with the company, a local fiddler stood by, able and willing to supply the music for dancing and singing.[52] In Wiscasset, Maine, Pardon Bowers's Tavern, ten miles out, was a favorite destination. When Bowers decided to charge admission, however, "five and sixpence lawful" for every male "and three four-pence ha' pennies" for every female, the sleighing parties refused to continue going there. Then George Peabody invited everybody to his farm without charge but suggested that they bring their own fiddler.[53]

New Yorkers were passionately fond of going off in evening parties of twenty or thirty to a place at a distance of six to eight miles, carrying a fiddler with them. After much dancing and singing, they would return home, often with the first light of day. A hushed city awakened to the tinkling of sleigh bells blending agreeably with the sound of songs and laughter.[54] Not to be outdone, Pittsburghers also took to their sleighs:

> For the night, an appointment is generally made by a large party
> (for instance, the company of twenty or thirty carioles) to meet at a
> tavern several miles distant; to which they go by torch-light, and ac-
> companied by music. On arriving there, the ladies cast off their fur
> pelisses, assume all their beauties, and with the men commence the
> mazy dance. This is followed by supper, songs, catches, and glees.[55]

The most fascinating sleighing incidents took place between the towns of Warsaw, Illinois, on one side of the Mississippi River, and Keokuk, Iowa, on the other. When winter arrived and the immense river froze over, a great deal of sociability was made possible between the two villages. When the ice was sufficiently thick, a road was broken through the snow that lay atop the ice. Sleighing parties went back and forth frequently. Warsaw House, in particular, was favored for supper, singing, and dancing. At times, as in the 1848–49 winter, a crossover remained possible for three months.[56]

African Americans rarely had the opportunity to picnic or engage in a boating excursion, and sleighing was unheard of. If they did picnic, it was not unusual for white folk also to be present. Whenever free blacks held their "annual colored picnic" in Paulding County, Ohio, there were white onlookers who came to enjoy the singing. On Southern plantations, most white masters were not given to allowing many picnics for the workers under their command. At the most, they approved one or two a year. Once in a while, a master weakened and agreed not only to the picnic but also to supplying the picnickers with more than the usual amount of food and occasionally drink. For example, one Virginia planter allowed a celebration for his return home after a long absence and furnished ample provisions, punch, and wine for the picnic. Jeff, the plantation's fiddler, was assisted by another black, Pompey, on

**196**  the banjo when playing for the dancing. Jeff then sang "Camptown Races," with the rest joining in the chorus. Pompey followed with another minstrel song, "Lucy Bell." This was succeeded by a great deal of dancing and singing.[57]

### Other Causes for Musical Celebration

All sorts of special occasions called for music, to an extent unheard of in later years. This did not mean a perfunctory performance of a piece or two by a standby band to which those present scarcely listened. People desired and welcomed the music. An illustrative case is the observance on 18 October 1854 connected with the completion of the first railroad through Cortland County, New York. Women had worked hard to ready a feast, which was laid out on tables set up around the station of the Central New York Railway. People came expecting not only to listen to speeches but also to derive joy from the music for the event. At last, the inaugural train arrived crowded with guests, a band, and a quartet of vocalists, who sang:

> No more we sing, as we sang of old, to the tune of lute or lyre,
>   For lo we live in an iron-age, in the age of steam and fire.
> The world is too busy for dreaming, and has grown too wise for war,
>   So today, for the glory of science, let us sing of the railway car.

The men and women present listened closely to the song and were so enthusiastic at its completion that the quartet decided to sing it at every station along the line, which it did from a special stage platform set up at the top of a railway car.[58]

One of the most ubiquitous special events requiring music was a wedding. To the class for whom decorum and an accepted code of etiquette were weighty considerations, the nuptial day unfolded in prescribed and staid fashion. An instrumental ensemble was hired to play forthrightly for dancing and softly as background to dining and conversation. Stylish dances learned from French dancing masters were produced. Airs in English, French, and Italian were warbled. Designing mothers of marriageable daughters herded their offspring to the piano for display. Sincere and insincere compliments were bestowed on the amateur attainments. The reception, on the whole, remained noisy with the conversation and laughter coming from the several cliques that had quickly formed.[59]

For the common people, however, the story was different. The general public of Kentucky celebrated "a real, genuine" wedding into "the early hours of the following day." Large gatherings of old and young commemorated the

turning point in a couple's lives with prayer, to be sure, but also with uncere-
monious feasting, drinking, singing, and dancing. The homespun weddings in
Georgia followed similar patterns. One Georgian said that at his wedding the
guests ate, sang, and danced "enough to make the fur fly in a tall coon-hunt."
Indeed, the wedding became an outstanding success only after "all got rid of
their shoes and stockings" and then "put in the double licks," which "beat
anything I ever saw afore in Georgia."[60]

Weddings in New England were little different but seem to have been
celebrated with less abandon. A New Hampshire woman wrote in 1845 of the
marriage of a farmer's daughter where the expected "vows, vittles, and fun-
ning" took place, though the circumstances she detailed were more sedate
than those of the Georgia marriage just mentioned. What is most informative
about this particular account is the mention of traditional ballads being
performed. These old songs had persisted here, as in all country places, of the
United States.

> Uncle Peter, the notorious singer, was called upon the board to fill
> the interim with songs such as the company should choose to select.
> The first that was called for was "Sweet William," as we thought this
> would be appropriate for the occasion [the groom's name was Wil-
> liam]; and a very excellent song it is, too, though as long as the
> moral law, containing about fifty verses; but who ever became weary
> of hearing it sung? It commences thus—
>
> > "A seaman of Plymouth, sweet William by name.
> > A wooing to beautiful Susan he came" etc.
>
> Then followed "Black-eyed Susan." I forgot to tell you that the newly-
> made bride was "Susan by name," and this was why the Susan
> songs took the lead. After these, the "Garden Gate," the "Yorkshire
> Bite," the "Lass of Richmond Hill," and "Merry Gordon," with oth-
> ers of like nature.[61]

Wedding celebrations for free black Americans paralleled those for white
Americans. Not so those of the slave population. At times a marriage was
forced on a black slave couple by masters who wished to unite two healthy
people for breeding purposes. Otherwise, when a black man and woman
desired to marry, certain potential impediments had to be removed. For one,
they needed the permission of one master, if he owned the two menials, or of
two masters, if the man and woman belonged to different plantations. For
another, the approval of the woman's parents might be sought if her parent-

198   age were known and the parents were nearby. Most marriages were of the perfunctory jump-the-broom variety, where the couple merely had to jump over a broom before the master and other witnesses to be declared married. When the ceremony was completed, little in the way of celebration might result. On rare occasion an elaborate party followed a black wedding. Edmund Kirke witnessed such a one, on a North Carolina plantation, near the Trent River. The master had authorized a wedding feast for around one hundred black attendees to take place in the black meetinghouse. Kirke saw "several sable gentlemen, with banjos and fiddles." The master himself was also seated on a raised platform, the better to see and enjoy the activity. People sang and danced vigorously. There were breakdowns—speedy and tumultuous shuffling dances, often with couples competing with one another—and even a waltz or two, for "some highfalutin dancin'," said the black leader, Boss Joe.[62]

More often, when African Americans on a plantation were allowed to indulge in pleasures of this sort, the wedding that had taken place was that of a member of the master's family. As James Weir said of a Kentucky wedding:

> Nor were the guests in the mansion the only revellers on that night;
> for the negroes on the plantation, and all those for miles around,
> were gathered in cabins and in the open green, celebrating with Afri-
> can hilarity and recklessness, the marriage of their young mistress.
> Their banjos, and fiddles, and songs made the silent woods echo
> with gladness.

The next morning, wrote Weir, the groggy and still tired field laborers were awakened at the usual early hour and sent back to work.[63]

In the antebellum years, music was vital to electioneering. A candidate on the campaign trail did so with a band in attendance, ready to play to attract an audience. His supporters sang campaign songs to boost his image. After the speeches, an invitation to the public to dance was considered a sure way to win votes by delivering instant happiness to those present. By no means rare were such aspirants as Congressman Cobb of Alabama, who serenaded voters in the 1850s with songs tailored to his candidacy.

> Mr. Cobb resorted to all sorts of tricks to catch the popular votes,
> such as the rattling of tinware and crockery . . . and he delighted in
> the singing of homely songs composed for stump purposes. One of
> these which he was wont to introduce at the end of a speech and
> which always seemed to be especially his own, was called "The

Homestead Bill." Of this remarkable composition there were a score
of verses, at least, that covered every possible possession which the
heart of the poor man [the voter] might crave, ranging from land
and mules to household furniture. The song began,

> "Uncle Sam is rich enough to give us all a farm!"

and Mr. Cobb would sing it in stentorian tones, winking as he did
so, to first one and then another of his admiring listeners, and punc-
tuating his phrases by chewing with great gusto, a piece of onion
and the coarsest of corn "pone."[64]

Those office seekers more skilled on an instrument than in singing made
do with a demonstration of their proficiency. Lew Wallace, the future author
of *Ben-Hur,* tells of stumping for the office of prosecuting attorney in 1852
against James Wilson. When both were appearing in Alamo, Indiana, Wallace
looked for a handle for getting the better of his opponent.

> At Alamo the opening of the discussion fell to me. The platform was
> just across the road in front of a tavern from which, while getting
> off my speech, I heard the notes of a violin wretchedly played. My
> competitor began his reply, and was yet in the introduction when I
> interviewed the fiddler.
> "Give me that violin," I said.
> He passed it to me.
> "Now throw the door and windows open—there at the front."
> Forthwith, I struck up the "Arkansas Traveller." The effect was
> instantaneous. The silver tongue of my antagonist lost its cunning.
> His hearers, partisans and enemies alike, were smitten with restless-
> ness. Presently they came streaming to my side of the road, and
> when, a little further on, he was driven to an untimely conclusion, I
> reached the conviction, held ever since, that the power of music is
> superior to that of eloquence—that the "Arkansas Traveller" in the
> right key and time and with the right expression, could have si-
> lenced Pericles, or Mirabeau, or any of those accounted of the di-
> vine in oratory.[65]

Political rallies were times for mass enthusiasm over a candidate. Candi-
dates tried to whip up that enthusiasm to a white heat. For example, Marion
Harland delineated a Whig rally in Powhatan, Virginia, that took place in the
presidential election of 1844:

The orations were interspersed with "patriotic songs." A quartette of young men, picked out by the committee of arrangements, for their fine voices and staunch Whiggery, stood on the platform and sang the body of the ballads. The choruses were shouted, with more force and good-will than tunefulness, by masculine voters of all ages and qualities of tone.

Doctor Henning, an able physician . . . stood near my father, his back against a tree, his mouth wide, and all the volume of sound he could pump from his lungs pouring skyward in the refrain of

"Get out of the way, you're all unlucky;
Clear the track for Old Kentucky!"[66]

Ann Stephens, posing as Jonathan Slick, wrote an amusing satire on meetings like the one just described. She claimed that a lot of "lower-class types" attended, and that a fiddler would play vigorous pieces such as "double shuffles and pigeon wings" to liven up the crowd.

There they were screaming, and a stamping, and a dancing, and a fiddling all in a heap, till a feller couldn't hear himself think. . . . Now, says a leetle man by the winder, clear your pipes, so that you can all jine in. Them that can't read or don't know the tune can sing Yankee Doodle or Hail Columbia.

With that he flung a hull grist of papers among the crowd and begun to raise his ebenezer rather strong afore the rest sot in. By-am-by they all got a going, and the way they roared out the song was awful, I can tell you. Some of 'em sung in one tune and some in another—every man went on his own hook. The pussy little feller pulled away on the fiddle like all natur, and the chap with the skewed nose made a plaguey squeaking with a split fife that he had. The feller that hadn't no crown in his hat bellered out Auld Lang Syne, and I see another chap holding the paper upside down and blowing away at Old Hundred like all natur. When they begun to drop off, for it warn't to be expected that such a heap of critters could stop altogether, the pussy feller with the fiddle yelled out, "Hurra for the song!—Three cheers for singing!" And then they went at it agin, a hooting and tossing up their hats—then that had 'em—as if Old Nick himself had kicked 'em on end.[67]

Presidential election campaign songs were popular in the years before the Civil War. John Adams in 1796 had gone on to victory with "Adams and

Liberty," sung to the melody of "To Anacreon in Heaven," which later would become the tune for "The Star-Spangled Banner." "Jefferson and Liberty," to the same tune, helped elect Thomas Jefferson in 1800. When Lincoln ran for president in 1860, his campaign song was "Lincoln and Liberty," to the tune of "Old Rosin, the Beau." Without question, however, the presidential election in which music was the most paramount and most significant in influencing the selection was that of 1840. The Log Campaign, mounted by the Whigs to a successful conclusion, was possibly the most high spirited and certainly the most absurd in the history of the United States. With General William Harrison as presidential candidate and John Tyler as vice presidential candidate, this political party succeeded in defeating the opposition Democrats and their candidate, Martin Van Buren, despite making no official declaration of principles and avoiding any discussion of publicly important matters. Music, emotionalism, and the upbuilding of popular excitement were the Whig weapons of choice. Harrison, the victorious general who defeated Tecumseh and his Indian allies in the Battle of Tippecanoe, 7 November 1811, had widespread enthusiasm awakened for him when a Richmond newspaper attacked his candidacy with: "Give him a barrel of hard cider, and a pension of two thousand dollars, and our word for it, he will sit the remainder of his days contented in a log cabin.'" Instantly, the Whig newspapers and orators initiated a "hard cider" and "log cabin" sloganeering offensive that won them votes throughout the United States. The barnstorm started in Maine with a campaign lyric set to the then-popular tune of "The Little Pigs":

What has caused this great commotion—motion—motion—motion,
Our country through,
It is a ball a-rolling on
For Tippecanoe and Tyler, too,
For Tippecanoe and Tyler, too.
And with them we'll beat little Van,
Van, Van, is a used up man.[68]

Extraordinary enthusiasm was generated wherever the song was produced, and the Whig masterminds saw to it that it was sung everywhere, by everyone. In New York City, George Templeton Strong heard it when he attended a concert given by a favorite vocalist, Henry Russell, then commented:

There is a certain degree of humbug about "The Maniac" [composed by Russell], though it's most effectively disagreeable, and the "Whig National Song" is unmitigated humbug. Quite a kickup it raised tonight. It was met at first by hisses, bahs, and penny trumpets from a miserable minority of Locofocos, but this opposition, though received again and again, was always overwhelmed utterly by thunderous applause; and it ended with hats off and in the air, and three cheers for Harrison. . . . Some slight attempt was made to get up a fight thereafter, but it failed.[69]

Disputes involving the Whig song were frequent. In New Orleans, William Timmons, a Locofoco Democrat, hailed a thick-set woman who lived next door into court. He claimed she was a Whig who had taught her parrot to torture him by singing, "Van, Van, Van—Van is a used-up man!" She rebutted by insisting that Mr. Timmons was often drunk, and when inebriated imagined the bird to be singing "Tippecanoe songs." The case was dismissed.[70]

Many a village and town had a log cabin built, with a raccoon chained to the door and with a keg of cider or whiskey close by, so that whoever wished could help himself. Log cabins were put on wheels and paraded through city streets. Minstrel bands were formed to popularize "Tippecanoe and Tyler, Too," and succeeded in having it "shouted in every street by all the musical and unmusical men and boys throughout the country."[71] Whig cookouts, picnics, boat rides, and hard-cider meetings used it to whip up those present. Shortly, Whig songsters with numerous lyrics pushing the party line to favorite tunes were printed in large numbers, and glee clubs sprang up everywhere to sing them.

Music quickly became a weapon of choice for all political parties, so that its effect became considerably diluted. Ruefully, Grace Greenwood (Sara Jane Clarke), in a letter dated 4 November 1848, complained that her "quiet corner of the world," New Brighton, Pennsylvania, was being shaken and thrown about "by that quadrennial political earthquake," the presidential campaign. Whether Whig, Democrat, or Free Soiler, meetings were held and songs persistently sung. However, the occasions were "nothing like the free-and-easy musical democracy of the Tippecanoe times! That dispensation of doggerel has passed away forever."[72]

Yet political partisans persisted in advancing their cause musically. One fascinating anecdote was related to the *Pittsburgh Press* on 11 July 1895 concerning the Buchanan presidential campaign of 1856. William Hamilton said that he and Stephen Foster had joined a Democratic campaign glee club to boost their candidate. The club had a bodyguard of fifty to one hundred men, who marched the streets with the glee club as it sang, alone or with other choruses, songs in favor of Buchanan. Sometimes they got into fights with opponents. Sometimes they were involved in ridiculous situations.

On our way home from one of these trips to East Liberty, we stopped at a residence this side of the forks of the road, Lawrenceville, to serenade a family with which some of us were acquainted. We sang a Foster song on this occasion, and I had the solo part. Some stranger joined the crowd and persisted in singing the solo part with me, although he was not familiar with it. He annoyed me, and I motioned to a member of the body guard to tell him to sing only the chorus. The guardsman misunderstood me . . . and promptly gave him a blow on the left ear, knocking him down.

The blow was a signal for universal fighting to begin. He, Foster, and the glee club rushed off, leaving the fisticuffs to the bodyguards.[73]

Political enemies set aside their antagonisms on one day of the year, the Fourth of July. Farmers and other country people converged on the nearest town to take part in whatever ceremonies were planned. North, south, east, and west, the usual way to celebrate the day was with military companies, firemen, town societies, distinguished citizens, Revolutionary War veterans, and bands parading to a church, town hall, or outdoor platform. Here the Declaration of Independence was read, orations given, odes to liberty declaimed, and patriotic songs performed. To see individuals shooting off handguns and rifles throughout the day was not at all unusual, especially in the areas well away from the Atlantic seaboard. Next came a public dinner, with numerous toasts and more music from instrumentalists, soloists, and choruses. As often as not, the men became drunk by the hour of their return home and the songs they sang were of a more rollicking nature. It was only after all of these activities had taken place that the national anniversary was thought to have been properly observed.[74] At one celebration, that held at the Concord battle monument in 1837, one year after the monument's dedication, singers, including Henry Thoreau, sang Emerson's hymn "Here once the embattled farmers stood,/And fired the shot heard round the world," to the tune of "Old Hundred."[75]

Since brawls and other loud, violent public disorders often broke out, the more staid citizens tried to introduce gentler ways of celebrating the holiday. On one Fourth of July, a midwestern town planned on bringing together all the Sunday school children and their parents "from far and near, to hear addresses, sing songs, and enjoy a rustic feast . . . but the opposition of the powder party was so bitter that very little was gained in the way of peace." Another year, the same town tried sending its celebrators off on a two-boat excursion and picnic. This effort seems to have gone over better, though the people in the second boat grew quite boisterous, with their loud talk, shouting, and lusty singing. An unrepentant person from the second boat said to

204   one from the first boat: "I wish you had been near us, that you might have
had the benefit of ours! The ladies sang 'Bonnie Doon,' and everything; and
'I see them on their winding way.'"[76]

Wagon trains on the western plains stopped to celebrate the Fourth. On
one occasion, a train camped nine miles out of Fort Laramie, broke out some
bottles of liquor, heard speeches, and sang songs accompanied by a fiddle, a
flute, and a drum made out of the skin of a dog. On another occasion, a train
stopped on the banks of the Green River, where a unit of the Sixth Ohio
Cavalry had also stopped. "Hail Columbia" was sung after a patriotic speech
by a Judge Drane. After this, whoever had an instrument was asked to strike
up some music. Later, the playing of football and chess began, while the
makeshift band played for the dances. Owing to the scarcity of women, some
men tied handkerchiefs around their arms and acted as "women partners."
In the evening, stories were told, followed by everybody singing "some parting
songs," such as "Home, Sweet Home." After the singing, all retired to rest.[77]

Further west, in Los Angeles, the Independence Day of 1853 kindled the
patriotic ardor of its American, French, and Mexican inhabitants, and the
three groups demonstrated their national loyalties, each after its own frenzied
fashion:

> The long dining table was kept going every hour night and day [the
> fourth and fifth of July]; the musicians and dancers relieved each
> other; those not engaged in eating or dancing were engaged in toast-
> ing, responding to toasts, speech-making or singing patriotic songs.
> A crowd of Americans roared "Hail Columbia," another crowd the
> "Star-Spangled Banner" and "Yankee Doodle," a knot of Frenchmen
> made night melodious with the soul inspiring "Marseillaise," while
> the patriotic Mexicans kept up the "Ponchada."[78]

On the other side of the continent, in New England, the celebration was
at the other extreme—sober, serious, and replete with moral exhortation. A
young woman working in the Lowell mills sent a letter in August 1844 to a
friend, saying:

> By the way, I almost forgot to tell you that we had a "Fourth of
> July" in Lowell, and a nice one it was, too. The Temperance celebra-
> tion was the chief dish in the entertainment. . . . In the evening we
> had the Hutchinsons, from our own Granite State, who discoursed
> sweet music *so sweetly*. They have become great favorites with the
> public. It is not on account of their fine voices only, but their pleas-
> ant modest manners—the perfect sense of propriety which they ex-

hibit in all their demeanor; and I think they are not less popular *here* because they sing the wrongs of the slave, and the praises of cold water.[79]

Without doubt, sweetness was not characteristic of most of the music heard on Independence Day. The sour sounds that James Fenimore Cooper listened to at a celebration in a New York town were undoubtedly more typical. As he gave ear to the instrumentalists, he decided that instrumental music was the weakest side of American civilization. The instruments were poor, the players musically illiterate, and no semblance of harmony or ensemble emerged from the performance. "Gentlemen" from the city and visitors from Europe found the proceedings hilarious and ludicrous, said Cooper.[80]

Music was also important to Christmas and New Year's Day observances. In New England, the gaiety tended to remain subdued. For example, Mrs. Alcott noted in her journal that in the days just before Christmas 1843, their Massachusetts neighborhood had experienced a series of severe snowstorms. December had remained cheerless. At the Alcotts' Fruitlands home, the holiday was passed quietly. She and Mr. Alcott played with the children, the children exchanged little gifts, and everyone sang a few songs—that was all. More than bitter weather inhibited the merrymaking. Harriet Beecher Stowe pointed out that celebrating Christmas was not in the tradition of New England's meetinghouse people, as it was with Episcopalians. To give one's self up to a week's amusement, from Christmas to New Year's, smacked of popery and showed irreverence toward God. Ministers warned those parishioners who were attracted to "these seductive festivities" to beware.[81]

New Year's Eve and Day, too, had nothing of exuberant merrymaking connected with them. New Englanders observed them tranquilly, without making a fuss. The women of Edgefield, Connecticut, prepared food for a shared New Year's Eve meal at the parish house. The minister's wife "delighted her guests with some of her rich songs, and music on the piano, and once the whole of the company sung together the sweet music of 'Auld Lang Syne.'" A prayer was heard; by 10 P.M. the old folks had gone; by 11 P.M. the young people had left for home.[82] That was all.

In the country outside New England, stricter sects, such as the Presbyterians, also were circumspect about the manner of their Christmas celebration. Virginia's Presbyterians permitted no dancing but did allow young people to visit and stay overnight at the homes of friends. As for music, what instrumentalists there were played accompaniments for the singers, who aired sacred songs, somber ballads like those in Moore's National Airs, and a lighthearted ditty or two, such as "Says the blackbird to the crow,/'What makes white folks hate us so?'" and "Whistle, daughter! Whistle!"[83]

Increasingly, after 1840, people rebelled against Presbyterian strictures. On 28 January 1847 D. F. Jamison, a member of the South Carolina State Legislature, wrote to a friend that William Simms had spent Christmas with him:

> To compensate for years of puritanical affectation, and eschewing of the devil and all his works, we frolicked throughout the holidays— had pleasant dancing parties every night for a week, to the great horror of Hanscombe Legare [a Presbyterian minister], who, on the successive Sundays anathematized all fiddles, triangles, and tamarinds (I believe that is the way to spell a certain instrument of music), that were ever invented and denounced all skipping turns or dancing as inventions of the evil one. But as every man, woman, and child of his congregation or audience were implicated more or less in the offense, his logic went unheeded, and his discourses were more amusing than edifying.[84]

Southern non-Presbyterian plantation owners tended to give elaborate and gay Christmas dinners, to which many guests were invited. After dinner came games, singing, and country dances, often with the Virginia reel at the close. Still more unconstrained celebration was found in the mining towns of California, where the restrictions that guided the eastern seaboard were not in effect. The India Bar miners in 1852 staged a "saturnalia" in the Humboldt barroom on Christmas Eve. A huge champagne supper began at 9 P.M. with countless toasts and songs. Two fiddlers then played for dancing. Liquor flowed freely and encouraged greater jollity. The festivities went on day after day. "On New Year's Day, when there was a grand dinner at Rich Bar, the excitement broke out, if possible, worse than ever."[85]

More than any other Americans, the African Americans on Southern plantations looked forward to the end of December, because it was the only time of the year when they were given a holiday extending longer than a day, usually over three or more days. Slaves would come to the master's mansion to be given a small drink of sweetened whiskey. Often, the master asked for entertainment on Christmas afternoon. Singing and dancing performances took place. Fiddlers requisitioned by the master produced tunes such as "Fisher's Hornpipe," "The Devil's Dream," and "Black-Eyed Susan" for the dancing. Those slaves born in Africa would sing their native songs to him, his family, and guests, tell stories and demonstrate the customs of Africa, and put on a dance show. When dismissed, each slave was given a present.

Some blacks would then get up their own parties, which would continue until they had to return to the fields. Others turned to making a little extra

money by manufacturing such items as brooms, baskets, mats, or ax handles. **207**
Still others, who were strict Methodists or Baptists, would spend their time at
revival meetings. More than a few chose simply to loaf and enjoy the luxury
of doing nothing at all.[86]

Metta Victor has given a detailed description of how blacks on one
Louisiana plantation spent the Christmas holidays. From this and other descriptions of the festivities attending the Christmas and New Year's holidays,
it would appear that the religious side of the celebration was frequently put
to one side. On Christmas Eve, Victor wrote, a frolic took place. An elderly
fiddler perched on a box in a large shed to play for the others, who arrived
dressed in their best clothing. Among them were blacks from other plantations. One dancer hurried up the fiddler with "Hi! Hi!" and a chorus of voices
shouted "Yah! Yah! Yah!" Somebody sang:

> De ladies in de parlour
> > Hey come a rollin' down—
> A drinkin' tea and coffee;
> > Good morning ladies all.

> De gemmen in de kitchen,
> > Hey come a rollin' down—
> A drinkin' brandy toddy;
> > Good morning ladies all.

The music went faster and faster, until the exhausted dancers had to pause.
Food and drink were served. A few dancers then tried the steps of the
"French-four, half-cotillion, and some of those regular dances which they had
copied" from the white balls, where they had acted as attendants.[87]

On Christmas morning the fiddler awakened everyone by marching

up and down the negro-quarters, playing and singing vociferously:

> Old Zip Coon, berry fine feller,
> Plays on de banjo, coon in de holler.

One of the awakened blacks came out with a banjo and proceeded to have a
playing contest with the fiddler. Later that day, the slaves were granted a
barbecue. A band made up of a fiddle, two banjos, a tambourine, a tin pan,
and a kettledrum made music that was "full of golden rhythm and delicious
sensibility." It "moved the African blood to responsive beats; it was simple and
natural as their own feelings, and as gay."[88]

208    During the rest of Christmas week, a long table was set up and everyone dined together. On a typical festive day, as the food was placed on the table, the fiddler would strike up a tune. Those standing around would join hands and utter "a wild chant, half song and half recitative, which it is almost impossible to put into words":

By de dark lagoon (*recitative*)

Huah! Huah! Huah! (*chorus*)

By de cane-brake's track (*recitative*)

Huah! Huah! Huah! (*chorus*)

By de cypress swamp (*recitative*)

Huah! Huah! Huah! (*chorus*)

|                 |                                      |
|-----------------|--------------------------------------|
| *First voice:*  | De darkness sleeps— (*tenor solo*)   |
| *Second voice:* | De winds make moan— (*bass solo*)    |
| *Third voice:*  | De waters dream— (*soprano solo*)    |
| *Fourth voice:* | De stars keep watch. (*alto solo*)   |
|                 | Hark! Hark! (*staccato chorus*)      |

The fiddler now played a plaintive tune, imitating "a woman's song":

|                 |                              |
|-----------------|------------------------------|
| *First voice:*  | My wife is dar, ober dar!    |
| *Second voice:* | My mother is dar, ober dar!  |
| *Third voice:*  | My sister is dar, ober dar!  |
| *Fourth voice:* | My true love is dar, ober dar! |
|                 | Hark! Hark!                  |

Next, the fiddler played a low but joyous strain, "which dies away on the strings":

By de dark lagoon—

By de cane-brake's track—

By de cypress swamp—

Huah! Huah! Huah!

Huah! Huah! Huah!

Huah! Huah! Huah!

The final chorus "was prolonged until it seemed to melt into the still air. The singers then all shook hands, and the feast began"—pork, potatoes, and hoecake.[89]

Caroline Gilman recalled similar incidents, entirely secular in nature, that took place on her Ashley River plantation, in South Carolina. She also added a thorough description of a courting dance between a woman, who enticed and backed away from suitors in a shuffling walk, and vigorously dancing men, who alternately whirled about and pleaded their cause—certainly not an appropriate activity for Christmas. Solomon Northup also observed a similar courting dance performed on Christmas Eve. Finally, Frederick Douglass also commented on the Christmas to New Year's Day festivities, with their fiddling, dancing, and "jubilee beating" done by a "juba beater." This performer

> improvised as he beat the instrument, marking the words as he sang so as to have them fall pat with the movement of his hands. Once in a while among a mass of nonsense and wild frolic, a sharp hit was given to the manners of slave holders. Take the following for example:

> We raise de wheat,
> Dey gib us de corn;
> We bake de bread,
> Dey gib us de crust.[90]

As can be seen, a holiday for these blacks was less a holy day set aside for special religious ceremonies and more a day when they were released from work and allowed some measure of freedom to do as they wished.

CHAPTER 7

# Education and Religion

N OT ALL BOYS AND GIRLS IN ANTEBELLUM AMERICA
went to school, and many attended only for a short while.
Because farm children had to help with a variety of tasks,
school attendance was suspended for prolonged periods. The young children
toiling in the burgeoning mills and factories of the new Industrial Age had no
moments or energy left over for schooling. To write their names was an
achievement. The young of pioneering families living far from settlements
had to get along as best they could with a mother who occasionally gave some
instruction. And education for slaves was strictly forbidden.

This said, the number of children from all walks of life who attended
school in the United States was high, especially when compared with Europe,
where to be poor was to be ignored or exploited, and where ignorance was a
tool for keeping the lower class in a submissive state. The citizens of the
United States would have none of Europe's rigid class system and regarded
education for all in a positive light. American educators dedicated themselves
to improving young minds not only mentally but also morally, and to developing skills useful in the workplace and home. Religious leaders called on
young and old to make a commitment to the rules of right conduct. All
schooling was aimed at abetting "honest" learning of this sort. All faiths tried
through education to promote unwavering devotion to God and to prepare
mortals for a promised life after death. Music had importance because it was
seen as promoting the goals of educators and the religious. The advancement
of aesthetics entered the equation only incidentally.

The usefulness of music making in school and in religious observances
was attested to again and again in the antebellum period. To this purpose,
songs, hymns, and instrumental pieces adapted to juvenile abilities and understanding and to the sensibilities and limited musical powers of most

Americans grew increasingly available. The sung texts for school and religious occasions emphasized what was inspirational, wholesome, and virtu-
ous. A premium was placed on lucid melodies that were likely to attract and
hold interest. It was hoped that whatever instrumental sounds were added
would jingle pleasantly on the ear. Whether a voice or instrument proved
inadequate when judged by purely musical standards was beside the point, so
long as a contribution was made toward realizing the objectives of teachers
and preachers.

## Music at School

The private academies for young women, for the most part, did retain
voice and piano teachers to cultivate in their pupils the musical accomplishments necessary for entry into polite society. On the other hand, public
schools open to all boys and girls, if they taught music at all, did so through
their regular teachers, most of whom had no, or scarcely any, musical background. Attempts were made to correct the musical shortcomings of teachers. In New England, annual musical conventions of a couple of weeks' du-
ration for those in need of training did gather strength in the 1830s, and the
introduction of music into the public school curriculum got a real start in the
1840s. It did not follow, however, that decently trained musicians would
invariably conduct the class lessons in music.

Also during these decades, teachers fanned out from New England to
staff public classrooms throughout the country. Few of them were truly
versed in music, though many did sing or attempt to play an instrument. J. L.
McConnel once described a schoolmaster, prepared to teach general subjects,
who had gone forth from New England with his flute in his pocket, which he
had taught himself to play. He was soon plying his trade in a village to the
west of New England. In leisure moments, he liked to sit at the door with boys
and girls gathered around him. Out would come the flute, and from it he
would draw "strains of concentrated mournfulness." He produced "The Mistletoe Bough" and "Barbara Allen" with such dismal tones they almost induced despair in his hearers. McConnell observed:

> He was not a scientific musician, then—fortunately for his useful-
> ness—because thorough musicians are generally "good-for-nothing"
> else. But music was not a science among the pioneers though the
> undertone of melancholy feeling, to which all sweet sounds appeal,
> was as easily reached in them as in any other people. Their wants in
> this, as in other things, were very easily satisfied—they were suscep-
> tible of pleasure from anything which was in the least commend-

able: and not feeling obliged by any captious canon, to condemn
nine true notes, because of the tenth false one, they allowed themselves to enjoy the best music they could get, without thinking of
the damage done their musical and critical reputation.[1]

Apparently this Yankee schoolmaster made no attempt to teach music in the
classroom itself.

To institute musical instruction in the schools of the hinterlands was far
more difficult than in those of the Atlantic seaboard. In *Zury*, an 1887 novel
that its author, Joseph Kirkland, affirms to be true to western life, Anne
Sparrow, a teacher from Boston, comes to instruct the boys and girls of
Spring Valley, Illinois. With her arrives the novel idea of introducing music
into the classroom. Regrettably, the students balk at the thought of singing.
On the first morning, she begins by asking her students what hymns they
know, but the answer is complete silence. She asks if they know "When Thee
I seek protecting power." Again silence. She suggests they join her anyway in
singing it and commences the first verse. No one joins in. The young ones
confer among themselves and reveal that they know "When I can read my
title clear." Immediately, she starts singing it, but she is alone. Asked why they
have not sung, the students reply that it was not the right tune. Surely, she
says, they all know "Old Hundred," and sings it to the words "From all that
dwell below the skies"—again alone. The text is different from theirs, the
students say. She sings the text they know; no one joins in. She begs them to
sing and gets the reply,

> "This ain't no singin'-scule. We didn't come h'yer t'learn t'sing. . . .
> Better go back whar ye come from."
> "I can't, now. I *must* keep on trying here. Now, if there are any
> of you who are willing to stand by me—like young ladies and gentle-
> men—please all sing with me this time."

One or two voices, barely audible, tentatively try the tune. Eventually, the ten
o'clock recess arrives, and she has them march out of the classroom as she
rhythmically claps her hands and commences "Hail Columbia." For the first
time, some students clap their hands with hers and parade out singing. She
has made a beginning in beating down their reserve.[2]

The parents are the next obstacle. Anne Sparrow arranges to hold a
school "exhibition" for the grown-ups, with songs, recitations, and the putting on of a skit. The curtain opens to no applause. Students sing "The Star-
Spangled Banner" with no reaction from the audience. Anne sings "The
Mellow Horn"; again, nothing. Confused, she asks a local friend what the

matter is and learns that the residents of Spring Valley know nothing about applauding. The friend then goes before the audience and teaches it to applaud. The people so love clapping that it proves difficult to silence them. Thus, "when Anne came on and sang 'The Mistletoe Bough,' the delight was so overwhelming that all almost forgot to stop."[3]

By the 1850s, school exhibitions featuring music were becoming prevalent in towns and villages outside New England. In June 1852 a reporter's "Notes of a Short Tour Westward" appeared in *Dwight's Journal of Music:*

> On the evening of my arrival in Rochester [N.Y.], Catharine Hayes gave a concert in the really fine hall, which is an honor to the city. I did not attend, but heard that the audience was very small. This was not true of another concert the next evening at the same place, at which two hundred and fifty sweet little creatures, from the girls' schools of the city, gave a selection of songs and duets. The pieces were such as usually form the staple on such occasions; popular airs adapted to children's (childish?) poetry. The "Spider and the Fly," "Marseilles Hymn," "Home, sweet Home," and such like common airs were sung, and were really sung exceedingly well, and greatly to the credit of their teacher.[4]

The sophisticated artistry of Catharine Hayes, a talented vocalist, failed to attract; the children did attract. Obviously, aesthetic considerations, which allowed only artistic music conforming to a refined standard to be taught and presented, failed to have an influence. Instead, popular songs arranged to accommodate young capacities and to please parents constituted the favored repertoire. The tunes sung by the children had already demonstrated their ability to hold general interest. Their texts, if altered, were directed toward promoting the well-being of mind and spirit. What is more, the writer liked what he heard and enjoyed the presentation without worrying about imperfections in the singing.

A more censorious correspondent wrote to *Dwight's Journal of Music* two years later, saying that he had attended "a common school exhibition" in Erie, Pennsylvania, on 9 February 1854. Girls from eight to fourteen years of age had appeared, performing the popular songs of the day. "Now this choir is not mentioned as being worse than others," he said; "it is just what I have found from Boston to the Mississippi. All sing the same sort of tunes; all sing them just alike," which is to say, with deficiencies.[5] He obviously was displeased that they did not embrace a "higher" art and achieve a better musical preparation. Equally obvious, those teaching the tunes, singing them, and listening to them did not share his values and concerns.

214     Some idea of what a typical public event involving children was like may be gained from the novel *Miss Gilbert's Career* (1860), in which the author, J. G. Holland, has recreated a school exhibition in a New England village during the 1830s. A temporary stage is erected in the meetinghouse, and on it sit an elderly bass violist and a young flautist—both of them barely competent players. Little boys and girls march from the schoolhouse to the church. The two instrumentalists are supposed to play for the procession but somehow get confused and remain silent. Adult speeches follow. Next, the children sing songs; this time the instrumentalists accompany them. The students also recite poetry in concert and go through the multiplication table to the tune of "Yankee Doodle." Ten years later, the village has grown, the school has grown, and a band has been added to the proceedings, which otherwise has not changed.[6]

Antebellum South Carolina was perhaps even looser than New England in what it thought fitting for children to sing. Rosser Taylor, writing about these early times, says that school commencements regularly treated the public to music. Furthermore, some popular numbers among the youngsters were "O Sing Once More That Melody," "Will You Love Me Then as Now," "Yes, I Have Dared to Love Thee," and "You Cannot Doubt My Love." These "ardent and romantic melodies enjoyed a great vogue among young people," he wrote. Taylor is evidently speaking only of the most settled areas of the state, however, for he adds that echoing "through the backwoods to the accompaniment of banjo and fiddle" were drinking songs and traditional ballads such as "The House Carpenter" and "Sweet William." In addition, "for solemn and worshipful moods, the doleful hymn brought solace to those in the humble walks of life."[7]

Like their public counterparts, the private academies also put on exhibitions, especially around Thanksgiving, Christmas, and the end of the academic year. Along with choral singing, individual students were usually singled out to execute piano solos or vocal pieces calling for some performing skill. This was particularly true for girls' academies, where students had the privilege of individual musical instruction from qualified teachers. There were also instances cited of young people engaging in benevolent musical deeds sponsored by their school. For example, Eliza Ripley writes that when an adolescent girl, in 1847, she left her New Orleans home to attend a girl's seminary in New York City. The school customarily sent out its students to entertain the elderly women of the Church Sewing Society. She states with tongue in cheek:

> I was the star performer. . . . My overture of "La Dame Blanche"
> was quite a masterpiece, but my "Battle of Prague" was simply stun-

ning. The "advance," the "rattle of musketry," the "beating of
drums" . . . I could render with such force that the dear, busy ladies
almost jumped from their seats. There were two Kentucky girls with
fine voices, also invited to entertain the guests. Alas! Our fun came
to an end. On one occasion, when I ended the "Battle of Prague"
with a terrific bang, there was an awful moment of silence, when
one of the ladies sneezed with such unexpected force that her false
teeth careered clear across the room! . . . Nothing was said to us of
the unfortunate contretemps, but the musical programs were discon-
tinued.[8]

Colleges were less given to engaging their students in musical exercises.
Their commencements always made room for singing, however, and if possible, performance by an instrumental ensemble. Then, as now, the graduating
class would have a class hymn to render, with the words commemorating the
occasion and set most often to an extant melody. The remaining music was
always of a solemn nature. At the 1843 commencement of Hampden-Sidney
College, in Virginia, a commendably prepared choir sang, but no band was
heard, because one did not yet exist. Appropriate sacred music graced the
ceremony, including such celebrated old anthems as

> Awake! Awake! Put on they strength, O Zion!
>     Put on thy beautiful garments.

and

> How beautiful upon the mountains
> Are the feet of him that publisheth salvation,
> That saith unto Zion
>     "Thy God reigneth!"[9]

Male students, when free of official control, demonstrated an opposite
side of college life. Charles Francis Adams, while attending Harvard College,
wrote an entry into his diary on 13 May 1824 of a meeting "at Shaefe's" for
a festive evening, with him and nine students of his Lyceum Club present.
First, they played whist. Then champagne was opened, one bottle for each.
The room got noisy and rough play occurred. An argument began about who
would pay for the broken glasses. When everybody calmed down, "we formed
a circle around the large table where we sung many songs, and finished the
wine. The rest of the scene was all riot." Adams drank one and a half bottles
of wine, got sick, and staggered to his bed at 1 A.M.[10]

The establishment of Sunday schools began in the United States about the turn of the century. With them came a pioneering effort to write music for children's use. Fifty years later, music written expressly for the young was flooding into the Sunday schools and affecting importantly the educational lives of juveniles.

Just before the turn of the century there were schools held on Sundays designed to keep children off the streets and teach them to read, using pages from the Bible. A different sort of evangelical Sunday school soon evolved whose predominant purpose was to transmit religious enlightenment. It put stress on the teachings and authority of the Scriptures and the achievement of salvation through personal faith. The commitment to teaching reading was minimized. The few men and many women voluntarily staffing these schools tried to fill their charges with a zealous enthusiasm for Christian conduct. Vocal music was an important means toward achieving this end. At first, the movement's growth was limited. Writing about the New England of around 1818, Harriet Beecher Stowe said that scarcely any Sunday schools existed and hymns for the young were unknown. Children were expected to live in an adult world where children's books and little sacred songs were irrelevant.[11]

Nevertheless, in 1817 the American Sunday School Union had been formed among the various Protestant denominations of the east. Its first mission was to situate Sunday schools without delay in the early towns and villages along the Mississippi. The Union took this action to counteract what it saw as the incipient lawlessness in frontier life. This undertaking swiftly met with extensive backing and substantial realization. The movement then expanded swiftly in the second and third decades of the nineteenth century, spreading to all religious denominations in all parts of the United States. By the end of the 1830s the Sunday school was a familiar element in almost all American children's lives.[12]

Proselytizing for young recruits became ceaseless. Typical was the 1850s advertising card of St. Louis's Benton Street Mission Sunday School, which invited new members to join because "it teaches the young people to sing the beautiful songs of Zion." Likewise, the advertising card of Boston's Davenport Sunday School read: "We have a pleasant school room; we learn to sing beautiful hymns."[13]

Adult and young African Americans had thronged to the earliest form of the Sunday school, for it opened the door not only to religion but also to reading and writing. When the Sunday schools began to play down reading and writing, however, black membership dropped. It dropped even more when racial prejudice and slave uprisings in the South resulted in shutting the door first on the adults and next on the children. Black-run Sunday schools that emphasized singing did rise to serve the excluded boys and girls, in the 1820s and 1830s. These were sponsored by black churches. Unfortunately, they accommodated mostly free African Americans, who remained small in number.[14] Nevertheless, this beginning would eventually lead to the establishment of African American churches throughout the nation as vital components of black life—religious, social, cultural, educational, and musical.

As one might expect, popular song tunes were readily available if anyone wanted to divert them to Sunday school use, and were of proven attractiveness if juvenile minds were to be engaged. Therefore, they supplied quite a few of the enticing melodies that effectively put across the religious texts. This, of course, upset the circumspect ministers and teachers who wished to decontaminate music intended for Sunday schools of its tainted secular elements. Sacred music reformers immediately took up the cudgels against what they defined as immoral sounds. One of these, Thomas Hastings, launched vociferous objections assailing the practice. In the *Musical Review and Choral Advocate* of May 1853, he criticized a Sunday school superintendent who had given minstrel music to a lady to use with her one hundred tender-aged students. She took issue with him and protested. "The children will never know it," he replied. Instead of accepting his word, she turned to the children, sang a line or two of one of the superintendent's Sunday school "songs" and asked, "Children, have you ever heard anything like that before?" They all shouted back, "Old folks at home! Old folks at home!," which she felt proved her point. Hastings ruefully admitted that it was a practice of long standing to supply the tunes of "merry dances, street ballads, bacchanalian songs, and negro melodies" for children to sing and learn corruption.[15]

Moves were made to get away from the use of popular tunes, especially in the 1850s, but change was sometimes illusory. As an example of one such action, the Reverend A. D. Merrill of Cambridge, Massachusetts, put into circulation in 1851 *The Sunday School Melodist,* "a collection of hymns and tunes specially designed for the use of Sabbath Schools and Juvenile Choirs." It is instructive to examine this collection closely, since it conforms to a pattern discernible in most tune books intended for use in Sunday schools that were issued by reformers. In his preface, Merrill assured anyone weighing the book's appropriateness that preachers in the Boston area had met to consider the publication, found it morally beneficial, and then had passed a resolution recommending its adoption. The melodies, he said, were generally original and so simple as to be easily learned by rote. Furthermore, the singing of the hymns would add "greatly to the interests of both teachers and children" and offer "strong inducements to other children to come in, who would not feel the force of higher motives."[16]

As with most such volumes, the majority of the melodies plod along at a slow pace until their final rest at the last cadence. Harmony remains clumsy though simple. Half notes and quarter notes maintain an unvaryingly tedious rhythm from beginning to end. The supposed attractions of the settings elude the listener. Some melodies are more attractive than most, like that to the hymn "Now that my journey's just begun," which sounds like a rollicking folk song in 6/8 time, and that for "I'm but a stranger here, Heaven is my home," which bounces along like a sprightly children's play song. Others could easily have substituted a sentimental ballad text, like the music for "Spared to another spring, We raise our grateful songs." Amazingly enough, one or two tilt toward the minstrel tunes that supposedly were anathema. For example, "Hark! The Sabbath bells are ringing" goes to a ditty that is little different from that to "Shinbone Alley" (also rearranged by Charles Horn and supplied with a sentimental text by George Morris as "Near the Lake Where Droop'd the Willow").[17]

The texts are overly sanctimonious, coming from adults busily constructing fantasies on how children think and behave:

> We are little children
> > Weak and apt to stray;
> Saviour, guide and keep us
> > In the heavenly way.

and admonishing them to do the right thing:

> O that it were my chief delight
> > To do the things I ought!
> Then let me try with all my might,
> > To mind what I am taught.

> Wherever I am told to go,
> > I'll cheerfully obey;
> Nor will I mind it much, although
> > I leave a pretty play.[18]

William Bradbury, Lowell Mason, Thomas Hastings, and George Root, all knowledgeable musicians, had pioneered the effort for sacred music reform. Bradbury, assisted by Hastings, had issued his first music book, the carefully thought-out *The Young Choir* (1841), to correct the profanation of the sacred. But none of these musicians could completely stem the populace's penchant for sounds akin to the secular music it loved. Indeed, Root had a foot in both camps, since he was also a songwriter responsible for some of the most popular secular songs of the 1850s and 1860s. Whatever the hymns intended expressly for the young, they came from well-meaning musicians who could not cancel out the secular sounds of sentimental and traditional ballads, of dance songs and minstrel tunes.

Inevitably, the excessive sentiment of popular songs carried over to psalmody. Honeyed hymns were offered children like musical sweets. Collections of these hymns, aimed at the juvenile market, proliferated. Many of their authors had the half-formed taste that characterized the multitudes, although they were sincerely convinced they aimed at a higher standard. Hundreds of thousands of copies were sold and took over the Sunday school classes entirely. When musical instruction was introduced into the public schools and instruction books were found to be lacking, the hymns intended for Sunday schools moved in to fill the void, for they were the only children's songs on offer. Their usefulness was maximized because their musical simplicity was telling, their idiom was familiar, and their texts sympathetic to contemporary values, however crude the first, trite the second, and maudlin the third seem today.

## White Church Services and Prayer Meetings

At the turn of the century, the breadth of mind discernable in the more tolerant, usually urban, churches was slow in arriving in the rural churches. Strict observance was still the rule, sometimes for an entire community. We find, for example, that in 1800 Benjamin Clough of Bluehill, Maine, was being accused of "breaking the Sabbath both by 'singing a dance tune' and by buying sugar and tea on that day; second, of a breach of truth; and, third, of 'speaking reproachfully of church members.'" When he responded in angry defiance that he could "glorify God in a dancing tune as well as by any other," the "Brethren" excommunicated him.[19]

Sometimes the rigidity involved individuals, who had to be circumvented in order to allow a bit of liberality to enter the service. In another Maine village, some twenty-five years after the Bluehill incident, an influential Major Murray opposed the introduction of the bass viol into the service as an aid to the singing, despite his having no ear for music and being unable to "tell the filing of a saw from a jewsharp." When the instrument first entered the church on Sunday and after it had accompanied the first hymn, "he took his hat and marched out of the meeting-house," because of the profanation.

220   Those in favor of the instrument's entrance would not give in. For the next few Sundays, the instrument was brought in secretly and played upon without the major detecting its presence. He learned of this subterfuge and, on a Sunday, listened carefully, thought he heard the bass viol, and marched out. Much to his embarrassment, he discovered that, on this one Sunday, a bass singer had imitated the instrument's sound. He was so mortified that he gave up his opposition and allowed the bass viol to return.[20]

Concerning one widespread activity, no opposition arose—the singing of hymns going to and from the meetinghouse. Elizabeth Oakes Smith once described how farming people walked on Sundays to and from the church she attended in Lewiston, Maine. She herself had to walk a two-mile distance from her grandparent's farm.

> Maids and youths and dependents of all ranks, took their way
> across the fields, through the fields, through the woods and pas-
> tures, and over the rustic bridge in the same direction. The young
> maids carried a pair of white stockings and slippers in their hands,
> which left their white, shapely feet to gleam through the green
> grass; arriving at the brook, the youths proceeded onward while the
> girls washed their feet and donned their slippers. All the way they
> sang in concert pious hymns, which were responded to by similar
> groups from other byways all tending in the same direction.[21]

During the antebellum period, the lustiest singers were the Methodists, Presbyterians, and Baptists. Few of their churches then had separate choirs, nor were organs plentiful. The entire congregation was accustomed to getting up to sing without the help of instruments or trained vocalists, which it did enthusiastically and sincerely. Onlookers were struck by the fact that the churchgoers "sang with all their might, and all their soul, and all their strength . . . [and] all their heart." In a typical description of a Sunday service, Sallie Rochester Ford said of a Presbyterian church in Kentucky, "The minister read a hymn and all the congregation joined in singing. There was no organ, no choir; all sung with the spirit, making melody with their hearts, and with their voices praising God."[22]

In the pioneer settlements to the west, no choice was given the worshipers. They had to get along without choir or organ and were fortunate if one or two singers were more knowledgeable than the rest and could keep them on the musical track. Francis Grierson states that his parents were new settlers in Illinois and he but a boy when, on Sundays, they would take him to the local log-house church. Here the Methodist minister would start off by calling for an old hymn, such as "In the Christian's home in glory/There remains a land of rest." Worshipers' faces would immediately brighten at the prospect of singing. One man, Silas Jordan, then tried to lead the congregational singing, although his voice was high and shrill and not at all pleasing. Two other people, Uriah Busby and Kezia Jordan, ameliorated the harshness with their melodious and expressive voices. Kezia Jordan's voice in particular moved Grierson's mother deeply during the singing, especially when the hymn was "There remains a land of rest."[23]

The penniless white settlers of Missouri also depended on one or more voices to lead the congregation in the singing. At one Missouri Sunday service in the 1840s, the Rev. Martin Louder gave a two-hour sermon, then called out, "Brother Creek, you don't seem to be doin' much of ennything, suppose you raise a tune!" Creek hawked and spit, then commenced the melody with quavering voice. Rev. Louder stopped him, saying, "'Pears to me, Brother Creek, you hain't got the right miter." Creek though about it and replied, "I'm confident she'll come out all right!" and tried singing again:

> When I was a mourner just like you,
>   Washed in the blood of the Lamb,
> I fasted and prayed till I got through,
>   Washed in the blood of the Lamb.

Evidently, it did "come out all right" on the second try. Men and women joined in, and quickly "the enthusiasm of the assembly was a white heat, and the shouting, with the loud 'Amen,' 'God, save the sinner,' 'Sing it, brother, sing it,' made the welkin ring."[24]

For a few, almost always more sophisticated witnesses of these services, the singing was an affliction to be endured. Ellen Rollins recalled the meeting-house services in the New England village of her childhood, at the beginning of the nineteenth century. She mentioned the nasal twang and bodily contortions that went with the music, but added that the worshipers were nevertheless "rich in faith and divine presence." They "might not have been good singers, but they were most devout choral worshippers of the Lord on the Lord's Day." Augustus Longstreet, of Georgia, was less magnanimous about the singing he heard in village and country churches. He said it resembled the caterwauling "with which a party of cats are wont to vex the dull ear of night, and the acute sensibilities of some sleepless victim." Startled and shocked by the sound, he could not compose himself for the solemnity of the service.[25]

Longstreet, ever hard to please and critical of his country brethren, mentioned an unpolished rustic, Ned Bruce, who visited Savannah for three days and, on a Sunday, attended a morning service. The minister invited the

222 entire congregation to sing and gave out the first lines of the hymn. After Ned joined in with one of the loudest, hoarsest, and most discordant voices ever heard in the church, the preacher commented, "I would observe that there are some persons who have not the gift of singing; such, of course, are not expected to sing." This shut Ned up.[26]

On more than one occasion the person responsible for giving out the first lines of the hymn went astray. George Templeton Strong, of New York, was not disposed to accept the informality of country worship. He was attending a service out on Long Island in July 1840 when the minister announced the hymn to be sung. At the announcement, the leader of the singing arose, "gave the first two lines, as of old, with the mellow tones of his nasal organ; and then stopped short, shut his book, and bolted out at the top of his lungs, 'There,' says he, 'I knowed I couldn't sing; I told you so afore I come. I 'as got a hoarse cold.' And down he sat."[27]

During the earliest years of the nineteenth century, New Englanders, too, were apt to sing quite sturdily, if at times imperfectly. In the Beverly, Massachusetts, of her childhood, Lucy Larcom says, the singing of the old hymns galvanized all the churchgoers, including herself: "How the meeting-house rafters used to ring to ['Rise, my soul, and stretch thy wings,/Thy better portion trace!'], sung to the tune of 'Amsterdam!' Sometimes it seemed as if the very roof was lifted off . . . as if the music had burst an entrance for our souls into the heaven of heavens."[28] This habit of lusty congregational singing would lessen when choirs began to dominate the proceedings, especially the paid quartet choirs that started to appear in urban and suburban churches.

It was the singing schools sponsored by churches that encouraged the formation of church choirs, whose members had trained in these schools. The quality of the singing did improve after the instruction. With these vocalists entered the fuguing tunes, anthems, and other sacred pieces that the singing masters had taught them, and that had been composed by New England tunesmiths such as William Billings, Timothy Swan, Oliver Holden, and Daniel Read. The fuguing tunes were in two parts, the first proceeding in block chords, the second, a repeated section, starting with staggered contrapuntal entries and ending with all voices singing together. Normally, they were set to four lines of psalm or hymn text. Most of them were distinguished for their energy, simple and unsophisticated harmonic designs, and rousing effect on hearers. Samuel Goodrich describes the church singing in Ridgefield, Connecticut, as flourishing at the beginning of the century. The choir, divided into four parts, was ranged on three sides of the meetinghouse gallery. Deacon Hawley would set the choir in motion with a pitch pipe of his own manufacture. The fuging tunes they sang ran "a little mad" but gave delight.[29]

The most notable description of the singing of fuguing tunes in the Sunday service came from Harriet Beecher Stowe. She wrote of a bitterly cold winter day when a shivering congregation gladly took shelter in the pews. The leader of the singing selected "Denmark" and "Majesty" for those "in the singers' seat." He beat time as he roared at first the treble singers, then the counters, then the basses, until "all the singers poured forth their voices with such ringing good-will that everybody felt sure they were better than any Episcopal organ in the world." She continued:

And as there is a place for all things in this great world of ours, so there was in its time and day a place and a style for Puritan music. If there were pathos and power and solemn splendor in the rhythmic movement of the churchly chants, there was a grand wild freedom, an energy of motion, in the old "fuguing" tunes of that day that well expressed the heart of a people courageous in combat and unshaken in endurance. The church chant is like the measured motion of the mighty sea in calm weather, but those old fuguing tunes were like that same ocean aroused by stormy winds, when deep calleth unto deep in tempestuous confusion, out of which at last is evolved union and harmony. It was a music suggestive of the strife, the commotion, the battle cries of a transition period of society, struggling onward toward dimly-seen ideals of peace and order. Whatever the trained musician might say of such a tune as old "Majesty," no person of imagination and sensibility could ever hear it well rendered by a large choir without deep emotion. And when back and forth from every side of the church came the different parts shouting,

"On cherubim and seraphim
    Full royally he rode.
And on the wings of mighty winds
    Came flying all abroad"

there went a stir and a thrill through many a stern and hard nature, until the tempest cleared off in the words,

"He sat serene upon the floods,
    Their fury to restrain,
And he, as sovereign Lord and King,
    Forever more shall reign."

And when the doctor rose to his sermon the music had done its work on his audience, in exalting their mood to listen with sympathetic ear to whatever he might have to say.[30]

The fuging tunes would gradually disappear from the church service, to be replaced by the more up-to-date, lockstep hymns, thought to be more correct in harmony and more dignified in character, which made their earliest appearances in such collections as Lowell Mason's influential *The Boston Handel and Haydn Society Collection of Church Music* (1822), and which a new breed of singing masters advocated for their students, and ministers for their choirs and congregations. Francis Underwood comments on the changeover that took place in the Quabbin area of Massachusetts:

> Sixty years ago [around 1830] the music of the Bridgewater Collection, or Billings and Holden, were in fashion, and there were frequent fugues, noisy and perverted reminiscences of Händel, or at times the quaint and melancholy strains of Ravenscroft, or the reverent and tender harmonies of Purcell. After that came the Boston Academy's Collection [published in 1835], consisting of music drawn from all schools and all sources, including gems from operas, symphonies, and sonatas; but all was tempered into monotony by cutting out any melodic ornaments, and by suppressing anything rich or inventive in harmony. . . . The people of Quabbin had not heard operas; and melodies from "The Magic Flute," "Don Giovanni," and "Der Frieschütz," were for them as sacred as any. Zerlina's "*Batti, batti*" became indissolubly linked with the hymn, "Saviour, Source of Every Blessing."[31]

It took a much longer time for the old-style music making to disappear in the sparsely settled areas a few hundred miles west of the Atlantic seaboard. Henry Riley gives a vivid description of this sort of musical execution in a western log-cabin meetinghouse, saying the choir there was like those of most villages. One or two members of the choir would get ready for the singing by nasally humming through the music as quietly as possible.

> But the hymn was at last given out; and there was a rustling of leaves, and a-hemming, and coughing, and spitting, and sounding of notes; and a toot on a cracked clarionet, which had been wound with tow; and a low grunt from a bass-viol, produced by a grave-looking man in the corner. Then all rose, and launched forth in one of those ancient pieces of church-harmony, "Coronation" [by Oliver

Holden], every voice and instrument letting itself go to its utmost extent. One airy-looking person was pumping out his bass by rising and falling on his toes; another, more solemn, was urging it up by crowding his chin on his breast; another jerked it out by a twist of his head; while one quiet old man, whose face beamed with tranquillity, just stood, in perfect ecstasy, and let the melody run out of his nose. The genius in the clarionet blew as if he were blowing his last. His cheeks were bloated, his eyes were wild and extended, and his head danced this way and that, keeping time with his fingers; and he who sawed the viol, tore away upon his instrument with a kind of ferocity, as if he were determined to commit some violence upon it. . . . Aunt Graves . . . put on the power of her voice and "drowned out" every thing around her at once . . . she rushed through the notes, the choir in full chase after her.

The settlers, Riley continues, were a rough, hardy, but honest lot. Their hours were taken up hewing down trees, clearing boulders from fields, and preparing the way "for a different class who would surely follow them." They had no time to spare for enriching their minds or refining their characters. If they were to be reached at all, it had to be in church and by means such as that just described.[32]

Scattered throughout the country were families whose custom it was to serve in their local choir. In Walpole, New Hampshire, Mr. And Mrs. Josiah Bellows and their children were ardent music lovers, and they displayed a well-cultivated discrimination for their time (around 1813) and place. Mrs. Bellows "for many years led with rare fidelity and success the choir at church, before any of her daughters were old enough to take part." Later, her oldest daughter, Ellen, "sang in the choir, or played the organ, or did both, in the old Walpole church every Sunday during thirty-five consecutive years." Another daughter, the musically gifted Anne, married Thomas Hill, who would later become president of Harvard College.[33]

Amateur choir directors were rather common in the years before the Civil War. Often their lack of expertise was all too apparent. The thirty-year-old Ebed Harrington, depicted in Samuel Gilman's *Memoirs of a New England Village Choir* (1829), was typical of most. Harrington had worked on a farm and directed the church choir in the nearby village. He now lived in a town and was apprenticed to study medicine with a local doctor. When members of his new church learned of his choir-directing experience, they asked him to take over the local choir. He agreed. On the first Sunday he forgot his pitch pipe and, not sure of himself, pitched the opening hymn too high. The choir strove for the high notes and disaster followed. He again gave the pitch, now

**226**  a little lower. Again, the choir foundered on the high notes. He lowered the
pitch even more, and at last the choir was able to sing the selection through.[34]

Democracy usually prevailed in the managing of church choirs. To cite
an instance, Herman Mann made a diary entry for 6 December 1819 that
went as follows:

> At a meeting of the singers [of the First Parish in Dedham, Massa-
> chusetts] this evening at Gragg and Alden's, Edmund M. Richards
> was chosen Clerk, Capt. P. Bingham and I. Whiting were chosen cho-
> risters for the ensuing year. J. Guild, P. Howard and J. Chickering Esq.
> were requested to play on the viol. An invitation was received from
> the Abbey or opposition singers to join them in learning pieces for
> the dedication of their meeting house; when it was voted that the
> singers act according to the dictates of their conscience with regard
> to singing in the new meeting house at the dedication.[35]

Since so many choir members, before the appearance of the quartet
choir, were unpaid volunteers coming from the broad masses, they insisted on
equality of rights and privileges. Unfortunately, a corollary was the right,
exercised by some, to disregard good manners or to behave petulantly. With
tongue in cheek, Josh Billings advised a young women that to be regarded as
a "good choir singer" she must giggle, prate about silly matters, object to
rehearsing anything she did not like, insist on singing only the tune, and
should write and pass along notes while the minister gave his sermon.[36]

Henry Brooks tells of two instances of misconduct. The first concerned a
visiting minister unfamiliar with the rules of the choir. As a result of what
they interpreted as his transgressions, the singers took offence. At the Sunday
service, the vocalists sat in their seats and would not sing. Growing impatient
with the intransigence, the minister read the hymn lines:

> Let those refuse to sing
>  Who never knew our God;
> But children of the heavenly King
>  May speak their joys abroad.

This admonition had the effect he hoped for. The second instance also involved a minister at loggerheads with his choir. The members of the choir, on
Sunday, occupied their seats but made not a sound. Provoked beyond endurance, the minister thundered out: "And are ye wretches yet alive?/And do ye
yet rebel?"[37]

In 1813 the *Salem* (*Massachusetts*) *Gazette* printed some suggestions on what constituted proper behavior for church choirs:

> Let persons who sing in the choir stand facing the pulpit. They should keep their eyes fixed on the book, except when it is proper to turn them up towards Heaven.—A rolling of the eyes around church, whilst singing, is very improper.
>
> Beating time with the hand so elevated as to be seen by the congregation has a very awkward appearance.
>
> As the place where the choir sits is very conspicuous, it is truly indecorous to indulge in whispering, laughing, or looking over the music during the prayer or sermon.
>
> Persons who occupy the pews should not attempt to sing loud, unless they understand the tune. It is enough to throw hale man or woman into a nervous fever to hear some wretched bawler in a neighboring pew literally murdering a tune.[38]

Altogether too many parishioners took to heart rebukes like the one above and ceased to sing. At least, this was so in those urban churches of ample means and with increasingly self-conscious and musically informed congregations. The old enthusiastic exhortation to make "a joyful noise unto the Lord" was set aside, whether in New York or New Orleans. Parishioners in these churches began to sit back in silence during church services and allow a trained choir, frequently a paid vocal quartet, to do all of the singing. Some might open their hymn books and quietly sing along with the choir. Others would just listen, like an audience attending a concert.[39]

In contrast, rural Americans, especially those living in the South and Southwest, continued to love, support, and enjoy singing fuging tunes and other homegrown sacred compositions. They kept up a custom of meeting for all-day or two-day song services featuring this sort of music. Some leader, more musically knowledgeable than the rest, would lead the singing, armed with a tuning fork or pitch pipe.[40] They often sang from shape-note hymnals, one of the earliest published being John Wyeth's *Repository of Sacred Music, Part Second* (1813). In these books, each tone was represented by a notehead with a specific shape, meant to aid amateur vocalists in sight-reading their parts.

During the antebellum period, too, prayer meetings took hold. These were services of worship held on weekdays that emphasized evangelical preaching and hymn singing. In newly settled lands, such as those in Indiana and Illinois, churches were few. Therefore, those desiring regular services took to gathering together for worship in any available building, whether a school,

228    tavern, or home. The driving force was usually the women, who feared the numbing of the senses and the spiritual backsliding that were concomitants of frontier life. Prayer meetings were also likely to take place in any American village or town, if only to get away from the more formalized structure of the church service. Thus, in Bluehill, Maine, the local minister held a "monthly concert prayer-meeting" so that worshipers could pray and sing free of all restraints.[41]

Prayer meetings aimed at the ill clothed, ill fed, and ill educated also took place in the cities, sponsored by the Methodists and Baptists mostly. During the economically distressful winter of 1857–58, when New York seemed frozen into numbness, the plight of the poor was severe. One day at noon, John Neal says, there came the sound of a large number of voices congregated in a Broadway theater and singing the hymn "Bring forth the royal diadem,/And crown him Lord of all!" The religious song was taken up by group after group standing around the doors of the theater, because there was no room inside. On inquiry, it was learned that the Methodists were holding a prayer meeting for those suffering from lack of employment.[42]

Assemblies for religious worship took place in most unlikely spots. One prayer meeting took place in July 1865 when several wagon trains came together on the northern bank of the South Platte River and ministers of different denominations carried out a service of thanksgiving "for their safe conduct through the perils of the road." Old familiar hymns were sung, prayers were said, then all retired for the night. On the next day, the site was deserted; all the companies had traveled on.[43]

Not all city- or rural-dwellers were amenable to the exhortations of ministers. Without question, evangelists in the tough Five Points section of New York City had a difficult time gathering people together and getting a message across. Even little girls, ragged, filthy, barefoot, and hungry as they were, resisted their efforts and taunted those men and women who came to the meetings to be saved. One girl would come every day to the door of the mission, called the "House of Industry," and whether the door was open or shut, "call over the names of the inmates, with all their catalogue of crimes, giving little scraps of their history, and their hateful nick-names—singing [not hymns but] some of the songs they used to sing in their drunken debauches at Peter Williams'."[44] Clearly, the missionaries were not up to the job of making tractable even the youngest of this undisciplined bunch.

These sermonizers would have fared much worse if they had been in the western parts of the nation. Adamantly resolute and brawny preachers alone were able to tame some of the wayward characters that peopled the frontier settlements. In the Georgia "border country," a formerly wild Tom Barker had experienced conversion, become a parson, and earned the nickname of

"Sledge Hammer" or "Old Sledge." He arrived one day at a village where
"Devil" Bill Jones "had sworn that no preacher should ever toot a horn or sing
a hymn." All the people of the area had gathered to see what would happen
when Old Sledge and Jones met and awaited the expected sport. At last, Old
Sledge appeared. Quickly, Bill Jones stopped him with "Now sing d———n you,
sing and dance as you sing," then proceeded to administer hard slaps to the
parson's face.

Old Sledge recoiled with pain and surprise. Recovering in a moment,
he said: "Well, Brother Jones, I did not expect so warm a welcome,
but if this be your crossroads manners, I suppose I must sing;" and
as Devil Bill gave him another slap on his other jaw he began with:

"My soul, be on thy guard."

And with his long arm suddenly and swiftly gave Devil Bill an open
hander that nearly knocked him off his feet, while the parson continued to sing in a splendid tenor voice:

"Ten thousand foes arise."

Never was a lion more aroused to frenzy than was Bill Jones.
With his powerful arm he made at Old Sledge, as if to annihilate
him with one blow, and many horrid oaths, but the parson fended
off the stroke as easily as a practiced boxer, and with his left hand
dealt Bill a settler on his peepers as he continued to sing:

"Oh, watch and fight, and pray,
The battle ne'er give o'er."

But Jones was plucky to desperation, and the settlers were
watching with bated breath. The crisis was at hand, and he squared
himself, and his clenched fist flew thick and fast upon the parson's
frame, and for a while disturbed his equilibrium and his song. But
he rallied quickly and began the offensive, as he sang:

"Ne'er think the victory won,
Nor lay thine armor down."

He backed his adversary squarely to the wall of his shop, and
seized him by the throat, and mauled him as he sang:

"Fight on, my soul till death."

> Well, the long and the short of it was that Old Sledge whipped
> him . . . and then begged a thousand pardons.

That night, Old Sledge held a "family prayer" meeting, and the next day, Sunday, he preached to a large crowd, singing his favorite hymns on both occasions.[45]

These anecdotes notwithstanding, American men and women, on the whole, did respect their clergymen, attend Sunday church services, and show up at weekday prayer meetings.

### Black Church Services and Prayer Meetings

African American prayer during the antebellum period often took on dimensions unfamiliar to white Americans. Many prayers were directed to a God who was expected to promise relief from suffering, if not in the present then in the hereafter. Some entreaties came from individuals who wondered whether prayer mattered at all. No praying came from more than a few who wondered about the nature or about even the existence of God. One Kentucky slave, Lindy, when told by a highly religious African American woman named Ann to pray to relieve her suffering, answered, "I doesn't know how to pray. I never seed God, and I is afraid of Him. He might be like master." Ann commented on Lindy's response by saying, "This begging of the poor negroes to the Lord to have mercy on them, though frequent, has no particular significance. It is more a plaint of agony than a cry for actual mercy; and, in Lindy's case, it most assuredly only expressed her grief, for she had no ripe faith in the power and willingness of Our Father to send mercy to her."[46]

In contrast to Lindy, some black Americans were so dedicated to their religion that they repudiated former secular pleasures. In this regard, one white preacher from South Carolina said that he had held prayer meetings for the slaves at his father's plantation, which once resounded "with the sound of jollity—the merry strains of the fiddle, the measured best of the 'quaw sticks,' and the rhythmical shuffling and patting of the feet in the Ethiopian jig." Shortly after these meetings began, this secular music making ceased, "and the light, carnal song gave way to psalms and hymns," which were enthusiastically sung. One improvised "spiritual" began: "My brother, you promised Jesus."[47]

This did not mean that religious musical practices were uniformly severe or solemn. Throughout the country, and especially among those Baptists and Methodists who possessed little money and less education, the singing was gay enough, the rhythms were novel and catching, and the tunes borrowed from their secular songs. By the 1850s two sorts of churches attended by free blacks could be distinguished. One was that of the "negro aristocracy," made up of better-educated, more affluent, and class-conscious urbanites, whose hymns, said Fredrika Bremer, sounded beautiful and were exquisitely sung. The service was quiet, very properly conducted, and "a little tedious." The other was that of the poor, where was found true ardor, said Bremer. The church overflowed with attendees, who sang their own hymns unaffectedly and enthusiastically, bodies swaying, hands and feet in motion, uttering verses such as:

What ship is this that's landed at the shore?
    Oh, glory hallelujah!
It's the old ship of Zion, hallelujah,
It's the old ship of Zion, hallelujah.[48]

At rural church services in the South, the membership oftentimes constituted plantation slaves and their white masters, the observances under white direction. Invariably, blacks, who might outnumber whites three to one, were made to sit in the rear.[49] In addition, all-black church services took place without white supervision. For example, around 1850, near North Carolina's Trent River, a "negro meeting house," containing benches able to seat two hundred people, witnessed the Sunday preaching of "Black Jack." African Americans from five miles around attended, when given permission, and sang such hymns as "From all dat dwell below de skies,/Leff de Creator's praise arise," assisted by a half-dozen fiddlers.[50]

More information about rural church services comes from the Rev. I. E. Lowery, formerly a slave on the Frierson plantation in South Carolina. Once a month, he writes, house servants and field hands went to a Sunday service at a Methodist church, eight miles away. On other Sundays, the service was conducted by Lowery and other black preachers and took place in the large yard in front of the Frierson "big house," where seating was provided for around 250 to 300 black people from the Frierson plantation and other nearby plantations, while the "white folks" observed them from the long piazza at the front of the house. Commonly, the preachers grew quite eloquent, singing and shouting in joy and in praise of the Lord. Furthermore:

While some colored sister would be jumping out in the audience,
some of the white ladies were known to act in a similar manner in
the piazza. . . . The singing by the colored folks on such occasions
was an important feature of the worship. It was not done by notes

nor always by words, but it was from the heart, and the melody seldom failed to stir the soul.[51]

White observers repeatedly commented on the beauty and sincerity of black singing in urban churches. Apparently, the repertoire and the singing that they heard conformed to white precepts of musical excellence. William Cullen Bryant listened to the singing of tobacco factory workers at a Baptist church in Richmond, Virginia, and wrote, "It has a congregation of twenty-seven hundred persons, and the best choir, I heard somebody say, in all Richmond." When in Charleston, South Carolina, visiting his sister Lucretia, Edward Everett Hale saw "negroes of the church meet for a service, like Methodist class meeting, in a hall attached to the house. You know the religious fervor of the blacks, and the musical enthusiasm. I never enjoyed any service more than I did this, to which I went as spectator for a little while. They speak admirably, and the singing—very Methodistical—is very fine." Further south, in Savannah, Georgia, Fredrika Bremer attended a black church service where a choir sang in the gallery, both correctly in harmony "and beautifully as can be imagined."[52]

Respected white musicians also attested to the musical excellence of African American singing. The composer and educator George Root was one who did so while visiting Richmond. Marion Harland, of Virginia, writes:

> The choir of the "Old African" [Church] was one of the shows of the city. Few members of it could read the words of the hymns and anthems. Every one of them could read the notes, and follow them aright. The parts were well-balanced and well-sustained. . . . On this afternoon, the then popular and always beautiful *Jerusalem, My Happy Home* was rendered with exquisite skill and feeling. George F. Root, who heard the choir more than once while he was our guest, could not say enough of the beauty of this anthem-hymn as given by the colored band. He declared that one soloist had the finest natural tenor he ever heard.[53]

Rural blacks were less staid in their musical manners and cultivated a more uninhibited way of singing. At baptisms, they worked themselves up to a high level of excitement. When Easter Lockhard was a young girl in South Carolina she went to a nearby pond for the Baptist ceremony. "When we got there, the banks of Austin's pond was lined with the negroes shouting and singing glory and praises. They sang all the songs they could think of and the preacher lined out songs to them." Sarah Felder, of Mississippi, says:

My old man was Jim Felder. . . . We bofe jined de Baptist Church an'
wus baptised at de same time. Dar wus er big crowd ter be baptised
wid us an' wus rainin' but we wus all so happy dat we didn't keer
one bit fur de rain; we jes kep' singing' an sum uf dem shouted. We
wus baptised in de creek. I 'member er song dat sung wus—

> O happy day, O happy day!
> When Jesus wash'd our sin er way.
> He taught me how ter sing an' pray,
> An' be rejoicin' ebery day.[54]

"Sum uf dem shouted." To "shout" during a religious engagement, a
ubiquitous reference in antebellum black narration, sometimes means simply
to raise one's voice and cry out exclamations and songs indicative of ecstatic
feeling. At other times it designates the "ring shout," a rapturous religious
dance with African antecedents that came into wide use in the South after
blacks were barred from the more vigorous dances involving the energetic
flinging about of legs and bodies to emphatic drum rhythms. Although most
descriptions involve men and women forming a ring and engaging in a
circular shuffling tread, now and again leaps were included.[55]

Frederick Olmsted writes of a New Orleans church service where shouting, in its first meaning, took place, then a dance by the minister that went
beyond just shuffling. For a long while, he states, he listened to an emotional
harangue from the black preacher.

> The speaker at length returned to the hymn, repeated the number
> and page and the first two lines. These were sung, and he repeated
> the next and so on, as in the Scotch Presbyterian service. The con-
> gregation sang; I think every one joined, even the children, and the
> collective sound was wonderful. The voices of one or two women
> rose above the rest, and one of these soon began to introduce vari-
> ations, which consisted mainly of shouts of Oh! Oh! At a piercing
> height. Many of the singers kept time with their feet, balancing
> themselves on each alternately, and swinging their bodies accord-
> ingly. . . . When the preacher had concluded reading the last two
> lines, as the singing again proceeded, he raised his own voice above
> all, turned around, clapped his hands, and commenced to dance.

The minister danced himself into a frenzy before he collapsed in exhaustion
on the floor.[56]

The second meaning of "shout," namely, the ring shout, enters H. G.

234    Spaulding's description of a Sea Islands, South Carolina, religious service and
its conclusion with a "very singular and impressive performance of the
'Shout,' or religious dance for the negroes." It began with three or four people
standing still, clapping their hands, beating time with their feet, and singing
in unison an odd shout melody. Others commenced walking about in single
file, in a ring, and also singing. Shortly, those walkers ceased their singing and
moved with greater vigor "into the shout step," which kept exact time with
the music.

> The step is sometimes halfway between a shuffle and a dance, as
> difficult for an uninitiated person to describe as to imitate. At the
> end of each stanza of the song the dancers stop short with a slight
> stamp on the last note, and then, putting the other foot forward, pro-
> ceed through the next verse. . . . The shout is a simple outburst and
> manifestation of religious fervor—a "rejoicing in the Lord"—making
> a "joyful noise unto the God of their salvation."[57]

A majority of slaves refused to adhere to their master's faith, preferring
to heed their own cravings and to realize their own religious needs in novel
ways, of which the ring shout was one. Churches by and for African Americans and ordained black ministers were few and far between, so the prayer
meeting, also called a praise meeting, was the usual venue for worship. It
could take place anywhere, outdoors or indoors, on any day or night of the
week, but more frequently on Saturday or Sunday night. Like the ring shout,
the prayer meeting service represented a reconciliation of African and common American religious tenets. Calm, self-contained worship was not a part
of the African inheritance. Deep passionate engagement was, and it resulted
in ceaseless activity during music making. Whatever inhibitions there were
disappeared, as ecstatic involvement took over. Participants would not sit still.
When carried away, they could not help but wave their arms, rock their
bodies, and throw their heads up and down and right to left. It was only
natural that they would make a joyful noise unto the Lord by clapping
rhythmically, stamping their feet, singing exuberantly, and shouting raptur-
ously.[58] The texts of their religious songs were cobbled together from biblical
phrases, hymns, familiar prayers, and their own experiences. The music
might come from white hymns and even secular music, but all was filtered
through black sensibilities. James Smith, a shoemaker in Heathsville, Virginia,
whose earnings went to his master, states that on Saturday evening he would
walk ten miles to attend a prayer meeting, where singing and praying went
on until daybreak. On Sunday morning he walked another two miles to a

second prayer meeting, returning home at 5 P.M. He says of the prayer meeting:

> The way in which we worshipped is almost indescribable. The
> singing was accompanied by a certain ecstasy of motion, clapping
> of hands, tossing of heads, which would continue without cessation
> about half an hour; one would lead off in a kind of recitative style,
> others joining in the chorus. The Old house partook of the ecstasy;
> it rang with their jubilation shouts, and shook in all its joints.[59]

The more religious and lenient plantation masters allowed their slaves to attend prayer meetings, sometimes even allotting a cabin on a plantation for the purpose. Those who were most effective at preaching led the assemblies. All who attended look forward to a release from the week's pains and burdens:

> All week the niggers worked plantin' and hoein' and carin' for the
> livestock. . . . On Sundays they had a meetin', sometimes at our
> house, sometimes at 'nother house. Right fine meetin's, too. They'd
> preach and pray and sing—shout, too. I heared them git up with a
> powerful force of the spirit, clappin' they hands and walkin' round
> the place. They'd shout, "I got the glory. I got that old time 'ligion in
> my heart." I seen some powerful 'figurations of the spirit in them
> days. Uncle Billy preached to us and he was right good at preachin'
> and nat'rally a good man anyways. He'd sing:
>
> Sisters, won't you help me bear my cross.[60]

White plantation masters did not always encourage or even allow prayer meetings for their slaves. Some claimed that however ardent the worship, blacks would continue to be untrustworthy, idling if not overseen and stealing if not watched. Other masters approved attendance only at white-supervised churches, where blacks were told their proper role was to serve and their proper virtue was to obey. Prayer meetings, they feared, might incite African Americans to revolt.[61]

Blacks, of course, saw things differently. Thomas Jones, a North Carolina slave, says that he was whipped if caught going to prayer meeting, but he sneaked away anyhow on Friday evenings. On one of these evenings

> Jack Cammon was there and opened the meeting with prayer. Then
> Binny Pennison gave out the sweet hymn, which begins in these
> words:

> Come, ye sinners, poor and needy,
> Weak and wounded, sick and sore.

I felt that it all applied most sweetly to my condition.[62]

Again and again, African Americans who had been slaves said they had felt exasperated at hearing white ministers in white churches making them promise to submit to their masters. They did what they considered their own real worshiping away from whites, hidden in the woods, out in the fields by night, sometimes even daring to gather around their cabins, if far enough from the "big house" and if their white masters were thought to be asleep or away. Then they could let loose after their own fashion, chanting, singing their own religious songs, shouting and dancing if they wished, and praying in meaningful ways—for succor from the miseries of this life, freedom from enslavement, and, all else failing, an afterlife where suffering would end. Sometimes they pleaded:

> O, Lord, cum free dis nigger,
> O, Lord, cum free dis nigger,
> O, Lord, cum free dis nigger,
> Fur I cany wurk all de day.

Sometimes they were close to despair:

> Hark from de tomb, it does resound
> Years ob tinder cry
> Livin', livin' come over de ground
> Where we shall lie.
> Prince in de clay mus' be our end
> In spite ob all our power.[63]

In descriptions of the worship of slaves, mention is often made of an iron pot, ostensibly to aid in smothering the sound so that whites would not hear the religious service. Yet it is doubtful that sound was really deadened, except in instances where a head was stuck into the pot itself. Possibly it had a symbolic meaning, an image whose meanings were hidden in African invocations of spirits and gods for protection. The pot's placement was indoors, or just outside the door of a cabin, or in the fields and woods. It rested bottom up or on its side.

In Texas, "de slaves didn' have no church den, but they'd take a big sugar kettle and turn it top down on de groun' and put logs roun' it to kill de soun'.

Dey'd pray to be free and sing and dance." In Alabama, "honey, I 'members when us had de big prayer meetin's. Dey would shut de door so de voice won't git out, an' dey would turn de wash pot down de door. It was to keep de voice inside, day tol' us." In Mississippi, "yes'm we had meetin at night at one house and next night at a nudder. Honey, we put a wash pot down in front ob de meetin house so's de overseer couldn't hear us a singing and a prayin. Dis wash pot caught de sound. De next mornin when de bugle blowed we'd slip by and ask de preacher how he feel. De Marster didn't low us to hab no kind of meetins if'n he knew it."[64]

### Camp Meetings

Evangelical denominations conducted camp meetings outdoors, on open ground or in a forested area cleared of undergrowth. Entire families came to worship, pitched tents for temporary shelter, and brought provisions for sojourns of two or more days, in order to listen to moral talks and exhortations from ministers and to become intensely involved in services of divine worship, which were deliberately kept open to as wide a public as wished to come. If a camp meeting was an annual event and had a fixed site, then shanties might replace tents.

One of the earliest verified camp meetings was sponsored by Presbyterians and took place in July 1800 in Logan County, Kentucky. The idea spread rapidly, especially among Methodists and Baptists. The preaching of salvation through change of heart and rebirth, the confession and obliteration of sin, and a firsthand communication with God were central to their faith. These last two denominations laid down few authoritarian doctrines of a definite nature. Their attraction was emotional rather than intellectual, and for that reason they were especially attractive to undereducated Americans. After 1840 the camp meeting would recede into the national background, as population growth encouraged the building of churches even in rural areas, as education and prosperity reached more and more people, and as Methodists and Baptists became less sects and more denominational institutions with clergy receiving training in seminaries.[65]

Black and white Americans attended, although they customarily occupied separate sections of the campgrounds. By themselves, black Americans were free to improvise their own verses and tunes, to cry out and exclaim noisily if they wished, and to address God as they pleased. Unfortunately for those men and women who were sincerely religious, others came to get away from their daily routines and find recreation by means of stimulating activities, whether in the excitement generated by the preachers or by the tippling, gaming, and whoring that went on around the peripheries of the camp. At

238    times, the larger camp meetings took on the appearance of fairgrounds, with
religion, however stressed, as one of several exhibitions. Often, on the peripheries of the campgrounds stood visitors who had come to observe the spectacle rather than participate in the religious ceremonies. Along with onlookers
who were seriously interested in the proceedings were scoffers who came for
amusement and to make fun of the uncouth dress, speech, manners, and
singing of the preachers and their flock.[66]

Francis Grierson went to a five-day Illinois camp meeting in the 1850s
and saw around two thousand white and black people gathered there, among
them "old reprobates and young rowdies." Unprincipled vendors had set up
whiskey barrels and demijohns for those wanting to buy a drink. At first
he thought he had come upon a gigantic picnic, with women cooking and
families eating by tents and covered wagons. All sorts of denominations were
in attendance, but mostly Methodists. Religious services took place three
times a day. People listened respectfully to the preachers and "exhorters" (two
of them African Americans), and sang hymns "with a hearty will." With each
succeeding service, the men and women grew more excited. On the third
evening, they really abandoned inhibitions—shouting, groaning, and avow-
ing their sins. Hymn after hymn sounded, insistently and passionately. The
skies began thundering; zigzag streaks of lightning flashed down; a huge elm
beside the preachers' platform took a bolt. With this there was a great shout
and hysterical throngs staggered to the platform. Throughout the night people roared out their sacred songs and forswore their sins.[67]

People participating in the religious activities had little use for hymn
books, even if they could read words and music, and a large number could do
neither. Many exercises took place after dark, in the dim light of torches, so
that reading was difficult, and it was in the night sessions that a great stress
on singing took place. Besides, without books, rapturous commitment to God
could be communicated more freely and the carried-away participants could
embrace each other without encumbrance. It follows that the camp meeting
hymns had to have simple, easily remembered melodies. Not surprisingly,
popular secular tunes also found their way into the repertoire. Much of the
music for camp meetings was transmitted by mouth from worshiper to worshiper. This newfound sacred music began to appear in hymnals from the
1830s on. The assemblers of these hymnals also conducted singing schools,
teaching mostly those spiritual pieces that were well liked, and capturing in
print what might have remained unrecorded and lost to later generations.
One such collection of religious songs, *The Southern Harmony*, was published
in 1835 and sold around 600,000 copies over the next twenty-five years.[68]

Fredrika Bremer has given a detailed description of a Methodist camp
meeting that took place eighteen miles out of Charleston, South Carolina, in

May 1850, during which a thunderstorm broke out. Around three or four
thousand people attended, a majority of them black Americans. Whites sat
on one side, blacks on the other.

Round the elevation, in the middle of which rose the pulpit, ran a
sort of low counter, forming a wide square. Within this, seated on
benches below the pulpit, and on the side of the whites, sat the
Methodist preachers . . . and on the side of the blacks their spiritual
leaders and exhorters, many among whom were mulattoes. . . .

The later it grew in the night, the more earnest grew the ap-
peals; the hymns short, but fervent, as the flames of the light-wood
ascending like them, with a passionate ardor. Again and again they
rose on high, like melodious, burning sighs from thousands of harmonious voices. The preachers increase in the fervor of their zeal;
two stand with their faces turned toward the camp of the blacks,
two toward that of the whites, extending their hands, and calling in
the sinners to come, come all, all of them, *now* at this time, at this
moment . . . to escape damnation! Midnight approaches, the fires
burn dimmer, but the exaltation increases and becomes universal.
The singing of hymns mingles with the invitations of the preachers,
and the exhortations of the class-leaders with the groans and cries
of the assembly. And now among the white people rise up young
girls and men, and go and throw themselves, as if overcome, upon
the low counter. These are met on the other side by the ministers,
who bend down to them, receive their confessions, encourage and
console them.

In the camp of the blacks is heard a great tumult and a loud
cry. Men roar and bawl out; women screech like pigs about to be
killed; many having fallen into convulsions, leap and strike about
them, so that they are obliged to be held down. It looks here and
there like a regular fight; some of the calmer participants laugh.
Many a cry of anguish may be heard, but you distinguish no words
excepting, "Oh, I am a sinner!" and "Jesus! Jesus!"

During all this tumult the singing continues loud and beautiful,
and the thunder joins in with its pealing kettledrum.

While this spectacle is going forward in the black camp . . . a
young [black] girl is lifted up by her friends and found to be "in a
trance." . . . Ten or twelve women—most of them young—stand
around her, singing softly and sweetly a hymn of the resurrection;
all watching the young girl, in whom they believe that something

great is now taking place. It is really a beautiful scene in that thunderous night.[69]

Similar Methodist camp meetings are described as taking place in Virginia, New York's Long Island, New Hampshire, and Indiana, where the young Abe Lincoln was an attendee. Singing is also described as taking place during travel back and forth to the campgrounds.[70] In one account, by a former South Carolina slave, Gus Feaster, the Methodist camp meeting took place near his plantation in the early summer after the crops were planted. The preachers who were conducting it stayed at his master's house:

> At night when de meeting dun busted till nex' day was when de darkies really did have dey freedom o' spirit. As de waggin be creeping along in de late hours o' moonlight an de darkies would raise a tune. Den de air soon be filled wid the sweetest tune as us rid on home and sung all de old hymns dat us loved. It was allus some big black nigger wid a deep bass voice like a frog dat ud start in de tune. Den de others mens jine in, followed up by de fine lil' voices o' de gals and de cracked voices o' de old wimmens and de grannies. When us reach near de big house us soften down to a deep hum dat de missus like! Sometime she hist up de window and tell us sing "Swing Low Sweet Cha'ot" for her and de visiting guests. Dat all us want to hear. Us open up and de niggers near de big house dat hadn't been to church would wake up and come out to de cabin door and jine in de refrain. From dat we'd swing on into all de old spirituals dat us love so well and dat us knowed how to sing. . . . Now and den some old mammie would fall out'n de waggin a shoutin' Glory and Hallelujah and Amen! After dat us went off to lay down fer der night.[71]

## Funerals, White and Black

Whether in Maine or South Carolina, the hymn most sung at antebellum funerals was "Why should we mourn departing friends," to the traditional tune of "China."

> Why should we mourn departing friends,
>     Or shake at Death's alarms?
> 'Tis but the voice that Jesus sends
>     To call them to His arms.[72]

Several descriptions of funerals note the solemnity of the church service and gravesite rite and the happy release of tension on the departure from the gravesite, a release that occasionally bordered on frivolity. For example, George Upton wrote in the *Chicago Tribune* about one funeral that he attended where the church service was conducted with all due sobriety, as was the graveside burial, which took place while a band played a dirge:

> To me there is something ineffably sad in the playing of a dirge in
> the open air. The funereal solemnity of the music contrasts so
> strangely with the beauty of the clear heavens and the joyous life of
> nature, and . . . the din and jargon of the busy street life, that I can-
> not keep the tears out of my eyes. . . . And somehow, although the
> dirge saddens me by sending a shadow across the brightness of the
> sunny day, I think I feel the better for having heard it.

Then quickly, the mood changed. In contrast to what had gone before, the mourners who had made up the procession thought nothing of singing a "quick tempo, frivolous popular song," on their return from the burial.[73]

Walt Whitman, when ten years old, witnessed the funeral held for sailors killed in an explosion aboard the steam frigate *Fulton* in 1829:

> It was a full military and naval funeral—the sailors marching two
> by two, hand in hand, banners tied up and bound in black crepe,
> the muffled drums beating, the bugles wailing forth the mournful
> peals of a dead march. We remember it all—remembered following
> the procession, boy-like, from beginning to end. We remember the
> soldiers firing the salute over the grave. And then how everything
> changed with the dashing and merry jig played by the same bugles
> and drums, as they made their exit from the grave-yard.[74]

In their anxiety to conduct a burial in accordance with what was proper, but limited to the few musical compositions they knew and were able to reproduce, mourners might introduce serious but perhaps unfitting music into the proceedings. This William Robyn points out about a funeral procession he watched in St. Louis in 1837. The settlement "was in a most primitive state." The deceased, a member of the Odd Fellows, was being taken to the cemetery to the sound of music, as was customary. "And what [do] you think the band consisted of? An E-flat clarinet, a violin and a bass drum. The funeral march they played was 'Adeste fidelis.'"[75]

On balance, written accounts of funerals usually direct the flow of the narration toward what was somberly impressive and leave out whatever may

242   have occurred that lacked seriousness. This is especially true of reports on urban funerals. All is dignified and somber formality in Richard Parker's version of the burial of Jonas Chickering in December 1853: the Episcopalian service at Boston's Trinity Church and the appropriate dirge played for the occasion; then the singing of the "124th hymn": "Hear what the voice from Heaven declares/To those in Christ who die." Next came the decorous procession, out of the church, over the Charles River, to the Mount Auburn Cemetery.[76] Nothing improper is mentioned. Indeed, nothing improper could be said to have taken place.

The same held true for many village burials. When a contemporary witness wrote about one of these, he told of the poignant beauty of the spectacle in a voice that bordered on the excessively sentimental. The procession from the church to the grave, he said, was led by twelve girls clad in white and bearing evergreen wreaths in their hands; next, the minister and the coffin carried by four men; then the mourners. Of course, there was singing, too. After the coffin was lowered into the grave, "the girls in white approached, and cast their wreaths upon it, and then lifted their voices in a low and mournful song, which gradually grew firmer and swelled louder till it closed in a full peal of triumph." At the song's conclusion, the pastor spoke, summarizing the meaning attached to funereal music: "It is well, it is fitting, that the fair and innocent should go to their home upon the wings of song, and that Christians should thus bid adieu to those whom they loved. While their spirits are welcomed by the hymns of angels above, it is right that our voices below should join the consoling and enrapturing strain."[77]

In some instances, any hint of impropriety was avoided, even if it went against the deceased's wishes. In this regard, Charles Benton's funeral in Virginia is informative. It was an extremely solemn and reverential affair. However, a friend commented:

> Poor fellow, little did he think his wishes would be so forgotten,
> when he used to sing . . .
>
> > I beg that no tear may be dropt when I'm dead,
> >   No *hic jacet* be graved on my stone,
> > But pour on my coffin a bottle of red,
> >   And say that his drinking is done.[78]

Whatever and wherever the funeral, whether seen as appropriate or inappropriate to the occasion, music was always present. One way or another, it helped assuage grief.

Africans brought full-fledged systems of religion and rich cultural pat-

terns with them when they arrived in America, none of which was ever  243
completely forgotten by following generations. Therefore, black American
behavior and music making at funerals was apt to be different from that of
white Americans. For one thing, African rather than European culture and
symbolism prompted significant differences in the funeral rite. One inherited
trait, for example, was the burial ceremony carried out at night:

> I members once 'bout a African preacher tellin' us how dey burried
> folks in Africy. Dey always burried dem at night. Dey would dig de
> grave and when night would come dey all carried a torch and fol-
> lowed single file atter de ones totin' de corpse. When dey throw de
> dirt in and fill up de grave, dey pile it up high, den dey all dance
> around on top of de grave and beat de dirt down smooth. Dey
> would sing at the same time.[79]

So it was in America—the nighttime burial with torchlight procession and
continual singing. Adele Frost, a South Carolina slave, made a typical statement:

> Fun'rals was at night an' w'en ready to go to the graveyard every
> body would light a lighted knot as torch while every body sing. This
> is one of the songs we 'n used to sing:

> > Goin' to carry dis body
> > To the grave-yard,
> > Grave-yard don' you know me?
> > To lay dis body down.[80]

Voodooism, arriving from Africa by way of Haiti as a ritual involving
ancestor worship and polytheism, was syncretized with Christianity (Catholic
in Louisiana, Methodist or Baptist, mostly, in other regions) by African Americans, especially those living in the Gulf states. The Reverend I. E. Lowery
noted this syncretism on South Carolina plantations. He tells of a young slave
mother, Mary, who had died after giving birth to her baby, despite a voodoo
doctor's attempt to cure her because she was "conjured." The funeral took
place at night. The rough homemade coffin was placed on a horse-drawn
cart. The mourners, in a file two deep and one-quarter of a mile long,
marched behind the cart and sang. Every fifteenth person carried an uplifted
torch. One of the hymns sung was Isaac Watts's "When I can read my title
clear/To mansions in the skies." Mary's grandmother took the baby to the
graveyard. Before the corpse was deposited into the grave, the baby, following

244    African tradition, was "passed from one person to another across the coffin," so "the mother's spirit would [not] come back for her baby and take it to herself." Another Watts hymn was sung; "Hark! From the tombs a doleful sound/My ears, attend the cry," as each person threw a handful of dirt into the grave. Lowery heard both "spirit and pathos . . . to move the heart" in the singing.[81]

Further differences with white practices could be found in how wakes were held: "At de wake we clapped our han's an' kep' time wid our feet—*Walking Egypt,* dey calls hit—an' we chant an' hum all night 'til de nigger was *funeralized.*"[82]

Some funerals were dignified affairs—friends and neighbors gathering around the coffin during the wake, singing recognizable hymns, talking quietly, and sharing the refreshments they had brought. The church service might differ little from that of whites. Afterward, the torchlight procession to the grave proceeded with a solemn, slow gait and more singing. At the gravesite, the preacher eulogized the deceased and the onlookers sang another hymn, not infrequently Watts's "Why do we mourn departing friends." Other favorite hymns, originating in the meetinghouse and camp meeting, included "Life is the time to serve the Lord," "Alas! and did my Saviour bleed," "On Jordan's stormy banks I stand," and "To Canaan's fair and happy land." The voices were consistently praised for their richness and fullness, and for their ability to blend "in perfect harmony."[83]

As many, if not more, African Americans showed far fewer inhibitions at funerals, the participants remaining truer to their African inheritance. White bystanders describe them as yelling their lamentations, rhythmically moving their feet or bodies, and producing what seemed a strange, barbaric music. At the "Old African Church" in Richmond, Virginia, Marion Harland says that on one occasion the front block of seats was occupied by women dressed entirely in black for a funeral. The preacher conducted the funeral service with a prayer, an anthem, and then a sermon, before sitting down.

> As he sat down, the audience arose . . . and broke into a funeral chant never written in any music-book, and in which the choir, who sang by note, took no part:
>
> "We'll pass over Jordan, O my brothers, O my sisters! De water's chilly an' cold, but Hallelujah to de Lamb! Honor de Lamb, my chillun, honor de Lamb!"
>
> This was shouted over and over, with upraised arms at one portion, and, as the refrain was repeated, all joined hands with those nearest to them and shook from head to foot in a sort of Dervish dance, without, however, raising the foot from the floor.[84]

In the same city, Frederick Olmsted watched a black funeral procession of about twenty to thirty people go to the cemetery. A prayer was said over the grave. Then:

> An old negro . . . raised a hymn, which soon became a confused chant—the leader singing a few words alone, and the company then either repeating them after him or making a response to them, in the manner of sailors heaving at the windlass. I could understand but few of the words. The music was wild and barbarous, but not without a plaintive melody. A new leader took the place of the old man, when his breath gave out (he had sung very hard with much bending of the body and gesticulation), and continued until the grave was filled, and a mound raised over it.[85]

White writers, normally those from the South, liked to depict slaves as mourning for a beloved master who had died. However fictional their account, they do testify to what was taken as the untamed character of black music and to the persistence of African traditions. One even suspects, after reading some of these accounts, that some black traditions were carried over to whites, as in the following account, given by Maria McIntosh, of a nighttime funeral procession of slaves bearing not a fellow slave but their Georgia plantation owner to his tomb:

> About midway in their sad march, there rose on the air of night, a wild mournful strain, sung by the blacks. Those who have ever heard this people sing, will not easily forget the wild melody of their music, or the readiness with which they improvised words to suit at once the music and the occasion. The music of this melancholy march required a stanza of eight lines, four of which were improvised by a leader, while the last four, in which all joined, was a chorus evidently familiar on such occasions. One stanza of it ran thus:

*Leader alone.*    We carry we massa to 'e long, long sleep,
        Tru de trees wid de torch a shinin' bright,
    An we lef' him dare in de grabe so deep
        All alone by hisself in de dark, dark night.

*Chorus.*    Jesus hab open de door in de heaben
        Higher dan eben de eagle fly,
    And to white wing angel de order giben
        To carry 'e soul clean up to de sky.[86]

CHAPTER 8

# Serenades and Other Outdoor Music

EVERYWHERE THE TRAVELER WENT IN ANTEBELLUM America, he heard music of a kind and to an extent unknown in later times. He would often be awakened in a hotel at night to the guitars and voices of serenaders or to the warbling of people returning home after a concert or theater presentation. He explored city and town streets to the sound of vendors' musical cries, street boys' whistling, street musicians' and organ grinders' performances, ballad hawkers' singing their wares, and military and club-sponsored bands constantly on the march, ceaselessly tooting. As he journeyed from town to town, he listened to the inveterate singing of fellow passengers in coaches, on trains, and on ships. Roaming through the countryside, on foot or horseback, he frequently caroled to himself as he went along and occasionally came upon music-making picnickers. Stopping overnight at an inn, he joined other travelers to provide the evening's entertainment, which included vocalizing, usually around a piano in the inn's common room. If he was fortunate, someone contributed the sound of a violin, flute, or guitar, since many Americans traveled with musical instruments and ached to play them. In short, music was likely to be heard anywhere and at any time.

## Serenades

America's obsession with serenading was at a peak in the antebellum years. Warm nights might find a lone individual or a group of several people wandering urban streets and rural stretches, with or without instruments, to regale friends or acquaintances with music. Some serenaders were gratifyingly musical; others brayed like donkeys. When the moon was at its full, so

were the streets with serenaders. Oliver Wendell Holmes in 1836 wrote a
poem about this night music:

> You're sitting on your window-seat,
>    Beneath a cloudless moon;
> You hear a sound that seems to wear
>    The semblance of a tune.
> As if a broken fife should strive
>    To drown a cracked bassoon.
> And nearer, nearer still, the tide
>    Of music seems to come,
> There's something like a human voice,
>    And something like a drum;
> You sit in speechless agony
>    Until your ear is numb.
> Poor "home, sweet home" should seem to be
>    A very dismal place;
> Your "auld acquaintance" all at once
>    Is altered in the face;
> Their discords sting through Burns and Moore,
>    Like hedgehogs dressed in lace.
> You think they are crusaders sent
>    From some infernal clime,
> To pluck the eyes of Sentiment,
>    And dock the tail of Rhyme,
> To crack the voice of Melody,
>    And break the legs of Time.[1]

The wanderers were most often young men, some of whom might have professional musicians along to add greater appeal to the serenading. The recipients of their attention were most often young women, who usually welcomed the homage paid them. When the sought-after window was discovered, the would-be musicians stood below it and began their concert. The music making beneath a window sometimes continued for one and a half to two hours, much to the annoyance of some neighbors. Carl Arfwedson, a Swedish visitor in Boston, witnessed a typical serenading situation:

> A custom very prevalent in Boston is to perform serenades at night
> time, for the edification of the fair sex. A young American proposed
> to me one evening to accompany him on a similar occasion. I ac-
> cepted the offer, and repaired to the spot agreed upon, where four or

five young men were already in attendance. Provided with a guitar and a flute, we started about midnight, and proceeded, in the first instance, to a house in the lower part of town, the residence of one of the belles of the city. In full imitation of the Italian fashion, we were wrapped up in cloaks, and formed a group exactly under the window stated to belong to the bedchamber of the lady. The first piece performed was a duo between the two instruments; subsequently followed songs, with accompaniments. Within a few moments our attention was arrested by the noise of a window softly opening. I tried in vain to recognize some of the listeners; the darkness of the room, however, prevented me from distinguishing any object within. Our persons must, however, have been easily discernible in the bright moonlight; for a few days afterwards, the same ladies told me unhesitatingly that I had formed one of the party. It may be easily imagined how sentimental were the tones which pierced the ears of the listening fair ones, enhanced as they were by a beautiful moon—an invariable friend to serenades—and in what a delightful mood the young gentlemen must have been, after singing and playing a dozen difficult airs. How the ladies in the window felt when the music ceased is not within my province to determine. The whole company, actors and audience, appeared, nevertheless, to part under the visible feelings of melancholy; and I hastened, half frozen, to my hotel.[2]

In a news item in the *Boston Musical Times* entitled "Music of the Night," the writer speaks of sitting alone by a window, after the rest of the household had retired. He could hear passersby singing and whistling; he heard bands tooting; and he listened to some serenader sweeping "the dull chords of his well-thumbed banjo to the chorus of his comrades."[3]

The recipients of the young men's attentions were flattered to be so singled out, as was the nineteen-year-old Eliza Southgate, visiting Albany in 1802:

About eleven o'clock, or rather twelve, I was surprised by some delightful music, a number of instruments and most elegantly playing "Rise! Cynthia! Rise!" I jumped up and by the light of the moon saw five gentlemen under the window. To Mr. Westelo I suppose we are indebted; "Washington March," "Blue Bells of Scotland," "Taste Life's glad moments," "Boston March," and many other charming tunes—played most delightfully. I have heard no music since I left Salem till this, and I was really charmed.[4]

Occasionally the selected recipients of the serenade were not completely satisfied with the musical compliment. Agnes McDowell, sister of Stephen Foster's wife, had obviously mixed feelings about a serenade to which she was subjected:

> We had a most delightful serenade last night, a parcel of plebeians
> were serenaders. They did not know the house exactly and they
> went up to Mrs. Townsend's, played at least an hour and a half and
> then they found our house out. I really think they must have played
> for two hours, most horrible music, at our house.[5]

In Frankfort, Kentucky, a Mr. Blissett was enraged at the serenade given him in 1815. Three or four young men had gotten through singing to some young ladies in various parts of the town. As a lark, on the way home they stopped to bellow a psalm tune beneath Mr. Blissett's window, knowing he hated psalm tunes. Their reward was a chamber pot emptied on their heads.[6]

As one might expect, college students enthusiastically joined the ranks of the serenaders. Some went out as individuals with particular lady friends in mind. Others went out in groups, lured outside by balmy moonlit nights and a reluctance to break up for the evening. Among them were future statesmen such as Charles Francis Adams and future composers such as William Henry Fry.[7]

So enthusiastic were some serenaders that they formed serenading clubs and went about regularly practicing their pastime. One club of twelve members, the Casco Serenading Club, of Portland, Maine, during the 1840s took a square piano on a wagon along with them. All of them not only sang but also played some instrument. They began their performances around eleven o'clock and went from window to window until about three in the morning. Apparently they were better received than an earlier serenading club, the Night Club, about which a writer to the *Portland Argus* complained in 1836, stating his desire to join forces with others to grab its members and dunk them in the horse pond. The journal's editor chimed in with, "We have no objections."[8]

"Serenading was a popular form of amusement for young men in those days," recalled William Hamilton, who once went serenading with Stephen Foster, in 1858 Cincinnati. Foster, when a young man, was known to strengthen various serenading parties both with his voice and with his portable melodeon.[9] If amateur serenaders felt their talents inadequate for the occasion, they engaged professional help, either for a fee or a donation. Thus, when a Mr. S. S. Stevens and his "Gentlemen Amateurs" needed such assistance in Schenectady, on 6 August 1842, they called upon the touring

250 Hutchinson Family Singers to help them serenade "a few private houses," writes Asa Hutchinson. He continues, naming four of the sung pieces, "Lady of Beauty &c. S. S. Stevens gave us 'Dempster's blind boy,' Woodsman Spare that Tree as a Trio, and Sleep on. . . . They also made a donation of 3.50 for Singing to a few of *their Friends.*" Three weeks later, the Hutchinsons were employed again, to serenade "the principle Editors" of Albany's newspapers. They received six dollars for their services.[10]

It follows that cities and larger towns would have resident professional serenaders, who were available for hire. In St. Louis, by no means a large city, two such ensembles were in operation in the 1840s, one formed by William Robyn, the other by Charles Balmer. Robyn says his band of six members were engaged sometimes two and three times a week, for five dollars at a time. Balmer's band had three members, Balmer playing a piano on a "furniture car," and the other two playing violin and guitar.[11] Aware of the universality of this music making, a tongue-in-cheek Charles Browne, posing as "Artemus Ward," commented:

> As several of our public men are constantly being surprised with
> serenades, I concluded I'd be surprised in the same way, so I made
> arrangements accordin. I asked the Brass Band how much they'd
> take to take me entirely by surprise with a serenade. They said
> they'd overwhelm me with an unexpected honour for seven dollars,
> which I accepted.[12]

Recently become a part of the United States, California had its own share of serenaders, both long-resident Mexicans and newly arrived civilians and soldiers from the East. Hot-blooded Mexican youths were forever wooing their ladyloves by moonlight. Americans were not vastly different. In 1854 an army colonel, wishing to serenade some ladies in San Diego, rounded up several officers to sing and play guitars, flutes, and other instruments. There had been a great deal of conviviality before the midnight hour, when the music making commenced. As a result, while most of the party had arranged themselves beneath the window and tried solemnly to intone "Oft in the Stilly Night," one blithely drunk person, a young surgeon, roared out an uncouth Bowery song, "Oh, my name is Jake Keyser."[13]

Rather unexpected was the serenading that went on at the California gold-mining camps, where tents and rude cabins with female occupants were apt to receive an evening's entertainment as a gesture of gallantry.[14] Most astonishing of all were the complimentary performances in the open air at night that took place among the wagon trains traversing the Great Plains and

Rocky Mountains. Sarah Herndon writes that her wagon train was on its way
to Montana when it met and made a joint camp with "the McMahan train,"
which harbored several chivalrous young men:

> There are several musicians in the McMahan train; Lyde says they
> serenaded me last night. She says they stood between our two wag-
> ons. I think she is trying to tease me.
> "Ask Dr. Howard, if you do not believe me. He was one of them."
> "Oh, no. I would be ashamed to acknowledge I did not hear
> them, and would feel like dunce if they had not been there."

Yet Dr. Howard shortly presented her with a bouquet of flowers he had
gathered on a nearby mountainside, a most extraordinary gesture, since
traveling conditions were rough and dangerous at best and at that time
"hostile Indians" were bent on killing what travelers they could find.[15]
Again and again we hear about suitors out at night to woo their beloveds
as best they knew how. One would do what he could to communicate his
ardor through a flute solo. A sophisticate would strum his guitar and offer up
Italian love songs. But most of the love-struck serenaders rendered sentimental ditties with lines like: "Come to my arms, my darling,/Come while the stars
are shining."[16] One of the most intriguing reports involved President John
Tyler. The poet and songwriter John Hewitt says that Tyler loved poetry and
music but was a good judge of neither. Further:

> I have set some of his effusions to music; one, a serenade which was
> sung under the window of Miss Gardner previous to their marriage.
> It was a beautiful moonlight night. . . . Mr. Tyler stood a short dis-
> tance off in the company with F. N. Thomas, the White House poet-
> laureate, while the serenaders *executed* the President's appeal to the
> sleeping beauty; who was wide awake all the while.

That night Miss Gardner was in a frivolous mood and had evidently anticipated the serenade, for she threw down to Tyler a bouquet consisting of
turnip tops, radishes, and cabbage leaves, tied to a turkey's gizzard and a
sunflower.[17]
The serenading of newlyweds was well established during these years.
Called "chivarees," "shivarees," or "charivoris," these were performances gotten up by friends, which often ended with the married couple inviting the
musical party indoors for a visit and for refreshments.[18] Quite a few men
banded together to form chivaree bands that were not at all welcome to

newlyweds and their neighbors. These bands sported a variety of noisemakers—tin cans, kettles, whistles, cowbells, and homemade "instruments" such as raucous "horse fiddles" (two large hoops heavily stringed and rosined, with an inflated bladder between the strings and the bow) and "great trombones" (a dry-goods box played upon with an eight-foot-long piece of timber). They deafened the newlyweds and outraged the neighbors with their banging, howling, whining, and clanging din. In one instance an Illinois bride took extreme umbrage at the refusal to stop and applied a rawhide whip to the leaders, forcing them to flee.[19]

Many Americans grew heartily sick of the constant serenading that interrupted their sleep. Like the Illinois bride, others acted forcibly to stop noise-making serenaders, as did the director of a college in Columbia, South Carolina, who became so incensed with the incessant din a band of college students was making that he discharged a shotgun at them, wounding one youth. Laws were passed regulating the hours when serenading was allowable, as happened in Richmond, Virginia, after members of a German glee club clashed with the night watch over their late-night singing. New Orleans tried putting teeth into its laws by arresting late-night singers and fiddlers for disturbing the peace.[20]

Slaves had almost no opportunity for serenading, except when a master drafted a talented fiddler or singer to accompany him for an evening's excursion.[21] The fanciful romanticizing that accompanied serenading was foreign to the thinking of African Americans and the reality that they had to embrace. For most of them, it was an extravagance to subscribe to irrelevant idealism, to display a desire for pointless adventure, or to exhibit the trappings of chivalry.

Yet, on occasion, a plantation menial is reported as seeking the hand of a young woman with music. In one instance, a Virginia slave, Dick, did court a girl who "went constantly to Meeting. She was daughter to old Solomon the Carter, and by moon-light I used to play my banger under her window, and sing a Guinea Love-song that my mother had taught me." In another instance, a man named Koba loved Yani, a pretty girl who was also admired by another man, Quince. One evening Quince boldly came to serenade Yani while she was engaged in conversation with an elderly woman, in Koba's presence. Strumming on his guitar, Quince improvised the following words:

> Koba thinks he's gonna git dis gal,
> One who'll mak' a beautiful pal,
> Yes, he thinks, he'll git 'er han',
> But I'm gonna beat Koba, if I can!

Yani ceased talking, listened a moment, smiled over at Koba, and quietly resumed her conversation with the old lady. Quince swaggered off, carrying on with his song, until he vanished behind the row of cabins.[22]

### Other Street and Outdoor Music

Antebellum Americans, whether city or village dwellers, encountered daily not only serenades but an extraordinary variety of other outdoor sounds. Walking about her village of Rahway, New Jersey, Ann Willson had listened to the music and mirth spilling out of the local inn. Doing the same in New Orleans, Liliane Crété heard a cacophony of sounds—the rattle and screech of wagons, ships' whistles, the constant tolling of church bells, the blare of brass instruments and thud of drums, the singing of a chain gang, and, everywhere, the musical cries of an oyster seller and other street vendors.[23]

In the village of Ridgefield, Connecticut, boys and girls gathered daily on the common to play games, dance, and sing play-songs and the popular songs of the day. Lydia Child complained of the noisy discords assailing her ears as she walked outdoors in New York. She was also left desolate by the weary voices of little waifs wandering the streets. These sounds, she says, were pleasantly modified by a female vendor singing out, "Hot corn! Hot corn! . . . Lily white corn! Buy my lily white corn." Then there was a Tyrolean plying his street organ, and a Scottish youth shrilling away on his bagpipe.[24]

Street vendors, like the "Hot corn!" lady, filled the urban air with musical sounds. New York's chimney sweeps announced their calling with: "Here goes old sweep what's got no money—/Here goes old sweep as sweet as honey."[25] A New Orleans oysterman sang out to buyers: "Ah-h-h-h-h-h-h-h-h-h a bonne marche—so cheep as nevair vas—toutes frais—var fresh. Ah-h-h un veritable collection—jentlemans and plack folks. Ah-h-h come and puy de veritable poisson de la mer—de bonne hûitres—Ah-h-h-h-h-h-h-h!"[26]

Organ-grinders, usually Italian, roamed throughout the United States, cranking forth operatic arias, dance music, marches, traditional airs, and popular songs. In New York, they assailed the ears of George Templeton Strong so frequently that he wished he had an effective cockroach powder that would exterminate these street cockroaches. In Boston, Margaret Fuller's mother once pitied a poor organ-grinder, who lived in a perpetual state of want, and constantly gave him money. Unfortunately for her, this resulted in all his fellow organ-grinders concentrating their musical efforts before her door and hoping for similar handouts. In 1848 musically starved San Franciscans heard their first organ-grinder playing in the street and received him eagerly. This Italian immediately became a person of considerable local importance, arousing "the enthusiasm of the homesick" while his monkey "served to amuse the leisure of" those rough miners to whom the music meant nothing. He was a welcome guest in all the hotels, playing jigs and reels, and arias of Bellini and Donizetti. Before long, real musicians came to the city and supplanted him.[27]

The streets allowed for every sort of musical expression. In contrast to the operatic strains, assorted musical vulgarities also accosted the ears of the more genteelly brought up men and women when they left their homes. Rough "b'hoys" riding on the streetcars shouted vulgar ditties out of the windows, the least offensive being a version of "Old Dan Tucker." Fragments of "senseless buffooneries," such as "Billy Barlow," "Jim Crow," and "Sittin' on a Rail," tweaked the sensibilities of the fastidious. In San Francisco, good citizens fled the streets when they saw the wild and lawless ruffians, known as the Hounds, advancing toward them and "shouting the most ribald songs," frequently "preceded by a violin or two, perhaps a horn, but always a banjo and several pairs of rib-bones."[28]

Outdoor singing was often an expression of an individual's feeling of well-being. Samuel Longfellow, when twenty-seven years of age (1846), once went swimming with a friend at the seashore near Portland, Maine. Afterward, they sunned themselves enjoyably on the rocks and watched the shipping go by. Next, Longfellow writes, "we sat under trees, singing, or weaving chaplets of bayberry leaves; we repeated snatches of sea-ballads—all the various employments of him whom the world calls idle." Seven months later, on the opposite side of the continent, Walter Colton met a Californian who was merrily strumming away on his guitar and singing. Colton asked him how he could possibly be so light-hearted when the Americans were taking over his country. "Oh," said the Californian, "give us the guitar and a fandango, and the devil take the flag." Hattie Nettles, a former Alabama slave, said her master revealed his state of health and happiness through song: "Honey, Ol' Master sho'ly did lak to sing, an' he was pretty good at dat. I 'members dat he useter git out in de back an' sing to de top of his voice: *I'se Gwine Home to Die No More.*"[29]

On holidays, no matter the temperature, a sizable number of Americans expressed their good cheer musically. One mild May Day morning the Alcotts went to Emerson's Concord home, where a maypole had been set up. The wagon on which they rumbled to their destination bore a maypole and was decorated with evergreens. The children wore evergreen wreaths on their heads. As they "passed along the road" they "sang, 'Merrily we go.'" Other parents and children awaited them on the Emerson grounds. After the maypole was raised and placed in position, the children sang and danced around it. At the opposite weather extreme, on a cold New Year's Eve in New York,

Lydia Child heard "nothing but merry glees and snatches of comic songs" outside, "as if a hundred theatres had emptied themselves into the streets. The watchmen were out in double force; a precaution which is deemed necessary to preserve public peace on this noisy anniversary."[30]

Boys throughout the land could be heard walking along the avenues and singing out from sheer joy—shop boys in San Francisco, bootblacks and printers' boys in New York.[31] Sadly, there was a reverse side to that coin— those boys and girls who sang joylessly and in order to solicit a pittance from onlookers. These were the "little waifs" wandering the streets of New York and other cities, whose weary voices left Lydia Child feeling desolate. One of them, an emaciated youngster in New York, played the accordion and presented such pieces as "Lily Dale" and "Auld Lang Syne" in a worn out, listless fashion that only seemed to annoy his auditors. He received nothing. It was not long after that he was reported to have accidentally drowned. Another friendless New York child was seen trying to sell matches by a New York curb, but no one heeded him. He seemed well on the way to dying from malnutrition and lack of care. Fortunately, Henry Ward Beecher came along and helped the boy by lifting his frail form up to his shoulder and telling him to continue his singing. This drew a more charitable crowd. It gave enough money to buy the boy clothes and stave off starvation, at least for a little while. More fortunate was the three-year-old street arab who lived an outdoor life of horror until the Home for the Friendless took him in. After the change, his whistling of "Yankee Doodle," "Old Dan Tucker," and "Pop Goes the Weasel" took on a far more cheerful quality.[32]

Competing with these children, ballad singers on street corners hawked broadsides fresh from the printers. Sheaves of the printed texts were draped over their arms, or individual copies were displayed on a wall or fence. The pieces might be traditional or newly composed, pious or obscene, hymns or popular songs. The singing peddlers of song texts had varying ages, from elderly to tiny seven-year-olds, like the little ballad boy observed on the New York streets in November 1845, bravely chanting his wares although he was freezing in a cold biting rain.[33]

The street scene was enlivened by bands making use of brass, percussion, and woodwind instruments. They appeared in parades on muster days, national holidays, and dates of local historical significance. Festivals, important wedding and funeral processions, dedicatory events, social and political organizations' outdoor demonstrations of unity all called for bands. On warm evenings, every town or village boasted its own group of instrumentalists, who performed from open-air bandstands.

At least annually, the local militia, part of the home guard, was called up for formal military inspection, on what was known as muster day. Troops

**256** drilled, firearms were discharged, and a march took place down the main street, minimally to the beat of drums and squeal of fifes, or ideally to the blare of a full band. In many a village the day took on a festive character, with a public meal served and quantities of liquor flowing freely down thirsty throats.[34]

When the new minister was ordained in Milford, New Hampshire, "a band of music escorted the candidate for ministerial honors from his boarding place." When several thousand advocates for temperance marched in Cincinnati, children from various schools marched with them singing temperance songs, and bands of music played compositions appropriate for the occasion. When Lafayette died in 1834, grief gripped the nation. Church bells tolled all day, flags were lowered to half mast, and slow "dead marches" were played as mourning processions moved along the streets.[35]

P. T. Barnum made a good thing out of the band he put together for his American Museum, on New York's Broadway, whose doors opened in 1841. The musicians called attention to the museum by performing from a balcony while above them glowed an obtrusive limelight, or "Drummond light," guaranteed to catch the attention of the throngs passing by:

> Here we are at the American Museum, crowned with its Drummond
> Light, sending a livid, ghastly glare for a mile up the street, and
> pushing the shadows of the omnibuses well-nigh to Niblo's. From
> the balcony of the third-story windows a cascade of horrent har-
> mony, issuing form an E flat bugle and three mismatched trom-
> bones, is tumbling down upon the up-turned faces of the boys and
> negro-women on the opposite walk—while that untiring chromatic
> wheel goes over round and round, twining and untwining its blue,
> red, and yellow wreaths of light in unvarying variety.[36]

Unlike New Yorkers, the trekkers to California and those who had arrived to mine for gold spent nearly all of their time outdoors. The wagons, tents, and blanket rolls in which most of them slept could hardly come under the heading of indoor living. The difficult journey westward and the hard labor at the mining sites would ostensibly have left little energy for recreation. Yet music was heard everywhere on the trail and in the mining camps. Andy Gordon wrote into his diary on 10 October 1949 that he was absolutely weary of hearing "Oh! Susannah" sung morning, noon, and night by members of his wagon train; indeed, he felt his mind was going with the repetition: "I have heard *Susannah* sung at least forty times today, and now it's bedtime and Tammy Plunkett is picking out the tune on his banjo and singing it loud enough to keep most of us awake. Don't he ever get tired of it? I used to like that song, but enough is enough, and I believe it will drive me crazy before we get to California."[37] A young woman from Amherst, Massachusetts, arrived at a California gold-mining camp and noted in February 1852 that a mulatto miner was leaving the camp with two pistols by his side and a violin and tambourine hanging behind him. He would be sorely missed, she wrote, because of "his beautiful music." Eight months later, she was delighted because a man who claimed he had once sung with Ossian Dodge's musical troupe was now living in her camp and regaled everyone with "a voice of remarkable purity and sweetness, which he was kind enough to permit us to hear now and then." Furthermore, "there was a little girl at one of the tents who had taught herself to play on the accordion on the way out. She was really quite a prodigy, singing very sweetly, and accompanying herself with much skill upon the instrument."[38]

Outdoor music making for black slaves could be an ordeal, if not a punishment. A white master could command them to play instruments, sing, and dance in the space before his veranda, where he, his family, and friends lounged in comfort. Little regard was paid to how unwilling or tired the enslaved toilers might be. In addition, when put up for sale they could be forced to perform in like manner within the slave pen, for viewing by potential buyers.[39]

Black plantation laborers, after their day's labor, usually passed their waking hours of leisure outdoors. Their small cabins were too hot, crowded, and uncomfortable to stay in. Sometimes as many as twelve people had to live in a room that contained next to no furniture. Explaining why not much music took place in their homes, one former Texas slave said, "De cabins where de slaves lived were not very big an' didn't have much furniture in 'em. Dey had jest one room and dirt flo's. . . . I recollect that my mother's house had one room an' dey was four beds in it. Ma, Aunt Cindy, Margaret, Dinah, an' seven children slept in dis room."[40] In the evening, whether it was Texas or Virginia, they customarily would sit before their doors or lounge on the grass, talking and singing hymns and secular ditties, some of them original. The music making was that of a soloist, or a chorus sounding in unison or in harmony, or a group vocalizing in call-and-response fashion. Banjos, violins, flutes, and guitars (homemade instruments were ever present) regularly made an appearance. Jugs and bottles were blown into, and skillet lids and frying pans were struck with knuckles, sticks, or bones. A few men, women, and children might choose to march about, clap their hands, slap their thighs, or dance. They chanted odd secular songs, such as:

Miss Ca'line gal,
    Yes, Ma'am,
Did you see dem buzzards?
    Yes, Ma'am,

258     Did you see dem floppin'
        How do ye' like 'em?
              Mighty well.

or:

        John, come down in de holler,
        Oh work and talk and holler.

and sacred songs, such as:

        Oh, yes, we'll gain de day,
        Oh, yes, we'll gain de day,
        Oh, yes, we'll gain de day,
        Po' sinners, flockin' home![41]

Game songs were also produced. Lawrence Evans, a former Mississippi slave, describes one:

    Now de slaves had pleasures 'long wid de wuk. Dey wuz allowed ter hab frolics an' times ter be off fer ammusements. One thing I can re-member de slaves use ter do, dat wuz ter light candles when de nites wuz dark an' go off in de woods an' build big fires an' play games by de firelight. One game wuz ter ketch hands an' go 'round in a circle an' sing some ole song dat dey would make up, lak dis:

    Run Liza Jane an' take her home,
    Run Liza Jane an' take her home,
    Run Liza Jane an' take her home,
    Run, run, run.

    A boy would be a running his gal, an' when he kotch her anuther couple would run.[42]

The most celebrated outdoor music making of the period took place in New Orleans's Congo Square. Homemade instruments, singing, and dances—often brazenly sexual—characterized the scene. James Creecy describes New Orleans as "the heaven of the negroes," free and enslaved, and Congo Square as the center of black free-time activities, especially on Sundays. The open area consisted of five or six shaded acres, with graveled paths crisscrossing grassy areas. The local African Americans, most of them Catholic, attended

Sunday mass in the morning and then took up hedonistic merrymaking in the afternoon, which continued until sunset:

> The "haut ton" attend operas, theatres, masquerades, etc. The qua-
> droons have their dashing fancy balls, dances, etc., and the lower or-
> der of colored people and negroes, bond and free, assemble in great
> numbers in Congo Square, on every Sunday afternoon, in good
> weather, to enjoy themselves in their own peculiar manner. Groups
> of fifties and hundreds may be seen in different sections of the
> square, with banjoes, tom-toms, violins, jawbones, triangles, and
> various other instruments, from which harsh or dulcet sounds may
> be extracted; and a variety of queer, grotesque, fantastic, strange,
> and merry dances are to be seen, to amuse and astonish, interest
> and excite, the risibles and wonder of "outside barbarians" unskilled
> in Creole or African manners and customs.
>
> Sometimes much grace, and often surprising activity and long-
> continued rapid motions, are seen. The dancers are most fancifully
> dressed with fringes, ribbons, little bells, shells, and balls, jingling
> and flirting about the performers' arms and legs, who sing a second
> or counter, to the music most sweetly—for all Africans have melody
> in their souls—and in all their movements, gyrations, and attitudi-
> nizing exhibitions, the most perfect time is kept; making the beats
> with the feet, head, or hands, or all, as correctly as a well-regulated
> metronome. Young and old join in the sport and dances. One will
> continue the rapid jig till nature is exhausted; then a fresh disciple
> leaps before him or her, and "cuts out" the fatigued one, who sinks
> down gracefully on the grass, out of the way, and is fanned by an as-
> sociate with one hand, while water and refreshment are tendered by
> the other.
>
> When a dancer or danseuse surpasses expectations, or is particu-
> larly brilliant in the execution of "flings" and "flourishings" of limb
> and body, shouts, huzzas, and clapping of hands follow, and numer-
> ous *piccallions* are thrown in the ring to the *performers* by (*strange*)
> spectators. . . . Hundreds of nurses with children of all ages attend;
> and many fathers and mothers, beaux and belles, are there to be
> found.[43]

## Boatmen

White and black men, fond of music and dance, formed the crews of rafts
and flatboats on the rivers and the narrow vessels on the canals of America.

**260** They were a rough-and-ready lot. During the day, corn whiskey, raucous singing, and rowdy jigging occupied their usually abundant leisure on board. In addition, the sound of a boatman's horn enlivened many a lonely forest bend, sometimes with a warning blast, sometimes with a rendition of an entire tune. In the evening, the crews anchored their craft, gathered around fires, and after eating, sang soft, sentimental songs between swallows of whiskey, until they bedded down for the night.[44] As illustration, James Weir tells of a boatman, Dick Murdock, who plied the Green River into the Ohio. He whiled away the time "by singing the many simple songs so common with boatmen. Often has his merry voice and mellow bugle-note, sounding far over the still waters of the deep-green river, as his heavily-laden boat floated lazily down the stream," gladdened the hearts of "denizens on either bank." Many of the "wild airs" he sang were "plaintive and beautiful. . . . I know nothing so sadly sweet, and so exquisitely delightful."[45]

Lew Wallace, the author of *Ben-Hur,* said that as a boy, growing up along the banks of the Wabash, he listened to and loved the sound of the tin horn used by boatmen. He quoted "the song of Butler, the soldier-poet of Kentucky," which remained "a favorite of mine, with powers to stir my pulse." A return to the joys of his childhood invariably accompanied his hearing again:

> Oh, boatman wind that horn again!
> > For never did the joyous air
> Upon its lambent bosom bear
> > So wild, so soft, so sweet a strain.[46]

Many songs were quite hearty and rendered with a swagger:

> We were forty miles from Albany,
> > Forget it I never shall,
> What a terrible storm we had one night
> > On the Erie Canal.
> Oh, the Erie was a rising,
> > And the gin was getting low,
> And I scarcely think we'll get a drink
> > Till we get to Buffalo. Till we get to Buffalo.

Or the music could be harmonious and soothing. From the shores of the Ashley River, in South Carolina, Caroline Gilman watched a flatboat manned by African Americans gently glide toward Charleston. As usual with

such crews, the men were not silent. In chorus they sang the well-known
hymn:

> When I can read my title clear
>> To mansions in the skies,
> I'll bid farewell to ev'ry fear,
>> And dry my weeping eyes.

She found the effect beautiful in the extreme: "I have since listened to the full
burst of orchestral harmony . . . and heard the rich strife of rival voices from
coral lips . . . but I have never forgotten that hymn upon the Ashley. As it
slowly receded, I mused on heaven until the happy past and the airy future
stole in, and mingled with my thoughts like the earth and sky before me."[47]

The Southern states were far more rural than those to the north. Roads
were few and frequently impassable. Rivers and lakes were plentiful. The most
convenient way for goods and people to go from plantation to plantation or to
a town was in small boats propelled by black oarsmen. Gilman says that one
day, when she and her brothers went to visit a neighboring plantation by
boat, the head oarsman sang a ditty and the other oarsmen struck in "with
a full but untaught counter at the last word of every line." The words were:

> Hi de good boat Neely?
> She row bery fast, Miss Neely!
> An't no boat like a' Miss Neely,
>> Ho yoi.[48]

A song that the Ashley River oarsmen always rendered with a rhythmic
swing had the lines "In case if I neber see you any mo', I'm hopes to meet you
on Canaan's happy sho'." Four other favorites were "Roll, Jordan, Roll," "Run,
Mary, Run," "Drinkin' Wine, Drinkin' Wine," and "Oh, Zion."[49]

For a visit to the South, it was more comfortable to go by sea to a port
town. This accomplished, one customarily set off in a boat rowed by four to
twelve African Americans to visit an outlying plantation. Thus, when Ward
McAllister visited his brother-in-law, who lived on a plantation near Savannah, Georgia, he rode there in a ten-oared boat called the *Rice Bird*, whose
crew rowed lustily because promised tobacco or money. The head oarsman
improvised songs and the others sang the refrains in chorus. The lyrics make
known the vexations they were put through and the recent happenings on
their plantation. They sang "about their 'Massa' and his family, as follows:
'Massa Ward marry our little Miss Sara, bring big buckra to Savannah, gwine
to be good times, my boys, pull boys, pull, over Jordan!'"[50]

The choruses that she heard, Frances Kemble writes, were all sung in unison, never in parts. The rowers kept precise time, perfect intonation, and accurate accentuation in their music. She states of her two-year sojourn, in 1838–39, on a Georgia plantation:

> My daily voyages up and down the river have introduced me to a great variety of new musical performances of our boatmen, who invariably, when the rowing is not too hard, moving up or down with the tide, accompany the stroke of their oars with the sound of their voices. I told you formerly that I thought I could trace distinctly some popular national melody with which I was familiar in almost all their songs, but I have been quite at a loss to discover any such foundation for many that I have heard lately, and which have appeared to me extraordinarily wild and unaccountable. The way in which the chorus strikes in with the burden, between each phrase of the melody chanted by a single voice, is very curious and effective, especially with the rhythm of the rowlocks for accompaniment. The high voices, all in unison, and the admirable time and true accent with which their responses are made, always make me wish that some great musical composer could hear these semi-savage performances. With a very little skillful adaptation and instrumentation, I think one or two barbaric chants and choruses might be evoked from them that would make the fortune of an opera.
>
> The only exception . . . to the high tenor which they seem all to possess is in the person of an individual named Isaac, a basso profundo of deepest dye, who nevertheless never attempts to produce with his different register any different effects in the chorus by venturing a second, but sings like the rest in unison. . . .
>
> You can not think . . . how strange some of their words are; in one, they repeatedly chanted the "sentiment" that "God made man and man makes"—what do you think?—"money!" Is not that a peculiar poetical proposition? Another ditty to which they frequently treat me they call Caesar's song; it is an extremely spirited war-song, beginning "The trumpets blow, the bugles sound—Oh, stand your ground!" . . . One of their songs displeased me not a little, for it embodied the opinion that "twenty-six black girls not make mulatto yellow-girl;" and as I told them I did not like it, they have omitted it since. This desperate tendency to despise and undervalue their own race and color, which is one of the very worst results of their abject condition, is intolerable to me.[51]

Horseback and muleback were an indispensable means for overland journeying, especially away from the Atlantic seaboard, when the absence of
roads and rivers offered no alternatives. On the wild western border of Missouri, Judge Hoss Allen rode circuit singing such ditties as:

Thar aint throughout this western nation,
    Another like old Hickory.
He was born fur his siteation—
    A bold leader of the free.[52]

On the Ouachita River of Arkansas, Davy Crockett heard a fiddler playing
"Hail Columbia" and "Over the River to Charley," and shortly discovered a
mounted parson, who was traveling around the district, in the midst of the
swift stream and about to be swept away, horse and all. After Crockett pulled
him to safety, the parson commented: "In times of peril I always fiddle because there is nothing in universal nature so well calculated to draw a crowd
together as the sound of a fiddler's tune."[53] In California a young wife
thought it hilarious that she and her husband were traveling on muleback to
the gold mines: "We sped merrily onward until nine o'clock, making the old
woods echo with song and story and laughter, for F. was unusually gay and I
was in tip-top spirits. It seemed to me so *funny* that we two people should be
riding on mules, all by ourselves . . . and, funniest of *all*, that we were going
to live in the Mines!"[54]

The antebellum years saw Americans constantly moving from one place
to another, much of the activity translating itself into a flood of individuals
and families emigrating to the West. Samuel Goodrich remembered the year
1817, in Connecticut, when family after family left for the western territories.
Some rode horseback or on wagons; others went on foot—fathers, mothers,
small children, and babes, along with kitchen utensils, bedding, "the family
Bible, Watts's Psalms and Hymns, and Webster's Spelling-book."[55] There were
also stagecoach passengers bowling along the oftentimes barely passable
roads, and wagoners hauling freight in plodding fashion. Along the national
road, stretching from Cumberland, Maryland, through the length of Pennsylvania to Ohio, inns were to be found every twelve miles or so, where food, rest,
and "the very best of entertainment" were offered the passengers. Taverns,
little more than wagon stands, did the same for the freighters.

A large number of wagoners played violin along the road or during stops.
Tavern owners, as often as not, were fiddlers, too, and volunteered their
services so the wagoners could have a friendly sing and take part in a hoe-

**264** down. When, finally, the railroad took over the hauling trade, the old wagoners lamented in chorus:

> Now all ye jolly wagoners, who have got good wives,
> Go home to your farms, and there spend your lives.
> When your corn is all cribbed, and your small grain is good,
> You'll have nothing to do but curse the railroad.[56]

Wagons conveyed not only freight but also people from one place to another. They were the least expensive and, in many areas, the only means of public transportation, however primitive. As the wagons slowly meandered toward a destination, passengers called on each other for a song. In July 1843, for example, William Cullen Bryant road a wagon with other passengers from Whitehall, New York, to Benson, Vermont:

> A third passenger was an emigrant from Vermont to Chataque county, in the state of New York, who was now returning to his native county, the hills of Vermont, and who entertained us by singing some stanzas of what he called the Michigan song, much in vogue, as he said, in these parts before he emigrated, eight years ago. Here is a sample:

> "They talk about Vermont,
>     They say no state's like that;
> 'Tis true the girls are handsome,
>     The cattle too are fat.
> But who amongst its mountains
>     Of cold and ice would stay,
> When he can buy paraira
>     In Michigan-*i-a?*"

> By "paraira" you must understand prairie. "It is a most splendid song," continued the singer. "It touches off one state after another."[57]

Songs of sentiment, such as "Home, Sweet Home" and "The Mistletoe Bough," were stuff for women to sing as they jogged over the lanes. Lachrymose older women, like the Mrs. Prouder of Illinois that Joseph Kirkland wrote about, preferred mournful hymns:

> Hark from the tombs a doleful sound!
>     Mine ears attend the cry.

Ye living men, come view the ground,
    Where ye must shortly lie.[58]

One rewarding wagon trip, at least for roadside onlookers, found members of the Hutchinson family of farmer-singers journeying from Weare Center to Hooksett, New Hampshire, in July 1842. Asa Hutchinson says they greeted the farmers working in the fields with music, which seemed to make them more cheerful and lively. Then, in the town of Dumberton, "we halted in front of a large Farm House under a beautiful shade. We sung one song. The inmates of the house came out. We asked for G[reen] Cheese, with bread. The ladies returned to the house but immediately appeared with three kinds of excellent bread, 2 of Cheese; a pitcher of Cool water."[59]

The most extraordinary traveling by wagon, of course, was the persistent movement of families westward from the Mississippi River. Account after account of the trek across the Great Plains and over the Rocky Mountains describes not only the dangers and hardships experienced but also the camaraderie and persistent music making along the way. Harriet Ward's journal entries of her difficult journey to California in 1853 constantly refer to singing and playing on the guitar. The first night out (20 April) from Dartford, Wisconsin, she writes, they enjoyed a picnic under the stars. Then "we seated ourselves by a blazing fire and Frank [her daughter] took out her Guitar and was playing 'Oft in the Stilly Night.'" Two weeks later they were "crossing interminable prairies" and had camped for the night. She found her situation ironically amusing: "Here I am, sitting on the front seat of the wagon, writing, Willie asleep beside me, Frank seated upon the bed playing her guitar and singing 'I've Something Sweet to Tell You,' and just a few rods from us, seated around a blazing fire, are the gentlemen of our company." A week later, she has her daughter Frank beside her, practicing a song that a young friend had asked her to play for him just before they had left home, "Oh! Where shall we meet them all again?" she wonders, "God alone can tell." In July, when they were crossing the mountains, the young people came together one evening— she names two girlfriends of Frank and a Major Clark. Guitars sounded pleasingly on the ear: "We could none of us realize we were almost at the summit of the Rocky Mountains. Evening very pleasant, the moon shining sweetly. Maj. Clark, a very pleasant gentleman from St. Louis, also accompanied the young ladies in their songs." In the Humboldt Sink, Nevada, the desert-like conditions presented real dangers to the company, which the young people took lightly: "At dawn of day we commenced our tedious march again. The young ladies, with Mr. Poland and myself, took a long walk which terminated very pleasantly indeed, in singing 'Begone, Dull Care;' but at its commencement all were just a little disposed to indulge in gloomy anticipa-

266   tion of the horrors of crossing the desert, with our teams not in very fine order, I assure you." At last, in October, they reached Indian Valley, California, where they decided to settle. To her surprise, they were surrounded with a "cultivated group of neighbors." She says: "Frequently our visitors were gentlemen of education and refinement . . . and often the mud walls of our little domicile echoed to the sweet sound of guitars and voices cultivated in the Handel and Haydn Society of Boston."[60]

Some wagon trains were fortunate to have trained musicians along. Sarah Herndon was delighted that a Mr. and Mrs. May, violinist and guitarist, crossed the plains with her in 1865; impromptu musicales ("The happiest features of the day") were possible all along the way. She was happier still when several different traveling companies came together near Plattsmouth, Nebraska:

> As the people from different camps were sitting around an immense camp-fire, not far from our wagons, someone proposed music. Some of the men in Mr. Clark's camp are fine musicians, they brought their violin and flute, and gave several instrumental pieces, then some familiar songs were sung and someone started "Just before the Battle, Mother." They had sung two verses when I heard a shriek from Gus's wagon. I hastened to see what was the matter. "Oh, Sallie, tell them to please not sing that, I cannot bear it. Dear Brother John used to sing it so much. It breaks my heart to hear it now." I sent Winthrop, who had followed me, to ask them to stop singing.

John had died the week before, on the road, killed when a rifle was accidentally fired.[61]

Other accounts of travelers with the wagon trains show that the most frequent instruments played during the journey were the violin, guitar, and flute; the most frequent participators in the music making and, when stopped, the dancing were young unmarried people, although married couples did not hesitate to participate. It is surprising how much singing took place even when perilous terrain, severe weather conditions, and hostile Indians made passage difficult. Favorite songs of the day, such as "Home, Sweet Home," "Sweet Betsy from Pike," and "Oh! Susannah"; dance tunes, such as "Money Musk" and "Zip Coon"; and hymns, such as "Old Hundred," "When I Survey the Wondrous Cross," and "Before Jehovah's Awful Throne," were common among the trekkers.[62]

Travel by stagecoach was a step above that by wagon in comfort and speed. Male passengers enjoyed singing patriotic, minstrel, and comic songs as they were borne along. Occasionally, a rough character offered a ditty

verging on ribaldry. Women produced sentimental ballads, and family groups
aired psalms and hymns. If the road was bad and the coach broke down,
passengers sang or pulled out musical instruments they were carrying with
them to amuse themselves as repairs were made to their vehicle.[63]

Sometimes it seemed as if the music would never cease. Herman Mann
entered a stagecoach in Boston on 11 February 1825 and "started for home;
excellent singing on the way; stopped at Taft's [tavern]; delectable 'bellows
stop'; arrived at Gragg's [tavern] about 10; sang a Te Deum." When an
overnight stay was required, so also was music. In 1816 passengers were
unloaded for the night in Harrodsburg, Kentucky. Mr. Koumar, of German
extraction and a traveling salesman for a jewelry firm, sang a "woodpecker's
song" in English, a thick accent notwithstanding. "During the symphony
between each verse, which he whistled, he would drum with his finger-nail on
the back of the guitar, giving a very good imitation of the sound the woodpecker usually makes on an old hollow tree." The night was warm, so everybody was sitting outside the inn. Another passenger sang Samuel Drake's
"Minute-Gun at Sea," to Koumar's improvised accompaniment, during which
"the note for the 'minute-gun'" was given out "by a loud rap of the knuckles
on the back of his guitar." Quickly, other songs were produced by the remaining members of the group, and the time passed agreeably until two or three
in the morning.[64]

Railroads and steam-powered trains began to proliferate in the 1830s and
became the favored means for travel in the 1850s. The passengers' music-
making propensities were transferred from stagecoach to train coach. Boys
and girls, men and women were recorded as singing secular and sacred songs
and playing instruments as they traveled. Among them were ordinary citizens
off to visit distant relatives, salesmen moving on to the next town, worshipers
going to or returning from a camp meeting, enlisted men transferring to
another camp, and politicians whistlestopping around the country. After arriving from England in August 1847, William Ryan rode a train from New
York City to Philadelphia and was subjected to the incessant singing of the
other rail users, among them a detachment of soldiers:

> The trip . . . was very pleasant, but outrageously noisy, for the entire
> detachment waxing patriotic, never ceased shouting "The Star-
> spangled Banner," "Columbia, The Gem of the Ocean," and similar
> national effusions; but as each individual—true to his republican
> principles—sang independently of every one else, and the melodies
> were arbitrarily disfigured by a running accompaniment of shakes,
> caused by the unevenness of the rails, the effect of the whole was
> rather more startling than imposing or harmonious.[65]

Fredrika Bremer in May 1850 returned to Charleston, South Carolina, from a camp meeting along with white and black returnees from the event. "At five in the afternoon we returned to Charleston by a train which conveyed certainly two thousand persons, two thirds of them black. They sang the whole way, and were in high spirits."[66]

Even presidents of the United States made music aboard trains. Abraham Lincoln, on his way to Washington with friends, invited his companions to join him in singing: "Between stops there was much gaiety and many hours were whiled away as Lamon lent his baritone voice to the sentimental and comic songs that Lincoln adored. Judge Davis, too, contributed to the hilarity."[67]

At times passengers wished for silence, but to no avail. George Derby writes of a train ride on a cold night in January 1857. As they went by New Brunswick, New Jersey, at 11 P.M., passengers trying to sleep were rudely awakened by a dirty, seedy-looking boy, who was working the coaches with his accordion. "I despise that instrument of music," said Derby, who endured torment as the boy played "the most awful version of that wretched 'Dog Tray' that I ever listened to." After the boy collected forty-two cents, he refused to leave, hoping to extract more money from the passengers. He went to the car's center, close to a red-hot stove, and played "Pop Goes the Weasel." Much to Derby's delight, the boy got burned by the stove.[68]

Obviously passengers aboard ships, a large number of them steam-driven paddle wheelers, would also amuse themselves with music. Informative in this regard is a comment of Mrs. N. P. Lasselle about a group taking a steamer down the Mississippi. Evenings, the men and women assembled "in the ladies' cabin" for music making around the piano. Several songs were sung, but a young man held back his voice. The company embarrassed him into taking up a guitar and singing, after being told: "You know, each one has to contribute something to the entertainment of the company, this evening, and you, as well as others." Every sort of song was likely to be sung. Dr. Thomas Nichols, traveling between New Orleans and Mobile in 1859, heard the men and women gathered around the piano "in the great saloon" produce "Ben Bolt," then "Casta Diva," and next "some negro melody or 'Old Dog Tray.'"[69] Sometimes a person insisted on sounding the piano in the saloon at an inappropriate hour. Amelia Murray tells of taking the Niagara Steamer from Milwaukee to Oswego, New York. One evening:

> Being much fatigued, I returned early, and the same thing was the case with a majority of passengers; but there was a piano in the saloon, close by my berth. After ten o'clock at night, a young girl sat down to perform—not harmonious music, for such a disturbance

might have been forgiven, but she perseveringly amused herself by striking the instrument in a style so utterly discordant, that, after a while of patient endurance, I opened my door and inquired whether it was right at that time of night to keep the passengers from sleeping? She repeated my words with an air of ludicrous impertinence, and, though she paused for a little while, before long the annoyance was continued, if not by her by others, without the smallest excuse or apology! Thus do the rising generation here mistake rudeness for Republicanism, and selfishness for independence; but we must not be too hard upon them. As this great and growing nation advances in life and experience, it will advance also in civilization and true Christian politeness. Rowdyism will cease to be considered manliness, or extravagance gentility.[70]

On the other hand, the next morning two black deckhands provided her with some agreeable "negro music" by singing duets and accompanying themselves with a guitar and violin. "Their voices good, and (like those of most of the negroes) in perfect tune. One song had a chorus imitative of barking dogs, which amused the younger passengers extremely."[71]

What of times when stormy weather at sea buffeted a ship and its passengers? Fredrika Bremer, on shipboard, going from New York to Georgia in October 1849, wrote a letter to her sister Agatha:

I am perfectly well; have not been sea-sick for a moment; but can not deny but that it seems to me rather unpleasant when, in the evening and at night, the waves thunder and strike above our heads, and the vessel heaves and strains. Fortunately, the ladies are all well and cheerful; and in the evening three of them sing, two of whom met here for the first time in the world, the "old lady" [from New York], who, after all, is not so old—only about fifty—and who has a splendid soprano voice, and the pale girl and her friend [both from Georgia], with their clear voices, sing hymns and songs remarkably well together. It is very charming and beautiful. The tones remain with me at night like consolatory waves.

Last night, when the sea was rough and there was even some danger, when every movable thing was tumbled about, and I thought of my home, and was in "a shocking humor," and acknowledged it even to my fellow-voyagers, those three voices sang hymns so exquisitely till about midnight, that every restless wave within me hushed itself to repose.[72]

If the passengers themselves did not sing or play, there were shipboard bands to keep them entertained. Ship bands were heard on the Hudson River, the Mississippi River, the Great Lakes, and the Atlantic Ocean. Their repertoire included marches, the popular hits of the day, dance pieces, and operatic selections.[73] In addition, an occasional ship possessed a steam-driven calliope, as did a vessel that visited Mobile, Alabama. Dr. Thomas Nichols was at the Mobile waterfront when he heard, in 1859, "the music of a steam organ on one of the boats, which was played by a German musical artist engaged by the year, at a handsome salary. It is a strange music that fills the air with a vast body of harmony, carrying with it the impression of the power that gives it birth." George Burns, a former slave who was put to work as a deckhand on a river ship around 1840, recalled the showboat *Banjo*, which called attention to itself by having someone play on its calliope while the black roustabouts danced on her deck. Other accounts describe the roustabouts themselves as singing some songs with newly invented texts to favorite tunes, such as that of "Dixie," and other songs where both tune and text were improvised.[74]

One of the most extraordinary descriptions of an American traveler engaged in music making was published in the *Newark Daily Advertiser* on 15 November 1852. The newspaper article concerned an unidentified correspondent traveling in Syria, who had entertained Arabs round a campfire by singing Foster's "Old Uncle Ned":

> Having excited the most profound interest in the history of Uncle
> Ned, I launched forth into the song, keeping as near the tune as pos-
> sible, and going through all the motions descriptive of the baldness
> of his head, the absence of his teeth, and the length of his fingers.
> At length, when I arrived at the final catastrophe, where Grim
> Death seizes the old gentleman by the heel, I made a sudden motion
> at the heel of one worthy who was sitting near by, completely upset-
> ting him with fright, and causing laughter from the audience.[75]

# CHAPTER 9

# Music for Work and Public Places

'Tis merry, 'tis merry, the livelong day,
To work. 'Tis better to work than play.
'Tis better to work, and to sing as I,
Than sit with nothing to do, and sigh.
'Tis merry with singing to earn our bread,
With the beetle below, and the lark overhead,
And sunshine around us the livelong day;
For singing and working are better than play.[1]

This song, which Sophie Damon says a young Vermont woman sang in the 1820s, gives working perhaps too affirmative a slant. Nevertheless, the lyric underlines the importance of singing in work situations during the early years of the United States. That this song had some prevalence is surmisable from a statement of Alice Carey. She writes that in the 1840s she came upon an Ohio man who "was spading the fresh earth, and the peculiar and invigorating odor impregnated all the air. He was singing to himself snatches of old songs." She then inserts the lines cited above as an example of what he was intoning.[2]

## Work and Song

During the entire antebellum era, traditional ballads, including those brought to America from the British Isles, continued to sound around American hearths and workplaces, especially rural ones. Simple strophic songs of sentimental or romantic nature and comic or gloomy narrations characterized most of them. To these were added revised songs, that is to say, texts pertinent to the New World and fitted to long-standing tunes. Moreover, there were traditional pieces with words and music ostensibly American in origin. Existing side by side with these types were hymns, ancient and new, and the recently composed or arranged secular music, mostly of a popular nature, that music publishers offered the public. All these categories of song figured in the singing of farmers in the fields and workers in the proliferating factories and mills. For example, Harriet Hanson Robinson, a Lowell, Massachusetts, mill worker, was quoted as saying that she and her friends, fresh from farms in northern New England, crooned "the old-time songs our mothers had sung, such as 'Barbara Allen,' 'Lord Lovell,' 'Captain Kid,' and 'Hull's Victory'" as they worked the factory looms.[3] John Trowbridge states that the farmer workers near Boston, whom he heard singing as they mowed a hay field, favored the contemporary minstrel ditties: "Hector marched at their head singing a negro melody. . . . Arriving at the edge of the field, the men rested their scythes upon the ground and began to whet them, having first wiped them with wisps of grass. The cheerful ring of the stone upon the metal beat a measured accompaniment to Hector's singing."[4]

Farm women did their share of the hard work in the fields, along with taking care of the children and doing the necessary household chores; persons journeying the country roads often saw them "hoeing, raking, digging." Fanny Fern speaks of one such woman, who allowed nothing to dishearten her. She went through the day cheerfully, "singing after the hay-cart, singing to the plow, singing to the barn-yard, singing to dinner, and singing to bed. That robbed labor of half its weariness, and winged the feet of every body about her."[5]

Whatever country people did together outdoors was accompanied with music. A customary chore for a community would be the raising of a barn, mill, or house. Neighbors would gather to accomplish the task. The men and boys, perhaps numbering one hundred, would engage in the actual building, while the sound "of merry laughter" mingled "with the cheering song of the workmen." The women would also be there, just as cheerfully laughing and singing as they saw to "the abundant refreshments."[6]

Indoors, men and women were just as vocal at their work. To this Harriet Beecher Stowe testifies. The Hartford school at which her sister Catherine taught was across from a harness store. Here a young man with "a most beautiful tenor voice" could be heard singing as he labored, delighting her with such compositions as:

> When in cold oblivion's shade
> Beauty, wealth, and power are laid,
> When, around the sculptured shrine,
> Moss shall cling and ivy twine,

Where immortal spirits reign,
There shall we all meet again.[7]

Standing for most workers, shoemakers were mentioned again and again as singing at their work. One writer speaks of a Maine farm, where "once a year, a cheery shoemaker appeared hammering at his last, and singing songs." Another writer, from Ridgefield, Connecticut, describes "Amby Benedict, the travelling shoemaker, [who] came with his bench, lapstone, and awls, and converted some little room into a shop, till the household was duly shod. He was a merry fellow, and threw in lots of singing gratis. He played all the popular airs upon his lapstone—as hurdygurdies and hand-organs do now [1864]." The barely settled western clearings also valued the labors of itinerant shoemakers, who went from isolated house to isolated house, "shoeing the family and mending the harness" as they went. One shoemaker, "a little, bald, twinkling-eyed fellow, made the smoky rafters ring with" his repertoire of songs, including that favorite ditty of the West: "All kinds of game to hunt, my boys, also the buck and doe,/All down by the banks of the river O-hi-o." "And children of all sizes, clattering in all keys, completed the picture and the concert."[8] Beginning with the late 1830s, the Industrial Revolution caught up with the roving shoemaker and gradually forced him to abandon his itinerancy and, instead, tend machines in shoe factories.

Women commonly resorted to song when doing their indoor chores, like the "Sally," who lived in a midwestern village, about whom Alice Carey says, "She was always good-natured as the day was long, and would sing all the time at her work. I remember, long before she was married, she used to sing one song a great deal, beginning 'I've got a sweetheart with bright black eyes,' and that she meant William McMicken by that."[9] The Reverend Elijah Sabin would have approved of guileless Sally. Indeed, he found considerable virtue in most women who inhabited the small country villages, most of which had not yet felt the corrupting influence of cities:

Miss was not put into the *papered room* [symbol of superficiality] to fold her hands, or do a little vanity needle work; nor did she stroll about the street in plaid silk, or white cambric; nor yet idle her time at tea parties, to retail scandal, and stab the envied innocent. Some sentimental song, or pious hymn, sung to the *buzz* of the wheel, and beat by the stroke of the loom, might be heard in every house.[10]

Women weaving clothing for their families were a familiar sight in rural America. While visiting her grandparents' Maine farm around 1815, Elizabeth Smith says,

I delighted to go into the weaving room, where the whir of the wheels and the bang of the loom was always relieved by the singing of the women. . . . Here I heard the "Nutbrown Maid," "Cruel Barbara Allen," "Fair Rosamond," "Queen Eleanor," "Braes of Yarrow," and other ballads which I afterward found in "Percy's Reliques of English Poetry." These of course were brought over from England by the Pilgrims, orally, and were passed about in manuscript.[11]

It was a logical progression for young women to leave off their home weaving to take their places before the factory looms in such places as Lowell. The wages paid them helped ease the lot of their families and allowed saving money for their dowries. The *Lowell Offering*, a periodical put out by the mill girls, is filled with descriptions of their music making. For example, the following item appeared in May 1844:

As soon as day broke I was awakened by one of the girls jumping out of bed, and beginning to crow. That awakened the others, and they bestirred themselves. One sung,

> Morning bells I hate to hear,
> Ringing dolefully, loud and clear, [etc.]

Then the other struck up with a loud voice,

> Now isn't it a pity,
> Such a pretty girl as I,
> Should be sent to the factory
> To pine away and die.[12]

On a more sorrowful note, one of the "real life" New York scenes described by Ned Buntline involved a poverty-stricken mother and her daughter who were deriving little relief from their singing as they sewed for a living in their freezing hovel during the winter. Yet the mother asked her daughter to persist in her singing. When the girl produced a sad song on the plight of a sewing girl, the older woman began to weep and requested a more hopeful song. The daughter then sang about never giving in to despair and always trusting in God.[13]

Black laborers loved to sing as they worked. In the South, some white masters encouraged their slaves to sing, believing that singing made them work better and with less resentment over their lot. If the singing centered on sacred song, so much the better. As Manda Boggan, a former Mississippi slave, tells us, her master, a preacher,

> got wuk a plenty out 'en us, fer when yo' turn a bunch ob niggers a loose an' let 'em sing, pray, an' shout all dey wants ter, he's sho' gwine ter turn de wuk off. . . . When I wuz put in de fields, hit wuz wuk from early till late. De fields would be full o' slaves a wukin' hard. Us would look up an see Mars [the master] accomin' across de field wid his bible under his arm. He would walk along whar us wuz a wukin' an' read a text, den us would sing an' pray. De song us liked bes' wuz, "De Day ob Jubilee is come."[14]

To give a second example, a former slave on a Texas plantation said his owner was pleased to hear the men happily singing away: "When old master come to the lot and hear the men singin' like that, he say, 'The boys is lively this mornin'. I's gwine git a big day's plowin' done.'"[15]

Likewise, in factory situations, some persons in charge encouraged their black workers to sing. The proprietor of a tobacco factory in Richmond, Virginia, said, "We encourage their singing as much as we can, for the boys work better while singing. . . . They must sing of their own accord, it is of no use to bid them do it." In this particular factory, the employees were mostly Baptists, with a few Methodists, and their taste ran exclusively to hymns.[16]

Music helped to make people work harder or more efficiently. A North Carolina master won bets from neighbors over his cow driver's, Sampson's, ability to sing a song that invariably started the entire herd running from the fields to the barn.[17] No one had to waste time and effort seeking out the animals and driving them home.

On the other hand, a few masters discouraged singing during working hours, believing there would be a slackening in the work pace. Typical of the experience that thousands of other enslaved African Americans encountered in the antebellum period, Tony Cox said he and his fellow field hands received only discouragement and punishment when they attempted to sing: "At times big fields full would be a workin', dey would be a singin', hollerin' an' a prayin'; de overseer would ride up on hes horse an' think 'nough wuk hadn't been done, den he would beat 'em till dey would fall in de field, an us would haf to tote water to 'em an' bring 'em to."[18]

Sometimes, songs were employed to convey hidden messages to and between the people in the fields. Richard Carruthers remembered one that he used for outwitting the overseers. He kept watch for the working men in the cotton patch when they took a break and lay down to rest, which they were forbidden to do. If he saw the overseer coming, he sang a song of warning,

**276** so that his friends would escape a whipping: "Hold up, hold up, American Spirit!/Hold up, hold up, H-o-o-o-o-o-o-o!" The overseer never caught on.[19]

In as many instances, the messages were not so hidden, as a former slave on the South Carolina plantation of "Maussa Johnnie Fripp" pointed out:

> Sometimes we sing w'en us wuk. One song we sing been lak dis:

> > Go way, Ole Man,
> > Go way, Ole Man,
> > We're you bin all day.
> > If you treat me good,
> > I'll stay 'till de Judgement day,
> > But if you treat me bad,
> > I'll sho' to run away.[20]

For the most part, when singing occurred, masters chose not to intervene, whether they approved or not. On a Georgia rice plantation, slaves flailed the rice stalks to the rhythm of an improvised song, which went on endlessly in call-and-response fashion as long as the task continued. Weeding cotton fields under a hot sun, field hands on an unidentified plantation moved along to:

> What y'u gwine t'do fo' June month?
> > Jerusalem, Jerusalem.
> Pull off y'u coat an' go t' work,
> > Jerusalem, Jerusalem.
> June month's a ha'd month,
> > Jerusalem, Jerusalem.

On a Virginia plantation at harvest time, the "young bucks" cut down "the yellow grain" while "chanting with mellow voices the harvest song 'Cool Water.'"[21]

Black women also labored to the sound of music. Marion Harland writes of one who, like her countless sisters, eased her household duties with song. The woman was observed doing the laundry, scrubbing, then wringing out the linen with energy as she sang:

> O young ladies, ain't you mighty sorry?
> De sun mos' down, an' I gwine away to-morry.

When she had to rub faster, she switched to another song that moved along
more quickly:

> O say, dear doctor, ken you tell
> What will make my sweetheart well?
> She am sick an' I are solly,
> Dat's what makes me melancholy.[22]

Not surprisingly, after breakfast, when everyone went off to begin their
work, they sang along the way, introducing lines such as:

> Old cotton, old corn, see you every morn,
> Old cotton, old corn, see you since I's born.
> Old cotton, old corn, hoe you till dawn,
> Old cotton, old corn, what for you born?

Returning home in the evening, the lines encompassed such words of relief
as:

> We is gwine er round—O, de las' round—
> We is gwine er round—De las' round—
> Ain't yo' glad we gwine round de las' round—
> We is gwine home.[23]

### Bees, Huskings, and Barn Raisings

Neighbors helped each other as a matter of course to accomplish tasks
that invited group effort. These were usually social gatherings of people to
achieve cooperatively a specific objective. The raising of a mill, mentioned
previously, is an example of this shared activity. Fun, frolic, and song attended
sugar maple parties, where young men and women gathered sap and boiled
it down at a central camp, and quilting parties, where women sewed and men
rolled up the sides of the quilts as needed and passed the thread and scissors.
Then there were apple-paring bees, to peel, core, quarter, and string apples up
to dry. Such parties and bees invariably introduced food, dancing, and more
singing after the tasks were accomplished. Sometimes a fiddler or guitarist
was on hand to aid in the music making.[24]

At one New England apple-paring bee in December 1845, the work went
on from late afternoon to 10 P.M., with much music and hilarity. Then came
pies, cheese, doughnuts, hard cider, and dancing in the parlor. The group
lacked a fiddler, so several voices joined in intoning dance songs for the

278    dancers. Nothing was known about waltzes and cotillions. But they did know "four-handed reels" and country dances such as "Chorus Jig," "French Tour," "Fisher's Hornpipe," "Rural Felicity," and "Soldier's Joy." Later came "an eight-handed reel, and an eight-handed 'hooter,' as the boys called it, with which to wind up. This last was danced to the tune of 'The girl I left behind me.'"[25]

The most commonly recorded cooperative activity was the corn-husking bee (or the corn shucking, as it was known in the South). During the months of winter, huskings took place almost every week at some farmhouse. Huge corn piles were stacked up, usually in a barn lighted with pine-knot torches or candles. Men and women, especially young unmarried ones, arrived from miles around, carrying lanterns and torches, singing and joking as they came. All hands then got on with the removal of the husks from the ears, making their labor pleasant with songs, yarns, banter, and the awareness that the chap who husked a red ear had the right to kiss the girl beside him. Then came the feasting and dancing to the music of fiddlers, playing pieces such as "Money Musk," "Money-in-Both-Pockets," and "Yankee Doodle."[26]

Corn shucking in the slave states was a noteworthy harvest observance that took place usually in November and December and had the nature of a slave festival. A master sent invitations to nearby plantations some six miles around, and on the agreed-upon evening about one hundred to three hundred African Americans came down the paths in groups, lighting their way with pine-knot torches and singing verses such as:

> You gwine, ain't you gwine,
> Ain't you gwine to the shuckin' of the corn?
> Oh, yes, I gwine to stay to morning. . . .

Their verse also envisaged the extensive meal to come after the shucking was finished.

To listen to several bands approaching from various routes, leaders lining out the words and entire companies responding with the refrain, could be awe-inspiring.

> When starting for the festivity—for the shuckings were so considered—a solitary refrain might be heard a mile or two away, then another would join, and as they approached, more and more, until they arrived, singing, at the corn-pile in a company of fifteen or twenty; sometimes two or three of such companies would approach at the same time, making the night air resonant with melody—I say

melody, for I know of no music so melodious to my ear, at a short distance, as an old time corn-song.[27]

After arrival, the workers often divided themselves into at least two teams, each assigned a huge corn pile and its team effort directed by a captain atop the pile. Each captain, his cap garnished with the inside shuck of an ear of corn, led the singing of his team, frequently improvising words and music, the team joining in a choral refrain. For example:

> My cow, Maria,
> She fell in de fire.
> (Chorus)    Go de corn! Go de corn!

A shucking contest ensued, with the winning team receiving a prize from the master and executing a walkaround, beating pots and pails and exuberantly strutting and singing. After hours of feeding, drinking, and dancing, all the celebrants departed for home in the early morning, not to rest but to carry on with their customary daily work. Their stamina had to have been extraordinary.[28]

Junius Quattlebaum, once a slave in South Carolina, says the shuckers on his plantation not only liked to sing as they worked but were commanded to sing by his master, who himself liked to join in. He also enjoyed his tipple and insisted that the shuckers drink with him:

> Us used to have big corn shuckin's on de plantation at night 'long 'bout de fust of November of every year. All de corn was hauled from de fields and put in two or three big piles on de barnyard and de slaves would get 'round them, sing and shuck de corn. De slave women would hang buckets of raw tar afire on staves drove in de ground 'round de crowd, to give light. Them was sho' happy times.
>
> Marster would give all de grown slaves a dram or two of pure apple brandy, on them corn shuckin' nights and take several smiles [drinks] hisself. I 'members so well one of them nights, dat marster come to de barnyard, where we was all lit up, a singing' fit to kill hisself. Us was s'prised to see marster settin' down wid us niggers and shuckin' corn as fas' as us was. After a spell, him stood up and took 'nother smile, then say: "Pass de jug 'round and let's all take a drink." Wid dat, one of de niggers grab de jug of liquor and passed it 'round to all de shuckers. Then marster say: "Everybody sing." Some of de niggers 'quire: "What you gwine to sing?" He say: "Sing dis song: 'Pas 'round de bottle and we'll all take a drink.'" Some of

*280*    them in de crowd 'jected to dat song, 'cause they had 'nough liquor in them to 'jist do anything. Marster kinda scratch his head and say: "Well, let me git a pole and you all is gwine to sing." And singin' dere was, as sho' as you's born. Them niggers 'round de corn piles dat night h'isted dat song right now; dere was no waitin' for de pole or nothin' else. They wanted to sing bad.[29]

William Cullen Bryant, visiting a plantation in South Carolina in 1843, witnessed a corn-husking evening to which African Americans came singing from nearby plantations. They continued to sing, and gleefully, too, as they stripped the husks from the ears, with an occasional joke added as a bonus. Most ditties were comic in character, the tunes only occasionally "wild and plaintive," as was the tune for the following:

> Johnny come down de hollow.
>     Oh hollow!
> Johnny come down de hollow.
>     Oh hollow!
> De nigger-trader got me.
>     Oh hollow!
> De speculator bought me.
>     Oh hollow!
> I'm sold for silver dollars.
>     Oh hollow!
> Boys, go patch de pony.
>     Oh hollow!
> Bring him round de corner.
>     Oh hollow!
> I'm goin' away to Georgia.
>     Oh hollow!
> Boys, good-by forever!
>     Oh hollow!

Next came a song called "Jenny Gone Away," then a "monkey-song, probably of African origin, in which the principal singer impersonated a monkey with all sorts of odd gesticulations, and the other negroes bore part in the chorus, 'Dan, dan, who's de dandy?'" Other animal songs followed. When work was finished, all adjourned to the kitchen. One man then commenced whistling and beating time with two sticks upon the floor. Although already having labored all day in the fields and then at the husking, several men entered into a series of sprightly and swaggering dances, rhythmically beating with heel and toe upon the floor. Also introduced was a ridiculous military parade, "a sort of burlesque of our militia trainings."[30]

### Music in Public Places

Places open to all persons included boardinghouses, hotels, resorts, saloons, taverns, and dance houses. They provided food and lodgings for let, dealt in agreeable diversions, or otherwise catered to the public at a price.

Living in boardinghouses was common in the decades prior to the Civil War, especially for those who could not get services owing to the shortage of help, were uncertain of the length of their stay in a place, or were unable to afford the purchase of a permanent residence. Lodgings offering room and board harbored mill girls in Lowell, students attending academies distant from home, single men and women, and even entire families. Some places barely covered the necessities; others offered every comfort and convenience. The more elegantly furnished boardinghouses boasted a parlor supplied with a piano, where it was customary for residents and their visitors to gather and entertain themselves at the end of the day. If they were fortunate, a capable singer, violinist, flutist, or guitarist was present to contribute to the diversions. Arriving from England for a visit to the United States in 1829, James Boardman observed:

> The *pensions,* or boarding-houses, are very agreeable places of residence. . . . All the various inmates meet at table as at the English watering places; and a well-furnished drawing-room, with its French timepiece, candelabra, and vases, is open to all during the day, as well as for the re-unions in the evening; where music and dancing for the young, and conversation for those who have passed the heyday of life, contribute to the enjoyment of these mixed but polite and agreeable circles.[31]

He also mentioned that he knew of unpleasant boardinghouses that ministered to the needs of the less affluent.

"After tea," wrote Harriet Martineau of boardinghouse living, "it is common practice to hand the young ladies to the piano, to play and sing to a party, composed chiefly of gentlemen and brought together on no principle of selection except mere respectability." In the summer months, with windows wide open, people occupying neighboring homes were a captive audience for such music making. A furious George Templeton Strong had his sleep interrupted one night in July 1836: "I was aroused by a fearful yelling. . . . Going to the window I found that the unearthly noises in question proceeded from . . . a 'young female lady,' at a house a considerable way off, yelling forth 'The Mellow Horn,' at the top of her voice, with a running accompaniment of what had once been (probably) a piano. . . . Some boarding school miss, probably."[32]

If lacking a public area to which they could resort, renters took to their rooms for their music making.

Hotels and inns accommodated a more transient population and offered more personal services. At the famous Willard's Hotel in Washington, D.C., a rainy morning in 1857 found the guests crowding the drawing room, wrote Mary Windle. She watched "the buoyant figure of a child of some eight years . . . flying through a waltz upon a young masculine's arm." Seated at the piano, "two bright-lipped Hebes were committing a grievous massacre upon the beauties of a new opera." At the same time, "in another direction a yawning masculine . . . listened to the notes of an old air on a guitar." Meanwhile, other guests gossiped and flirted, while little girls played with dolls.[33]

At one time Fanny Fern was asked about hotel etiquette and the "rights of persons occupying rooms" whose windows opened on the veranda. Could they complain when "a person draws a chair in front and commences singing 'Pop goes the Weasel,' with variations, or whistles 'Yankee Doodle' for an hour?" Furthermore, on an uncomfortably hot and humid night, if one was sweating and tossing in bed at midnight, was it proper to protest if "some enterprising individual, in the parlor opposite your door, played with one hand, the inspiring tune of 'Lanigan's Ball,' or rattled discordantly through 'I love but Thee'?" Fern's answer was an unequivocal *yes!*[34]

In small towns and villages, the local inn provided not only food and shelter for travelers but also a place where local citizens could come to amuse themselves. A spacious chamber was usually available for communal activities such as balls, concerts, theatrical presentations, and town meetings. Thomas Ashe says he was staying at an inn in Wheeling, West Virginia, where he decided to enter the large common room. He found, to his dismay, that it was filled with people, only a few of them guests, noisily playing cards, drinking, smoking, dancing, and singing. "The *music* consisted of two bangies [banjos?], played by negroes nearly in a state of nudity, and a [f]lute, through which a Chickesaw breathed with much occasional exertion and violent gesticulation." The social gathering broke up after a fight began over politics. The innkeeper told Ashe that these affairs often ended with a brawl, if not duels, and some fatalities had resulted.[35]

The designations *inn* and *tavern* were used interchangeably during the antebellum years. The latter term gradually was understood to mean those lodging houses that were also convenient meeting places for the local citizens, and that emphasized conviviality and specialized in alcohol to be drunk on the premises.

Hotels in resorts were places offering recreational facilities, to which vacationers went to relax or seek pleasure. The English novelist Anthony Trollope visited Newport, Rhode Island, and loathed the music making in the "huge, dismal, and depressing" drawing room of the resort hotel where he was staying. The piano always to be found in such rooms constantly left him at the mercy of "forlorn ladies" who insisted on playing it and singing. Harsh, loud, and unmusical sounds assailed his ears and produced "exceptional mental depression":

> The ladies, or probably some one lady, will sing, and as she hears her own voice ring and echo through the lofty corners and round the empty walls, she is surprised at her own force, and with increased efforts sings louder and still louder. She is tempted to fancy that is suddenly gifted with some power of vocal melody unknown to her before, and filled with the glory of her own performance shouts till the whole house rings. At such moments she at least is happy, if no one else is.[36]

On the other hand, another English traveler, Amelia Murray, found the music quite agreeable at the Flume House, in the White Mountains of New Hampshire. Two or three ladies and one gentleman entertained the company with solo songs, duets, and trios during a rainy morning. In the afternoon, some people played cards and one or two women did needlework in the drawing room. At the same time, "a young lady played nursery songs at the piano" while "six little children belonging to different visitors" joined "their voices in the choruses, one as young as four, but all were in tune." In the evening dancing and more singing took place.[37]

The most celebrated watering place in America was Saratoga Springs, New York, where even the more straitlaced visitors enjoyed its gaiety and lightness. "I see in it," said Charles Sedgwick, "a great compensation to those who at home are weary and worn with care, and, if possible, a still more merciful promise for those who, in the variety and excitement of a crowd, for a time forget their own insignificance." Bands tootled outdoors; one or two hotels maintained their own instrumental ensembles; amateurs sang and played on piano and guitar in the hotel music room.[38]

Like city hotels, Saratoga hotels had their share of singers and instrumentalists whose musical cravings were irrepressible, though unwelcome to other lodgers. In a few instances, no reprimand was forthcoming however

284  disruptive the sounds, because of the wealth or standing of the guest. In July
1833 George Morris sent a letter from Saratoga, saying:

> Young ——— is famous for his flute, his dog, and the number of ser-
> vants. . . . He plays the German flute with great unction. . . . He
> lodges at ——— hotel, near the top of the house—that apartment
> having been assigned him on account of his musical propensities.
> . . . He is the horror of the surrounding country; and complaints
> have frequently been lodged against him for annoying quiet, well-dis-
> posed citizens throughout the day, and keeping them awake during
> most of the night. Wherever he goes he pays double board, as all
> fluting gentlemen undoubtedly ought to do, and therefore enjoys a
> kind of privilege to blow away as loud and as often as he thinks
> proper.[39]

Three institutions open to the public, none of them usually held in the
highest repute, were saloons, brothels, and dance houses. The patrons of
these establishments, almost exclusively men, expected to find music, among
other things, when they entered their doors. Any one of the types could
embrace the other two, the difference in the nomenclature indicating where
the emphasis lay.

The saloon, in some instances, was a designation for a richly ornamented
hall where balls and formal dinners were held and to which respectable men
and women could come without any twinge of guilt. Indicative of its nature,
the saloon we talk about here was variously also called a barroom, taproom,
beer cellar, groggery, watering hole, and rum mill. Its raison d'être was the
alcoholic drinks freely purchased and consumed on the premises. A youthful
reporter, Walt Whitman, inveighed against such saloons in the *Brooklyn Daily
Eagle* in November 1846. Undergoing a fit of righteousness, he warned of the
dangers that young men encountered in the city:

> On all sides, and at every stop, some temptation assails them; but all
> the others joined together are nothing compared with the seductive
> enchantments which have been thrown around the practice of in-
> toxication, in some five or six of the more public and noted taverns
> called "musical saloons," or some other name which is used to hide
> their hideous nature. These places are multiplying. The persons en-
> gaged in the sale of ardent spirits are brought to see that their trade,
> unless they can join something to it, as a make-weight, will shortly
> vanish into thin air, and their gains along with it. Thus they have
> hit upon the expedient of MUSIC, as a lure to induce customers, and
> in too many cases with fatally extensive success.[40]

Was the Opera Hotel Saloon one of these? It advertised in 1848 that it promised "Free Concerts. Sweet music and a social glass may be enjoyed at the Opera Hotel Saloon, No. 43 Chambers Street, every evening. Hear ye that, ye bachelors and widowers, who ain't got any homes? Just call in and spend an hour tonight. The charming Miss ———— and her sweet notes will drive dull care away."[41]

Saloons, wherever they might be, tried to provide some musical entertainment, no matter how primitive. In Mobile, Alabama, the Revolver Saloon offered a peripatetic fiddler who had commenced playing his instrument only six weeks before. The performance was terrible and not helped by an accompaniment of bells set ringing with one foot, a triangle with the other, and a pair of cymbals made to clash by bringing his knees together. Few of the men present seemed to mind. In Clarksville, Georgia, a black fiddler, Lewie, was much in demand in the "rude saloons" because he attracted customers, even though he was constantly drunk and given to outrageous conduct. While visiting Pittsburgh, the actor Noah Ludlow could find "no place or places of rational amusement open to the public." So he and his fellow actor Aleck Drake strolled over to a beer cellar where they heard a good singer rendering "Willie Brewed a Peck o' Maut," "John Anderson, My Jo," and other Scottish songs. With beer mugs in hand, Ludlow, Drake, and several other men were soon joining in on such ballads as "Auld Robin Gray" and "Curly-Headed Plough-Boy."[42]

In one instance, the music in a saloon imparted knowledge of a sort. A gold prospector left California and landed in New York City in 1855, but did not know where to stay. He did, nevertheless, remember "a song, sung by a pretty dancing girl in a saloon in Sacramento." The verse she sang entered his mind: "I'm Going to the Astor House to Dine,/And I won't be back 'til half past nine." After which she had done a double-shuffle. He acted on the information, went to the Astor House, and stayed there until he was ready to complete his travel home.[43]

A brothel off Broadway, in the New York City of the late 1840s, can stand as an example of establishments also known as whorehouses, stews, sporting houses, bawdy houses, cathouses, bordello, call houses, cribs, and fancy houses. A pretty servant girl greeted clients at the door and led them into a cozy parlor furnished with comfortable ottomans and sofas, splendid Brussels carpets, and voluptuous paintings. A stunning young woman was entertaining on a fine Chickering piano. In an adjoining room were about thirty attractive women. The clients were plied with alcoholic beverages; the pianist struck up a variety of popular tunes and vivacious dances. One drank, sang, danced, then proceeded to a negligée-clad madame for the "business" to follow.[44]

A dance house, also called a dance hall, was a place open to the public, sometimes charging an admission fee, that provided its customers with music, space for dancing, drink and other refreshments, and, often, dancing partners, who might double as bed partners for a price. All too often they were shabby and disreputable places, like the "lowlife" New York dance house called the "Star and Garter." The music came from "one fiddle scraped by a blind negro, a tambourine played by a very fat Dutch girl, and a harp touched not very lightly by 'a German travelling *artiste*,' and to the concord of sound thus produced, many a lively measure was stepped over the rather . . . greasy floor. Cotillions, fore-and-afters, reels, and waltzes were danced."[45]

The most widely known dance house was that operated by an African American, Pete Williams, in the Five Points section of New York City. It was also dubbed Dickens' Place, after Charles Dickens visited it in 1842. Here were found a black band (at various times, a fiddler, guitarist, trumpet player, bass fiddler, and drummer were named), waitresses who sang and danced, and prostitutes. The coarse entertainment, raucous singing, bawdy dancing, and recurrent fisticuffs that spilled over into the street occasioned many complaints from neighbors. As many as two hundred African Americans would come of a night for entertainment. The upper-class white men who made frequent excursions to the hangout seeking pleasure prevented its being shut down.

George Foster described the building Pete Williams occupied as looking shabby and rickety, and the dance hall itself as giving the impression of being huge and desolate. Wooden benches lined the walls, a wobbly platform in the middle of the room held the instrumental players, and women, three-quarters of them black and one-quarter of them white, awaited the male customers. The white women, in particular, looked like "bleary-eyed, idiotic, beastly wretches." Sailors, present in large numbers, were easy prey for the thieves and prostitutes.

Piercing trumpet blasts and frenetic drumming assailed Foster's ears when he paid the "one shilling" admission fee and entered. As he watched:

> Each gentleman, by a simultaneous and apparently preconcerted
> movement now 'drawrs' his 'chawr' of tobacco and depositing it
> carefully in his trowsers pocket, flings his arms about his buxom
> inamorata and salutes her whiskey-breathing lips with a chaste kiss,
> which extracts a scream of delight from the delicate creature, something between the whoop of an Indian and the neighing of a horse.
> And now the orchestra strikes up "Cooney in de Holler" and the
> company "cavorts to places." Having taken their positions and saluted each other with the most ludicrous exaggeration of ceremony,
> the dance proceeds for a few moments in tolerable order. But soon

the excitement grows—the dancers begin contorting their bodies and accelerating their movements, accompanied with shouts of laughter and yells of encouragement and applause, until all observance of the figure is forgotten and every one leaps, stamps, screams and hurras on his or her own hook. Affairs are now at their height. The black leader of the orchestra increases the momentum of his elbow and calls out the figures in convulsive efforts to be heard, until shining streams of perspiration roll in cascades down his ebony face; the dancers now wild with excitement . . . leap frantically about like howling dervishes, clasp their partners in their arms, and at length conclude the dance in hot confusion and disorder. As soon as things have cooled off a little each cavalier walks up to the bar, pays his shilling for the dance, and the floor is cleared for a new set; and so it goes all night.[46]

One cannot help wondering what prompted his New York hosts to take Charles Dickens to Pete Williams's dance house, and how he reacted to this scene.

### Amateurs in Public Performance

Musical ladies and gentlemen of high reputation were known to lend their talents to benefit charity causes, though circumspectly. So long as their good characters were not compromised, they consented to appear as singers and instrumentalists at formal public concerts. Mr. and Mrs. George Templeton Strong and their friends, all prominent in New York society, were in the habit of holding private meetings to rehearse music of high caliber. In April 1854 they graciously contributed their services to a charity affair. A reporter who wrote up the event, possibly Richard Storrs Willis, was awed by the social eminence of the performers and described their voices as having "uncommon power and richness." Although the sound was often "thrilling" and "magnificent," he thought the amateur musicians would have been still more effective if their "natural unwillingness to appear before a critical and numerous audience had not rendered an intervening curtain of silk necessary to their comfort and self-possession."[47]

Other leading citizens were somewhat less circumspect, like the group of "young gentlemen of the city" of Richmond, Virginia, who openly participated in a "dramatic and musical entertainment," assisted by "some professional Ladies and Gentlemen." In Charlestown, a suburb of Boston, citizens staged a "Festival of Beauty" that consisted of amateur singing and dancing. "Throngs of fairy-dressed young ladies, attired in white, and decorated with

**288**  a profusion of every variety of roses, made the hall echo with their joyous tones." The performance met with such enthusiastic approval that it was repeated in several other cities and towns.[48] Whether in Richmond or Charlestown, the public appearances were not prompted by charitable causes. There is every reason, however, to believe that decorum was duly observed.

Amateur musicians of less than exalted status did not worry overly about their social reputations. There was a Jack Power, recognized as "an excellent performer on the banjo," who one evening in 1848, "with three or four others, gave a 'nigger' concert in the dining-saloon at the Parker House." George Templeton Strong would never have approved. He would have approved even less of the fifteen-year-old Daniel Emmett, on the threshold of musical professionalism. A traveling show had arrived in his Ohio village minus its violinist. Daniel, then working for his blacksmith father, was asked to replace the violinist and, as an inducement, was allowed to sing a song he had composed. The company with Daniel performed on the village green before the entire village. Nobody present was taken aback to find the boy playing upon his fiddle, but "when he appeared as a black-faced character and sang OLD DAN TUCKER, the town folks roared and cheered with delight," according to H. Ogden Wintermute.[49] With this appearance, Daniel Emmett was believed to have crossed over the line, from amateur to professional.

Sarah Royce, who thought of herself as a lady, was recently arrived in San Francisco. She was immediately shocked at the avaricious disposition of some local women, who constantly looked for presents from men. These women were at the opposite end of the social spectrum from Strong and his friends. Amateur musicians they and their daughters might be; ladies they were not. In their public appearances, they showed a lack of prudence and a lapse of ethical conduct.

> There were instances of women watching each other, jealously, each afraid the other would get more or richer presents than herself. This evil became painfully prominent, as time went on and more families came to the coast, in connection with musical and literary entertainments, school exhibitions, etc. Little girls and young ladies who sung, played, or recited on such occasions often received, thrown at their feet before they left the stage, expensive jewelry, or even pieces of coin. They commonly accepted them; often with looks of exultation; and, still worse, there were mothers who not merely countenanced the thing, but even boasted of the amount their daughters had thus received.[50]

# Denouement

GEORGE ROOT WAS AN EMINENT MUSIC EDUCATOR AC-
tive during the middle of the nineteenth century. A knowledgeable musician, he composed several simple songs, from
1852 through 1862, that achieved great popularity: "Hazel Dell," "There's
Music in the Air," "Rosalie, the Prairie Flower," "The Battle Cry of Freedom,"
and "Tramp! Tramp! Tramp!" Root limited himself to writing only uncomplicated works, although he had the capacity to create large-scale compositions.
Why did he hold himself back? Because he was an astute observer of his
fellow Americans, aware of their cultural wants and limitations. He thought
sensibly about the likely role of music in their lives and created works in
accord with that role. At first, he concealed the authorship of his songs,
feeling guilty that he was not writing something "better." Later, encouraged
by the music educator and hymn writer Lowell Mason, he learned to be happy
about his ability to reach his fellow Americans with music they could truly
enjoy.

Root wrote in his autobiography that some compositions, whether modest ballad or complex symphony, had a "mysterious quality" that caused them
to continue in people's favor while the vast remainder swiftly passed out of
mind. The most learned students of music could analyze a work's structure,
true. Analysis did not unlock a work's secrets, however. No scholar was
capable of discovering what that puzzling yet wonderful attribute is that
brings music alive. Furthermore, it is not enough for pundits to tell us that a
work is worthy of high regard, he said. We must feel that it is so. The capacity
to feel thusly is shared by all people, sophisticated and unsophisticated. A
variety of fine compositions, from the most multifaceted to the most modest,
elicited that feeling from people, depending on their experience, education,
and background. Americans in humble circumstances and living under con-

ditions unlike anything in Europe found it difficult to become lovers of highly artistic music. Thorough musical training in America was close to impossible. Exceptionally well trained performing groups were scarce. The money to maintain them was difficult to find. Americans were insufficiently prepared to appreciate the offerings of the few that existed.

The majority of Americans of his time did love music, Root insisted, but could assimilate only "the little way-side flowers and simple scenery of the land of tonic, dominant and subdominant." Music more complicated than this was "a kind of desert" that they found "entirely unfit to live in." He warned the few whose tastes were more developed not to despise the simpler songs. "The way-side flower has its place in the economy of God's creation as truly as the oak, and the little hill and the brooklet are as truly beautiful as the mountain and torrent are grand." As for rubbish, it was found in all kinds of music.

Root had in mind the distinction that a few Americans of higher refinement and education, such as John Sullivan Dwight, insisted on making between noble and commonplace art. Yes, a Handel oratorio and a Beethoven symphony achieved the highest reaches of the human spirit. With that, Root agreed. Nevertheless, he had no use for the untruth that passed as wisdom which decreed that the tragic and majestic music of cultivated beings was transformed by corrupt means into the sentimental and vulgar music of the common herd, especially if the herd was American.

To him and, as we have seen in the previous nine chapters, to the vast majority of men and women of his day, the value of a musical work did not lie in its complexity and sophisticated structure but in the way it met people's needs: in its usefulness, in addition to the feelings it brought forth. His underlying message was, Let people employ music according to their capacities and desires, so long as it communicates something to them. If you can educate them to appreciate more complex works, fine. But if they cannot respond, do not condemn them.[1] There was danger in this attitude. Taken to its extreme, it allowed for no demands on listeners. They could always remain in safe and familiar territory. Therefore, it could lead to perpetual philistinism.

Note the concern and also the optimism of the New Orleans–born pianist and composer Louis Moreau Gottschalk when he wrote in 1862:

There is no doubt that there are immense lacunae in certain details of our civilization. Our appreciation of the *beax-arts* is not always enlightened, and we treat them like parasites occupying a usurped place. The wheels of our government are, like our manners, too new not to grate upon the ear sometimes. We perhaps worship a little too much the golden calf, and do not kill the fatted calf often enough to feast the elect of thought. Each of us thinks himself as good as (if not better than) any other man—an excellent faith that engenders self-respect but often leads us to wish to reduce to our own level those to whose level we cannot attain. These little faults happily are not national traits; they appertain to all young societies. We are, in a word, like the beautiful children of whom Montaigne speaks, who bite the nurse's breast, and whom the exuberance of health sometimes renders turbulent.[2]

Root was also confident that the young American society would eventually mature into a people who would nurture and cherish the arts.

The previous chapters of this study have established one indisputable fact: music, in the uncomplicated mode that Root described, was indeed prominent in the lives of almost all Americans. As already noted, a traveler could journey anywhere, from eastern city to wagon train to California settlement, and find music encouraged and practiced whenever possible. Whatever that music, it always fitted the conditions in which the individuals who employed it found themselves. Little by little, the musical usages in the newly settled lands acknowledged, by force of circumstances, a dependence and trust in cultural equality for all. By midcentury the young American democracy, too, had articulated shared concepts of cultural beliefs and sentiments, in harmony with its principles of political and social equality for all. The one tragic exception involved the institution of slavery. Even here, however, a certain ambivalence was manifest. Bondage exacted heavy and degrading labor, true. Yet it did not necessarily demand musical conformity. African Americans therefore were able to develop a parallel art to that of white Americans, borrowing freely from white sources and synthesizing it with their African backgrounds and shaping it to meet their own requirements.

On balance, we gather from the evidence that democracy meant noninterference with any person's chosen relationship to art. Early nineteenth-century Americans saw themselves as a people for whom leisure was a luxury and working a necessity. They were uneasy if idle, pleased to find some activity that would occupy them, and especially pleased if that activity provided exhilaration of some sort. Music, to them, provided reasonable and satisfying exhilaration. All men and women found themselves receptive to music's appeal and welcomed it into their lives, but each in his or her own way.

Cultural freedom allowed a citizen to choose to go in the direction of his or her own desires, however contradictory to that of another person, thereby meeting the needs of the greatest number. From the democratic viewpoint of the time, this dynamic, which attempted to balance different interests, was thought to achieve cultural harmony. Each citizen cultivating the particular music that most satisfied him would contribute to a result profitable for all citizens. In this way alone could a democratic nation arrive at maturity. With regard to that happiness whose pursuit the Declaration of Independence advocated, all Americans had the right to share in it so long as morality was not transgressed. Different musics gave different hapinesses to different people. Let everyone achieve happiness through whatever music proved effective; that was the consensus.

If citizens turned away from music or if they wished to define it in their own terms, it was their right to do so. If they chose to see it simply as a small accomplishment, a pleasing endowment or only a minor skill expected in polite society, one could not gainsay them. If they chose to use it for momentary diversion, something with which to idle away an hour or two around a piano or on the dance floor, they had to be allowed that freedom. In short, most Americans thought they should avoid meddling with one another's taste preferences and should insist on freedom from cultural control. It is true that these pages have quoted from the writings of critics who attacked one or more of these positions. However, none of those critics would have dared to force his or her opinion on others. Opinions were in the nature of proposals that the cultural electorate could vote up or down.

Believers in democracy upheld the right to perform and listen to music according to choice. The well-to-do and well-educated found happiness in their opera and symphony; the middle class's happiness came through sentimental and lightweight comic songs; the lower class happily sponsored its minstrel songs and racy ballads; and country folk continued to preserve their traditional airs, some of ancient provenance, that gave them pleasure. Anyone was free to cross over from one type of music to another, experimentally or permanently.

Thousands of men, women, boys, and girls did go beyond the more limited purposes of music. Again and again, we have quoted individuals saying they valued music for its extraordinary aesthetic appeal, its deliverance of a sense of beauty that defied categorization. Nevertheless, this beauty was always joined to sensibility. An effective composition succeeded in calling forth their deepest emotions. It eased their minds in moments of mental turmoil and maintained their links to the past and hopes for the future. Furthermore, educated and uneducated people alike discovered in music a transcending experience not realizable in the usual course of events—in a string quartet by Beethoven for one, in a hymn by Lowell Mason for another. The carried-away listener felt close to a supreme being, whether apprehended as God, sublime spirit, soul, truth, or love. When an out-of-the-ordinary musical composition affected listeners, these pages have quoted them as saying that it touched them in an inexpressible but profoundly moving fashion. The sounds they heard seemed to delineate the human condition, especially in its highest aspirations. The Americans of these decades remained united about what dimension that experience took, but attempted no explanation of it. The phenomenon went beyond words.

John Moore, a New Hampshire music educator and compiler of the first music encyclopedia in English (1854), summarizes the effect of music on the Americans of his time:

> The art of music has special claims upon the American people. All men have been endowed with susceptibility to its influence. The child is no sooner born than the nurse begins to soothe its repose by music. Through life, music is employed to animate the depressed, to inspire the timid with courage, to lend new wings to devotion, and to give utterance to joy or sorrow. It is predominantly the language of the heart.[3]

What no American would accept was the notion that a musical work took on an independent value with no link to what might be considered beautiful, pleasureful, or useful. He or she would have scorned the idea, advanced a hundred years later by aestheticians and musicians who favored modern ways, that a composition's reason for existence centered on itself and needed no justification beyond itself, and that beauty was not a valid criterion for judgment of its worth. In the words of John Cage, to say a work was beautiful only meant that it had "clicked" in one's mind, that it had made a hit and was found agreeable, nothing more. A nineteenth-century American would have replied, If that is your belief, fine, but do not try to force it on others.

The urge to become acquainted with and make music of some sort remained strong throughout the first half of the nineteenth century. We know that pianos and melodeons by the thousands entered American parlors during the antebellum years. Failing these, there were violins, flutes, and guitars. As the years went by and demand increased, native manufacture of instruments grew tremendously and the price of instruments dropped significantly. Their acquisition became all the more easy. For the penniless, homemade banjos, reed pipes, fiddles, and percussion instruments answered. The drive to fashion a musical instrument out of whatever materials were on hand was found in isolated farmhouse, slave cabin, and wilderness camp. And always there was the voice, which called for no expense of money and time. Untrained, it could still make music. Moreover, in these decades characterized

**294**  by constant movement, the voice was undeniably transportable. Nobody had to remain without song, and nobody did.

Older children passed on to younger children a repertoire of play-songs. Boys and girls learned sacred and secular songs from the lips of parents and grandparents. Relatives, friends, and visitors opened children's minds to wider musical worlds. The love for and knowledge about favored songs was also transferred from one generation to the next. This important avenue for music learning was certainly a determinant of taste. Moreover, it ensured cultural continuity and steadied taste to withstand swift changes in style and fashion.

To an extent unknown today, hymn singing prevailed in nearly all households as well as in church. Antebellum Americans were by and large a religious people devoted to praising God through sacred songs. Hymn singing was seen both to facilitate entrance to heaven and also to promote blessed harmony in individuals and communities, thus abetting happiness. Moreover, as Moore pointed out:

> When we look at church music, as we now enjoy it in the United States, and compare it with its infancy, we cannot but wonder at the progress it has made. One of the most essential preparations for eternity is delight in praising God; to be able to do this acceptably, in sacred song, is a higher requirement than even devotedness in prayer.[4]

For those who desired more formal musical education, there was the possibility of private or class instruction at a private academy or public school or by attendance at a singing school. Contemporary educators insisted that happiness came to any child directed toward better comprehension of musical sounds, and that all youngsters derived a healthy contentment from the ability to sing and listen. Those who possessed sufficient financial means studied with European musicians resident in the United States. As steamships proved their utility and capability to transport people over long distances more swiftly and dependably than before, a handful of enterprising Americans crossed the Atlantic to get their musical education. On the other hand, most people, of necessity, were self-taught. Depending on the manner of education or noneducation and exposure to music, discrimination formed. Some individuals expressed preferences narrowly centered on "Art" but were otherwise intolerant. Others, whose appreciation was broadly based, embraced ditty and artistic statement. Still others, whose discernment was rudimentary in development, confined themselves only to what was taken in from rather crude surroundings.

Thoroughly trained professional musicians scarcely existed anywhere, and the very few on hand were almost always European émigrés. These took pride in their talent and in an artistic repertoire imported entirely from Europe. The number of opera companies and symphony associations in the United States was no more than a dozen for the entire nation. Chamber ensembles numbered less than half that. It remained for traveling virtuoso performers such as the violinist Ole Bull and the distinguished singer Jenny Lind to sow the seed of "high art" in various sections of the country.

What was far more freely available to Americans, at least in urban areas, was the music purveyed by oratorio societies, whose reliance for the most part was on amateur singers, though regularly aided by professional vocalists in the solo parts. A piano, organ, or when feasible, an orchestra supported the vocalists. Oratorio concerts presented anthems, cantatas, oratorios, and occasionally motets and masses. As a result, the introduction to music other than the undemanding songs and dances that made up the popular fare came mainly from the oratorio societies.

The distinction between art, popular, and folk music that became established in the twentieth century hardly entered the considerations of antebellum Americans. Given the opportunity and having the admission fee, men and women wanted to and did attend symphony concerts, operatic productions, and oratorio offerings. If their backgrounds left them unprepared to deal with what was offered, they might feel that their curiosity was satisfied and cease attending. They would freely admit their failure to understand, but this did not lead to aversion of this music. On balance, animosity against the artistic genres was expressed mainly by those who were highly religious. Yet the criticism was limited mainly to opera singers whose remuneration was thought exorbitant and attitudes undemocratic, and to operas whose themes delved into uncontrollably passionate emotions, sexual desire, and other forms of unethical and immoral behavior. About such issues, many men and women did feel strongly. However, we must keep in mind that most Americans had never experienced operas or symphonies, never seen a prima donna, and had no opinions whatsoever about them.

Americans were more likely to have heard traveling professional singers, English and American, who introduced them to easily understood and remembered vocal pieces. They would also have taken instruction from leaders of sacred music, who guided them toward hymns of the plainest variety. Although certain musical individuals, such as the Hutchinson Family Singers and Lowell Mason, did occupy positions of influence, they did not speak for any social class or distinguishable group. They could recommend a song or cultural reform; they could not command its acceptance. Music was disseminating itself throughout the land in a fashion that made the directing of musical culture by one person, one group, or one urban cultural center impossible. Cultural authority was in no way exercisable, as it was in Europe.

296 Indeed, the repudiation of cultural authority was a revolutionary notion, and one especially put forth during the Jacksonian era.

Because the appearances of even the professional singers were unpredictable and usually far between, Americans most often were left to their own resources for entertainment, singing to themselves or to and with family and friends. These pages have chronicled what Walt Whitman meant when he wrote, "I hear America singing":

> I hear America singing, the varied carols I hear;
> Those of mechanics—each one singing his, as it should be, blithe
> and strong;
> The carpenter singing his, as he measures his plank or beam,
> The mason singing his, as he makes ready for work, or leaves off
> work;
> The boatman singing what belongs to him in his boat—the deck-
> hand singing on the steamboat deck;
> The shoemaker singing as he sits on his bench—the hatter singing
> as he stands;
> The wood-cutter's song—the ploughboy's, on his way in the morn-
> ing, or at the noon intermission, or at sundown;
> The delicious singing of the mother—or of the young wife at work—
> or of the girl sewing or washing—Each singing what belongs to
> her, and to none else;
> The day what belongs to the day—At night the party of young fel-
> lows, robust, friendly,
> Singing, with open mouths, their strong melodious songs.[5]

Whitman's words were literally true. The United States was indeed a music-making nation.

Differences are easily discernable between Americans then and now. Self-entertainment is no longer the necessity that it was then. We now have ample trained professional musicians and actors, theaters, performance centers, motion pictures, television, radio, and recordings to keep us perpetually amused. Organized sports events and museum exhibitions provide further diversion. The availability of rapid air transportation has made tourism a major source for recreation.

The life of a musical composition is much briefer today. Then, a composition did not swiftly outwear its welcome. Children delighted in the music their grandparents had treasured. In addition, Americans took a lively interest in new music of every type—a song of Henry Russell, a walkaround of Dan Emmett, a symphony of Beethoven, an oratorio of Mendelssohn, a noc-

turne of Chopin. In contrast, popular songs and styles now come and go at a
dizzying rate. A new artistic work is heard reluctantly and incuriously once
and then is forgotten. The variety of different musics available to the public
today is stupendous and even confusing, when compared to what was available a century and a half ago. The role of parents, school, and religion in
shaping musical attitudes is nil. The influence of advertising, of insistently
publicizing popular pieces to elicit predictable responses, has become a well-
honed skill. At the same time the multicultural infusions and intrusions from
every part of today's globe were unheard of in the antebellum years. Now
every group—ethnic, class, racial, ideological—pushes for the acceptance of
its cultural value system by others. There are some critics today who advocate
openness to all musical experience—although to be open to all may mean a
commitment to none. The cultural message we bring children is diffuse,
lacking in focus. Not infrequently, the young flounder about, acquire a bit of
flotsam here a piece of jetsam there, and must seek cultural salvation on their
own.

Yet similarities between then and now also exist. Music is still ubiquitous
throughout the country. However, the tendency is toward more passive listening, not active participation. The reign of popular music is as strong as ever,
despite the increased art music and operatic offerings. Music continues to be
valuable in commemorations, anniversaries, national and religious holidays,
public and private ceremonies, and special occasions such as weddings, funerals, and the like. Dancing is as popular as ever, and music is still intimately
allied to it. Finally, music persists in living within the context of feeling, not
intellect—no matter what some contemporary art composers say. It is still a
vehicle for nostalgia and remembrance. Musical therapy is now, as then, a
recognized treatment of disorders. Moreover, for many, music endures as
a means toward transcendence, toward attaining to deity.

Whatever the future of America, music will be there, as it was in the past
and is in the present. What forms it will take cannot be predicted. On the
other hand, as in the America of the antebellum years, one can predict that
it will run the gamut from the most simple to the most knotty.

# Notes

**Preface**

1. David Grimsted, "Introduction," in *Notions of the Americans, 1820–1860* (New York: Braziller, 1970), 7.

**Chapter 1. Shaping Music for an American Society**

1. George P. Rawick, ed. *The American Slave: A Composite Autobiography*, vol. 4, *Texas Narratives, Part 2* (Westport, Conn.: Greenwood, 1972), 189. Although the autobiographies contained in this and other volumes of this entire series are reprints of the original type-written interviews conducted by the WPA Federal Writers Project, only an occasional volume records that it is a reprint.

2. Ira Berlin, Marc Favreau, and Steven F. Miller, eds., *Remembering Slavery* (New York: New Press, 1998), 12–13, 170–71.

3. Richard Green Parker, *A Tribute to the Life and Character of Jonas Chickering* (Boston: Tewksbury, 1854), 13–14.

4. David Grimsted, "Introduction," in *Notions of the Americans, 1820–1860* (New York: Braziller, 1970), 3–4.

5. M. A. DeWolfe Howe, *Memories of a Hostess* (Boston: Atlantic Monthly, 1922), 5.

6. Stuart Chase, *The Proper Study of Mankind* (New York: Harper, 1948), 65.

7. Harriet Martineau, *Society in America*, vol. 1 (New York: Saunders & Otley, 1837), 20.

8. Carl Bode, *American Life in the 1840s* (Garden City, N.Y.: Anchor, 1967), 3.

9. Ira Berlin, *Slaves without Masters* (New York: Pantheon, 1974), 136.

10. Kenneth T. Jackson, ed., *The Encyclopedia of New York City* (New Haven, Conn.: Yale University Press, 1995), s.v. "Population."

11. Robert Douglas Mead, *New Promised Land* (New York: New American Library, 1974), 37.

12. J. G. Holland, *Miss Gilbert's Career* (New York: Scribners, 1860), 369.

13. Robert Ernst, *Immigrant Life in New York City, 1825–1863* (New York: Octagon, 1979), 184.

14. James Fenimore Cooper, *Home as Found* (1838; reprint, New York: Townsend, 1860), 150.

15. Dr. Thomas L. Nichols, *Forty Years of American Life*, vol. 1 (London: Maxwell, 1864), 396.

16. Martineau, *Society in America* 1:108.

17. Michel Chevalier, *Society, Manners, and Politics in the United States*, ed. John William

**300**   Wood, trans. after the T. G. Bradford ed. (Ithaca, N.Y.: Cornell University Press, 1961), 96, 305.

18. Francis C. Sheridan, *Galveston Island*, ed. Willis W. Pratt (Austin: University of Texas Press, 1954), 90–92.

19. S. Margaret Fuller, *Papers on Literature and Art*, part 2 (New York: Wiley & Putnam, 1846), 4.

20. Cooper, *Home as Found*, 79.

21. D. R. Hundley, *Social Relations in Our Southern States* (New York: Price, 1860), 98–99.

22. See the *Boston Euterpeiad* 1 (1820): 7; Charles T. Congdon, *Reminiscences of a Journalist* (Boston: Osgood, 1880), 198.

23. Vera Brodsky Lawrence, *Strong on Music*, vol. 1 (New York: Oxford University Press, 1988), 243–44. Walt Whitman would also experience a taste change, at first enjoying the concerts of the American singing families and speaking disapprovingly of opera, later succumbing completely to the opera performances.

24. Carl David Arfwedson, *The United States in 1832, 1833, and 1834*, vol. 2 (London: Bentley, 1834), 363–65; John Neal, *True Womanhood* (Boston: Ticknor & Fields, 1859), 130.

25. Arthur Farwell and W. Dermot Darby, eds., *Music in America*, The Art of Music, 4 (New York: National Society of Music, 1915), 127.

26. Chevalier, *Society, Manners, and Politics in the United States*, 46, 181–82.

27. Francis Pulszky and Theresa Pulszky, *White, Red, Black*, vol. 2 (Clinton Hall, N.Y.: Redfield, 1853), 11; Isaac C. Pray, *Memoirs of James Gordon Bennett and His Times* (New York: Stringer & Townsend, 1855), 65–66.

28. Solon Robinson, *Selected Writings*, vol. 1, ed. Herbert A. Kellar (Indianapolis: Indiana Historical Bureau, 1936), 421–22.

29. A Young Gent, *Squints through an Opera Glass* (New York: Merchant's Day-Book, 1850), 43.

30. Neal, *True Womanhood*, 8–9, 15.

31. Thomas Colley Grattan, *Civilized America*, vol. 2 (London: Bradbury & Evans, 1859), 108.

32. John W. Francis, *Old New York*, rev. ed. (New York: Roe, 1858), 254–56.

33. Charles Fraser, *Reminiscences of Charleston* (Charleston, S.C.: Russell, 1854), 96.

34. Alexis de Tocqueville, *Democracy in America*, vol. 2, Henry Reeve text, rev. Frances Bowen, further rev. Phillips Bradley (New York: Vintage, 1954), 41.

35. Roger D. Abrahams, *Singing the Master* (New York: Pantheon, 1992), 107–8.

36. Ibid., 123.

37. Sarah Harvey Porter, *The Life and Times of Anne Royall* (Cedar Rapids, Iowa: Torch Press Book Shop, 1908), 79.

38. Walt Whitman, "Art-Singing and Heart-Singing," in *The Uncollected Poetry and Prose of Walt Whitman*, vol. 1, ed. Emory Holloway (Gloucester, Mass.: Peter Smith, 1972), 104. An editorial comment states that Edgar Allan Poe agreed with this Whitman position. Whitman would develop a strong taste for Italian opera several years later, however.

39. Nathaniel Parker Willis, *Hurry-Graphs* (London: Bohn, 1851), 162.

40. Lawrence, *Strong on Music* 1:6.

41. Augusta J. Evans, *Beulah* (New York: Derby & Jackson, 1859), 409–10.

42. William Hancock, *The Emigrant's Five Years in the Free States of America* (London: Newby, 1860). Hancock arrived at New York City in June 1852.

43. In this regard, see A. B. Longstreet, *Georgia Scenes*, 2d ed. (New York: Harper, 1851), 65.

44. H. W. Shaw, *Josh Billings: His Sayings* (New York: Carleton, 1866), 119.

45. Samuel G. Goodrich, *Peter Parley's Own Story* (New York: Sheldon, 1864), 41–42. This autobiography of Goodrich states that his father was the Congregational minister in the town.

46. Ralph Waldo Emerson, "Poetry and Imagination," in *Letters and Social Aims* (Boston: Houghton Mifflin, 1894), 41.

47. William Atson, *Heart Whispers . . . A Series of Letters to His Wife* (Philadelphia: Cowperthwait, 1859), 166.

48. Fuller, *Papers on Literature and Art*, part 2, 108, 110.

49. George Root, *The Story of a Musical Life* (Cincinnati: Church, 1891), 96.

50. Tocqueville, *Democracy in America* 2:50.

51. E. Douglas Branch, *The Sentimental Years, 1836–1860* (New York: Appleton-Century, 1934), 304–5.

52. Charles Godfrey Leland, *Memoirs* (New York: Appleton, 1893), 15.

53. Fred Folio, *Lucy Boston, or Woman's Rights and Spiritualism* (Boston: Shepard, Clark, 1855), 227, 231–32, respectively.

54. The need for poetic simplicity was underlined by Thomas Hastings in his *Dissertation on Musical Taste* (Albany, N.Y.: Websters & Skinners, 1822), 11; the need to address people's own experiences was underlined in a discussion that took place between members of the Hutchinson Family Singers, Henry Russell, and G. P. Morris in New York City in 1843, as reported in Philip D. Jordan, *Singin' Yankees* (Minneapolis: University of Minnesota Press, 1946), 78.

55. Charles H. Kaufman, *Music in New Jersey, 1655–1860* (Rutherford, N.J.: Fairleigh Dickinson University Press, 1981), 201.

56. John H. Hewitt, *Shadows on the Wall* (Baltimore: Turnbull, 1877), 88; Mary B. Claflin, *Personal Recollections of John G. Whittier* (New York: Crowell, 1893), 116–17; Nathaniel Parker Willis, *The Miscellaneous Works* (Clinton Hall, N. Y.: Redfield, 1847), 45; and Samuel Longfellow, *Memoir and Letters*, ed. Joseph May (Boston: Houghton Mifflin, 1894), 18–19.

57. Longstreet, *Georgia Scenes*, 671–68.

58. [Hutchinson Family], *Excelsior: Journals of the Hutchinson Family Singers, 1842–1846*, ed. and annotated Dale Cockrell (Stuyvesant, N.Y.: Pendragon, 1986), 6.

59. John Wallace Hutchinson, *Story of the Hutchinsons*, vol. 1 (Boston: Lee & Shepard, 1896), 51.

60. Kaufman, *Music in New Jersey*, 176–77.

## Chapter 2. Why Americans Did or Did Not Cultivate Music

1. Julius Hawthorne, *Nathaniel Hawthorne and His Wife*, vol. 1 (Boston: Houghton Mifflin, 1884), 103; John Hewitt, *Shadows on the Wall* (Baltimore: Turnbull, 1877), 94.

2. Julia Ward Howe, *Reminiscences, 1819–1899* (1899; reprint, New York: Negro Universities Press, 1969), 162–63.

3. Thurlow Weed, *Life of Thurlow Weed, Including His Autobiography and a Memoir*, vol. 1, ed. Harriet A. Weed (Boston: Houghton Mifflin, 1883), 467.

4. Grant Thorburn, *Fifty Years' Reminiscences of New-York* (New York: Fanshaw, 1845), 70, 147–48.

302       5. Mrs. Sue (Petigrue) Bowen, *Busy Moments of an Idle Woman* (New York: Appleton, 1854), 239–40.

6. Charles Brockden Brown, *Memoirs of Charles Brockden Brown . . . with Selections from His Original Letters and Miscellaneous Writings,* ed. William Dunlap (London: Colburn, 1822), 309–15.

7. John Randolph, *Letters to a Young Relative* (Philadelphia: Carey, Lea & Blanchard, 1834), 26. Randolph did not dislike music; he simply felt that, enjoyable as it might be, it should remain a pastime.

8. Amelia M. Murray, *Letters from the United States, Cuba, and Canada* (New York: Putnam, 1856), 143–44.

9. Charles Quill, *The American Mechanic* (Philadelphia: Perkins, 1838), 132.

10. Howe, *Reminiscences,* 15; Thomas Hastings, *Dissertation on Musical Taste* (Albany, N.Y.: Websters & Skinners, 1822), 14.

11. John Donald Wade, *Augustus Baldwin Longstreet* (New York: Macmillan, 1924), 252–53.

12. Caroline Howard Gilman, *Love's Progress* (New York: Harper, 1840), 23.

13. Elizabeth W. Allston Pringle, *Chronicles of Chicora Wood* (New York: Scribners, 1922), 144.

14. Dr. Thomas L. Nichols, *Forty Years of American Life,* vol. 1 (London: Maxwell, 1864), 75–76.

15. Richard B. Kimball, *Was He Successful?* (New York: Carleton, 1864), 183.

16. Susan Dabney Smedes, *Memorials of a Southern Planter* (Baltimore: Cushings & Bailey, 1887), 161–62; Rawick, ed. *American Slave,* supp. ser. 1, vol. 7, *Mississippi Narratives, Part 2* (Westport, Conn.: Greenwood, 1977), 791.

17. *Boston Euterpeiad* 1 (8 April 1820): 7; Margaret Bayard Smith, *The First Forty Years of Washington Society,* ed. Gaillard Hunt (New York: Ungar, 1965), 261; Hewitt, *Shadows on the Wall,* 95; Vera Brodsky Lawrence, *Strong on Music,* vol. 1 (New York: Oxford University Press, 1988), 422–23; George William Curtis, *Early Letters of George Wm. Curtis to John S. Dwight,* ed. George Willis Cooke (New York: Harper, 1898), 235–36; Walt Whitman, *The Uncollected Poetry and Prose of Walt Whitman,* vol. 1, collected and edited by Emory Holloway (Gloucester, Mass.: Smith, 1972), 256.

18. Meade Minnigerode, *The Fabulous Forties* (New York: Putnam, 1924), 273.

19. Eliza Ripley, *Social Life in Old New Orleans* (New York: Appleton, 1912), 92; A. B. Longstreet, *Georgia Scenes,* 2d ed. (New York: Harper, 1851), 65–66. For further confirmation of fashion-driven taste, see Curtis, *Early Letters,* 167–68, 176; Charles Fraser, *Reminiscences of Charleston* (Charleston, S.C.: Russell, 1854), 147; Edward E. Hale Jr., *The Life and Letters of Edward Everett Hale,* vol. 1 (Boston: Little, Brown, 1917), letter dated 1 January 1841 to Edward Everett; Thomas Hamilton, *Men and Manners in America* (Philadelphia: Carey, Lea & Blanchard, 1833), 131; "Fashionable Music," in *The Singer's Companion* (New York: Stringer & Townsend, 1854), 51.

20. H. W. Shaw, *Josh Billings: His Sayings* (New York: Carleton, 1866), 118.

21. Max Maretzek, "Crotchets and Quavers" (1855), in *Reflections of an Opera Manager in 19th-Century America* (New York: Dover, 1968), 25–26, 66–67; Nathaniel Parker Willis, *The Miscellaneous Works* (Clinton Hall, N.Y.: Redfield, 1847), 50, 191, 147–48, 216; A Young Gent, *Squints through an Opera Glass* (New York: Merchants' Day-Book, 1850), 1–3, 9–10.

22. Seba Smith, *The Life and Writings of Major Jack Downing* (Boston: Lilly, Wait, Col-

man & Holden, 1834), 100; William R. Ryan, *Personal Adventures in Upper and Lower California, in 1848–9*, vol. 2 (London: Shoberl, 1851), 284.

23. Lydia H. Sigourney, *Letters to Young Ladies*, 2d ed. (Hartford, Conn.: Watson, 1835), 62; Longstreet, *Georgia Scenes*, 68–71.

24. Evelyn Foster Mornewick, *Chronicles of Stephen Foster's Family*, vol. 1 (Pittsburgh: University of Pittsburgh Press, 1944), 31–32. That Molly Murphy was not altogether wrong in her assessment is made clear by reports like that of Thurlow Weed, of a "beautiful and accomplished young lady," in Schenectady, New York, who "rejected wealthy suitors for the sake of the fine person and melodious voice of a music teacher, preferring, it would seem, musical to circulating notes"; see Weed, *Life of Thurlow Weed* 1:155.

25. William Gilmore Simms, *The Letters of William Gilmore Simms*, vol. 1, ed. Mary C. Simms Oliphant, Alfred Tayler Odell, and T. C. Duncan Eaves (Columbia: University of South Carolina Press, 1952), 90.

26. Marion Harland, *Marion Harland's Autobiography* (New York: Harper, 1910), 22–32.

27. Harriet Beecher Stowe, *My Wife and I* (New York: Ford, 1871), 187; *The Young Lady's Own Book* (Philadelphia: Key, Mielke & Biddle, 1832), 51.

28. H. Marion Stephens, *Home Scenes and Home Sounds* (Boston: Fetridge, 1854), 180–81. For a commentary on genteel education of this sort, see Daniel Pierce Thompson, *Locke Amsden, or The Schoolmaster* (Boston: Sanborn, Carter & Bazin, 1855), 150–51.

29. Walter Colton, *Three Years in California* (New York: Evans, 1860), 34–35. Colton wrote this in his journal on 18 August 1846, while in Monterey, California.

30. Joseph C. Neal, *Charcoal Sketches, or Scenes in a Metropolis*, new ed. (New York: Burgess & Stringer, 1844), 21.

31. George Lippard, *N.Y.: Its Upper Ten and Lower Million* (Cincinnati: Rulison, 1853), 53.

32. Anna Hanson Dorsey, *Woodreve Manor* (Philadelphia: Hart, 1852), 39.

33. Donald Fraser, *The Mental Flower Garden* (New York: Southwick, 1808), 157; Sigourney, *Letters to Young Ladies*, 60; John Pintard, *Letters from John Pintard to His Daughter*, vol. 2 (New York: New-York Historical Society, 1940), 155; *The Young Lady's Own Book*, 7–8.

34. Frances Trollope, *Domestic Manners of the Americans*, 5th ed. (1839; reprint, New York: Dodd, Mead, 1927), 39; Whitman quoted in Gay Wilson Allen, *The Solitary Singer* (New York: Macmillan, 1955), 71; Charles H. Smith, *The Farm and the Fireside* (Atlanta: Constitution Publishing House, 1892), 283, 327.

35. R. L. B., *An Autobiography: Being Passages from a Life Now Progressing in the City of Boston* (n.p.: n.p., 1871), 124 [copyright holder, Harriet G. Storer]; John P. Kennedy, *Memoirs of the Life of William Wirt*, rev. ed., vol. 1 (Philadelphia: Lippincott, 1860), 144; Charles Burleigh Galbreath, *Daniel Decatur Emmett* (Columbus, Ohio: Galbreath, 1904), 9; Fanny Fern, *The Play-Day Book* (New York: Mason, 1857), 205.

36. Sophie M. Damon, *Old New-England Days* (Boston: Cupples & Hurd, 1887), 73; Samuel Upham, *Notes of a Voyage to California via Cape Horn, Together with Scenes of El Dorado, in the Years 1849-'50* (Philadelphia: Upham, 1878), 271; Timothy Dwight, *Travels in New-England and New-York*, vol. 4 (New Haven: author, 1822), 354; "Preface" to *The Singer's Companion*. See also Rev. Elijah R. Sabin, *The Life and Reflections of Charles Observator* (Boston: Rowe & Hooper, 1816), 49, where he makes observations identical to those of Sophie Damon.

37. Lew Wallace, *An Autobiography*, vol. 1 (New York: Harper, 1906), 215; Daniel

*304*  Mann, *Wolfsden* (Boston: Phillips, Sampson, 1856), 59; and John B. Jones, *Wild Western Scenes* (Philadelphia: Grigg, Elliot, 1849), 145.

38. W. Gilmore Simms, *Charlemont* (New York: Redfield, 1856), 39; Robert Kemp, *Father Kemp and His Old Folks* (Boston: Kemp, 1868), 16–17.

39. *Boston Euterpeiad* 1 (15 July 1820): 64; Charles T. Congdon, *Reminiscences of a Journalist* (Boston: Osgood, 1880), 303–4; Philip D. Jordan, *Singin' Yankees* (Minneapolis: University of Minnesota Press, 1946), 181–82; Thomas Chandler Haliburton, *The Americans at Home*, vol. 3 (London: Hurst & Blacket, 1854), 96–100.

40. William Wells Brown, *My Southern Home* (1880; reprint, Upper Saddle River, N.J.: Gregg, 1968), 66. Fredrika Bremer, *The Home of the New World*, vol. 1, trans. Mary Howitt (New York: Harper, 1853), 372, mentions "hearing negro songs" sung by a young black man trained as a musician owing to his weak lungs, which left him "not able to do much work."

41. Solomon Northup, *Twelve Years a Slave* (New York: Miller, Orton & Mulligan, 1855), 181–82.

42. Henry T. Tuckerman, *The Optimist* (New York: Putnam, 1852), 20; see also pp. 5, 7–8, 13–14.

43. James Russell Lowell, *The Function of the Poet and Other Essays*, ed. Albert Mordell (Boston: Houghton Mifflin, 1920), 28.

44. John Moore, *Complete Encyclopaedia of Music* (Boston: Ditson, 1854), s.v. "Ballad"; Frederic Saunders, *Mosaics* (New York: Scribners, 1859), 370–71.

45. *Dwight's Journal of Music* 3 (13 August 1853): 151; Lydia Maria Child, *Letters from New York*, 2d ser. (New York: Francis, 1845), 20–22.

46. Eliza Southgate Browne, *A Girl's Life Eighty Years Ago* (New York: Scribners, 1887), 24–25.

47. Mrs. N. P. Lasselle, *Annie Grayson, or Life in Washington* (New York: Bunce, 1853), 70; Fanny Fern, *Folly as It Flies* (New York: Carleton, 1868), 205; Annie Fields, ed., *Life and Letters of Harriet Beecher Stowe* (Boston: Houghton Mifflin, 1897), 23; Child, *Letters from New York*, 187.

48. Candace Wheeler, *Yesterdays in a Busy Life* (New York: Harper, 1918), 49–50.

49. Susan Warner, *The Hills of Shatemuc* (New York: Appleton, 1856), 325–28; David Sower Jr., *Village Sketches* (Morristown, Pa.: David Sower Jr., 1825), 43; Caroline Gilman, *Recollections of a New England Bride and of a Southern Matron*, rev. ed. (New York: Putnam, 1852), 112; Marie Jane McIntosh, *Praise and Principle* (New York: Harper, 1847), 222; Samuel Osgood, *Mile Stones* (New York: Appleton, 1855), 97.

50. S. Trevena Jackson, *Fanny Crosby's Story of Ninety-Four Years* (New York: Revell, 1915), 154–55; John Townsend Trowbridge, *My Own Story* (Boston: Houghton Mifflin, 1903), 33–34; Howe, *Reminiscences*, 17–18.

51. Rawick, ed., *American Slave*, vol. 2, *South Carolina Narratives, Part 1* (Westport, Conn.: Greenwood, 1972), 76.

52. Brown, *My Southern Home*, 43; Metta V. Victor, *Maum Guinea and Her Plantation "Children"* (London: Beadle, [1860?]), 35–36; Frederick Douglass, *Life and Times of Frederick Douglass* (1892; reprint, New York: Collier, 1962), 54–55.

53. Gilbert Osofsky, ed. *Puttin' on Ole Massa: The Slave Narratives of Henry Bibb, William Welss Brown, and Solomon Northup* (New York: Harper, 1969), 197.

54. Caroline Howard Gilman, *A Balcony in Charleston*, ed. Mary Scott Saint-Amand (Richmond, Va.: Garrett & Massie, 1941), 30–31. The incident was originally reported in the *Rose Bud*, 2 March 1833.

55. Mary J. Windle, *Life in Washington* (Philadelphia: Lippincott, 1859), 106; Dorsey, *Woodreve Manor,* 49. "Love Not," words by Mrs. Norton, music by John Buckley, was published in New York around 1833–36 and warns that everything one loves must die.

56. Joseph C. Neal, *Charcoal Sketches* (New York: Burgess & Stringer, 1844), 108–9; Frederic S. Cozzens, *Prismatics,* 2d ed. (New York: Appleton, 1854), 85.

57. In this manner was a young but wealthy widow courted; see Mrs. Rhoda E. White, *Portraits of My Married Friends* (New York: Appleton, 1858), 81. *Pintard, Letters* 3:179–80, tells of a suitor whose "heart is in the safe keeping of Miss Carr, to whom he sent some music as a love token."

58. Rosser H. Taylor, *Ante-Bellum South Carolina: A Social and Cultural History* (Chapel Hill: University of North Carolina Press, 1942), 62–63; Wallace, *Autobiography* 1:217; Sower, *Village Sketches,* 151. See also Ellen K. Rothman, *Hands and Hearts: A History of Courtship in America* (New York: Basic, 1984), 26; John B. Jones, *The Winkles* (New York: Appleton, 1855), 248–49; Catharine Maria Sedgwick, *Married or Single,* vol. 1 (New York: Harper, 1857), 61–62.

59. J. Hawthorne, *Nathaniel Hawthorne and His Wife* 1:208.

60. Marian Harland, *Judith: A Chronicle of Old Virginia* (Philadelphia: Our Continent Publishing Co., 1883), 251. The book narrates episodes in Harland's life.

61. James Weir, *Lonz Powers, or The Regulators,* vol. 1 (Philadelphia: Lippincott, Grambo, 1850), 31.

62. H. M. Brackenbridge, *Recollections of Persons and Places in the West* (Philadelphia: Lippincott, 1868), 75.

63. Saunders, *Mosaics,* 381–82.

64. Sabin, *Life and Reflections of Charles Observator,* 112.

65. Ann Willson, *Familiar Letters* (Philadelphia: Parrish, 1850), 53.

66. See, for example, *The Clifford Family, or A Tale of the Old Dominion,* by one of her daughters (New York: Harper, 1852), 392; John Townsend Trowbridge, *Neighbor Jackwood* (Boston: Lee & Shepard, 1888), 78.

67. Oliver Wendell Holmes, *The Autocrat of the Breakfast-Table* (Boston: Houghton Mifflin, 1916), 182. The book was first published in 1858. The Tuckerman information comes from Tuckerman, *The Optimist,* 65.

68. Charles Dickens, *American Notes* (Leipzig: Tauchnitz, 1842), 52–53.

69. Bremer, *The Homes of the New World* 1:402.

70. "Mr. Bray," in the *Boston Euterpeiad* 1 (15 April 1820): 11.

71. Harriet Beecher Stowe, *We and Our Neighbors* (Boston: Houghton Mifflin, 1898), 245. The book first appeared in 1873. The reference to hymns is from Stowe, *Flowers and Fruit from the Writings of Harriet Beecher Stowe,* arr. Abbie H. Fairfield (Boston: Houghton Mifflin, 1888), 163.

72. Sigourney, *Letters to Young Ladies,* 63.

73. Quill, *American Mechanic,* 10; John Wallace Hutchinson, *Story of the Hutchinsons,* vol. 1 (Boston: Lee & Shepard, 1896), 139; Harriet Martineau, *Retrospect of Western Travels,* vol. 1 (London: Saunders & Otley, 1838), 137.

74. Liliane Crété, *Daily Life in Louisiana, 1815–1830,* trans. Patrick Gregory (Baton Rouge: Louisiana State University Press, 1981), 92.

75. Rawick, ed., *American Slave,* vol. 3, *South Carolina Narratives, Part 3* (Westport, Conn.: Greenwood, 1972), 283.

76. Northup, *Twelve Years a Slave,* 217.

77. Jacob Stroyer, *My Life in the South*, 3d ed. (Salem, Mass.: Salem Observer Book, 1885), 42–43.

78. Augusta J. Evans, *Beulah* (New York: Derby & Jackson, 1859), 220.

79. George P. Upton, *Letters of Peregrine Pickle* (Chicago: Western News Co., 1869), 223.

80. Pintard, *Letters* 2:167, 3 (1941): 150; Lucius Fairchild, *California Letters*, ed. Joseph Schafer (Madison: State Historical Society of Wisconsin, 1931), 18; Ripley, *Social Life in Old New Orleans*, 5–6.

81. Sallie Rochester Ford, *Grace Truman* (New York: Sheldon, Blakeman, 1857), 39.

82. Mary B. Claflin, *Personal Recollections of John G. Whittier* (New York: Crowell, 1893), 76–77.

83. Ruth Painter Randall, *Mary Lincoln* (Boston: Little, Brown, 1953), 30.

84. Weir, *Lonz Powers* 2:91.

85. Garnett Andrews, *Reminiscences of an Old Georgia Lawyer* (Atlanta: Franklin Steam Printing House, 1870), 72.

86. Tuckerman, *The Optimist*, 60.

87. Moore, "Preface," in *Complete Encyclopaedia of Music*, 6.

88. Stowe, *Flowers and Fruit*, 162.

89. Bronson Alcott, *The Journals of Bronson Alcott*, ed. Odell Shepard (Boston: Little, Brown, 1938), 218–19; James F. Otis, "Musings on Music," in *The Portland Sketch Book*, ed. Mrs. Ann S. Stephens (Portland, Maine: Colman & Chisholm, 1836), 185–86; Misses Mendell and Hosmer, *Notes of Travel and Life* (New York: the authors, 1854), 171–72.

90. S. Margaret Fuller, *Papers on Literature and Art*, part 2 (New York: Wiley & Putnam, 1846), 2; S. Margaret Fuller, *Memoirs*, vol. 1 (Boston: Phillips, Sampson, 1852), 343; and Child, *Letters from New York*, 25.

91. Saunders, *Mosaics*, 374–75.

92. Upton, *Letters of Peregrine Pickle*, 123–24.

93. Rawick, ed., *American Slave*, vol. 2, *South Carolina Narratives, Part 2*, 313–14.

## Chapter 3. Becoming Acquainted with Music

1. Catherine Maria Sedgwick, *A New England Tale and Miscellanies* (New York: Putnam, 1852), 15–16.

2. Sophie M. Damon, *Old New-England Days* (Boston: Cupples & Hurd, 1887), 207; Lydia Maria Child, *Letters from New York*, 2d ser. (New York: Francis, 1845), 192.

3. N. P. Willis, *The Miscellaneous Works* (Clinton Hall, N.Y.: Redfield, 1847), 151 (Willis's italics).

4. See, for example, what is said about Richmond's newspapers in Albert Stoutamire, *Music of the Old South* (Rutherford, N.J.: Fairleigh Dickinson University Press, 1972), 95–96; Charles Cist, *The Cincinnati Miscellany*, vol. 2 (Cincinnati: Robinson & Jones, 1846), 216; Howard Swan, *Music in the Southwest, 1825–1950* (San Marino, Calif.: Huntington Library, 1952), 101.

5. Eliza Southgate Browne, *A Girl's Life Eighty Years Ago* (New York: Scribners, 1887), 173–74.

6. Henry M. Brooks, *Olden-Time Music* (Boston: Ticknor, 1888), 108; Thomas Ashe, *Travels in America* (Newburyport, Mass.: Sawyer, 1808), 52–53; Timothy Dwight, *Travels in New-England and New-York*, vol. 4 (New Haven, Conn.: author, 1822), 354; Joel H. Ross, *What I Saw in New-York* (Auburn, N.Y.: Derby & Miller, 1851), 231.

7. Evelyn Foster Mornewick, *Chronicles of Stephen Foster's Family*, vol. 1 (Pittsburgh:

University of Pittsburgh Press, 1944), 39–40; Cornel Lengyel, ed., *Music in the Gold Rush Era*, History of Music in San Francisco, vol. 1 (San Francisco: WPA, 1939), 96.

8. Annie Fields, ed., *Life and Letters of Harriet Beecher Stowe* (Boston: Houghton Mifflin, 1897), 41–42.

9. Henry Wadsworth Longfellow, *The Letters of Henry Wadsworth Longfellow*, vol. 2, ed. Andrew Hilen (Cambridge, Mass.: Belknap, 1966), 113.

10. Laura E. Richards and Maud Howe Elliott, assisted by Florence Howe Hall, *Julia Ward Howe, 1819–1910*, vol. 1 (Boston: Houghton Mifflin, 1916), 120–21.

11. Emily R. Barnes, *Narratives, Traditions, and Personal Reminiscences* (Boston: Ellis, 1888), 114–16.

12. Lew Wallace, *An Autobiography*, vol. 1 (New York: Harper, 1906), 206–7.

13. *Boston Musical Times* 1 (25 January 1860): 15 carried an advertisement for Prince & Co., Buffalo, New York, offering portable melodeons for sale: 4 octaves for $45, $4\frac{1}{2}$ octaves for $60, and 5 octaves for $75.

14. Asa Greene, *A Yankee among the Nullifiers* (New York: Stodart, 1833), 48–49.

15. William Cullen Bryant, *The Letters of William Cullen Bryant*, vol. 1, ed. William Cullen Bryant II and Thomas G. Voss (New York: Fordham University Press, 1975), 3; Harriet Martineau, *Society in America*, vol. 1 (New York: Saunders & Otley, 1837), 169.

16. Charles Quill, *The American Mechanic* (Philadelphia: Perkins, 1838), 126 (Quill's italics).

17. William Johnson, *William Johnson's Natchez: The Ante-Bellum Diary of a Free Negro*, ed. William Ransom Hogan and Edwin Adams Davis (Baton Rouge: Louisiana State University Press, 1951), 86–87, 114, 431.

18. George P. Rawick, ed., *The American Slave: A Composite Autobiography*, vol. 4, *Texas Narratives, Part 1* (Westport, Conn.: Greenwood, 1972), 121.

19. Harry Smith, *Fifty Years of Slavery* (Grand Rapids: West Michigan Printing Co., 1891), 14; John W. Blassingame, *The Slave Community* (New York: Oxford University Press, 1972), 32; Rawick, ed. *American Slave*, supp. ser. 1, vol. 6, *Mississippi Narratives, Part 2* (Westport, Conn.: Greenwood, 1977), 86.

20. Roger Abrahams, *Singing the Master* (New York: Pantheon, 1992), 310; Rawick, ed. *American Slave*, vol. 2, *South Carolina Narratives, Part 1* (Westport, Conn.: Greenwood, 1972), 152; Rawick, ed., *American Slave*, supp. ser. 1, vol. 7, *Mississippi Narratives, Part 2* (Westport, Conn.: Greenwood, 1977), 431.

21. John Davis, *Travels of Four Years and a Half in the United States of America* (London: Edwards, 1803), 414 (Davis's italics).

22. *Boston Euterpeiad* 1 (1 April 1820): 4; John Donald Wade, *Augustus Baldwin Longstreet* (New York: Macmillan, 1924), 49–50; Quill, *American Mechanic*, 83–84 (Quill's italics).

23. Richard Green Parker, *A Tribute to the Life and Character of Jonas Chickering* (Boston: Tewksbury, 1854), 35; Julius H. Ward, *The Life and Letters of James Gates Percival*, (Boston: Ticknor & Fields, 1866), 478–79; Misses Mendell and Hosmer, *Notes of Travel and Life* (New York: the authors, 1854), 49; Quill, *American Mechanic*, 127.

24. Nicholas E. Tawa, in *The New Grove Dictionary of American Music*, ed. H. Wiley Hitchcock and Stanley Sadie (London: Macmillan, 1986), s.v. "Winner, Septimus."

25. Lucy Larcom, *A New England Girlhood* (1889; reprint, Boston: Northeastern University Press, 1986), 47.

26. Samuel G. Goodrich, *Peter Parley's Own Story* (New York: Sheldon, 1864), 25; Frederic S. Cozzens, "Autobiographical Sketch," in *Sayings, Wise and Otherwise* (New York: Lovell, 1870), xxii; Carl Sandburg, *Abraham Lincoln*, vol. 1, *The Prairie Years* (New York:

Harcourt, Brace, 1926), 32. On page 70 Sandburg adds, "Among the best remembered favorites in the neighborhood around the Lincoln farm in Indiana were 'Skip to My Lou,' 'Old Sister Phoebe,' 'Thus the Farmer Sows His Seed,' and 'Weave Wheat.'"

27. Rawick, ed., *American Slave*, supp. ser. 1, vol. 8, *Mississippi Narratives, Part 3* (Westport, Conn.: Greenwood, 1977), 1097; ibid., vol. 3, *South Carolina Narratives, Part 4* (Westport, Conn.: Greenwood, 1972), 105.

28. *An Autobiography*, 2d ed. (Boston: Williams, 1871), 31–32; Quill, *American Mechanic*, 10.

29. Fred Lewis Pattee, *The Feminine Fifties* (New York: Appleton-Century, 1940), 58–59; Elizabeth W. Allston Pringle, *Chronicles of Chicora Wood* (New York: Scribners, 1922), 20–21.

30. Susan Dabney Smedes, *Memorials of a Southern Planter* (Baltimore: Cushings & Bailey, 1887), 42.

31. John Wallace Hutchinson, *Story of the Hutchinsons*, vol. 1 (Boston: Lee & Shepard, 1896), 283; Mornewick, *Chronicles of Stephen Foster's Family* 1:42. The last quotation comes from John Tasker Howard, *Stephen Foster, America's Troubadour* (New York: Crowell, 1962), 29.

32. Eliza Ripley, *Social Life in Old New Orleans* (New York: Appleton, 1912), 153; F. B. Sanborn, *Recollections of Seventy Years*, vol. 1 (Boston: Badger, 1909), 15–16; George A. Ramsdell, *A History of Milford* (Concord, N.H.: Rumford, 1901), 484. John Hutchinson writes: "At the age of seven I had learned many hymns of my mother, and at the church I took my place in the choir, and carried my part, the alto, ere I could read a note of music"; see Hutchinson, *Story of the Hutchinsons* 1:21.

33. Richards et al., *Julia Ward Howe, 1819–1910*, 1:146–48, 216–17.

34. George Henry Tripp, *Student-Life at Harvard* (Boston: Lockwood & Brooks, 1876), 121–22. Benjamin Carr had composed a "Hymn to the Virgin," which he published as no. 3 of *Six Ballads from the Poem of "The Lady of the Lake,"* op. 7 (Philadelphia: Carr & Schetky, 1810). The habit of copying music that had already been published was endemic during the early nineteenth century.

35. Richard Henry Stoddard, *Recollections, Personal and Literary* (New York: Barnes, 1903), 4–5.

36. Rawick, ed., *American Slave*, supp. ser. 1, vol. 7, *Mississippi Narratives, Part 2*, 400–401; Rawick, ed., *American Slave*, vol. 6, *Indiana Narratives* (Westport, Conn.: Greenwood, 1972), 193.

37. Charles Godfrey Leland, *Memoirs* (New York: Appleton, 1893), 19, 73.

38. M. R. G., "Uncle Peter," *Lowell Offering* 5 (April 1845): 84–85; Stoddard, *Recollections*, 14.

39. Mrs. Lydia Huntley Sigourney, *Letters of Life* (New York: Appleton, 1867), 44–45.

40. Rawick, ed., *American Slave*, vol. 2, *South Carolina Narratives, Part 1* (Westport, Conn.: Greenwood, 1972), 43.

41. Larcom, *New England Girlhood*, 43–44.

42. Julia Ward Howe, *Reminiscences, 1819–1899* (1899; reprint, New York: Negro Universities Press, 1969), 29.

43. Mornewick, *Chronicles of Stephen Foster's Family* 1:41; the antebellum private music collections are examined in great detail in Nicholas E. Tawa, *Sweet Songs for Gentle Americans: The Parlor Song in America, 1790–1860* (Bowling Green, Ohio: Bowling Green University Popular Press, 1980). Charles T. Congdon, *Reminiscences of a Journalist* (Boston: Osgood, 1880), 299–300; Congdon was born in New Bedford, Massachusetts, attended

Brown University in Providence, Rhode Island, and moved to Boston after graduation in 1854. Philip Hone, *The Diary of Philip Hone, 1828–1851,* vol. 1, ed. Bayard Tuckerman (New York: Dodd, Mead, 1889), 272. Levi Beardsley, *Reminiscences* (New York: Vinten, 1852), 88.

44. W. Gilmore Simms, *Charlemont* (New York: Redfield, 1856), 72; J. P. Kennedy, *Swallow Barn,* rev. ed. (New York: Putnam, 1851), 376–80.

45. Fanny Appleton Longfellow, *Mrs. Longfellow: Selected Letters and Journals,* ed. Edward Wagenknecht (New York: Longmans, Green, 1856), 17; Leland, *Memoirs,* 60.

46. For a discussion of this phenomenon, see Tawa, *Sweet Songs for Gentle Americans,* 158–97.

47. Julius H. Ward, *The Life and Letters of James Gates Percival* (Boston: Ticknor & Fields, 1866), 432–33.

48. E. Douglas Branch, *The Sentimental Years, 1836–1860* (New York: Appleton-Century, 1934), 9.

49. Leland, *Memoirs,* 10–11.

50. *The Singer's Companion* (New York: Stringer & Townsend, 1854), 111; Henry Russell, *Cheer! Boys, Cheer!* (London: Macqueen, 1895), 184; "Musical Gossip: Domestic," *Boston Musical Times* 2 (23 February 1861): 5; Charles F. Browne, *Complete Works* (London: Chatto & Windus, n.d.), 90.

51. Charles H. Haswell, *Reminiscences of New York by an Octogenarian (1816 to 1860)* (New York: Harper, 1896), 89; John Townsend Trowbridge, *My Own Story* (Boston: Houghton Mifflin, 1903), 127–28.

52. Marion Harland, *Judith: A Chronicle of Old Virginia* (Philadelphia: Our Continent, 1883), 234.

53. Bowne, *A Girl's Life Eighty Years Ago,* 171; John P. Kennedy, *Memoirs of the Life of William Wirt,* rev. ed., vol. 2 (Philadelphia: Lippincott, 1860), 128.

54. Longfellow, *Letters* 2:33, 135.

55. Kate Leonard, *Clara Temple Leonard: A Memoir of Her Life by Her Daughter* (Springfield, Mass.: Loring-Axtoll, 1908), 22.

56. Haswell, *Reminiscences,* 447; Mornewick, *Chronicles of Stephen Foster's Family* 1:111.

57. Rawick, ed., *American Slave,* vol. 6, *Mississippi Narratives, Part 1,* 73, *Part 2,* 514–15.

58. Edward Augustus Kendall, *Travels through the Northern Parts of the United States, in the Years 1807 and 1808,* vol. 1 (New York: Riley, 1809), 328.

59. A. D. Merrill, *The Sunday School Melodist* (Boston: Peirce, 1851); Maria Cummins, *Mabel Vaughan* (Boston: Jewett, 1857), 178.

60. Augusta J. Evans, *Beulah* (New York: Derby & Jackson, 1859), 18.

61. Fields, ed., *Life and Letters of Harriet Beecher Stowe,* 8–9.

62. Sigourney, *Letters of Life,* 128–32.

63. James Boardman, *America, and the Americans* (London: Longman, Rees, Orme, Brown, Green & Longman, 1833), 131–32; Henry David Thoreau, *Familiar Letters,* ed. F. B. Sanborn (Boston: Houghton Mifflin, 1895), 367.

64. Francis H. Underwood, *Quabbin: The Story of a Small Town* (1893; reprint, Boston: Northeastern University Press, 1986), 168.

65. Cist, *The Cincinnati Miscellany* 2:51–53; Mary Ellen Chase, *Jonathan Fisher, Maine Parson, 1768–1847* (New York: Macmillan, 1948), 139–40; James L. Smith, *Autobiography* (Norwich, Conn.: Press of the Bulletin Co., 1881), 72.

66. "Notes of a Short Tour Westward," *Dwight's Journal of Music* 1 (19 June 1852): 84;

**310**    "The Musical Trade," *Dwight's Journal of Music* 3 (11 June 1853): 75–76, 79; news item taken from the *Musical Review*, in *Dwight's Journal of Music* 3 (16 July 1853): 116. One hopes that this singing master was not the Levi M'Clean mentioned earlier in these pages.

67. Seba Smith, *'Way Down East, or Portraitures of Yankee Life* (Philadelphia: Potter, 1854), 77–91.

68. Daniel Drake, *Pioneer Life in Kentucky, 1785–1800*, ed. Emmett Field Horne (New York: Schuman, 1948), 189–90.

69. Candace Wheeler, *Yesterdays in a Busy Life* (New York: Harper, 1918), 67–68.

70. Sigourney, *Letters of Life*, 132; Mrs. Ellen Chapman Hobbs Rollins, *New England Bygones* (Philadelphia: Lippincott, 1880), 209.

71. Marion Harland, *Marion Harland's Autobiography* (New York: Harper, 1910), 114–16. Marion Harland was the pen name of Mrs. Mary Virginia (Hawes) Terhune. The singing book mentioned is either Lowell Mason's *The Boston Academy's Collection of Church Music* (1835) or *Selections for the Choir of the Boston Academy* (1836).

72. Parke Godwin, *A Biography of William Cullen Bryant*, vol. 1 (1883; reprint, New York: Russell & Russell, 1967), 113; Betsy, "Recollections of My Childhood," in *The Lowell Offering*, vol. 1 (Lowell: Powers & Bagley, n.d.), 81–82 (the volume covers the period from October 1840 through December 1841); Charles H. Kaufman, *Music in New Jersey, 1655–1860* (Rutherford, N.J.: Fairleigh Dickinson University Press, 1981), 113.

73. Garnett Andrews, *Reminiscences of an Old Georgia Lawyer* (Atlanta: Franklin Steam Printing House, 1870), 79.

74. Longfellow, *Letters*, vol. 3, ed. Andrew Hilen (Cambridge, Mass.: Belknap, 1972), 69; preface, *The Singer's First and Second Book* (Boston: Bird, 1845).

75. Whitman quoted in Gay Wilson Allen, *The Solitary Singer* (New York: Macmillan, 1955), 70; John Moore, *Complete Encyclopedia of Music* (Boston: Ditson, 1854), s.v. "Ballad."

76. Kaufman, *Music in New Jersey*, 108, 110.

77. Howe, *Reminiscences*, 16–17.

78. D. R. Hundley, *Social Relations in Our Southern States* (New York: Price, 1860), 100; Caroline Gilman, *Recollections of a New England Bride and of a Southern Matron*, rev. ed. (New York: Putnam, 1852), 60, 62; Pringle, *Chronicles of Chicora Wood*, 180; Ripley, *Social Life in Old New Orleans*, 10–11.

79. Sara A. Wentz, *Smiles and Frowns* (New York: Appleton, 1857), 18.

80. Susan I. Lesley, *Recollections of My Mother* (Boston: Ellis, 1886), 40; Barnes, *Narratives, Traditions, and Personal Reminiscences*, 114.

81. Kennedy, *Memoirs of the Life of William Wirt* 1:145.

82. See "Letter from a Teacher at the South," *Dwight's Journal of Music* 2 (26 February 1853): 164, 196; Underwood, *Quabbin*, 197–99.

83. Lady Emmeline Stuart Wortley, *Travels in the United States, etc., during 1849 and 1850* (New York: Harper, 1851), 69; Ross, *What I Saw in New-York*, 289–90; Fanny J. Crosby, *Memories of Eighty Years* (Boston: Earle, 1906), 39, 57, 102, 111.

84. Marion Harland, *The Hidden Path* (New York: Derby, 1856), 112.

85. Vera Brodsky Lawrence, *Strong on Music*, vol. 1 (New York: Oxford University Press, 1988), 571; John Esten Cooke, *Ellie, or The Human Comedy* (Richmond: Morris, 1855), 480.

86. Isaac C. Pray, *Memoirs of James Gordon Bennett and His Times* (New York: Stringer & Townsend, 1855), 63; John W. Francis, *Old New York*, rev. ed. (New York: Roe, 1858), 253–54; Ripley, *Social Life in Old New Orleans*, 65.

87. Ralph Waldo Emerson, W. H. Channing, and J. F. Clarke, *Memoirs of Margaret*

*Fuller Ossoli*, vol. 1 (Boston: Roberts Brothers, 1884), 33; Margaret Fuller, *Memoirs*, vol. 1 (Boston: Phillips, Sampson, 1852), 33–34; Sigourney, *Letters of Life*, 53.

88. Charles Fraser, *Reminiscences of Charleston* (Charleston, S.C.: Russell, 1854), 44, 106.

89. The letter to his father may be found in Longfellow, *Letters* 2:263; that to Charles Sumner, dated 21 September 1854, in 3:447. Carlo Dolce (1616–86) was a Florentine responsible for little religious paintings.

90. George William Curtis, *Early Letters of George Wm. Curtis to John S. Dwight*, ed. George Willis Cooke (New York: Harper, 1898), 46.

91. Pringle, *Chronicles of Chicora Wood*, 141–43; A. B. Longstreet, *Georgia Scenes*, 2d ed. (New York: Harper, 1851), 71–72; Mrs. Rhoda E. White, *Mary Staunton* (New York: Appleton, 1860), 227, 234–35; Maria Jane McIntosh, *Praise and Principle* (New York: Harper, 1847), 241–42.

92. Fanny Longfellow, *Mrs. Longfellow: Selected Letters and Journals*, 7; Henry Wadsworth Longfellow, *Letters* 3:258; Samuel Longfellow, ed., *Life of Henry Wadsworth Longfellow*, vol. 2 (Boston: Houghton Mifflin, 1887), 303.

93. James Weir, *Lonz Powers*, vol. 1 (Philadelphia: Lippincott, 1850), 29.

94. Hundley, *Social Relations in Our Southern States*, 345, 348.

95. Metta V. Victor, *Maum Guinea and Her Plantation "Children"* (London: Beadle, [1860?]), 127.

96. Robert C. Toll, *Blacking Up* (New York: Oxford University Press, 1974), 50, 45.

97. J. G. Clinkscales, *On the Old Plantation: Reminiscences of His Childhood* (1916; reprint, New York: Negro Universities Press, 1969), 100.

98. Amelia M. Murray, *Letters from the United States, Cuba, and Canada* (New York: Putnam, 1856), 199; Fredrika Bremer, *The Homes of the New World*, vol. 1, trans. Mary Howitt (New York: Harper, 1853), 369–70.

99. "Letter from a Teacher at the South," 164.

100. T. Lindsay Baker and Julie B. Baker, eds., *The WPA Oklahoma Slave Narratives* (Norman: University of Oklahoma Press, 1996), 453–54.

101. Gilman, *Recollections*, 89.

102. Francis C. Sheridan, *Galveston Island*, ed. Willis W. Pratt (Austin: University of Texas Press, 1954), 93–94.

103. See, for example, Henry A. Kmen, *Music in New Orleans* (Baton Rouge: Louisiana State University Press, 1966), 230–33.

## Chapter 4. Listening to Professional Musicians

1. Jane Grey Swisshelm, *Half a Century*, 2d ed. (Chicago: Jansen, McClurg, 1880), 206.

2. Louis Moreau Gottschalk, *Notes of a Pianist*, ed. Jeanne Behrend (New York: Knopf, 1964), 75.

3. "Letter from a Teacher at the South," *Dwight's Journal of Music* 2 (26 February 1853): 164.

4. "Happy Hours at Home," words and music by Stephen C. Foster (New York: Daly, 1862).

5. "Sambo's Address," as sung by Mr. Brower (New York: Birch, 1833).

6. "The Old Granite State," composed and sung by the Hutchinson Family (New York: John Hutchinson, 1843).

7. Philip D. Jordan, *Singin' Yankees* (Minneapolis: University of Minnesota Press, 1946), 225.

8. Henry Wadsworth Longfellow, *The Letters of Henry Wadsworth Longfellow*, vol. 3, ed. Andrew Hilen (Cambridge, Mass.: Belknap, 1972), 130, 207.

9. Noah Ludlow writes that performers often had to stay overnight in whatever lodgings, public or private, that they could find. One evening in 1815 he, Sam Drake, and their troupe were put up in a western Pennsylvania farmhouse, in which a doctor and his family now lived. Drake played violin variations on a song from *The Beggar's Opera* for the musically starved family. "The lady was in ecstasies, the doctor delighted; the two night-caps, and the two little bob-tails had got fairly out into the parlor before the mother saw them and drove them back to their room." See Noah M. Ludlow, *Dramatic Life as I Found It* (1880; reprint, New York: Blom, 1966), 35.

10. Walt Whitman, "Art-Singing and Heart-Singing," *Broadway Journal* (29 November 1845), reprinted in *The Uncollected Poetry and Prose of Walt Whitman*, vol. 1, ed. Emory Holloway (Gloucester, Mass.: Peter Smith, 1972), 105. On page 106, Whitman writes that the criticisms he has made are not aimed at the "musical connoisseur."

11. Robert Kemp, *Father Kemp and His Old Folks* (Boston: Kemp, 1868), 64–65; Henry Hiram Riley, *The Puddleford Papers* (New York: Derby & Jackson, 1860), 281–82.

12. Philip Hone, *The Diary of Philip Hone, 1828–1851*, vol. 1, ed. Bayard Tuckerman (New York: Dodd, Mead, 1889), 265; Nathaniel Parker Willis, *The Miscellaneous Works* (Clinton Hall, N.Y.: Redfield, 1847), 59.

13. Albert Stoutamire, *Music of the Old South* (Rutherford, N.J.: Fairleigh Dickinson University Press, 1972), 149.

14. See Robert C. Toll, *Blacking Up* (New York: Oxford University Press, 1974), 3–11.

15. Walter Austin, *Tales of a Dedham Tavern* (Cambridge, Mass.: privately printed, 1912), 127–28.

16. Lew Wallace, *An Autobiography*, vol. 1 (New York: Harper, 1906), 31–32.

17. William Johnson, *William Johnson's Natchez: The Ante-Bellum Diary of a Free Negro*, ed. William Ransom Hogan and Edwin Adams Davis (Baton Rouge: Louisiana State University Press, 1951), 114, 513; George P. Rawick, ed., *The American Slave: A Composite Autobiography*, supp. ser. 1, vol. 5, *Ohio Narratives* (Westport, Conn.: Greenwood, 1977), 328.

18. The California incident is described in Jordan, *Singin' Yankees*, 185; the St. Louis one, in Dr. Thomas L. Nichols, *Forty Years of American Life*, vol. 1 (London: Maxwell, 1864), 397.

19. J. D. Borthwick, *The Gold Hunters*, ed. Horace Kephart (New York: Macmillan, 1924), 212–13.

20. Ludlow, *Dramatic Life as I Found It*, 268.

21. Kemp, *Father Kemp and His Old Folks*, 36.

22. Ludlow, *Dramatic Life as I Found It*, 213.

23. John Wallace Hutchinson, *Story of the Hutchinsons*, vol. 1 (Boston: Lee & Shepard, 1896), 329–30.

24. News item in *Dwight's Journal of Music* 1 (19 June 1852): 84.

25. H. Earle Johnson, *Hallelujah, Amen!* (Boston: Humphries, 1965), 10–11.

26. David Still, "Patterns of Mid-Nineteenth Century Urbanization in the Middle West," in Raymond A. Mohl and Neil Betten, eds., *Urban America in Perspective* (New York: Weybright & Talley, 1970), 174.

27. Louis C. Madeira, *Annals of Music in Philadelphia and History of the Musical Fund Society*, ed. Philip H. Goepp (Philadelphia: Lippincott, 1896), 86.

28. Letter dated 23 January 1837, written to Thomas Gold Appleton, from Cambridge, in Longfellow, *Letters* 2:9.

29. George F. Root, *The Story of a Musical Life* (Cincinnati: Church, 1891), 17.

30. Johnson, *Hallelujah, Amen!*, 63.

31. Ibid., 55.

32. John Moore, *Complete Encyclopaedia of Music* (Boston: Ditson, 1854), s.v. "Oratorio."

33. Hone, *Diary* 1:169–70, 172–73.

34. John Donald Wade, *Augustus Baldwin Longstreet* (New York: Macmillan, 1924), 52.

35. Letter to his wife, Frances, from New York City, dated 29 July 1826, in William Cullen Bryant, *The Letters of William Cullen Bryant*, ed. William Cullen Bryant II and Thomas G. Voss (New York: Fordham University Press, 1977), 206–7.

36. Charles Francis Adams, *The Diary of Charles Francis Adams*, vol. 2, ed. Aida DiPace Donald and David Donald (Cambridge, Mass.: Belknap, 1964), 58–60, 70.

37. Stoutamire, *Music in the Old South*, 207–8.

38. Charles T. Congdon, *Reminiscences of a Journalist* (Boston: Osgood, 1880), 198–99.

39. Thomas Ryan, *Recollections of an Old Musician* (New York: Dutton), 132–34.

40. Bronson Alcott, *The Journals of Bronson Alcott*, ed. Odell Shepard (Boston: Little, Brown, 1938), 233; Nathaniel Parker Willis, *Hurry-Graphs* (London: Bohn, 1851), 121–22.

41. As told in S. J. Fitz-Gerald, *Stories of Famous Songs*, vol. 1 (Philadelphia: Lippincott, 1910), 30.

42. Stoutamire, *Music of the Old South*, 145.

43. Charles F. Browne, *Complete Works* (London: Chatto & Windus, n.d), 91–92.

44. Longfellow, *Letters* 3:318.

45. Whitman, *Uncollected Poetry and Prose* 2:100.

46. John Neal, *True Womanhood* (Boston: Ticknor & Fields, 1859), 30.

47. Eliza Ripley, *Social Life in Old New Orleans* (New York: Appleton, 1912), 68–69.

48. Johnson, *William Johnson's Natchez*, 125, 521; George G. Ripley, *New York by Gas-Light and Other Urban Sketches*, ed. Stuart M. Blumin (Berkeley and Los Angeles: University of California Press, 1990), 145–46. Ripley's book was originally published in 1850.

49. Henry Wikoff, *The Reminiscences of an Idler* (New York: Fords, Howard & Hulbert, 1880), 34–35.

50. Gottschalk, *Notes of a Pianist*, 50.

51. Thomas Hastings, *Dissertation on Musical Taste* (Albany, N.Y.: Websters & Skinners, 1822), 138.

52. Ibid., 139.

53. Gottschalk, *Notes of a Pianist*, 58.

54. Rosser Taylor, *Ante-Bellum South Carolina* (Chapel Hill: University of North Carolina Press, 1942), 137.

55. Letter to Mrs. Child, October 1844, quoted in George Willis Cooke, *John Sullivan Dwight* (Boston: Small, Maynard, 1898), 80–81.

56. John Tasker Howard, *Our American Music*, 4th ed. (New York: Crowell, 1965), 222–23.

57. Journal entry for 25 April 1849, in Samuel Longfellow, ed., *Life of Henry Wadsworth Longfellow*, vol. 2 (Boston: Houghton Mifflin, 1887), 149.

58. Bliss Perry, *Life and Letters of Henry Lee Higginson*, vol. 1 (Boston: Atlantic Monthly, 1921), 78.

59. Stoutamire, *Music of the Old South*, 201.

60. Virginia Clay-Clopton, *A Belle of the Fifties*, ed. Ada Sterling (New York: Doubleday, Page, 1904), 49–50.

61. Ryan, *Recollections of an Old Musician*, 163, 164 (Ryan's italics).

62. Vera Brodsky Lawrence, *Strong on Music*, vol. 1 (New York: Oxford University Press, 1988), 370, 372.

63. Harriet Martineau, *Retrospect of Western Travels*, vol. 2 (London: Saunders & Otley, 1838), 54.

64. Bryant, *Letters* 2:438.

65. Congdon, *Reminiscences of a Journalist*, 196–97.

66. George William Curtis, *Early Letters of George Wm. Curtis to John S. Dwight*, ed. George Willis Cooke (New York: Harper, 1898), 119–20.

67. George R. Stewart, *John Phoenix, Esq.* (New York: Holt, 1937), 142.

68. Printed in the *San Diego Pioneer*, 10 July 1854; see George H. Derby, *Phoenixiana* (New York: Appleton, 1855), 44–46.

## Chapter 5. Amateur Music Making at Home

1. Frances Trollope, *Domestic Manners of the Americans*, 5th ed. (1839; reprint, New York: Dodd, Mead, 1927), 175.

2. Francis Baily, *Journal of a Tour in Unsettled Parts of North America in 1796 and 1797* (London: Baily, 1856), 121.

3. Samuel Osgood, *Mile-Stones* (New York: Appleton, 1855), 97.

4. Quoted in Arthur Loesser, *Men, Women, and Pianos* (New York: Simon & Schuster, 1954), 456–57.

5. Hardin E. Taliaferro, *Fisher's River (North Carolina)* (New York: Harper, 1859), 114–15; Marion Harland, *Marion Harland's Autobiography* (New York: Harper, 1910), 220.

6. F. B. Sanborn, *Recollections of Seventy Years*, vol. 2 (Boston: Badger, 1909), 535.

7. "Preface," in Sally and Pamela Brown, *The Diaries of Sally and Pamela Brown, 1832–1838*, ed. Blanche Bryant and Gertrude Elaine Baker (Springfield, Vt.: Bryant Foundation, 1970), 3; Benjamin P. Thomas, *Lincoln's New Salem*, rev. ed. (New York: Knopf, 1954), 42.

8. George P. Rawick, ed. *The American Slave: A Composite Autobiography*, vol. 4, *Texas Narratives, Part 2* (Westport, Conn.: Greenwood, 1972), 43.

9. Mrs. Lydia Huntley Sigourney, *Letters of Life* (New York: Appleton, 1867), 74; Mrs. Sue (Petigrue) Bowen, *Busy Moments of an Idle Woman* (New York: Appleton, 1854), 9–10.

10. Letter from Hill Rowan to Ann Eliza, sister of Stephen Foster, dated 19 November 1829, in Evelyn Foster Mornewick, *Chronicles of Stephen Foster's Family*, vol. 1 (Pittsburgh: University of Pittsburgh Press, 1944), 106.

11. Susan Dabney Smedes, *Memorials of a Southern Planter* (Baltimore: Cushings & Bailey, 1887), 177.

12. George F. Root, *The Story of a Musical Life* (Cincinnati: Church, 1891), 4.

13. J. Marion Sims, *The Story of My Life*, ed. H. Marion Sims (New York: Appleton, 1884), 66–67.

14. Richard Green Parker, *A Tribute to the Life and Character of Jonas Chickering* (Boston: Tewksbury, 1854), 43–44; Lady Emmeline Stuart Wortley, *Travels in the United States, etc., during 1844 and 1850* (New York: Harper, 1851), 43; Eliza Ripley, *Social Life in Old New Orleans* (New York: Appleton, 1912), 154.

15. Jessie Benton Frémont, *Souvenirs of My Time* (Boston: Lothrop, 1887), 59–60.

16. Carl Sandburg, *Abraham Lincoln*, vol. 1, *The Prairie Years* (New York: Harcourt, Brace, 1926), 53; Joseph C. Neal, *Charcoal Sketches*, new ed. (New York: Burgess & Stringer, 1844), 144; Julius H. Ward, *The Life and Letters of James Gates Percival* (Boston: Ticknor &

Fields, 1866), 433; Misses Mendell and Hosmer, *Notes of Travel and Life* (New York: the authors, 1854), 217.

17. Vera Brodsky Lawrence, *Strong on Music*, vol. 1 (New York: Oxford University Press, 1988), 4–5.

18. Frances M. Whitcher, *The Widow Bedott Papers* (New York: Derby & Jackson, 1856), 207–8.

19. Oliver Wendell Holmes, *The Autocrat of the Breakfast-Table* (Boston: Houghton Mifflin, 1916), 116–17.

20. Fredrika Bremer, *The Homes of the New World*, trans. Mary Howitt, vol. 2 (New York: Harper, 1853), 36, 41.

21. George William Curtis, *Early Letters of George Wm. Curtis to John S. Dwight*, ed. George Willis Cooke (New York: Harper, 1898), 18–19.

22. Root, *Story of a Musical Life*, 18; H. Earle Johnson, *Musical Interludes in Boston, 1795–1830* (New York: Columbia University Press, 1943), 73; *The Singer's Companion* (New York: Stringer & Townsend, 1854), 117.

23. Howard Swan, *Music in the Southwest, 1825–1950* (San Marino, Calif.: Huntington Library, 1852), 40–41, 48.

24. Cornel Lengyel, ed., *A San Francisco Songster*, History of Music in San Francisco, vol. 2 (San Francisco: WPA, 1939), 16, 19–20.

25. Nicholas E. Tawa, *Sweet Songs for Gentle Americans: The Parlor Song in America, 1790–1860* (Bowling Green, Ohio: Bowling Green University Popular Press, 1980), has as its main object a thorough study of such bound volumes and their owners.

26. Laura E. Richards and Maud Howe Elliott, assisted by Florence Howe Hall, *Julia Ward Howe, 1819–1910*, vol. 2 (Boston: Houghton Mifflin, 1916), 26.

27. Hans Nathan, *Dan Emmett and the Rise of Early Negro Minstrelsy* (Norman: University of Oklahoma Press, 1962), 104; Albert Stoutamire, *Music in the Old South* (Rutherford, N.J.: Fairleigh Dickinson University Press, 1972), 55; W. E. Woodward, *The Way Our People Lived* (New York: Dutton, 1944), 189.

28. Smedes, *Memorials of a Southern Planter*, 110.

29. John Townsend Trowbridge, *My Own Story* (Boston: Houghton Mifflin, 1903), 164; Major Horace Bell, *Reminiscences of a Ranger* (Santa Barbara, Calif.: Hebberd, 1927), 465–67.

30. Fanny J. Crosby, *Memories of Eighty Years* (Boston: Earle, 1906), 81; Curtis Dahl, *Robert Montgomery Bird* (New York: Twayne, 1963), 37–38.

31. Rev. E. H. Chapin, *Humanity in the City* (New York: De Witt, 1854), 126.

32. Lydia H. Sigourney, *Letters to Young Ladies*, 2d ed. (Hartford, Conn.: Wilson, 1835) 64–65.

33. Oliver Wendell Holmes, *The Complete Poetical Works* (Boston: Houghton Mifflin, 1908), 166–67.

34. Ibid., 254.

35. Samuel Longfellow, ed., *Life of Henry Wadsworth Longfellow*, vol. 1 (Boston: Houghton Mifflin, 1887), 14.

36. "Life as It Is," *The Lowell Offering*, vol. 2 (Lowell: Powers & Bagley, 1842), 321–22.

37. Rufus Rockwell Wilson, *Intimate Memories of Lincoln* (Elmira, N.Y.: Primavera, 1945), 399–400.

38. M. E. Dodge, *Irvington Stories*, 4th ed. (New York: O'Kane, 1865), 57.

39. Edgar Allan Poe, *The Letters of Edgar Allan Poe*, ed. John Ward Ostrom, vol. 2 (Cambridge, Mass.: Harvard University Press, 1940), 350.

40. *The Parish-Side*, by the Clerk of the Parish of Edgefield (New York: Mason, 1854), 39.

41. Charles Quill, *The American Mechanic* (Philadelphia: Perkins, 1838), 157–58.

42. Ralph Waldo Emerson, W. H. Channing, and J. F. Clarke, *Memoirs of Margaret Fuller Ossoli*, vol. 1 (Boston: Roberts, 1884), 52–53.

43. Bronson Alcott, *The Journals of Bronson Alcott*, ed. Odell Shepard (Boston: Little, Brown, 1938), 174.

44. Rosser H. Taylor, *Ante-Bellum South Carolina: A Social and Cultural History* (Chapel Hill: University of North Carolina Press, 1942), 17; Smedes, *Memorials of a Southern Planter*, 117.

45. Susan I. Lesley, *Recollections of My Mother* (Boston: Ellis, 1886), 89–90 (her parents lived in Milton, Mass.); Lew Wallace, *An Autobiography*, vol. 1 (New York: Harper, 1906), 209–10.

46. Carl David Arfwedson, *The United States in 1832, 1833, and 1834*, vol. 1 (London: Bentley, 1834), 135.

47. Mrs. Sarah J. Hale, *Traits of American Life* (Philadelphia: Carey & Hart, 1835), 149; Ripley, *Social Life in Old New Orleans*, 157–58.

48. W. L. G. Smith, *Life at the South* (Buffalo, N.Y.: Derby, 1852), 121. The author claims to be depicting "the passions and sentiments as . . . are usually found to exist in the every-day scenes of life."

49. Emily R. Barnes, *Narratives, Traditions, and Personal Reminiscences* (Boston: Ellis, 1888), 125.

50. See Richards and Elliott, *Julia Ward Howe* 1:60; Mary H. Eastman, *Aunt Phillis's Cabin, or Southern Life as It Is* (Philadelphia: Lippincott, Grambo, 1852), 52; Bowen, *Busy Moments of an Idle Woman*, 35–36; Mrs. Rhoda (Eastman) White, *Portraits of My Married Friends* (New York: Appleton, 1858), 310; Quill, *American Mechanic*, 18.

51. Lawrence, *Strong on Music* 1:571.

52. Curtis, *Early Letters*, 185–86.

53. Richards and Elliott, *Julia Ward Howe* 1:116, 122, 126.

54. Sallie Rochester Ford, *Grace Truman* (New York: Sheldon, Blakeman, 1857), 493; James Weir, *Lonz Powers*, vol. 1 (Philadelphia: Lippincott, Grambo, 1950), 90; Mornewick, *Chronicles of Stephen Foster's Family* 1:34.

55. Anna Hanson Dorsey, *Woodreve Manor* (Philadelphia: Hart, 1852), 166.

56. Dodge, *Irvington Stories*, 55.

57. Mornewick, *Chronicles of Stephen Foster's Family* 1:40; John Tasker Howard, *Stephen Foster, America's Troubadour* (New York: Crowell, 1962), 40.

58. Lesley, *Recollections of My Mother*, 303; Eastman, *Aunt Phillis's Cabin*, 197; Caroline Lee Hentz, *The Planter's Northern Bride*, vol. 1 (Philadelphia: Hart, 1854), 98–99.

59. Henry David Thoreau, *Writings*, vol. 11, *Familiar Letters*, ed. F. B. Sanborn (Boston: Houghton Mifflin, 1895), 311.

60. Sanborn, *Recollections of Seventy Years* 2:397–98.

61. Julia Ward Howe, *Reminiscences, 1819–1899* (1899; reprint, New York: Negro Universities Press, 1969), 24.

62. Francis H. Underwood, *Quabbin: The Story of a Small Town* (1893; reprint, Boston: Northeastern University Press, 1986), 204–6.

63. Jack Larkin, *The Reshaping of Everyday Life, 1790–1940* (New York: Harper & Row, 1988), 233.

64. Horace Greeley, *Recollections of a Busy Life* (New York: Ford, 1868), 51.

65. Virginia Clay-Clopton, *A Belle of the Fifties*, ed. Ada Sterling (New York: Doubleday, Pate, 1904), 25–26; John Pintard, *Letters from John Pintard to His Daughter*, vol. 2 (New York: New-York Historical Society, 1940), 90–91.

66. Ellen K. Rothman, *Hands and Hearts: A History of Courtship in America* (New York: Basic Books, 1984), 23–24; Bliss Perry, *Life and Letters of Henry Lee Higginson*, vol. 1 (Boston: Atlantic Monthly, 1921), 81; Harland, *Marion Harland's Autobiography*, 203.

67. Letitia Burwell, *A Girl's Life in Virginia before the War*, (New York: Stokes, 1895), 130–31; Edmund Kirke, *My Southern Friends* (New York: Tribune Association, 1863), 152–53.

68. Metta V. Victor, *Maum Guinea and Her Plantation "Children"* (London: Beadle, [1860?]), 57–58.

69. Quoted in Eileen Southern, *The Music of Black Americans*, 3d edition (New York: Norton, 1997), 101.

70. *Autobiography of a Female Slave* (1857; reprint, New York: Negro Universities Press, 1969), 339–40.

71. Emily P. Burke, *Reminiscences of Georgia* (Oberlin, Ohio: Fitch, 1850), 152; Rawick, ed. *American Slave*, supp. ser. 1, vol. 7, *Mississippi Narratives, Part 2* (Westport, Conn.: Greenwood, 1977), 646.

72. Rawick, ed. *American Slave*, supp. ser. 1, vol. 5, *Indiana Narratives* (Westport, Conn.: Greenwood, 1977), 177–78.

73. Ibid., vol. 3, *South Carolina Narratives, Part 3* (1941; reprint, Westport, Conn.: Greenwood, 1972), 56–57.

74. Longfellow, ed. *Life of Henry Wadsworth Longfellow* 1:13; Caroline Gilman, *Recollections of a New England Bride and of a Southern Matron*, rev. ed. (New York: Putnam, 1852), 92. Also see Henry Ware Jr., *The Recollections of Jonathan Anderson*, 2d ed. (Boston: Christian Register Office, 1828), 138.

75. Sigourney, *Letters to Young Ladies*, 63; Ford, *Grace Truman*, 39.

76. Barnes, *Narratives, Traditions, and Personal Reminiscences*, 234.

77. Elizabeth Oakes Smith, *Riches without Wings*, 3d ed. (Boston: Light, 1839), 48.

78. Parke Godwin, *A Biography of William Cullen Bryant*, vol. 1 (1883; reprint, New York: Russell & Russell, 1967), 21.

79. *The Lowell Offering*, vol. 5 (Lowell: Misses Curtis & Farley, 1843), 149.

80. Harriet Beecher Stowe, *We and Our Neighbors* (Boston: Houghton Mifflin, 1898), 115–16.

81. Barnes, *Narratives, Traditions, and Personal Reminiscences*, 171–72, 225.

82. Alice Carey, *Clovernook, or Recollections of Our Neighborhood in the West* (Clinton Hall, N.Y.: Redfield, 1852), 196.

83. Trowbridge, *My Own Story*, 34.

84. Susan Warner [Elizabeth Wetherell], *The Wide, Wide World*, vol. 1 (New York: Putnam, 1851), 67; Maria Jane McIntosh, *Evenings at Donaldson Manor* (New York: Appleton, 1851), 136, and *Two Pictures* (New York: Appleton, 1863), 85; Hentz, *The Planter's Northern Bride* 1:69.

85. Samuel G. Goodrich, *Peter Parley's Own Story* (New York: Sheldon, 1864), 38–39.

86. Marion Harland, *Judith: A Chronicle of Old Virginia* (Philadelphia: Our Continent, 1883), 217–19.

87. Harriet Beecher Stowe, *Oldtown Folks* (Boston: Houghton Mifflin, 1869), 348, 351.

88. Fanny Fern, *Fern Leaves* (Boston: Miller, Orton & Mulligan, 1854), 200; Lucy Larcom, *A New England Girlhood* (1889; reprint, Boston: Northeastern University Press, 1986), 138.

89. Harland, *Marion Harland's Autobiography*, 350–51.

90. Fanny Appleton Longfellow, *Mrs. Longfellow: Selected Letters and Journals*, ed. Edward Wagenknecht (New York: Longmans, Green, 1956), 9; Sophie M. Damon, *Old New-England Days* (Boston: Cupples & Hurd, 1887), 95.

91. Emerson et al., *Memoirs of Margaret Fuller Ossoli* 1:884–85.

92. Eastman, *Aunt Phillis's Cabin*, 87; John W. Blassingame, ed., *Slave Testimony* (Baton Rouge: Louisiana State University Press, 1977), 593.

93. Bremer, *The Homes of the New World* 1:124 (Bremer's italics).

## Chapter 6. Parties, Frolics, and Other Celebrations

1. Kate Leonard, *Clara Temple Leonard: A Memoir of Her Life by Her Daughter* (Springfield, Mass.: Loring-Axtoll, 1908), 6–7.

2. Letters of 19 and 31 January 1822, in John Pintard, *Letters from John Pintard to His Daughter*, vol. 2 (New York: New-York Historical Society, 1940), 123–24.

3. Frances Trollope, *Domestic Manners of the Americans*, 5th ed. (1839; reprint, New York: Dodd, Mead, 1927), 256.

4. David Macrae, *Americans at Home* (1870; reprint, N.Y.: Dutton, 1952), 53.

5. Harriet Beecher Stowe, *We and Our Neighbors* (Boston: Houghton Mifflin, 1898), 215.

6. William Cullen Bryant, *The Letters of William Cullen Bryant*, vol. 1, ed. William Cullen Bryant II and Thomas G. Vose (New York: Fordham University Press, 1975), 100.

7. A journal entry, dated 24 January 1840, in Francis C. Sheridan, *Galveston Island*, ed. Willis W. Pratt (Austin: University of Texas Press, 1954), 23–25.

8. Trollope, *Domestic Manners of the Americans*, 49–50; Lydia H. Sigourney, *Letters to Young Ladies*, 2d ed. (Hartford, Conn.: Watson, 1835), 182–83.

9. Sophie M. Damon, *Old New-England Days* (Boston: Cupples & Hurd, 1887), 207–8.

10. Harriet Beecher Stowe, *My Wife and I* (New York: Ford, 1871), 166.

11. Sally Brown and Pamela Brown, *The Diaries of Sally and Pamela Brown, 1832–1838*, ed. Blanche Brown Bryant and Gertrude Elaine Baker (Springfield, Vt.: Bryant Foundation, 1970), 21; Henry Hiram Riley, *The Puddleford Papers* (New York: Derby & Jackson, 1860), 125–26.

12. George P. Rawick, ed., *The American Slave: A Composite Autobiography*, supp. ser. 1, vol. 7, *Mississippi Narratives, Part 2* (Westport, Conn.: Greenwood, 1977), 685.

13. Virginia Wilcox Ivins, *Pen Pictures of Early Western Days* (Keokuk, Iowa: n.p., 1909), 54; Daniel Drake, *Pioneer Life in Kentucky, 1785–1800*, ed. Emmett Field Horne (New York: Schuman, 1948), 185.

14. Evelyn Foster Mornewick, *Chronicles of Stephen Foster's Family*, vol. 1 (Pittsburgh: University of Pittsburgh Press, 1944), 55; Rufus Rockwell Wilson, *Intimate Memories of Lincoln* (Elmira, N.Y.: Primavera, 1945), 121.

15. Amelia M. Murray, *Letters from the United States, Cuba, and Canada* (New York: Putnam, 1856), 82. In her letters Murray reveals a sense of superiority to Americans, except perhaps for some Southern "aristocrats." She was also an apologist for slavery.

16. John P. Kennedy, *Memoirs of the Life of William Wirt*, rev. ed., vol. 2 (Philadelphia: Lippincott, 1860), 95–96.

17. Philip Hone, *The Diary of Philip Hone, 1828–1851*, ed. Bayard Tuckerman (New York: Dodd, Mead, 1889), 1:345, 347–48; 2:56.

18. Kemble quoted in ibid., 1:128.

19. H. M. Brackenbridge, *Recollections of Persons and Places in the West* (Philadelphia: Lippincott, 1868), 132.

20. John Neal, *True Womanhood* (Boston: Ticknor & Fields, 1859), 68–69.

21. Theodore S. Fay, *Norman Leslie*, vol. 1 (New York: Harper, 1835), 39–42.

22. *Tales of an American Landlord, Containing Sketches of Life South of the Potomac*, vol. 1 (New York: Gilley, 1824), 168–69.

23. Laura E. Richards and Maud Howe Elliott, assisted by Florence Howe Hall, *Julia Ward Howe, 1819–1910*, vol. 1 (Boston: Houghton Mifflin, 1916), 32; Samuel Longfellow, ed., *Life of Henry Wadsworth Longfellow*, vol. 2 (Boston: Houghton Mifflin, 1887), 34, 41; Anne C. L. Botta, *Memoirs of Anne C. L. Botta* (New York: Tait, 1894), 175.

24. Thomas Colley Grattan, *Civilized America*, 2d ed., vol. 1 (London: Bradbury, 1859), 127.

25. Charles Francis Adams, *Diary of Charles Francis Adams*, vol. 1, ed. Aida DiPace Donald and David Donald (Cambridge, Mass.: Belknap, 1964), 83–84; Richards and Elliott, *Julia Ward Howe* 1:123–24.

26. Vera Brodsky Lawrence, *Strong on Music*, vol. 2 (New York: Oxford University Press, 1988), 444–45.

27. Henry M. Brooks, *Olden-Time Music* (Boston: Ticknor, 1888), 239; Daniel Mann, *Wolfsden* (Boston: Phillips, Sampson, 1856), 462; Walter Austin, *Tales of a Dedham Tavern* (Cambridge, Mass.: privately printed, 1912), 75.

28. Elizabeth W. Allston Pringle, *Chronicles of Chicora Wood* (New York: Scribners, 1922), 145–46.

29. N. Parker Willis, *Fun-Jottings* (New York: Scribners, 1853), 230; A. B. Longstreet, *Georgia Scenes*, 2d ed. (New York: Harper, 1851), 119; Henry A. Kmen, *Music in New Orleans* (Baton Rouge: Louisiana State University Press, 1966), 15.

30. Grace Greenwood, *Greenwood Leaves*, 2d ed. (Boston: Ticknor, Reed & Fields, 1850), 6.

31. Edward Augustus Kendall, *Travels through the Northern Parts of the United States, in the Years 1807 and 1808*, vol. 1 (New York: Riley, 1809), 240; Christopher Columbus Baldwin, *Diary*, Transactions and Collections of the American Antiquarian Society, 8 (Worcester, Mass.: American Antiquarian Society, 1901), 11; Austin, *Tales of a Dedham Tavern*, 73; Sheridan, *Galveston*, 75.

32. Rawick, ed., *American Slave*, vol. 4, *Texas Narratives, Part 1* (Westport, Conn.: Greenwood, 1972), 110.

33. Charles Dickens, *American Notes* (Leipzig: Tauchnitz, 1842), 52–53.

34. Jonathan Slick [Ann S. Stephens], *High Life in New York* (New York: Bunce, 1854), 63.

35. Longstreet, *Georgia Scenes*, 12–17.

36. Constance Rourke, *Davy Crocket* (New York: Harcourt, Brace, 1934), 125–26; William T. Porter, ed., *A Quarter Race in Kentucky and Other Sketches* (Philadelphia: Peterson, 1854), 83–88.

37. D. R. Hundley, *Social Relations in Our Southern States* (New York: Price, 1860), 213–14.

38. George W. Harris, *Sut Lovingood* (New York: Dick & Fitzgerald, 1867), 182–89.

39. W. E. Woodward, *The Way Our People Lived* (New York: Dutton, 1944), 249.

40. Rawick, ed., *American Slave*, supp. ser. 1, vol. 6, *Mississippi Narratives, Part 1* (Westport, Conn.: Greenwood, 1977), 157.

41. Solomon Northup, *Twelve Years a Slave* (New York: Miller, Orton & Mulligan, 1855), 216.

42. Rawick, ed., *American Slave*, vol. 3, *South Carolina Narratives, Part 3* (Westport,

**320**    Conn.: Greenwood, 1972), 151–52; ibid., *Mississippi Narratives, Part 2*, 120; ibid., *Texas Narratives, Part 1*, 10.

43. Harry Smith, *Fifty Years of Slavery* (Grand Rapids: West Michigan Printing Co., 1891), 76; Rawick, ed., *American Slave*, supp. ser. 1, vol. 8, *Mississippi Narratives, Part 3* (Westport, Conn.: Greenwood, 1977), 843–44.

44. [James Boardman], *America and the Americans, by a Citizen of the World* (London: Longman, Rees, Orme, Brown, Green & Longman, 1833), 336–37; N. Parker Willis, *Rural Letters and Other Records of Thought at Leisure* (Auburn, N.Y.: Alden, Beardsley, 1853), 342.

45. Lady Emmeline Stuart Wortley, *Travels in the United States, etc., during 1849 and 1850* (New York: Harper, 1851), 55; James Weir, *Lonz Powers*, vol. 1 (Philadelphia: Lippincott, Grambo, 1850), 356.

46. Charles Sealsfield, *Flirtations in America*, trans. from the German (New York: Taylor, 1847), 141–42.

47. Frederic S. Cozzens, *The Sparrowgrass Papers* (Philadelphia: Lippincott, 1865), 163–64; Walt Whitman, *The Uncollected Poetry and Prose of Walt Whitman*, vol. 1, ed. Emory Holloway (Gloucester, Mass.: Peter Smith, 1972), 49; Grace Greenwood, *Greenwood Leaves* (Boston: Ticknor, Reed, & Fields, 1850), 350; Mrs. Lydia Huntley Sigourney, *Letters of Life* (New York: Appleton, 1867), 134; *Boston Musical Gazette*, 27 June 1838, 37.

48. Ward McAllister, *Society as I Found It* (New York: Cassell, 1890), 102–3; Lydia Maria Child, *Letters from New York*, 2d ser. (New York: Francis, 1845), 195; Lawrence, *Strong on Music* 1:78.

49. Dr. Thomas L. Nichols, *Forty Years of American Life*, vol. 1 (London: Maxwell, 1864), 142. The excursion took place in the summer of 1839.

50. Samuel C. Upham, *Notes of a Voyage to California via Cape Horn, Together with Scenes in El Dorado, in the Years 1849–'50* (Philadelphia: Upham, 1878), 323–25.

51. John Esten Cooke, *Ellie, or The Human Comedy* (Richmond, Va.: Morris, 1855), 422–23.

52. Sigourney, *Letters of Life*, 120–21; also see, Nichols, *Forty Years of American Life* 1:17–18.

53. Thomas Chandler Haliburton, *The Americans at Home*, vol. 3, ed. by the author of "Sam Slick" (London: Hurst & Blackett, 1854), 104–5.

54. William Hancock, *An Emigrant's Five Years in the Free States of America* (London: Newby, 1860), 184; Francis Baily, *Journal of a Tour in Unsettled Parts of North America in 1796 and 1797* (London: Baily, 1856), 122.

55. Thomas Ashe, *Travels in America, performed in 1806* (Newburyport, Mass.: Sawyer, 1808), 30.

56. Ivins, *Pen Pictures of Early Western Days*, 56.

57. Rawick, ed., *American Slave*, supp. ser. 1, vol. 5, *Ohio Narratives* (Westport, Conn.: Greenwood, 1977), 325; W. L. G. Smith, *Life at the South* (Buffalo, N.Y.: Derby, 1852), 53–55.

58. Bertha Eveleth Blodgett, *Stories of Cortland County* (Cortland, N.Y.: Cortland Historical Society, 1952), 201–2.

59. The details of one such wedding may be found in John B. Jones, *The Winkles* (New York: Appleton, 1855), 104–5. In this instance the crowd fell silent only when an unassuming girl sang naturally "one of the songs of other days."

60. Weir, *Lonz Powers* 2:243; Haliburton, *The Americans at Home* 3:283–84.

61. *The Lowell Offering*, vol. 2 (Lowell: Powers & Bagley, 1842), 51–52.

62. Edmund Kirke, *My Southern Friends* (New York: Tribune Association, 1863), 208–9.

63. Weir, *Lonz Powers* 2:243.

64. Virginia Clay-Clopton, *A Belle of the Fifties*, ed. Ada Sterling (New York: Doubleday, Page, 1904), 21.

65. Lew Wallace, *An Autobiography*, vol. 1 (New York: Harper, 1906), 226.

66. Marion Harland, *Marion Harland's Autobiography* (New York: Harper, 1910), 135.

67. Slick, *High Life in New York*, 33–35.

68. Thurlow Weed, *Life of Thurlow Weed Including His Autobiography and a Memoir*, vol. 1, ed. Harriet A. Weed (Boston: Houghton Mifflin, 1883), 490–93. Arthur M. Schlesinger Jr., in *The Age of Jackson* (Boston: Little, Brown, 1945), 290, says a pro-Democrat paper in Baltimore, not Richmond, made the statement about the pension and hard cider.

69. Lawrence, *Strong on Music* 1:68.

70. D. Corcoran, *Pickings from . . . the New Orleans "Picayune"* (Philadelphia: Carey & Hart, 1846), 23–25.

71. Grattan, *Civilized America* 1:322.

72. Greenwood, *Greenwood Leaves*, 379. New Brighton was on the Ohio River, about thirty miles northwest of Pittsburgh.

73. John Tasker Howard, *Stephen Foster, America's Troubadour* (New York: Crowell, 1962), 258–59.

74. See, for example, Mrs. C. M. Kirkland, *Western Clearings* (New York: Wiley & Putnam, 1845), 25–27; Rosser H. Taylor, *Ante-Bellum South Carolina* (Chapel Hill: University of North Carolina Press, 1942), 52; Nichols, *Forty Years of American Life* 1:39.

75. F. B. Sanborn, *Recollections of Seventy Years*, vol. 2 (Boston: Badger, 1909), 432–33.

76. Ibid., 27, 33.

77. Dale Morgan, ed., *Overland in 1846*, vol. 2 (Georgetown, Calif.: Talisman, 1963), 586; Mrs. Catharine V. Waite, *Adventures on the Far West, and Life among the Mormons* (Chicago: Waite, 1882), 55–57.

78. Major Horace Bell, *Reminiscences of a Ranger* (Santa Barbara, Calif.: Hebberd, 1927), 62.

79. *The Lowell Offering*, vol. 4 (Lowell: Curtis & Farley, 1844), 237–40.

80. James Fenimore Cooper, *Home as Found* (New York: Townsend, 1860), 353–54.

81. Bronson Alcott, *The Journals of Bronson Alcott*, ed. Odell Shepard (Boston: Little, Brown, 1938), 155; Harriet Beecher Stowe, *Poganuc People: Their Loves and Lives* (New York: Fords, Howard & Hulbert, 1878), 85.

82. *The Parish-Side*, by the Clerk of the Parish of Edgefield (New York: Mason, 1854), 79.

83. Marion Harland, *Judith: A Chronicle of Old Virignia* (Philadelphia: Our Continent, 1883), 154–60.

84. William Gilmore Simms, *The Letters of William Gilmore Simms*, vol. 2, ed. Mary C. Simms Oliphant, Alfred Taylor Udell, and T. C. Duncan Eaves (Columbia: University of South Carolina Press, 1953), 252 n. 8.

85. Thomas Nelson Page, *Social Life in Old Virginia* (1897; reprint, Freeport, N.Y.: Books for Libraries, 1970), 96–97; Louise A. K. S. Clappe, *The Shirley Letters from California Mines in 1851–52* (San Francisco: Russell, 1922), 167–70.

86. William Wells Brown, *My Southern Home* (1880; reprint, Upper Saddle River, N.J.: Gregg, 1968), 95–97; Rev. I. E. Lowery, *Life on the Old Plantation in Ante-Bellum Days* (Columbia, S.C.: State Co. Printers, 1911), 65; Jacob Stroyer, *My Life in the South*, 3d ed. (Salem, Mass.: Salem Observer Books, 1885), 46–48.

87. Metta V. Victor, *Maum Guinea and Her Plantation "Children"* (London: Beadle, [1860?]), 20–24.

88. Ibid., 43–45.

89. Ibid., 129–30.

90. Caroline H. Gilman, *Recollections of a Housekeeper* (New York: Harper, 1836), 116–17; Northup, *Twelve Years a Slave*, 218–20; Frederick Douglass, *Life and Times of Frederick Douglass* (1892; reprint, New York: Collier Books, 1962), 145–46.

**Chapter 7. Education and Religion**

1. J. L. McConnel, *Western Characters* (New York: Redfield, 1852), 308–10.

2. Joseph Kirkland, *Zury* (Boston: Houghton Mifflin, 1887), 155–58.

3. Ibid., 192–94.

4. *Dwight's Journal of Music* 1 (19 June 1852): 84.

5. *Dwight's Journal of Music* 4 (18 February 1854): 156.

6. J. G. Holland, *Miss Gilbert's Career* (New York: Scribners, 1860), 5–10, 404–5.

7. Rosser H. Taylor, *Ante-Bellum South Carolina* (Chapel Hill: University of North Carolina Press, 1942), 136.

8. Eliza Ripley, *Social Life in Old New Orleans* (New York: Appleton, 1912), 20–21.

9. Marion Harland, *Marion Harland's Autobiography* (New York: Harper, 1910), 109.

10. Charles Francis Adams, *Diary of Charles Francis Adams*, ed. Aida DiPace Donald and David Donald (Cambridge, Mass.: Belknap, 1964), 136–37.

11. Harriet Beecher Stowe, *Poganuc People* (New York: Fords, Howard & Hulbert, 1878), 19, 291.

12. Anne M. Boylan, *Sunday School* (New Haven, Conn.: Yale University Press, 1988), 7–10, 20.

13. Ibid., 41, 157.

14. Ibid., 23, 26–28.

15. Quoted in John Tasker Howard, *Stephen Foster, America's Troubadour* (New York: Crowell, 1962), 218–19.

16. Reverend A. D. Merrill, "Preface," in *The Sunday School Melodist* (Boston: Peirce, 1851).

17. Ibid., 56, 176, 74, 19.

18. Ibid., 3, 9.

19. Mary Ellen Chase, *Jonathan Fisher, Maine Parson, 1768–1847* (New York: Macmillan, 1948), 84.

20. Daniel Mann, *Wolfsden* (Boston: Phillips, Sampson, 1856), 59–60. On the title page, the author says the book contains "an authentic account of things there and thereunto pertaining as they are and have been."

21. Elizabeth Oakes Smith, *Selections from the Autobiography of Elizabeth Oakes Smith*, ed. Mary Alice Wyman (Lewiston, Maine: Lewiston Journal, 1924), 31.

22. Samuel Gilman, *Memoirs of a New England Village Choir* (Boston: Goodrich, 1829), 40–42; Sallie Rochester Ford, *Grace Truman* (New York: Sheldon, Blakeman, 1857), 101.

23. Francis Grierson, *The Valley of Shadows*, new ed. (London: Lane, 1893), 12–14.

24. William Wells Brown, *My Southern Home* (1880; reprint, Upper Saddle River, N.J.: Gregg, 1968), 89–90.

25. Ellen Chapman Hobbs Rollins, *New England Bygones* (Philadelphia: Lippincott, 1880), 153; John Donald Wade, *Augustus Baldwin Longstreet* (New York: Macmillan, 1924), 64–65.

26. Augustus B. Longstreet, *Georgia Scenes*, 2d ed. (New York: Harper, 1851), 45–46.

27. Vera Brodsky Lawrence, *Strong on Music*, vol. 1 (New York: Oxford University Press, 1988), 78.

28. Lucy Larcom, *A New England Girlhood* (1889; reprint, Boston: Northeastern University Press, 1986), 68.

29. Samuel G. Goodrich, *Peter Parley's Own Story* (New York: Sheldon, 1864), 38.

30. Stowe, *Poganuc People*, 72–74.

31. Francis H. Underwood, *Quabbin: The Story of a Small Town* (1893; reprint, Boston: Northeastern University Press, 1986), 169–70.

32. Henry Hiram Riley, *The Puddleford Papers* (New York: Derby & Jackson, 1860), 59–64.

33. Emily R. Barnes, *Narratives, Traditions, and Personal Reminiscences* (Boston: Ellis, 1888), 130, 133–34.

34. Gilman, *Memoirs of a New England Village Choir*, 6–7, 11.

35. Walter Austin, *Tales of a Dedham Tavern* (Cambridge, Mass.: privately printed, 1912), 30.

36. Henry M. Brooks, *Olden-Time Music* (Boston: Ticknor, 1888), 219–21.

37. Ibid., 212–13.

38. Ibid., 210–11.

39. See the letter dated 2 March 1850, sent from New York City, in Fredrika Bremer, *The Homes of the New World*, vol. 1, trans. Mary Howitt (New York: Harper, 1853), 241; also see Ripley, *Social Life in Old New Orleans*, 121–22.

40. See, for example, Taylor, *Ante-Bellum South Carolina*, 79. South Carolinians called these events "singings."

41. John Mack Faragher, *Women and Men on the Overland Trail* (New Haven, Conn.: Yale University Press, 1979), 119; Chase, *Jonathan Fisher*, 109.

42. John Neal, *True Womanhood* (Boston: Ticknor & Fields, 1859), 7.

43. Sarah Raymond Herndon, *Days on the Road: Crossing the Plains in 1865* (New York: Burr, 1902), 125–26.

44. Solon Robinson, *Hot Corn: Life Scenes in New York* (1854; reprint, New York: Pollard & Moss, 1888), 52–53.

45. Charles H. Smith, *The Farm and the Fireside* (Atlanta: Constitution Publishing House, 1892), 245–51. The book gives an account of northwestern Georgia from around 1835 to 1890.

46. *Autobiography of a Female Slave* (1857; reprint, New York: Negro Universities Press, 1969), 156–57.

47. R. Q. Mallard, *Plantation Life before Emancipation* (Richmond, Va.: Whittet & Shepperson, 1892), 162–63.

48. Bremer, *Homes of the New World* 2:157–58.

49. See Mallard, *Plantation Life before Emancipation*, 75.

50. Edmund Kirke, *My Southern Friends* (New York: Tribune Association, 1963), 137–39.

51. Rev. I. E. Lowery, *Life on the Old Plantation in Ante-Bellum Days* (Columbia, S.C.: State Co. Printers, 1911), 70–73.

52. William Cullen Bryant, *The Letters of William Cullen Bryant*, vol. 2, ed. William Cullen Bryant II and Thomas G. Voss (New York: Fordham University Press, 1977), 200; Edward E. Hale Jr., *The Life and Letters of Edward Everett Hale*, vol. 1 (Boston: Little, Brown, 1917), 98; Bremer, *Homes of the New World* 1:354.

53. Harland, *Autobiography*, 234.

54. George P. Rawick, ed., *The American Slave: A Composite Autobiography*, vol. 3, *South Carolina Narratives, Part 3* (1941; reprint, Westport, Conn.: Greenwood, 1972), 108–9; ibid.,

**324** supp. ser. 1, vol. 7, *Mississippi Narratives, Part 2* (Westport, Conn.: Greenwood, 1977), 721–22.

55. Roger D. Abrahams, *Singing the Master* (New York: Pantheon, 1992), 44–45.

56. Frederick Law Olmsted, *The Cotton Kingdom*, vol. 1 (New York: Mason, 1861), 315–16.

57. From "Under the Palmetto," *Continental Monthly* 4 (August 1863): 196–97, reprinted in John Blassingame, ed., *Slave Testimony* (Baton Rouge: Louisiana State University Press, 1977), 65–66.

58. See John W. Blassingame, *The Slave Community* (New York: Oxford University Press, 1972), 64.

59. James L. Smith, *Autobiography* (Norwich, Conn.: Bulletin, 1881), 26–27.

60. Rawick, ed., *American Slave*, vol. 4, *Texas Narratives, Part 2* (Westport, Conn.: Greenwood, 1972), 170; also see 62.

61. See, e.g., Brown, *My Southern Home*, 58–59.

62. *The Experience of Thomas H. Jones, Who Was a Slave for Forty-Three Years*, written by a friend (New Bedford, Mass.: Anthony, 1871), 25–26.

63. Rawick, ed., *Mississippi Narratives, Part 2*, 715–16, 757; see also 744.

64. Rawick, ed., *Texas Narratives, Part 2*, 10; Rawick, ed., *American Slave*, vol. 6, *Alabama Narratives* (Westport, Conn.: Greenwood, 1972), 1; ibid., supp. ser. 1, vol. 8, *Mississippi Narratives, Part 3* (Westport, Conn.: Greenwood, 1977), 1307.

65. Dickson D. Bruce Jr., *And They All Sang Hallelujah* (Knoxville: University of Tennessee Press, 1974), 56–57.

66. Chandler R. Gilman, *Legends of a Log Cabin* (New York: Dearborn, 1835), 77–79.

67. Grierson, *The Valley of Shadows*, 152–71.

68. Ibid., 91–92.

69. Letter of 7 May 1850, in Bremer, *Homes of the New World* 1:306–9.

70. Benjamin Henry Latrobe, *The Journal of Latrobe* (New York: Appleton, 1905), 256–57; James Stuart, *Three Years in North America*, vol. 1 (Edinburgh: Cadell, 1833), 413–15; Dr. Thomas L. Nichols, *Forty Years of American Life*, vol. 1 (London: Maxwell, 1864), 78–79; Carl Sandburg, *Abraham Lincoln*, vol. 1, *The Prairie Years* (New York: Harcourt, Brace, 1926), 61.

71. Rawick, ed., *American Slave*, vol. 2, *South Carolina Narratives, Part 2* (Westport, Conn.: Greenwood, 1972), 58, 63.

72. This is the usual hymn that is cited, as in Marion Harland, *Judith* (Philadelphia: Our Continent, 1883), 341; Harland, *Autobiography*, 59; Stowe, *Poganuc People*, 284–87.

73. Reprinted in George P. Upton, *Musical Memories* (Chicago: McClurg, 1908), 211–12, from a *Tribune* article published 17 April 1869.

74. Whitman quoted in Gay Wilson Allen, *The Solitary Singer* (New York: Macmillan, 1955), 11.

75. Ernst C. Krohn, *Missouri Music* (New York: Da Capo, 1971), 233.

76. Richard Green Parker, *A Tribute to the Life and Character of Jonas Chickering* (Boston: Tewksbury, 1854), 123.

77. Henry Ware Jr., *The Recollections of Jonathan Anderson*, 2d ed. (Boston: Christian Register Office, 1828), 160–61.

78. *Tales of an American Landlord*, vol. 1 (New York: Gilley, 1824), 15. The anonymous author describes the work as "containing sketches of life south of the Potomac."

79. Told by Lucy Galloway, former Mississippi slave, in Rawick, ed., *American Slave*, supp. ser. 1, vol. 8, *Mississippi Narratives, Part 3*, 810.

80. Ibid., vol. 2, *South Carolina Narratives, Part 2,* 89.

81. Lowery, *Life on the Old Plantation,* 85–86.

82. Rawick, ed., *American Slave,* supp. ser. 1, vol. 8, *Mississippi Narratives, Part 3,* 1273.

83. Mary H. Eastman, *Aunt Phillis's Cabin, or Southern Life as It Is* (Philadelphia: Grambo, 1852), 155–57; Caroline Howard Gilman, *Recollections of a Housekeeper* (New York: Harper, 1836), 90–93; Grierson, *The Valley of Shadows,* 148–49. Grierson describes the burial of a runaway slave in Illinois.

84. Harland, *Autobiography,* 233.

85. Olmsted, *Cotton Kingdom* 1:43–45.

86. Maria Jane McIntosh, *Two Pictures* (New York: Appleton, 1863), 327–28.

## Chapter 8. Serenades and Other Outdoor Music

1. Oliver Wendell Holmes, "The Music-Grinders," in *The Complete Poetical Works* (Boston: Houghton Mifflin, 1908), 12–13.

2. Carl David Arfwedson, *The United States in 1832, 1833, and 1834,* vol. 1 (London: Bentley, 1834), 150–52.

3. *Boston Musical Times* 1 (2 April 1860): 56.

4. Eliza Southgate Bowne, *A Girl's Life Eighty Years Ago* (New York: Scribners, 1887), 135.

5. Letter to her sister Marion, sent July 1850, reprinted in John Tasker Howard, *Stephen Foster, America's Troubadour* (New York: Crowell, 1962), 165.

6. Noah M. Ludlow, *Dramatic Life as I Found It* (1880; reprint, New York: Blom, 1966), 84.

7. Charles Francis Adams, *Diary of Charles Francis Adams,* ed. Aida DiPace Donald and David Donald (Cambridge, Mass.: Belknap, 1964), 124; William Treat Upton, *William Henry Fry* (New York: Crowell, 1954), 12; George Henry Tripp, *Student-Life at Harvard* (Boston: Lockwood, Brooks, 1876), 288–89; Julius H. Ward, *The Life and Letters of James Gates Percival* (Boston: Ticknor & Fields, 1866), 435.

8. George Thornton Edwards, *Music and Musicians of Maine* (1928; reprint, New York: AMS, 1970), 87–88.

9. Howard, *Stephen Foster,* 288; Evelyn Foster Mornewick, *Chronicles of Stephen Foster's Family,* vol. 2 (Pittsburgh: University of Pittsburgh Press, 1944), 505.

10. [Hutchinson Family], *Excelsior: Journals of the Hutchinson Family Singers, 1842–1846,* ed. Dale Cockrell (Stuyvesant, N.Y.: Pendragon, 1986), 46–47, 68–69.

11. Ernst C. Krohn, *Missouri Music* (New York: Da Capo, 1971), 242.

12. Charles F. Browne, *Complete Works* (London: Chatto & Windus, n.d.), 267.

13. George H. Derby, *Phoenixiana* (New York: Appleton, 1855), 213.

14. See Louise A. K. S. Clappe, *The Shirley Letters from California Mines in 1851–52* (San Francisco: Russell, 1922), 107–9.

15. Sarah Raymond Herndon, *Days on the Road: Crossing the Plains in 1865* (New York: Burr, 1902), 158.

16. Caroline Howard Gilman, *Recollections of a Housekeeper* (New York: Harper, 1836), 21; Grace Greenwood, *Greenwood Leaves,* 2d ed. (Boston: Ticknor, Reed & Fields, 1850), 178–79; Peggy Eaton, *Autobiography* (New York: Scribners, 1932), 15.

17. John H. Hewitt, *Shadows on the Wall* (Baltimore: Turnbull, 1877), 103.

18. James Stuart, *Three Years in North America,* vol. 1 (Edinburgh: Cadell, 1833), 117–18; Christopher Columbus Baldwin, *Diary,* Transactions and Collections of the American Antiquarian Society, 8 (Worcester: American Antiquarian Society, 1901), 65; Jack Larkin, *The Reshaping of Everyday Life, 1790–1840* (New York: Harper, 1988), 64.

*326*        19. Francis Grierson, *The Valley of Shadows*, new ed. (London: Lane, 1893), 125–26; see also Henry Hiram Riley, *The Puddleford Papers* (New York: Derby & Jackson, 1860), 94.

20. J. Marion Sims, *The Story of My Life*, ed. H. Marion Sims (New York: Appleton, 1884), 102–3; Albert Stoutamire, *Music of the Old South* (Rutherford, N.J.: Fairleigh Dickinson University Press, 1972), 181; D. Corcoran, *Pickings from . . . the New Orleans "Picayune"* (Philadelphia: Carey & Hart, 1846), 34–35, 85–86.

21. J. P. Kennedy, *Swallow Barn*, rev. ed. (New York: Putnam, 1851), 101–2.

22. John Davis, *Travels of Four Years and a Half in the United States of America* (London: Edwards, 1803), 416; Virgil S. Powell, *From the Slave Cabin of Yani* (Hicksville, N.Y.: Exposition Press, 1977), 78.

23. Ann Willson, *Familiar Letters* (Philadelphia: Parrish, 1850), 96; Liliane Crété, *Daily Life in Louisiana, 1815–1830*, trans. by Patrick Gregory (Baton Rouge: Louisiana State University Press, 1981), 63.

24. Fanny J. Crosby, *Memories of Eighty Years* (Boston: Earle, 1906), 33–34; Lydia Maria Child, *Letters from New York*, 2d ser. (New York: Francis, 1845), 14–17.

25. Joel H. Ross, *What I Saw in New-York* (Auburn, N.Y.: Derby & Miller, 1851), 67.

26. Whitman, *The Uncollected Poetry and Prose of Walt Whitman*, ed. Emory Holloway (Gloucester, Mass.: Peter Smith, 1972), 1:48.

27. Vera Brodsky Lawrence, *Strong on Music*, vol. 2 (New York: Oxford University Press, 1988), 577; Ralph Waldo Emerson, W. H. Channing, and J. F. Clarke, *Memoirs of Margaret Fuller Ossoli* (Boston: Roberts, 1884), 383; William R. Ryan, *Personal Adventures in Upper and Lower California, 1848–9*, vol. 2 (London: Shoberl, 1851), 290–92.

28. Whitman, *Uncollected Poetry and Prose* 1:226; Charles Quill, *The American Mechanic* (Philadelphia: Perkins, 1838), 126; Ryan, *Personal Adventures in Upper and Lower California* 2:260.

29. Samuel Longfellow, *Memoirs and Letters*, ed. Joseph May (Boston: Houghton Mifflin, 1894), 68–69; Walter Colton, *Three Years in California* (New York: Evans, 1860), 56; George P. Rawick, ed., *The American Slave: A Composite Autobiography*, vol. 6, *Alabama Narratives* (Westport, Conn.: Greenwood, 1972), 297.

30. Bronson Alcott, *The Journals of Bronson Alcott*, ed. Odell Shepard (Boston: Little, Brown, 1938), 178; Child, *Letters from New York*, 27–28.

31. Ryan, *Personal Adventures in Upper and Lower California* 2:174; Fanny Fern, *Folly as It Flies* (New York: Colton, 1868) 191; *The Singer's Companion* (New York: Stringer & Townsend, 1854), 12.

32. Fanny Fern, *The Play-Day Book* (New York: Mason, 1857), 124; David Macrae, *Americans at Home* (1870; reprint, New York: Dutton, 1952), 60–61; Samuel B. Halliday, *The Little Street Sweeper, or Life among the Poor* (New York: Phinney, Blakeman & Mason, 1861), 151.

33. Edmund Kirke, *My Southern Friends* (New York: Tribune Association, 1863), 9–10. See also Stoutamire, *Music of the Old South*, 180, and *Tales of an American Landlord*, vol. 2 (New York: Gilley, 1824), 12.

34. William T. Thompson, *Chronicles of Pineville* (Philadelphia: Carey & Hart, 1849), 44–45; James Weir, *Lonz Powers*, vol. 1 (Philadelphia: Lippincott, Grambo, 1850), 241; Marion Harland, *Marion Harland's Autobiography* (New York: Harper, 1910), 56; Samuel Goodrich, *Peter Parley's Own Story* (New York: Sheldon, 1864), 48.

35. George A. Ramsdell, *A History of Milford* (Concord, N.H.: Rumford, 1901), 81; Charles Dickens, *American Notes* (Leipzig: Tauchnitz, 1842), 196; Arfwedson, *The United States in 1832, 1833, and 1834*, 2:405.

36. George G. Foster, *New York by Gaslight and Other Sketches*, ed. Stuart M. Blumin (1850; reprint, Berkeley and Los Angeles: University of California Press, 1990), 71.

37. W. E. Woodward, *The Way Our People Lived* (New York: Dutton, 1944), 265.

38. Clappe, *Shirley Letters*, 179, 324–35.

39. Solomon Northup, *Twelve Years a Slave* (New York: Miller, Orton & Mulligan, 1855), 79; John Brown, *Slave Life in Georgia*, ed. F. N. Boney (Savannah, Ga.: Beehive Press, 1972), 95–96.

40. T. Lindsay Baker and Julie B. Baker, eds., *The WPA Oklahoma Slave Narratives* (Norman: University of Oklahoma Press, 1996), 452.

41. Ibid., 153, 286–87; Metta V. Victor, *Maum Guinea and Her Plantation "Children"* (London: Beadle, [1860?]), 91–92; Rawick, ed., *American Slave*, supp. ser. 1, vol. 6, *Mississippi Narratives, Part 1* (Westport, Conn.: Greenwood, 1977), 58. See also Mary H. Eastman, *Aunt Phillis's Cabin, or Southern Life as It Is* (Philadelphia: Grambo, 1852), 29; Thomas Nelson Page, *Social Life in Old Virginia* (1897; reprint, Freeport, N.Y.: Books for Libraries, 1970), 124; William T. Thompson, *Chronicles of Pineville* (Philadelphia: Carey & Hart, 1849), 95–96.

42. Rawick, ed., *American Slave*, supp. ser. 1, vol. 7, *Mississippi Narratives, Part 2* (Westport, Conn.: Greenwood, 1977), 704–5.

43. James R. Creecy, *Scenes in the South and Other Miscellaneous Pieces* (Washington, D.C.: McGill, 1860), 19–21. Other descriptions of the Congo Square scene are found in Benjamin Henry Latrobe, *The Journal of Latrobe* (New York: Appleton, 1905), 180–81, and Crété, *Daily Life in Louisiana*, 220–28. The famous pianist and composer Louis Moreau Gottschalk, when a youngster, was one of the hundreds of "children of all ages" who attended with his black nurse. A "piccallion," also known as a picayune, was a Spanish coin of small value that was formerly current in New Orleans.

44. N. Parker Willis, *Rural Letters and Other Records of Thought at Leisure* (Auburn, N.Y.: Alden, Beardsley, 1853), 128; [James Boardman], *America and the Americans* (London: Longman, Rees, Orme, Brown, Green & Longman, 1833), 169; Constance Rourke, *American Humor: A Study of National Character* (Garden City, N.J.: Doubleday, 1953), 42–44; Constance Rourke, *Davy Crockett* (New York: Harcourt, Brace, 1934), 31.

45. Weir, *Long Powers* 1:163.

46. Lew Wallace, *An Autobiography*, vol. 1 (New York: Harper, 1906), 11.

47. Caroline Gilman, *Recollections of a New-England Bride and of a Southern Matron*, rev. ed. (New York: Putnam, 1852), 121–22.

48. Ibid., 76–77.

49. Elizabeth W. A. Pringle, *Chronicles of Chicora Wood* (New York: Scribners, 1922), 69.

50. Ward McAllister, *Society as I Found It* (New York: Cassell, 1890), 84.

51. Frances Anne Kemble, *Journal of a Residence on a Georgian Plantation in 1838–1839* (New York: Harper, 1863), 218–19.

52. John S. Robb, *Streaks of Squatter Life and Far-West Scenes* (Philadelphia: Peterson, 1846), 76.

53. Rourke, *Davy Crockett*, 160–62.

54. Letter dated 13 September 1851, in Clappe, *Shirley Letters*, 17–18.

55. Goodrich, *Peter Parley's Own Story*, 155. See also Asa Greene, *A Yankee among the Nullifiers* (New York: Stodart, 1833), 7.

56. Thomas B. Searight, *The Old Pike* (Uniontown, Pa.: author, 1894), 17, 119–20, 130, 145, 148.

*328*   57. William Cullen Bryant, *The Letters of William Cullen Bryant*, vol. 2, eds. William Cullen Bryant II and Thomas G. Voss (New York: Fordham University Press, 1977), 236–37.

58. Joseph Kirkland, *Zury: The Meanest Man in Spring Country* (Boston: Houghton Mifflin, 1887), 340.

59. [Hutchinson Family], *Excelsior*, 5.

60. Harriet Sherrill Ward, *Prairie Schooner Lady: The Journal of Harriet Sherrill Ward, 1853*, ed. Ward G. DeWitt and Florence Stark DeWitt (Los Angeles: Westernlore, 1959), 21, 27, 36, 93–95, 154, 169.

61. Herndon, *Days on the Road*, 58, 110–11.

62. See John Mack Faragher, *Women and Men on the Overland Trail* (New Haven, Conn.: Yale University Press, 1979), 84, 145; Mrs. Catharine V. Waite, *Adventures in the Far West and Life among the Mormons* (Chicago: Waite, 1882), 14–15, 37–38; Virginia Wilcox Ivins, *Pen Pictures of Early Western Days* (Keokuk, Iowa: n.p., 1908), 71; Samuel C. Upham, *Notes of a Voyage to California via Cape Horn, Together with Scenes in El Dorado, in the Years 1849–'50* (Philadelphia: Upham, 1878), 243.

63. Fredrika Bremer, *The Homes of the New World*, vol. 1, trans. Mary Howitt (New York: Harper, 1853), 649; John Melish, *Travels through the United States of America* (London: Cowie, 1818), 90; Frederick Law Olmsted, *The Cotton Kingdom*, vol. 2 (New York: Mason, 1861), 60; Annie Fields, ed., *The Life and Letters of Harriet Beecher Stowe* (Boston: Houghton Mifflin, 1897), 75; Harriet Martineau, *Society in America*, vol. 1 (New York: Saunders & Otley, 1837), 236.

64. Walter Austin, *Tales of a Dedham Tavern* (Cambridge, Mass.: privately printed, 1912), 55; Ludlow, *Dramatic Life as I Found It*, 92–93.

65. Ryan, *Personal Adventures in Upper and Lower California* 1:27.

66. Bremer, *Homes of the New World* 1:317.

67. Rufus Rockwell Wilson, *Intimate Memories of Lincoln* (Elmira, N.Y.: Primavera, 1945), 115.

68. George H. Derby, *The Squibb Papers* (New York: Carleton, 1865), 148–49.

69. Mrs. N. P. Lasselle, *Anne Grayson, or Life in Washington* (New York: Bunce, 1853), 230–32; Dr. Thomas L. Nichols, *Forty Years of American Life*, vol. 1 (London: Maxwell, 1864), 221.

70. Amelia M. Murray, *Letters from the United States, Cuba, and Canada* (New York: Putnam, 1856), 394.

71. Ibid., 395.

72. Bremer, *Homes of the New World* 1:7.

73. Stuart, *Three Years in North America* 1:429; Theodore S. Fay, *Hoboken*, vol. 1 (New York: Harper, 1843), 123; Nichols, *Forty Years of American Life* 1:122–23.

74. Nichols, *Forty Years of American Life* 1:229; James Russell Lowell, *Letters of James Russell Lowell*, vol. 1, ed. Charles Eliot Norton (New York: Harper, 1894), 216; Rawick, ed., *American Slave*, supp. ser. 1, vol. 5, *Indiana Narratives* (Westport, Conn.: Greenwood, 1977), 28, 32; *Tales of an American Landlord* 2:47–48.

75. Mornewick, *Chronicles of Stephen Foster's Family* 2:488.

## Chapter 9. Music for Work and Public Places

1. Sophie M. Damon, *Old New-England Days* (Boston: Cupples & Hurd, 1887), 336.

2. Alice Carey, *Clovernook, or Recollections of Our Neighborhood in the West* (Clinton Hall, N.Y.: Redfield, 1852), 150.

3. Jack Larkin, *The Reshaping of Everyday Life, 1790–1840* (New York: Harper & Row, 1988), 239.

4. John Townsend Trowbridge, *Neighbor Jackwood* (1857; reprint, Boston: Lee & Shepard, 1888), 99.

5. Fanny Fern, *The Play-Day Book* (New York: Mason, 1857), 257.

6. Thomas Chandler Haliburton, *The Americans at Home*, vol. 2 (London: Hurst & Black, 1854), 310.

7. Annie Fields, ed., *Life and Letters of Harriet Beecher Stowe* (Boston: Houghton Mifflin, 1897), 42.

8. Elizabeth Oakes Smith, *Selections from the Autobiography of Elizabeth Oakes Smith*, ed. Mary Alice Wyman (Lewiston, Maine: Lewiston Journal, 1921), 17; Samuel G. Goodrich, *Peter Parley's Own Story* (New York: Sheldon, 1864), 40; Mrs. C. M. Kirkland, *Western Clearings* (New York: Wiley & Putnam, 1845), 10.

9. Carey, *Clovernook*, 73.

10. Reverend Elijah R. Sabin, *The Life and Reflections of Charles Observator* (Boston: Rowe & Hooper, 1816), 53.

11. Smith, *Selections from the Autobiography*, 17.

12. *The Lowell Offering*, vol. 4 (Lowell: Misses Curtis & Farley, 1844), 147.

13. Ned Buntline, *The Mysteries and Miseries of New York: A Story of Real Life* (New York: Berford, 1848), 26–27.

14. George P. Rawick, ed., *The American Slave: A Composite Autobiography*, supp. ser. 1, vol. 6, *Mississippi Narratives, Part 1* (Westport, Conn.: Greenwood, 1977), 155–56.

15. Rawick, ed., *American Slave*, vol. 4, *Texas Narratives, Part 2* (Westport, Conn.: Greenwood, 1972), 166–67.

16. William Cullen Bryant, *The Letters of William Cullen Bryant*, vol. 2, ed. William Cullen Bryant II and Thomas G. Voss (New York: Fordham University Press, 1977), 200.

17. Rawick, ed., *American Slave*, supp. ser. 1, vol. 5, *Ohio Narratives* (Westport, Conn.: Greenwood, 1977), 486.

18. Ibid., vol. 7, *Mississippi Narratives, Part 2*, 523.

19. Ibid., vol. 4, *Texas Narratives, Part 1*, 199.

20. Ibid., vol. 3, *South Carolina Narratives, Part 3*, 274–75.

21. R. Q. Mallard, *Plantation Life before Emancipation* (Richmond, Va.: Whittet & Shepperson, 1892), 22; Edward D. C. Campbell Jr. and Kym S. Rice, eds., *Before Freedom Came* (Richmond, Va.: Museum of the Confederacy, 1991), 52; Thomas Nelson Page, *Social Life in Old Virginia* (1897; reprint, Freeport, N.Y.: Books for Libraries Press, 1970), 31.

22. Marion Harland, *Judith: A Chronicle of Old Virginia* (Philadelphia: Our Continent, 1883), 312–13.

23. Rawick, ed., *American Slave* 4:99; ibid., supp. ser. 1, 6:46–47.

24. Joseph William Schmitz, *In the Days of the Republic: Texas Culture, 1836–1846* (San Antonio, Tex.: Naylor, 1960), 130; Jane Grey Swisshelm, *Half a Century*, 2d ed. (Chicago: Jansen, McClurg, 1880), 38–39; Dr. Thomas L. Nichols, *Forty Years of American Life*, vol. 1 (London: Maxwell, 1864), 27–28.

25. *The Lowell Offering*, vol. 5 (Lowell: Misses Curtis & Farley, 1845), 269–70.

26. Mrs. Ann S. Stephens, *Old Homestead* (New York: Bunce, 1855), 372–73; Nichols, *Forty Years of American Life* 1:27; Henry Hiram Riley, *The Puddleford Papers* (New York: Derby & Jackson, 1860), 93; Carl David Arfwedson, *The United States in 1832, 1833, and 1834*, vol. 1 (London: Bentley, 1834), 208; D. R. Hundley, *Social Relations in Our Southern States* (New York: Price, 1860), 197.

27. Garnett Andrews, *Reminiscences of an Old Georgia Lawyer* (Atlanta: Franklin, 1870), 10–11.

28. Roger D. Abrahams, *Singing the Master* (New York: Pantheon, 1992), 3–19; Wil-

**330** liam Wells Brown, *My Southern Home* (1880; reprint, Upper Saddle River, N.J.: Gregg, 1968), 91–92; Letitia Burwell, *A Girl's Life in Virginia before the War* (New York: Stokes, 1895), 131–32; John M. Blassingame, *The Slave Community* (New York: Oxford University Press, 1972), 52–53; Harry Smith, *Fifty Years of Slavery* (Grand Rapids: West Michigan Printing Company, 1891), 38; Reverend I. E. Lowery, *Life on the Old Plantation in Ante-Bellum Days* (Columbia, S.C.: State Co. Printers, 1911), 96–98. The quoted lines are from Marion Harland's description of a Virginia corn shucking in *Marion Harland's Autobiography* (New York: Harper, 1910), 145–47.

29. Rawick, ed., *American Slave* 3:283–84.

30. Bryant, *The Letters of William Cullen Bryant* 2:206–7.

31. [James Boardman], *America and the Americans, by a Citizen of the World* (London: Longman, Rees, Orme, Brown, Green & Longman, 1833), 26.

32. Harriet Martineau, *Society in America*, vol. 2 (New York: Saunders & Otley, 1837), 246; Vera Brodsky Lawrence, *Strong on Music*, vol. 1 (New York: Oxford University Press, 1988), 4.

33. Mary J. Windle, *Life in Washington* (Philadelphia: Lippincott, 1859), 68–69.

34. Fanny Fern, *Ginger-Snaps* (New York: Carleton, 1870), 206, 208.

35. Thomas Ashe, *Travels in America* (Newburyport, Mass.: Sawyer, 1808), 100.

36. Anthony Trollope, *North America* (New York: Harper, 1862), 23.

37. Amelia M. Murray, *Letters from the United States, Cuba, and Canada* (New York: Putnam, 1856), 51.

38. Charles Sedgwick, *Letters* (Boston: privately printed, 1870), 183–84. See also N. Parker Willis, *Fun-Jottings* (New York: Scribners, 1853), 26, 30.

39. George P. Morris, *Sketches of the Times* (Philadelphia: Lea & Blanchard, 1839), 66–67.

40. Walt Whitman, *The Uncollected Poetry and Prose of Walt Whitman*, vol. 2, ed. Emory Holloway (Gloucester, Mass.: Peter Smith, 1972), 221.

41. Lawrence, *Strong on Music* 2:556. Pages 231–32 cite four other saloons where alcoholic "singing parties" were taking place in 1843: Rainbow, Wiedemeyer's Saloon, Climax Saloon, and Luscomb and Sanborn's Cornucopia. Temperance societies tried to counter them by offering cheap, alcohol-free "Shilling Concerts" in and around the Bowery.

42. Trowbridge, *Neighbor Jackwood*, 44–45; Andrews, *Reminiscences of an Old Georgia Lawyer*, 74–76; Noah M. Ludlow, *Dramatic Life as I Found It* (1880; reprint, New York: Blom, 1966), 58–59.

43. Lucius Fairchild, *California Letters*, ed. Joseph Schafer (Madison: State Historical Society of Wisconsin, 1931), 197.

44. Ned Buntline, *The B'Hoys of New York* (New York: Dick & Fitzgerald, 1950), 160–61.

45. Buntline, *Mysteries and Miseries of New York*, 60.

46. George G. Foster, *New York by Gas-Light and Other Urban Sketches*, ed. Stuart M. Blumin (1850; reprint, Berkeley and Los Angeles: University of California Press, 1990), 141–43. See also Buntline, *Mysteries and Miseries of New York*, 89–91; Roi Ottley and William J. Weatherby, eds., *The Negro in New York* (New York: New York Public Library, 1967), 78–79.

47. Lawrence, *Strong on Music* 2:451.

48. Albert Stoutamire, *Music of the Old South* (Rutherford, N.J.: Fairleigh Dickinson University Press, 1972), 194; *Dwight's Journal of Music* 3 (9 July 1853): 109.

49. William R. Ryan, *Personal Adventures in Upper and Lower California in 1848–9*, vol. 2 (London: Shoberl, 1851), 290; H. Ogden Wintermute, *Daniel Decatur Emmett* (Mount Vernon, Ohio: Wintermute, 1955), 27.

50. Sarah Royce, *Frontier Lady: Recollections of the Gold Rush and Early California* (New
Haven, Conn.: Yale University Press, 1932), 115.

## Chapter 10. Denouement

1. George F. Root, *The Story of a Musical Life* (Cincinnati: Church, 1891), 10, 54–55.

2. Louis Moreau Gottschalk, *Notes of a Pianist*, ed. Jeanne Behrend (New York: Knopf, 1964), 52.

3. John W. Moore, *Complete Encyclopedia of Music* (Boston: Ditson, 1854), s.v. "Ballad."

4. Ibid., s.v. "Church Music."

5. Walt Whitman, *Leaves of Grass* (New York: Books, Inc., n.d.), 230.

# Bibliography

Abrahams, Roger D. *Singing the Master.* New York: Pantheon, 1992.

Adams, Charles Francis. *Diary of Charles Francis Adams.* Edited by Aida DiPace Donald and David Donald. Cambridge, Mass.: Belknap Press, 1964.

Addington, Henry Unwin. *Youthful America: Selections from Henry Unwin Addington's Residence in the United States of America, 1822, 23, 24, 25.* Edited by Bradford Perkins. University of California Publications in History, 65. Berkeley and Los Angeles: University of California Press, 1960.

Alcott, Bronson. *The Journals of Bronson Alcott.* Selected and edited by Odell Shepard. Boston: Little, Brown, 1938.

Allen, Gay Wilson. *The Solitary Singer.* New York: Macmillan, 1955.

Andrews, Garnett. *Reminiscences of an Old Georgia Lawyer.* Atlanta: Franklin Steam Printing House, 1870.

Arfwedson, Carl David. *The United States in 1832, 1833, and 1834.* 2 vols. London: Bentley, 1834.

Ashe, Thomas. *Travels in America, Performed in 1806.* Newburyport, Mass.: Sawyer, 1808.

Atson, William. *Heart Whispers . . . A Series of Letters to His Wife.* Philadelphia: Cowperthwait, 1859.

Austin, Walter. *Tales of a Dedham Tavern: History of the Norfolk Hotel.* Cambridge, Mass.: privately printed, 1912.

*An Autobiography,* 2d ed. Boston: Williams, 1871.

*Autobiography of a Female Slave.* 1857. Reprint. New York: Negro Universities Press, 1969.

Bagby, George W. *The Old Virginia Gentleman and Other Sketches.* 1884. Reprint. New York: Scribners, 1911.

Baily, Francis. *Journal of a Tour in Unsettled Parts of North America in 1796 and 1797.* London: Baily, 1856.

Baker, T. Lindsay, and Julie B. Baker, eds. *The WPA Oklahoma Slave Narratives.* Norman: University of Oklahoma Press, 1996.

Baldwin, Christopher Columbus. *Diary.* Transactions and Collections of the American Antiquarian Society, 8. Worcester: American Antiquarian Society, 1901.

Baldwin, Joseph. *The Flush Times of Alabama and Mississippi.* New York: Appleton, 1858.

Barnes, Emily R. *Narratives, Traditions, and Personal Reminiscences.* Boston: Ellis, 1888.

Beardsley, Levi. *Reminiscences.* New York: Vinten, 1852.

Bell, Major Horace. *Reminiscences of a Ranger.* Santa Barbara, Calif.: Hebberd, 1927.

Berlin, Ira. *Slaves without Masters.* New York: Pantheon, 1974.

**334**   Berlin, Ira, Marc Favreau, and Steven F. Miller, eds. *Remembering Slavery*. New York: New Press, 1998.

Blassingame, John W. *The Slave Community*. New York: Oxford University Press, 1972.

———. *Slave Testimony*. Baton Rouge: Louisiana State University Press, 1977.

Blodgett, Bertha Eveleth. *Stories of Cortland County*. Cortland, N.Y.: Cortland County Historical Society, 1952.

[Boardman, James]. *America and the Americans, by a Citizen of the World*. London: Longman, Rees, Orme, Brown, Green & Longman, 1833.

Bode, Carl. *Antebellum Culture*. Carbondale: Southern Illinois University Press, 1959.

Bode, Carl, ed. *American Life in the 1840s*. Garden City, N.Y.: Anchor Books, 1967.

Borthwick, J. D. *The Gold Hunters*. Edited by Horace Kephart. New York: Macmillan, 1924.

Botta, Anne C. L. *Memoirs of Anne C. L. Botta*. New York: Tait, 1894.

Bouldin, Powhatan. *Home Reminiscences of John Randolph of Roanoke*. Danville, Va.: published for the author, 1876.

Bowen, Mrs. Sue (Petigrue). *Busy Moments of an Idle Woman*. New York: Appleton, 1854.

Bowne, Eliza Southgate. *A Girl's Life Eighty Years Ago*. New York: Scribners, 1887.

Boylan, Anne M. *Sunday School*. New Haven, Conn.: Yale University Press, 1988.

Brackenbridge, H. M. *Recollections of Persons and Places in the West*. Philadelphia: Lippincott, 1868.

Bradford, Gamaliel. *Wives*. New York: Harper, 1925.

Branch, E. Douglas. *The Sentimental Years, 1836–1860*. New York: Appleton-Century, 1934.

Bremer, Fredrika. *The Homes of the New World*. 2 vols. Translated by Mary Howitt. New York: Harper, 1853.

Brooks, Henry M. *Olden-Time Music*. Boston: Ticknor, 1888.

Brown, Charles Brockden. *Memoirs of Charles Brockden Brown . . . with Selections from His Original Letters and Miscellaneous Writings*. Edited by William Dunlap. London: Colburn, 1822.

Brown, John. *Slave Life in Georgia*. Edited by F. N. Boney. Savannah, Ga.: Beeline Press, 1972.

Brown, Sally, and Pamela Brown. *The Diaries of Sally and Pamela Brown, 1832–1838*. Edited by Blanche Brown Bryant and Gertrude Elaine Baker. Springfield, Vt.: Bryant Foundation, 1970.

Brown, William Wells. *My Southern Home*. 1880. Reprint. Upper Saddle River, N.J.: Gregg Press, 1968.

Browne, Charles F. *Complete Works of Charles F. Browne*. London: Chatto & Windus, n.d.

Bruce, Dickson D., Jr. *And They All Sang Hallelujah*. Knoxville: University of Tennessee Press, 1974.

Bryant, William Cullen. *The Letters of William Cullen Bryant*. Edited by William Cullen Bryant II and Thomas G. Vose. 2 vols. New York: Fordham University Press, 1975, 1977.

Buntline, Ned [Edward Judson]. *The B'Hoys of New York*. New York: Dick & Fitzgerald, 1850.

———. *The G'Hals of New York*. New York: DeWitt, 187–.

———. *The Mysteries and Miseries of New York: A Story of Real Life*. New York: Berford, 1848.

Burke, Emily P. *Reminiscences of Georgia*. Oberlin, Ohio: Fitch, 1850.

Burwell, Letitia. *A Girl's Life in Virginia before the War*. New York: Stokes, 1895.

Campbell, Edward D. C., Jr., and Kym S. Rice, eds. *Before Freedom Came*. Richmond, Va.: Museum of the Confederacy, 1991.

Carey, Alice. *Clovernook, or Recollections of Our Neighborhood in the West*. Clinton Hall, N.Y.: Redfield, 1852.

Chapin, Rev. E. H. *Humanity in the City.* New York: De Witt, 1854.

Chase, Mary Ellen. *Jonathan Fisher, Maine Parson, 1768–1847.* New York: Macmillan, 1948.

Chase, Stuart. *The Proper Study of Mankind.* New York: Harper, 1948.

Chevalier, Michel. *Society, Manners, and Politics in the United States.* Edited by John William Ward. Translated after the T. G. Bradford ed. Ithaca, N.Y.: Cornell University Press, 1961.

Child, Lydia Maria. *Letters from New York.* 2d ser. New York: Francis, 1845.

Cist, Charles. *The Cincinnati Miscellany.* Vol. 1. Cincinnati: Clark, 1845. Vol. 2. Cincinnati: Robinson & Jones, 1846.

Claflin, Mary B. *Personal Recollections of John G. Whittier.* New York: Crowell, 1893.

Clappe, Louise A. K. S. *The Shirley Letters from California Mines in 1851–52.* San Francisco: Russell, 1922.

Clay-Clopton, Virginia. *A Belle of the Fifties.* Gathered and edited by Ada Sterling. New York: Doubleday, Page, 1904.

*The Clifford Family, or A Tale of the Old Dominion.* By one of her daughters. New York: Harper, 1852.

Clinkscales, J. G. *On the Old Plantation: Reminiscences of His Childhood.* 1916. Reprint. New York: Negro Universities Press, 1969.

Colton, Walter. *Three Years in California.* New York: Evans, 1860.

Comfield, Amelia S. *Alida.* 4th ed. New York: Angell & Engel, 1849.

Congdon, Charles T. *Reminiscences of a Journalist.* Boston: Osgood, 1880.

Cooke, George Willis. *John Sullivan Dwight.* Boston: Small, Maynard, 1898.

Cooke, John Esten. *Ellie, or The Human Comedy.* Richmond, Va.; Morris, 1855.

Cooper, James Fenimore. *Home as Found.* 1838. Reprint. New York: Townsend, 1860.

Corcoran, D. *Pickings from . . . The New Orleans "Picayune."* Philadelphia: Carey & Hart, 1846.

Cozzens, Frederic S. *Prismatics.* 2d ed. New York: Appleton, 1854.

———. *Sayings, Wise and Otherwise.* New York: Lovell, 1870.

———. *The Sparrowgrass Papers.* Philadelphia: Lippincott, 1865.

Crafts, William. *A Selection in Prose and Poetry from the Miscellaneous Writings.* Charleston, S.C.: Sebring & Burges, 1828.

Creecy, James R. *Scenes in the South and Other Miscellaneous Pieces.* Washington, D.C.: McGill, 1860.

Crété, Liliane. *Daily Life in Louisiana, 1815–1830.* Translated by Patrick Gregory. Baton Rouge: Louisiana State University Press, 1981.

Crosby, Fanny J. [Mrs. Alexander Van Alstyne]. *Memories of Eighty Years.* Boston: Earle, 1906.

Cummins, Maria. *Mabel Vaughan.* Boston: Jewett, 1857.

Curtis, George William. *Early Letters of George Wm. Curtis to John S. Dwight.* Edited by George Willis Cooke. New York: Harper, 1898.

———. *Prue and I.* 1856. Reprint. New York: Harper, 1898.

Dahl, Curtis. *Robert Montgomery Bird.* New York: Twayne, 1963.

Damon, Sophie M. *Old New-England Days.* Boston: Cupples & Hurd, 1887.

Davis, John. *Travels of Four Years and a Half in the United States of America.* London: Edwards, 1803.

Derby, George. *Phoenixiana.* New York: Appleton, 1855.

———. *The Squibb Papers.* New York: Carleton, 1865.

Dickens, Charles. *American Notes.* Leipzig: Tauchnitz, 1842.

336  Dizikes, John. *Opera in America.* New Haven, Conn.: Yale University Press, 1993.

Dodge, M. E. *Irvington Stories.* 4th ed. New York: O'Kane, 1865.

Dorsey, Anna Hanson. *Woodreve Manor.* Philadelphia: Hart, 1852.

Drake, Daniel. *Pioneer Life in Kentucky, 1785–1800.* Edited by Emmett Field Horne. New York: Schumann, 1948.

Dwight, Timothy. *Travels in New-England and New-York.* 4 vols. New Haven, Conn.: author, 1821–22.

Eastman, Mary H. *Aunt Phillis's Cabin, or Southern Life as It Is.* Philadelphia: Lippincott, Grambo, 1852.

Eaton, Peggy. *Autobiography.* New York: Scribners, 1932.

Edwards, George Thornton. *Music and Musicians of Maine.* 1928. Reprint. New York: AMS, 1970.

Emerson, Ralph Waldo. *Letters and Social Aims.* Boston: Houghton Mifflin, 1894.

Emerson, Ralph Waldo, W. H. Channing, and J. F. Clarke. *Memoirs of Margaret Fuller Ossoli.* 2 vols. Boston: Roberts, 1884.

Ernst, Robert. *Immigrant Life in New York City, 1825–1863.* New York: Octagon Books, 1979.

Evans, Augusta J. *Beulah.* New York: Derby & Jackson, 1859.

*The Experience of Thomas H. Jones, Who Was a Slave for Forty-Three Years.* Written by a friend. New Bedford, Mass.: Anthony & Sons, 1871.

Fairchild, Lucius. *California Letters.* Edited by Joseph Schafer. Madison: State Historical Society of Wisconsin, 1931.

Faragher, John Mack. *Women and Men on the Overland Trail.* New Haven, Conn.: Yale University Press, 1979.

Fay, Theodore S. *Hoboken.* 2 vols. New York: Harper, 1843.

———. *Norman Leslie.* 2 vols. New York: Harper, 1835.

Fern, Fanny [Mrs. Sarah P. W. F. Parton]. *Fern Leaves.* Auburn, N.Y.: Miller, Orton & Mulligan, 1854.

———. *Folly as It Is.* New York: Carleton, 1868.

———. *Ginger-Snaps.* New York: Carleton, 1870.

———. *The Play-Day Book.* New York: Mason, 1857.

Ferris, Mrs. B. G. *The Mormons at Home.* New York: Dix & Edwards, 1856.

Fields, Annie, ed. *Life and Letters of Harriet Beecher Stowe.* Boston: Houghton Mifflin, 1897.

Folio, Fred. *Lucy Boston, or Woman's Rights and Spiritualism.* Boston: Shepard, Clark, 1855.

Ford, Sallie Rochester. *Grace Truman.* New York: Sheldon, Blakeman, 1857.

Foster, George G. *New York by Gas-Light and Other Urban Sketches.* Edited by Stuart M. Blumin. Berkeley and Los Angeles: University of California Press, 1990.

Francis, John W. *Old New York.* Rev. ed. New York: Roe, 1858.

Fraser, Charles. *Reminiscences of Charleston.* Charleston, S.C.: Russell, 1854.

Flower, Donald. *The Mental Flower Garden.* New York: Southwick, 1808.

Frémont, Jessie Benton. *Souvenirs of My Time.* Boston: Lothrop, 1887.

Fuller, Sarah Margaret. *Papers on Literature and Art.* New York: Wiley & Putnam, 1846.

Galbraith, Charles Burleigh. *Daniel Decatur Emmett.* Columbus, Ohio: Galbraith, 1904.

Gilman, Caroline Howard. *A Balcony in Charleston.* Edited by Mary Scott Saint-Amand. Richmond, Va.: Garrett & Massie, 1941.

———. *Love's Progress.* New York: Harper, 1840.

———. *Recollections of a Housekeeper.* New York: Harper, 1836.

———. *Recollections of a New England Bride and of a Southern Matron.* Rev. ed. New York: Putnam, 1852.

Gilman, Chandler R. *Legends of a Log Cabin.* New York: Dearborn, 1835.

Gilman, Samuel. *Memoirs of a New England Village Choir.* Boston: Goodrich, 1829.

Godwin, Parke. *A Biography of William Cullen Bryant.* 2 vols. 1883. Reprint. New York: Russell & Russell, 1967.

Goodrich, Samuel G. *Peter Parley's Own Story.* New York: Sheldon, 1864.

Gottschalk, Louis Moreau. *Notes of a Pianist.* Edited by Jeanne Behrend. New York: Knopf, 1964.

Grattan, Thomas Colley. *Civilized America.* 2d ed. 2 vols. London: Bradbury & Evans, 1859.

Greeley, Horace. *Recollections of a Busy Life.* New York: Ford, 1868.

Greene, Asa. *Travels in America.* New York: Pearson, 1833.

———. *A Yankee among the Nullifiers.* New York: Stodart, 1833.

Greenwood, Grace [Sara Jane Clarke]. *Greenwood Leaves.* 2d ed. Boston: Ticknor, Reed & Fields, 1850.

Grierson, Francis. *The Valley of Shadows.* New ed. London: Lane, 1893.

Grimsted, David, ed. *Notions of the Americans, 1820–1860.* New York: Braziller, 1970.

Grund, Francis J. *Aristocracy in America.* New York: Harper & Row, 1959.

Haight, Gordon S. *Mrs. Sigourney.* New Haven, Conn.: Yale University Press, 1930.

Hale, Edward Everett. *James Russell Lowell and His Friends.* Boston: Houghton Mifflin, 1899.

Hale, Edward E., Jr. *The Life and Letters of Edward Everett Hale.* Vol. 1. Boston: Little, Brown, 1917.

Hale, Mrs. Sarah J. *Traits of American Life.* Philadelphia: Carey & Hart, 1835.

Haliburton, Thomas Chandler. *The Americans at Home.* 3 vols. Edited by the author of "Sam Slick." London: Hurst & Blackett, 1854.

Halliday, Samuel B. *The Little Street Sweeper, or Life among the Poor.* New York: Phinney, Blakeman & Mason, 1861.

Hamilton, Thomas. *Men and Manners in America.* Philadelphia: Carey, Lea & Blanchard, 1833.

Hancock, William. *An Emigrant's Five Years in the Free States of America.* New York: T. Cautley Newby, 1860.

Harland, Marion [Mrs. Mary Virginia (Hawes) Terhune]. *The Hidden Path.* New York: Derby, 1856.

———. *Judith: A Chronicle of Old Virginia.* Philadelphia: Our Continent Publishing Co., 1883.

———. *Marion Harland's Autobiography.* New York: Harper, 1910.

Harris, George W. *Sut Lovingood.* New York: Dick & Fitzgerald, 1867.

Hastings, Thomas. *Dissertation on Musical Taste.* Albany, N.Y.: Websters & Skinners, 1822.

Haswell, Charles H. *Reminiscences of New York by an Octogenarian (1826 to 1860).* New York: Harper, 1896.

Hawthorne, Julius. *Nathaniel Hawthorne and His Wife.* Vol. 1. Boston: Houghton Mifflin, 1884.

Hentz, Caroline Lee. *The Planter's Northern Bride.* 2 vols. Philadelphia: Hart, 1854.

Herndon, Sarah Raymond. *Days on the Road.* New York: Burr, 1902.

Hewitt, John H. *Shadows on the Wall.* Baltimore: Turnbull, 1877.

Holland, J. G. *Miss Gilbert's Career.* New York: Scribners, 1860.

Holmes, Oliver Wendell. *The Autocrat of the Breakfast-Table.* Boston: Houghton Mifflin, 1916.

———. *The Complete Poetical Works.* Boston: Houghton Mifflin, 1908.

Hone, Philip. *The Diary of Philip Hone, 1828–1851.* 2 vols. Edited by Bayard Tuckerman. New York: Dodd, Mead, 1889.

Howard, John Tasker. *Our American Music.* 4th ed. New York: Crowell, 1965.

338 ————. *Stephen Foster, America's Troubadour.* New York: Crowell, 1962.

Howe, Julia Ward. *Reminiscences, 1819–1899.* 1899. Reprint. New York: Negro Universities Press, 1969.

Hundley, D. R. *Social Relations in Our Southern States.* New York: Price, 1860.

[Hutchinson Family]. *Excelsior: Journals of the Hutchinson Family Singers, 1842–1846.* Edited and annotated by Dale Cockrell. Stuyvesant, N.Y.: Pendragon Press, 1986.

Hutchinson, John Wallace. *Story of the Hutchinsons.* 2 vols. Boston: Lee & Shepard, 1896.

Ivins, Virginia Wilcox. *Pen Pictures of Early Western Days.* Keokuk, Iowa: n.p., 1908.

Jackson, Kenneth T., ed. *The Encyclopedia of New York City.* New Haven, Conn.: Yale University Press, 1995.

Jackson, S. Trevena. *Fanny Crosby's Story of Ninety-Four Years.* New York: Revell, 1915.

Johnson, H. Earle. *Hallelujah, Amen!* Boston: Humphries, 1965.

————. *Musical Interludes in Boston, 1795–1830.* New York: Columbia University Press, 1943.

Johnson, William. *William Johnson's Natchez: The Ante-Bellum Diary of a Free Negro.* Ed. William Ransom Hogan and Edwin Adams Davis. Baton Rouge: Louisiana State University Press, 1951.

Jones, John B. *Wild Western Scenes.* Philadelphia: Grigg, Elliot, 1849.

————. *The Winkles.* New York: Appleton, 1855.

Jordan, Philip D. *Singin' Yankees.* Minneapolis: University of Minnesota Press, 1946.

Kaufman, Charles H. *Music in New Jersey, 1655–1860.* Rutherford, N.J.: Fairleigh Dickinson University Press, 1981.

Kemble, Frances Anne. *Journal of a Residence on a Georgian Plantation in 1838–1839.* New York: Harper, 1863.

Kemp, Robert. *Father Kemp and His Old Folks.* Boston: Kemp, 1868.

Kendall, Edward Augustus. *Travels through the Northern Parts of the United States, in the Years 1807 and 1808.* 3 vols. New York: Riley, 1809.

Kennedy, John P. *Memoirs of the Life of William Wirt.* Rev. ed. 2 vols. Philadelphia: Lippincott, 1860.

————. *Swallow Barn.* Rev. ed. New York: Putnam, 1951.

Kimball, Richard B. *Was He Successful?* New York: Carleton, 1864.

Kirke, Edmund. *My Southern Friends.* New York: Tribune Association, 1863.

Kirkland, Mrs. C. M. *Western Clearings.* New York: Wiley & Putnam, 1845.

Kirkland, Joseph. *Zury: The Meanest Man in Spring Country.* Boston: Houghton Mifflin, 1887.

Kmen, Henry A. *Music in New Orleans.* Baton Rouge: Louisiana State University Press, 1966.

Krohn, Ernst C. *Missouri Music.* New York: Da Capo Press, 1971.

Larcom, Lucy. *A New England Girlhood.* 1889. Reprint. Boston: Northeastern University Press, 1986.

Larkin, Jack. *The Reshaping of Everyday Life, 1790–1840.* New York: Harper & Row, 1988.

Lasselle, Mrs. N. P. *Anne Grayson, or Life in Washington.* New York: Bunce, 1853.

Latrobe, Benjamin Henry. *The Journal of Latrobe.* New York: Appleton, 1905.

Lawrence, Vera Brodsky. *Strong on Music.* 2 vols. New York: Oxford University Press, 1988.

Leland, Charles Godfrey. *Memoirs.* New York: Appleton, 1893.

Lengyel, Cornel, ed. *Music in the Gold Rush Era.* History of Music in San Francisco, vol. 1. San Francisco: WPA, 1939.

————. *A San Francisco Songster, 1849–1939.* History of Music in San Francisco, vol. 2. San Francisco: WPA, 1939.

Leonard, Kate. *Clara Temple Leonard: A Memoir of Her Life by Her Daughter.* Springfield, Mass.: Loring-Axtall, 1908.

Lesley, Susan I. *Recollections of My Mother.* Boston: Ellis, 1886.

Lippard, George. *New York: Its Upper Ten and Lower Million.* Cincinnati: Rulison, 1853.

Loesser, Arthur. *Men, Women, and Pianos.* New York: Simon & Schuster, 1954.

Longfellow, Fanny Appleton. *Mrs. Longfellow: Selected Letters and Journals.* Edited by Edward Wagenknecht. New York: Longmans, Green, 1956.

Longfellow, Henry Wadsworth. *The Letters of Henry Wadsworth Longfellow.* Edited by Andrew Hilen. 3 vols. Cambridge, Mass.: Belknap Press, 1966–72.

Longfellow, Samuel, ed. *Life of Henry Wadsworth Longfellow.* 3 vols. Boston: Houghton Mifflin, 1887.

———. *Memoir and Letters.* Edited by Joseph May. Boston: Houghton Mifflin, 1894.

Longstreet, A. B. *Georgia Scenes.* 2d ed. New York: Harper, 1851.

Lowell, James Russell. *Letters of James Russell Lowell.* Vol. 1. Edited by Charles Eliot Norton. New York: Harper, 1894.

*The Lowell Offering.* Vols. 1–2. Lowell, Mass.: Powers & Bagley, n.d. Vol. 3, Lowell, Mass.: Schouler, 1843. Vols. 4–5. Lowell, Mass.: Misses Curtis & Farley, 1844–45.

Lowery, Rev. I. E. *Life on the Old Plantation in Ante-Bellum Days.* Columbia, S.C.: State Co. Printers, 1911.

Ludlow, Noah M. *Dramatic Life as I Found It.* 1880. Reprint. New York: Blom, 1966.

McAllister, Ward. *Society as I Found It.* New York: Cassell, 1890.

McConnel, J. L. *Western Characters.* New York: Redfield, 1853.

Mcintosh, Maria Jane. *Evenings at Donaldson Manor.* New York: Appleton, 1851.

———. *Praise and Principle.* New York: Harper, 1847.

———. *Two Pictures.* New York: Appleton, 1863.

Macrae, David. *Americans at Home.* 1870. Reprint. New York: Dutton, 1952.

Madeira, Louis C. *Annals of Music in Philadelphia and History of the Musical Fund Society.* Edited by Philip H. Goepp. Philadelphia: Lippincott, 1896.

Mallard, R. Q. *Plantation Life before Emancipation.* Richmond, Va.: Whittet & Shepperson, 1892.

Mann, Daniel. *Wolfsden.* Boston: Phillips, Sampson, 1856.

Mann, Dennis Alan, ed. *The Arts in a Democratic Society.* Bowling Green, Ohio: Popular Press of Bowling Green University, 1977.

Martineau, Harriet. *Retrospect of Western Travels.* 2 vols. London: Saunders & Otley, 1838.

———. *Society in America.* 2 vols. New York: Saunders & Otley, 1837.

Melish, John. *Travels through the United States of America.* London: Cowie, 1818.

Mendell and Hosmer, Misses. *Notes of Travel and Life.* New York: published by the authors, 1854.

Mitchell, Donald G. *Dream-Life.* New York: Scribners, 1889.

Moore, John. *Complete Encyclopaedia of Music.* Boston: Ditson, 1854.

Morgan, Dale, ed. *Overland in 1846.* 2 vols. Georgetown, Calif.: Talisman Press, 1963.

Mornewick, Evelyn Foster. *Chronicles of Stephen Foster's Family.* 2 vols. Pittsburgh: University of Pittsburgh Press, 1944.

Morris, George P. *Sketches of the Times.* Philadelphia: Lea & Blanchard, 1839.

Murray, Amelia M. *Letters for the United States, Cuba, and Canada.* New York: Putnam, 1856.

Nathan, Hans. *Dan Emmett and the Rise of Early Negro Minstrelsy.* Norman: University of Oklahoma Press, 1962.

Neal, John. *True Womanhood.* Boston: Ticknor & Fields, 1899.

Neal, Joseph C. *Charcoal Sketches, or Scenes in a Metropolis.* New ed. New York: Burgess & Stringer, 1844.

Nichols, Dr. Thomas L. *Forty Years of American Life.* 2 vols. London: Maxwell, 1864.

**340**   Northup, Solomon. *Twelve Years a Slave.* New York: Miller, Orton & Mulligan, 1855.

Olmsted, Frederick Law. *The Cotton Kingdom.* 2 vols. New York: Mason, 1861.

Osgood, Samuel. *Mile Stones.* New York: Appleton, 1855.

Ossoli, Margaret Fuller. *Memoirs.* 2 vols. Boston: Phillips, Sampson, 1852.

Ottley, Roi, and William J. Weatherby. *The Negro in New York.* New York: New York Public Library, 1967.

Page, Thomas Nelson. *Social Life in Old Virginia.* 1897. Reprint. Freeport, N.Y.: Books for Libraries Press, 1970.

*The Parish-Side.* By the Clerk of the Parish of Edgefield. New York: Mason, 1854.

Parker, Richard Green. *A Tribute to the Life and Character of Jonas Chickering.* Boston: Tewksbury, 1854.

Pattee, Fred Lewis. *The Feminine Fifties.* New York: Appleton-Century, 1940.

Perry, Bliss. *Life and Letters of Henry Lee Higginson.* 2 vols. Boston: Atlantic Monthly Press, 1921.

Pintard, John. *Letters from John Pintard to His Daughter.* 4 vols. New York: New-York Historical Society, 1940–41.

Poe, Edgar Allan. *The Letters of Edgar Allan Poe.* Edited by John Ward Ostrom. Cambridge, Mass.: Harvard University Press, 1940.

Porter, Sarah Harvey. *The Life and Times of Anne Royall.* Cedar Rapids, Iowa: Torch Press Book Shop, 1908.

Porter, William T., ed. *A Quarter Race in Kentucky and Other Sketches.* Philadelphia: Peterson, 1854.

Powell, Virgil S. *From the Slave Cabin of Yani.* Hicksville, N.Y.: Exposition Press, 1977.

Pray, Isaac C. *Memoirs of James Gordon Bennett and His Times.* New York: Stringer & Townsend, 1855.

Pringle, Elizabeth W. A. *Chronicles of Chicora Wood.* New York: Scribners, 1922.

Pulszky, Francis, and Theresa Pulszky. *White, Red, Black.* 2 vols. New York: Redfield, 1853.

Quill, Charles. *The American Mechanic.* Philadelphia: Perkins, 1838.

Ramsdell, George A. *A History of Milford.* Concord, N.H.: Rumford Press, 1901.

Randall, Ruth Painter. *Mary Lincoln.* Boston: Little, Brown, 1953.

Randolph, John. *Letters to a Young Relative.* Philadelphia: Carey, Lea & Blanchard, 1834.

Rawick, George P., ed. *The American Slave: A Composite Autobiography.* 19 vols. Westport, Conn.: Greenwood Press, 1972–76.

———. *The American Slave: A Composite Autobiography.* Supplement ser. 1. 12 vols. Westport, Conn.: Greenwood Press, 1977.

Richard, Laura E., and Maud Howe Elliott, assisted by Florence Howe Hall. *Julia Ward Howe, 1819–1910.* 2 vols. Boston: Houghton Mifflin, 1916.

Riley, Henry Hiram. *The Puddleford Papers.* New York: Derby & Jackson, 1860.

Ripley, Eliza. *Social Life in Old New Orleans.* New York: Appleton, 1912.

R. L. B. *An Autobiography: Being Passages from a Life Now Progressing in the City of Boston.* N.P.: n.p., 1871.

Robb, John S. *Streaks of Squatter Life and Far-West Scenes.* Philadelphia: Peterson, 1846.

Robinson, Solon. *Hot Corn: Life Scenes in New York.* 1853. Reprint. New York: Pollard & Moss, 1888.

———. *Selected Writings.* 2 vols. Edited by Herbert A. Kellar. Indianapolis: Indiana Historical Bureau, 1936.

Rollins, Mrs. Ellen Chapman Hobs. *New England Bygones.* Philadelphia: Lippincott, 1880.

Root, George. *The Story of a Musical Life.* Cincinnati: Church, 1891.

Ross, Joel H. *What I Saw in New-York.* Auburn, N.Y.: Derby & Miller, 1851.

Rothman, Ellen K. *Hands and Hearts: A History of Courtship in America.* New York: Basic Books, 1984.

Rourke, Constance. *American Humor: A Study of the National Character.* 1931. Reprint. Garden City, N.Y.: Doubleday, 1953.

——. *Davy Crockett.* New York: Harcourt, Brace, 1934.

——. *The Roots of American Culture and Other Essays.* New York: Harcourt, Brace, 1942.

Royce, Sarah. *A Frontier Lady: Recollections of the Gold Rush and Early California.* New Haven, Conn.: Yale University Press, 1932.

Russell, Henry. *Cheer! Boys, Cheer!* London: Macqueen, 1895.

Ryan, Thomas. *Recollections of an Old Musician.* New York: Dutton, 1899.

Ryan, William R. *Personal Adventures in Upper and Lower California, in 1848–9.* 2 vols. London: Shoberl, 1850–51.

Sabin, Rev. Elijah R. *The Life and Reflections of Charles Observator.* Boston: Rowe & Hooper, 1816.

Sanborn, F. B. *Recollections of Seventy Years.* 2 vols. Boston: Badger, 1909.

Sandburg, Carl. *Abraham Lincoln.* Vol. 1. *The Prairie Years.* New York: Harcourt, Brace, 1926.

Saunders, Frederic. *Mosaics.* New York: Scribners, 1859.

Schlesinger, Arthur M., Jr. *The Age of Jackson.* Boston: Little, Brown, 1945.

Schmitz, Joseph William. *In the Days of the Republic: Texas Culture, 1836–1846.* San Antonio, Tex.: Naylor, 1960.

Sealsfield, Charles. *Flirtations in America.* Translated from the German. New York: Taylor, 1847.

Searight, Thomas B. *The Old Pike.* Uniontown, Pa.: author, 1894.

Sedgwick, Catharine Maria. *Married or Single.* Vol. 1. New York: Harper, 1857.

——. *A New England Tale and Miscellanies.* New York: Putnam, 1852.

Sedgwick, Charles. *Letters.* Boston: privately printed, 1870.

Shaw, H. W. *Josh Billings: His Sayings.* New York: Carleton, 1866.

Sheridan, Francis C. *Galveston Island.* Edited by Willis W. Pratt. Austin: University of Texas Press, 1954.

Sigourney, Mrs. Lydia Huntley. *Letters of Life.* New York: Appleton, 1867.

——. *Letters to Young Ladies.* 2d ed. Hartford, Conn.: Watson, 1835.

Simms, W. Gilmore. *Charlemont.* New York: Redfield, 1856.

——. *The Letters of William Gilmore Simms.* 2 vols. Edited by Mary C. Simms Oliphant, Alfred Taylor Odell, and T. C. Duncan Eaves. Columbia, S.C.: University of South Carolina Press, 1952–53.

Sims, J. Marion. *The Story of My Life.* Edited by H. Marion Sims. New York: Appleton, 1884.

*The Singer's Companion.* New York: Stringer & Townsend, 1854.

Slick, Jonathan [Mrs. Ann S. Stephens]. *High Life in New York.* New York: Bunce, 1854.

Smedes, Susan Dabney. *Memorials of a Southern Planter.* Baltimore: Cushings & Bailey, 1887.

Smith, Charles H. *The Farm and the Fireside.* Atlanta: Constitution Publishing House, 1892.

Smith, Elizabeth Oakes. *Selections from the Autobiography of Elizabeth Oakes Smith.* Edited by Mary Alice Wyman. Lewiston, Maine: Lewiston Journal, 1921.

——. *Riches without Wings.* 3d ed. Boston: Light, 1839.

Smith, Harry. *Fifty Years of Slavery.* Grand Rapids: West Michigan Printing Co., 1891.

Smith, James L. *Autobiography.* Norwich, Conn.: Press of the Bulletin Co., 1881.

342    Smith, Margaret Bayard. *The First Forty Years of Washington Society.* Edited by Gaillard Hunt. New York: Ungar, 1965.

Smith, Seba. *The Life and Writings of Major Jack Downing.* 2d ed. Boston: Lilly, Wait, Colman & Holden, 1834.

———. *'Way Down East, or Portraitures of Yankee Life.* Philadelphia: Potter, 1854.

Smith, W. L. G. *Life at the South.* Buffalo, N.Y.: Derby, 1852.

Southern, Eileen, *The Music of Black Americans.* 3d ed. New York: Norton, 1997.

Sower, David, Jr. *Village Sketches.* Norristown, Pa.: Sower, Jr., 1825.

*Squints through an Opera-Glass.* By a young gent. New York: Merchants' Day-Book, 1850.

Stephens, Mrs. Ann S. *Old Homestead.* New York: Bunce, 1855.

———, ed. *The Portland Sketch Book.* Portland, Maine: Colman & Chisholm, 1836.

Stephens, H. Marion. *Home Scenes and Home Sounds.* Boston: Fetridge, 1854.

Stewart, George R. *John Phoenix, Esq.* New York: Holt, 1937.

Stoddard, Richard Henry. *Recollections, Personal and Literary.* New York: Barnes, 1903.

Stoutamire, Albert. *Music of the Old South.* Rutherford, N.J.: Fairleigh Dickinson University Press, 1972.

Stowe, Harriet Beecher. *Flowers and Fruit from the Writings of Harriet Beecher Stowe.* Arranged by Abbie H. Fairfield. Boston: Houghton Mifflin, 1888.

———. *My Wife and I.* New York: Ford, 1871.

———. *Oldtown Folks.* Boston: Houghton Mifflin, 1869.

———. *Poganuc People: Their Loves and Lives.* New York: Fords, Howard & Hulbert, 1878.

———. *We and Our Neighbors.* Boston: Houghton Mifflin, 1898.

Stroyer, Jacob. *My Life in the South.* 3d ed. Salem, Mass.: Salem Observer Books, 1885.

Stuart, James. *Three Years in North America.* 2 vols. Edinburgh: Cadell, 1833.

Swan, Howard. *Music in the Southwest, 1825–1950.* San Marino, Calif.: Huntington Library, 1952.

Swisshelm, Jane Grey. *Half a Century.* 2d ed. Chicago: Jansen, McClurg, 1880.

*Tales of an American Landlord.* 2 vols. New York: Gilley, 1824.

Taliaferro, Hardin E. *Fisher's River (North Carolina).* New York: Harper, 1859.

Tawa, Nicholas. *Sweet Songs for Gentle Americans: The Parlor Song in America, 1790–1860.* Bowling Green, Ohio: Bowling Green University Popular Press, 1980.

Taylor, Rosser H. *Ante-Bellum South Carolina: A Social and Cultural History.* Chapel Hill: University of North Carolina Press, 1942.

Thomas, Benjamin P. *Lincoln's New Salem.* Rev. ed. New York: Knopf, 1954.

Thompson, Daniel Pierce. *Locke Amsden, or The Schoolmaster.* Boston: Sanborn, Carter & Bazin, 1855.

Thompson, William T. *Chronicle of Pineville.* Philadelphia: Carey & Hart, 1849.

Thorburn, Grant. *Fifty Years' Reminiscences of New-York.* New York: Fanshaw, 1845.

Thoreau, Henry David. *Familiar Letters.* Edited by F. B. Sanborn. *Writings* 11. Boston: Houghton Mifflin, 1895.

Tocqueville, Alexis de. *Democracy in America.* 2 vols. Henry Reeve text, revised by Francis Bowen, further revised by Phillips Bradley. New York: Vintage Books, 1954.

Toll, Robert C. *Blacking Up.* New York: Oxford University Press, 1974.

Tripp, George Henry. *Student-Life at Harvard.* Boston: Lockwood, Brooks, 1876.

Trollope, Anthony. *North America.* New York: Harper, 1862.

Trollope, Frances. *Domestic Manners of the Americans.* 5th ed. 1839. Reprint. New York: Dodd, Mead, 1927.

Trowbridge, John Townsend. *My Own Story.* Boston: Houghton Mifflin, 1903.

————. *Neighbor Jackwood.* 1857. Reprint. Boston: Lee & Shepard, 1888.

Tuckerman, Henry T. *The Optimist.* New York: Putnam, 1852.

Underwood, Francis H. *Quabbin: The Story of a Small Town.* 1893. Reprint. Boston: North-eastern University Press, 1986.

Upham, Samuel C. *Notes of a Voyage to California via Cape Horn, Together with Scenes in El Dorado, in the Years 1849–'50.* Philadelphia: Upham, 1878.

Upton, George P. *Letters of Peregrine Pickle.* Chicago: Western News Co., 1869.

————. *Musical Memories.* Chicago: McClurg, 1908.

Victor, Metta V. *Maum Guinea and Her Plantation "Children."* London: Beadle, [1860?].

Wade, John Donald. *Augustus Baldwin Longstreet.* New York: Macmillan, 1924.

Waite, Mrs. Catharine V. *Adventures in the Far West and Life among the Mormons.* Chicago: Waite, 1882.

Wallace, Lew. *An Autobiography.* New York: Harper, 1906.

Ward, Harriet Sherrill. *Prairie Schooner Lady: The Journal of Harriet Sherrill Ward, 1853.* Edited by Ward G. DeWitt and Florence Stark DeWitt. Los Angeles: Westernlore Press, 1959.

Ward, Julius H. *The Life and Letters of James Gates Percival.* Boston: Ticknor & Fields, 1866.

Ware, Henry, Jr. *The Recollections of Jotham Anderson.* 2d ed. Boston: Christian Register Office, 1828.

Warner, Susan. *The Hills of Shatmuc.* New York: Appleton, 1856.

————. *The Wide, Wide World.* 2 vols. New York: Putnam, 1851.

Weed, Thurlow. *The Life of Thurlow Weed, Including His Autobiography and a Memoir.* 2 vols. Edited by Harriet A. Weed. Boston: Houghton Mifflin, 1883.

Weir, James. *Lonz Powers, or The Regulators.* 2 vols. Philadelphia: Lippincott, Grambo, 1850.

Wentz, Sara A. *Smiles and Frowns.* New York: Appleton, 1857.

Wheeler, Candace. *Yesterdays in a Busy Life.* New York: Harper, 1918.

Whitcher, Frances M. *The Widow Bedott Papers.* New York: Derby & Jackson, 1856.

White, Mrs. Rhoda E. (Waterman). *Mary Staunton.* New York: Appleton, 1860.

————. *Portraits of My Married Friends.* New York: Appleton, 1858.

Whitman, Walt. *The Uncollected Poetry and Prose of Walt Whitman.* 2 vols. Collected and edited by Emory Holloway. Gloucester, Mass.: Peter Smith, 1972.

Wikoff, Henry. *The Reminiscences of an Idler.* New York: Fords, Howard & Hulbert, 1880.

Willis, Nathaniel Parker. *Fun-Jottings.* New York: Scribners, 1853.

————. *Hurry-Graphs.* London: Bohn, 1851.

————. *The Miscellaneous Works.* Clinton Hall, N.Y.: Redfield, 1847.

————. *Rural Letters and Other Records of Thought at Leisure.* Auburn, N.Y.: Alden, Beardsley, 1853.

Willson, Ann. *Familiar Letters.* Philadelphia: Parish, 1850.

Wilson, Rufus Rockwell. *Intimate Memories of Lincoln.* Elmira, N.Y.: Primavera Press, 1945.

Windle, Mary J. *Life in Washington.* Philadelphia: Lippincott, 1859.

Wintermute, H. Ogden. *Daniel Decatur Emmett.* Mount Vernon, Ohio: Wintermute, 1955.

Woodward, W. E. *The Way Our People Lived.* New York: Dutton, 1944.

Wortley, Lady Emmeline Stuart [Charlotte Elizabeth Manners]. *Travels in the United States, etc., during 1849 and 1850.* New York: Harper, 1851.

*The Young Lady's Own Book.* Philadelphia: Key, Mielke & Biddle, 1832.

# Index